THE WORKS
AND CORRESPONDENCE OF
DAVID RICARDO

VOLUME IV

PLAN OF THE EDITION

A General Index is in preparation.

THE WORKS
AND CORRESPONDENCE OF
DAVID RICARDO

EDITED BY
PIERO SRAFFA

WITH THE COLLABORATION OF
M. H. DOBB

VOLUME IV

PAMPHLETS AND PAPERS
1815–1823

CAMBRIDGE UNIVERSITY PRESS

CAMBRIDGE

LONDON   NEW YORK   NEW ROCHELLE

MELBOURNE   SYDNEY

FOR THE ROYAL ECONOMIC SOCIETY

Published by the Press Syndicate of the University of Cambridge
The Pitt Building, Trumpington Street, Cambridge CB2 1RP
32 East 57th Street, New York, NY 10022, USA
296 Beaconsfield Parade, Middle Park, Melbourne 3206, Australia

First published 1951
Reprinted 1962 1966 1980

Printed in Great Britain at the
University Press, Cambridge

ISBN 0 521 06069 9

CONTENTS OF VOLUME IV

PAMPHLETS AND PAPERS WRITTEN FOR PUBLICATION 1815–1823

NOTES FROM RICARDO'S MANUSCRIPTS 1818–1823

APPENDIX

FACSIMILES

PAMPHLETS AND PAPERS
WRITTEN FOR PUBLICATION
1815–1823

AN

ESSAY

ON

*The Influence of a low Price of Corn on
the Profits of Stock;*

SHEWING THE

INEXPEDIENCY OF RESTRICTIONS
ON IMPORTATION:

WITH

𝕽𝖊𝖒𝖆𝖗𝖐𝖘

ON

MR. MALTHUS' TWO LAST PUBLICATIONS:

" An Inquiry into the Nature and Progress of Rent;" and " The
Grounds of an Opinion on the Policy of restricting the Importation of Foreign Corn."

———

By DAVID RICARDO, Esq.

———

LONDON:

PRINTED FOR JOHN MURRAY, ALBEMARLE STREET.

1815.

AN

ESSAY

ON

*The Influence of a low Price of Corn on
the Profits of Stock;*

INEXPEDIENCY OF RESTRICTIONS
ON IMPORTATION:

WITH

𝕶𝖊𝖒𝖆𝖗𝖐𝖘

ON

MR. MALTHUS' TWO LAST PUBLICATIONS:

"An Inquiry into the Nature and Progress of Rent;" and "The
Grounds of an Opinion on the Policy of restricting the Importation of Foreign Corn."

═══

BY DAVID RICARDO, Esq.

═══

SECOND EDITION.

═══

LONDON:

PRINTED FOR JOHN MURRAY, ALBEMARLE STREET.

1815.

[Title page to ed. 2]

NOTE ON 'ESSAY ON PROFITS'

Up to March 1813 both his letters and his published writings show Ricardo to have been concerned only with currency questions. By August 1813, however, the question under discussion between Malthus and himself had become the relation between the increase of capital and the rate of profits. Ricardo's letters at this time contain the essential elements of what he already calls his 'theory': that ˙ ˙is only improvements in agriculture, or new facilities for the production of food, that can prevent an increase of capital from lowering the rate of profits.[1] At this stage, and up to March 1814, Ricardo and Malthus were not explicitly concerned with the question of the importation of corn, which had not yet aroused the public interest. The Committee on the Corn Trade, which had been appointed on 22 March 1813 and had reported on 11 May 1813, had been concerned chiefly with Ireland, and it was not until after the great fall of prices due to the huge harvest of 1813 and the further fall after the peace of March 1814 that their Report was made the occasion for the debate which, after a new Committee had reported in 1814, ended in the Corn Law of 1815.

In February 1814 Ricardo had written some 'papers on the profits of Capital' which he had shown to Malthus, Trower and Mill.[2] These papers have not survived, but a summary of their contents, contained in a letter to Trower of 8 March 1814, shows that the theory of profits, which was to appear in the pamphlet of the following year, was already fully developed:

'I will endeavor to state the question itself. When Capital increases in a country, and the means of employing Capital already exists, or increases, in the same proportion, the rate of interest and of profits will not fall.

'Interest rises only when the means of employment for Capital

---

[1] To Malthus, 17 Aug. 1813, below, VI, 94–5. In the previous letter, of 10 August, he had argued that the extension of foreign trade does not by itself increase profits. The light thrown on the origin of the theory of profits by these two letters has been obscured hitherto by their having been misdated 1810 in *Letters to Malthus*, Oxford, 1887.
[2] See Trower's letter of 2 March 1814, below, VI, 102.

bears a greater proportion than before to the Capital itself, and falls when the Capital bears a greater proportion to the arena, as Mr. Malthus has called it, for its employment. On these points I believe we are all agreed, but I contend that the arena for the employment of new Capital cannot increase in any country in the same or greater proportion than the Capital itself, unless Capital be withdrawn from the land[,] unless there be improvements in husbandry,—or new facilities be offered for the introduction of food from foreign countries;—that in short it is the profits of the farmer which regulate the profits of all other trades,—and as the profits of the farmer must necessarily decrease with every augmentation of Capital employed on the land, provided no improvements be at the same time made in husbandry, all other profits must diminish and therefore the rate of interest must fall.'[1]

When in February 1815 Malthus's pamphlets appeared, Ricardo was able to write within a few days his *Essay on the Influence of a Low Price of Corn on the Profits of Stock*,[2] by using his already developed theory of profits, incorporating Malthus's theory of rent, and adding a refutation of the protectionist arguments put forward by Malthus in his *Grounds of an Opinion*.[3] It was published about 24 February 1815.[4]

Ricardo's *Essay* was one of the many pamphlets which were prepared in anticipation of the debates in the House of Commons on the question of the Corn Laws.[5] Among these pamphlets some were particularly connected with Ricardo's and it may be useful to establish the sequence of their publication. The following table is constructed mainly from publishers' advertisements in the newspapers.[6]

---

[1] Below, VI, 103–4.

[2] Referred to hereafter as the *Essay on Profits*.

[3] It is remarkable that in the first half of the *Essay on Profits* there is an unusually large number of footnotes, and that most references to Malthus are contained in them: this suggests that it is the revised version of a text prepared before the appearance of Malthus's pamphlets. The second half, on the other hand, is a direct reply to these pamphlets.

[4] See below, p. 5, n. 5.

[5] The debate began on 17 February and ended with the passing of the new Corn Law on 10 March 1815.

[6] At that time there was no fixed 'day of publication'. The earliest advertisement stating 'this day is published' and giving the price of the pamphlet has been taken to indicate the date of publication.

3 February 1815			Malthus, *Inquiry into Rent.*[1]
10	„	„	Malthus, *Grounds of an Opinion.*[2]
13	„	„	[West], *Essay on the Application of Capital to Land.*[3]
24	„	„	Torrens, *Essay on the External Corn Trade.*[4]
24	„	„	Ricardo, *Essay on Profits.*[5]

Of the pamphlets that preceded Ricardo's, that of West has the most striking similarity with it. Indeed Ricardo's theory of profits is the same as West's. West says that the theory had occurred to him 'some years ago' and his pamphlet was undoubtedly published before Ricardo's. That Ricardo, nevertheless, formed his theory independently is shown by his letters to Malthus and Trower in 1813 and 1814, which contain its essential elements. Ricardo made no claim to independence in his published writings, but recorded the fact on

[1] Advertisement in *Morning Post*, 3 February. Ricardo had read the pamphlet by 6 February (see below, VI, 172). There appear to be four issues of this pamphlet, differing only in the imprint on the title-page and the advertisements on the last page.

[2] Advertised as 'This day is published, price 2/6' in the *Morning Post* of 10 February. It had been advertised in the same paper on 3 February as 'This day is published' price 1/6, but this was undoubtedly premature, as on 8 February another advertisement in the same paper announced it as 'In a few days will be published', no price being given: the price of 1/6 is that of all the preliminary announcements, but in fact all the copies of the pamphlet examined bear the price of 2/6, either imprinted or corrected in ink from 1/6. There is some doubt as to the exact date of publication, which may have been a few days earlier, since newspaper advertisements were often delayed: on 17 February Mr Brand in the House of Commons quoted it as having been published 'ten days

ago' (*Hansard*, XXIX, 834). What is certain is that the *Grounds* was published after the *Inquiry into Rent*: for in the three earliest issues of the *Inquiry into Rent* the *Grounds* is advertised as 'In a few days will be published, price 1*s*. 6*d*.', and in the fourth issue (which bears the imprint of Murray and Johnson) the *Grounds* is advertised as 'Just published', no price being given. Ricardo had read the *Grounds* by 13 February.

[3] Advertisement in the *Morning Chronicle*, 13 February. The same paper had advertised it on 7 February as to be published 'in a few days'. Ricardo had read it by 9 March 1815.

[4] Advertisement in *Morning Post*, 24 February. It had been advertised in *The Monthly Literary Advertiser* of 10 February as to be 'speedily' published. The preface is dated 17 Feb. 1815. Ricardo had read it by 14 March 1815.

[5] Advertisement in *Morning Post*, 24 February. It had been advertised in the *Morning Chronicle* of 23 February as 'published this day', but no price was stated.

his own copy of West's pamphlet, which is in the Library at Gatcombe: 'This was published before my Essay on the Profits of Stock, but it never came into my hands till after I had published my Essay. D. Ricardo'.[1]

All the pamphlets in question have in common the principle of rent based on diminishing returns from the extension of cultivation to inferior qualities of land; and also (all of them with the exception of Torrens's) from the employment of successive portions of capital on the same land. West certainly, and Torrens possibly,[2] arrived at the principle independently of Malthus; Ricardo, however, says in his Introduction that he is very much indebted to Malthus for the theory of rent, and he repeats this in his preface to the *Principles*.

The popular belief that Ricardo actually invented the theory of rent (whence the phrase 'the Ricardian theory of rent')[3] derives some support from the Note on Rent in McCulloch's edition of the *Wealth of Nations*:[4] 'The theory of rent... was first announced to the world in two pamphlets, published in 1815, by Mr. West, (now Sir Edward West, chief-justice of Bombay) and Mr. Malthus. A pamphlet explanatory of the same doctrine was published by Mr. Ricardo, two years after:[5] but, although he was posterior to the authors above named, in promulgating the doctrine, and less happy in his mode of explaining it than Sir Edward West, it is well known to many of his friends that he was in possession of the principle, and was accustomed to communicate it in conversation several years prior to the publication of the earliest of these works.'

[1] See the facsimile opposite. Cp. also Ricardo's letter to Malthus of 9 March 1815 (below, VI, 179–80): 'I have read his [West's] book with attention and I find that his views agree very much with my own.'

[2] Torrens, in his *Essay on the External Corn Trade*, pp. x and 281, quotes Malthus's *Grounds of an Opinion*, published after the *Inquiry into Rent*.

[3] Among the further consequences of this mistaken notion is that of regarding Ricardo as the originator of the whole marginal theory. 'The Ricardian law of rent....is the first great example of the marginal method, later to become the keystone of the entire Austrian system of economic theory.' (J. M. Clark, art. 'Distribution', in *Encyclopaedia of the Social Sciences*, 1931.)

[4] Edinburgh, Black, 1828, vol. IV, pp. 124–5.

[5] The writer here confuses the *Essay* of 1815 with the *Principles* of 1817.

ESSAY

ON THE

APPLICATION OF CAPITAL

TO

LAND,

WITH

OBSERVATIONS

SHEWING THE

IMPOLICY

OF

ANY GREAT RESTRICTION OF THE IMPORTATION OF CORN,

AND

THAT THE BOUNTY OF 1688 DID NOT LOWER THE PRICE OF IT.

Edward West Esq.

BY

A FELLOW OF UNIVERSITY COLLEGE, OXFORD.

LONDON:

PRINTED FOR T. UNDERWOOD, 32, FLEET STREET;

By C. Roworth, Bell Yard, Temple Bar.

1815.

This was published before my Essay on the Profits of Stock, but it never came into my hands till after I had published my Essay.

D. Ricardo

As the Note was written in the main by John Stuart Mill,[1] who had presumably derived the information from his father, it might be supposed to be authoritative. There is, however, no evidence to confirm its contention. The letters of Ricardo up to the time of the publication of Malthus's *Inquiry into Rent* contain no dicussion of the subject of rent.[2] What Ricardo had been familiar with for many years was the principle of diminishing returns on land;[3] but in his letters of 1813 and 1814 he had applied this principle only to his theory of profits.[4] This is borne out by the writer of Ricardo's obituary in the *Globe and Traveller* (Torrens's newspaper) of 16 September 1823, who, after saying that Adam Smith had left unexplained the principles of the distribution of wealth and that Malthus and West had discovered the laws of rent, adds: 'Mr. Ricardo, who appears, from frequent conversations with his friends, to have been previously investigating the effects of the gradations of soil, immediately discovered[5] the principles which determine the rate of profit and thus completed the theory of the distribution of wealth.'

Although Ricardo opens his Introduction with the statement that in treating the subject of profits it is necessary to consider the principles of rent, the fact is that for the previous two years in his letters he had been working out his theory of profits without ever finding it necessary explicitly to mention rent. Indeed, the theory of profits presented in the pamphlet adds little to what was already

[1] See an entry in MS list of published writings of J. S. Mill, in the Mill-Taylor papers in the Library of the London School of Economics: '1827. A dissertation on Rent, in the notes subjoined to MacCulloch's edition of Smith's Wealth of Nations. Some parts of this note were however altered by MacCulloch.' [The list has been printed as *Bibliography of the Published Writings of J. S. Mill*, ed. by N. MacMinn and others, Northwestern University, Evanston, Ill., 1945; the item in question is mistaken by the editors for McCulloch's Note on Taxes on Rent.]

[2] The letter to Malthus of 6 Feb. 1815, however, refers to some discussion of rent between them at an earlier time: see below, VI, 173.
[3] He stated it as early as 1810 or 1811 in his Notes on Bentham, above, III, 287.
[4] It is remarkable that West also, in the first 48 pages of his pamphlet, applies the principle of diminishing returns on land exclusively to the theory of profits: it is only in the last 7 pages that he applies it to rent.
[5] It was Ricardo's publication of the theory of profits, rather than his discovery of it, that followed Malthus's pamphlet.

contained in his letters of 1813 and 1814, before his attention had been directed to the connection between rent and profits.[1]

A 'Second Edition' of the *Essay on Profits*, also published in 1815, contains no alterations, not even the correction of misprints, and would be more accurately described as a reprint. As the same type appears to have been used, it probably followed the first edition within a few days.

In the summer of 1815 Ricardo was considering the preparation of a revised edition of the *Essay on Profits*. On 18 August he wrote to Say: 'Mr. Mill wishes me to write it over again more at large. I fear the undertaking exceeds my power.' He started work on the project, but it finally took shape, not as a new edition of the pamphlet, but as the *Principles of Political Economy, and Taxation*.[2]

[1] 'The law of rent came into Ricardo's system, *not as a basis, but as a better proof of a theory already developed*.' (S. N. Patten, 'The Interpretation of Ricardo', in *Quarterly Journal of Economics*, April 1893, vol. VII, p. 329.)
[2] In the early editions of his *Life and Writings of Mr. Ricardo*, McCulloch emphasised the connection between the two works: 'This Essay is particularly worthy of attention, as it contains a brief statement of some of the fundamental principles subsequently demonstrated in the "*Principles of Political Economy and Taxation*."' But in the later versions (including the one prefixed to Ricardo's *Works*, 1846) he omitted this passage.

INTRODUCTION

In treating on the subject of the profits of capital, it is necessary to consider the principles which regulate the rise and fall of rent; as rent and profits, it will be seen, have a very intimate connexion with each other. The principles which regulate rent are briefly stated in the following pages, and differ in a very slight degree from those which have been so fully and so ably developed by Mr. Malthus in his late excellent publication,[1] to which I am very much indebted. The consideration of those principles, together with those which regulate the profit of stock, have convinced me of the policy of leaving the importation of corn unrestricted by law. From the general principle set forth in all Mr. Malthus's publications, I am persuaded that he holds the same opinion as far as profit and wealth are concerned with the question;—but, viewing, as he does, the danger as formidable of depending on foreign supply for a large portion of our food, he considers it wise, on the whole, to restrict importation. Not participating with him in those fears, and perhaps estimating the advantages of a cheap price of corn at a higher value, I have come to a different conclusion. Some of the objections urged in his last publication,—"Grounds of an Opinion," &c.[2] I have endeavoured to answer; they appear to me to be unconnected with the political danger he apprehends, and to be inconsistent with the general doctrines of the advantages of a free trade, which he has himself, by his writings, so ably contributed to establish.

[1] *An Inquiry into the Nature and Progress of Rent, and the Principles by which it is Regulated*, London, Murray, 1815.

[2] *The Grounds of an Opinion on the Policy of Restricting the Importation of Foreign Corn*. London, Murray, 1815.

ON THE

INFLUENCE, &c.

Mr. Malthus very correctly defines, "the rent of land to be that portion of the value of the whole produce which remains to the owner, after all the outgoings belonging to its cultivation, of whatever kind, have been paid, including the profits of the capital employed, estimated according to the usual and ordinary rate of the profits of agricultural stock at the time being."[1]

Whenever, then, the usual and ordinary rate of the profits of agricultural stock, and all the outgoings belonging to the cultivation of land, are together equal to the value of the whole produce, there can be no rent.

And when the whole produce is only equal in value to the outgoings necessary to cultivation, there can neither be rent nor profit.

In the first settling of a country rich in fertile land, and which may be had by any one who chooses to take it, the whole produce, after deducting the outgoings belonging to cultivation, will be the profits of capital, and will belong to the owner of such capital, without any deduction whatever for rent.

Thus, if the capital employed by an individual on such land were of the value of two hundred quarters of wheat, of which half consisted of fixed capital, such as buildings, implements, &c. and the other half of circulating capital,—if, after replacing the fixed and circulating capital, the value of the remaining produce were one hundred quarters of wheat, or of equal value with one hundred quarters of wheat, the neat profit to the owner of capital would be fifty per cent. or one hundred profit on two hundred capital.

[1] *Inquiry into...Rent*, pp. 1–2.

For a period of some duration, the profits of agricultural stock might continue at the same rate, because land equally fertile, and equally well situated, might be abundant, and therefore, might be cultivated on the same advantageous terms, in proportion as the capital of the first, and subsequent settlers augmented.

Profits might even increase, because the population increasing, at a more rapid rate than capital, wages might fall; and instead of the value of one hundred quarters of wheat being necessary for the circulating capital, ninety only might be required: in which case, the profits of stock would rise from fifty to fifty-seven per cent.

Profits might also increase, because improvements might take place in agriculture, or in the implements of husbandry, which would augment the produce with the same cost of production.

If wages rose, or a worse system of agriculture were practised, profits would again fall.

These are circumstances which are more or less at all times in operation—they may retard or accelerate the natural effects of the progress of wealth, by raising or lowering profits—by increasing or diminishing the supply of food, with the employment of the same capital on the land.*

* Mr. Malthus considers, that the surplus of produce obtained in consequence of diminished wages, or of improvements in agriculture, to be one of the causes to raise rent. To me it appears that it will only augment profits.

"The accumulation of capital, beyond the means of employing it on land of the greatest natural fertility, and the greatest advantage of situation, must necessarily lower profits; while the tendency of population to increase beyond the means of subsistance must, after a certain time, lower the wages of labour.

"The expense of production will thus be diminished, but the value of the produce, that is, the quantity of labour, and of the other products of labour besides corn, which it can command instead of diminishing, will be increased.

"There will be an increasing number of people demanding subsistance,

We will, however, suppose that no improvements take place in agriculture, and that capital and population advance in the proper proportion, so that the real wages of labour, continue uniformly the same;—that we may know what peculiar effects are to be ascribed to the growth of capital, the increase of population, and the extension of cultivation, to the more remote, and less fertile land.

In this state of society, when the profits on agricultural stock, by the supposition, are fifty per cent. the profits on all other capital, employed either in the rude manufactures, common to such a stage of society, or in foreign commerce, as the means of procuring in exchange for raw produce, those commodities which may be in demand, will be also, fifty per cent.*

If the profits on capital employed in trade were more than fifty per cent. capital would be withdrawn from the land to be employed in trade. If they were less, capital would be taken from trade to agriculture.

and ready to offer their services in any way in which they can be useful. The exchangeable value of food will therefore be in excess above the cost of production, including in this cost the full profits of the stock employed upon the land, according to the actual rate of profits, at the time being. And this excess is rent."—*An Inquiry into the Nature and Progress of Rent*, page 18.

In page 19, speaking of Poland, one of the causes of rent is again attributed to cheapness of labour. In page 22 it is said that a fall in the wages of labour, or a reduction in the number of labourers necessary to produce a given effect, in consequence of agricultural improvements, will raise rent.

* It is not meant, that strictly the rate of profits on agriculture and manufactures will be the same, but that they will bear some proportion to each other. Adam Smith has explained why profits are somewhat less on some employments of capital than on others, according to their security, cleanliness, and respectability, &c. &c.[1]

What the proportion may be, is of no importance to my argument, as I am only desirous of proving that the profits on agricultural capital cannot materially vary, without occasioning a similar variation in the profits on capital, employed on manufactures and commerce.

[1] *Wealth of Nations*, Bk. I, ch. x, pt. i; Cannan's ed., vol. I, pp. 102–20.

After all the fertile land in the immediate neighbourhood of the first settlers were cultivated, if capital and population increased, more food would be required, and it could only be procured from land not so advantageously situated. Supposing then the land to be equally fertile, the necessity of employing more labourers, horses, &c. to carry the produce from the place where it was grown, to the place where it was to be consumed, although no alteration were to take place in the wages of labour, would make it necessary that more capital should be permanently employed to obtain the same produce. Suppose this addition to be of the value of ten quarters of wheat, the whole capital employed on the new land would be two hundred and ten, to obtain the same return as on the old; and, consequently the profits of stock would fall from fifty to forty-three per cent. or ninety on two hundred and ten.*

On the land first cultivated, the return would be the same as before, namely, fifty per cent. or one hundred quarters of wheat; but, the general profits of stock being regulated by the profits made on the least profitable employment of capital on agriculture, a division of the one hundred quarters would take place, forty-three per cent. or eighty-six quarters would constitute the profit of stock, and seven per cent. or fourteen quarters, would constitute rent. And that such a division must take place is evident, when we consider that the owner of the capital of the value of two hundred and ten quarters of wheat would obtain precisely the same profit, whether he cultivated the distant land, or paid the first settler fourteen quarters for rent.

* Profits of stock fall because land equally fertile cannot be obtained, and through the whole progress of society, profits are regulated by the difficulty or facility of procuring food. This is a principle of great importance, and has been almost overlooked in the writings of Political Economists. They appear to think that profits of stock can be raised by commercial causes, independently of the supply of food.

In this stage, the profits on[1] all capital employed in trade would fall to forty-three per cent.

If, in the further progress of population and wealth, the produce of more land were required to obtain the same return, it might be necessary to employ, either on account of distance, or the worse quality of land, the value of two hundred and twenty quarters of wheat, the profits of stock would then fall to thirty-six per cent. or eighty on two hundred and twenty, and the rent of the first land would rise to twenty-eight quarters of wheat, and on the second portion of land cultivated, rent would now commence, and would amount to fourteen quarters.

The profits on all trading capital would also fall to thirty-six per cent.

Thus by bringing successively land of a worse quality, or less favourably situated into cultivation, rent would rise on the land previously cultivated, and precisely in the same degree would profits fall; and if the smallness of profits do not check accumulation, there are hardly any limits to the rise of rent, and the fall of profit.

If instead of employing capital at a distance on new land, an additional capital of the value of two hundred and ten quarters of wheat be employed on the first land cultivated, and its return were in like manner forty-three per cent. or ninety on two hundred and ten; the produce of fifty per cent. on the first capital, would be divided in the same manner as before forty-three per cent. or eighty-six quarters would constitute profit, and fourteen quarters rent.

If two hundred and twenty quarters were employed in addition with the same result as before, the first capital would afford a rent of twenty-eight; and the second of fourteen quarters, and the profits on the whole capital of six hundred

[1] Misprinted 'in'; corrected by Ricardo in his copy at Gatcombe.

and thirty quarters would be equal, and would amount to thirty-six per cent.

Supposing that the nature of man was so altered, that he required double the quantity of food that is now necessary for his subsistence, and consequently, that the expenses of cultivation were very greatly increased. Under such circumstances the knowledge and capital of an old society employed on fresh and fertile land in a new country would leave a much less surplus produce; consequently, the profits of stock could never be so high. But accumulation, though slower in its progress, might still go on, and rent would begin just as before, when more distant or less fertile land were cultivated.

The natural limit to population would of course be much earlier, and rent could never rise to the height to which it may now do; because, in the nature of things, land of the same poor quality would never be brought into cultivation;—nor could the same amount of capital be employed on the better land with any adequate return of profit.*

The following table is constructed on the supposition, that the first portion of land yields one hundred quarters profit on a capital of two hundred quarters; the second portion, ninety quarters on two hundred and ten, according to the foregoing calculations.† It will be seen that during the pro-

---

* In all that I have said concerning the origin and progress of rent, I have briefly repeated, and endeavoured to elucidate the principles which Mr. Malthus has so ably laid down, on the same subject, in his "Inquiry into the Nature and Progress of Rent;" a work abounding in original ideas,—which are useful not only as they regard rent, but as connected with the question of taxation; perhaps, the most difficult and intricate of all the subjects on which Political Economy treats.

† It is scarcely necessary to observe, that the data on which this table is constructed are assumed, and are probably very far from the truth. They were fixed on as tending to illustrate the principle,—which would be the same, whether the first profits were fifty per cent. or five,—or, whether an additional capital of ten quarters, or of one hundred, were

gress of a country the whole produce raised on its land will increase, and for a certain time that part of the produce which belongs to the profits of stock, as well as that part which belongs to rent will increase; but that at a later period, every accumulation of capital will be attended with an absolute, as well as a proportionate diminution of profits,—though rents will uniformly increase. A less revenue, it will be seen, will be enjoyed by the owner of stock, when one thousand three hundred and fifty quarters are employed on the different qualities of land, than when one thousand one hundred were employed. In the former case the whole profits will be only two hundred and seventy, in the latter two hundred and seventy five; and when one thousand six hundred and ten are employed, profits will fall to two hundred and forty-one and a half.*

This is a view of the effects of accumulation which is exceedingly curious, and has, I believe, never before been noticed.

It will be seen by the table, that, in a progressive country, rent is not only absolutely increasing, but that it is also increasing in its ratio to the capital employed on the land; thus

required to obtain the same produce from the cultivation of new land. In proportion as the capital employed on the land, consisted more of fixed capital, and less of circulating capital, would rent advance, and property fall less rapidly.[1]

* This would be the effect of a constantly accumulating capital, in a country which refused to import foreign and cheaper corn. But after profits have very much fallen, accumulation will be checked, and capital will be exported to be employed in those countries where food is cheap and profits high. All European colonies have been established with the capital of the mother countries, and have thereby checked accumulation. That part of the population too, which is employed in the foreign carrying trade, is fed with foreign corn. It cannot be doubted, that low profits, which are the inevitable effects of a really high price of corn, tend to draw capital abroad: this consideration ought therefore to be a powerful reason to prevent us from restricting importation.

[1] No doubt should read 'rent advance, and profits fall, less rapidly.'

TABLE, shewing the Progress of Rent and Profit under an assumed Augmentation of Capital.

Capital estimated in quarters of wheat.	Profit per cent.	Neat produce in quarters of wheat after paying the cost of production on each capital.	Profit of 1st portion of land in quarters of wheat.	Rent of 1st portion of land in quarters of wheat.	Profit of 2d portion of land in quarters of wheat.	Rent of 2d portion of land in quarters of wheat.	Profit of 3d portion of land in quarters of wheat.	Rent of 3d portion of land in quarters of wheat.	Profit of 4th portion of land in quarters of wheat.	Rent of 4th portion of land in quarters of wheat.	Profit of 5th portion of land in quarters of wheat.	Rent of 5th portion of land in quarters of wheat.	Profit of 6th portion of land in quarters of wheat.	Rent of 6th portion of land in quarters of wheat.	Profit of 7th portion of land in quarters of wheat.	Rent of 7th portion of land in quarters of wheat.	Profit of 8th portion of land in quarters of wheat.
200	50	100	100	none.													
210	43	90	86	14	90	none.											
220	36	80	72	28	76	14	80	none.									
230	30	70	60	40	63	27	66	14	70	none.							
240	25	60	50	50	$52\frac{1}{2}$	$37\frac{1}{2}$	55	25	$57\frac{1}{2}$	$12\frac{1}{2}$	60	none.					
250	20	50	40	60	42	48	44	36	46	24	48	12	50	none.			
260	15	40	30	70	$31\frac{1}{2}$	$58\frac{1}{2}$	33	47	$34\frac{1}{2}$	$35\frac{1}{2}$	36	24	$37\frac{1}{2}$	$12\frac{1}{2}$	40	none.	
270	11	30	22	78	23	67	24	56	25.3	44.7	26.4	33.6	$27\frac{1}{2}$	$22\frac{1}{2}$	27.6	12.4	29.7

	When the whole capital employed is	Whole amount of rent received by landlords in quarters of wheat.	Whole amount of profits in quarters received by owners of stock.	Profit per cent. on the whole capital.	Rent per cent. on the whole capital.	Total produce in quarters of wheat, after paying the cost of production.
1st Period	200	none.	100	50		100
2d Ditto	410	14	176	43	$3\frac{1}{2}$	190
3d Ditto	630	42	228	36	$6\frac{3}{4}$	270
4th Ditto	860	81	259	30	$9\frac{1}{2}$	340
5th Ditto	1100	125	275	25	$11\frac{1}{2}$	400
6th Ditto	1350	180	270	20	$13\frac{1}{4}$	450
7th Ditto	1610	$248\frac{1}{2}$	$241\frac{1}{2}$	15	$15\frac{1}{2}$	490
8th Ditto	1880	$314\frac{1}{2}$	$205\frac{1}{2}$	11	$16\frac{1}{2}$	520

when four hundred and ten was the whole capital employed, the landlord obtained three and a half per cent.; when one thousand one hundred—thirteen and a quarter per cent.; and when one thousand eight hundred and eighty—sixteen and a half per cent. The landlord not only obtains a greater produce, but a larger share.

*Rent then is in all cases a portion of the profits previously obtained on the land. It is never a new creation of revenue, but always part of a revenue already created.

Profits of stock fall only, because land equally well adapted to produce food cannot be procured; and the degree of the fall of profits, and the rise of rents, depends wholly on the increased expense of production.

If, therefore, in the progress of countries in wealth and population, new portions of fertile land could be added to such countries, with every increase of capital, profits would never fall, nor rents rise.†

If the money price of corn, and the wages of labour, did not vary in price in the least degree, during the progress of the country in wealth and population, still profits would fall and rents would rise; because *more* labourers would be employed on the more distant or less fertile land, in order to obtain the same supply of raw produce; and therefore the cost of production would have increased, whilst the value of the produce continued the same.

---

* By rent I always mean the remuneration given to the landlord for the use of the original and inherent power of the land. If either the landlord expends capital on his own land, or the capital of a preceding tenant is left upon it at the expiration of his lease, he may obtain what is indeed called a larger rent, but a portion of this is evidently paid for the use of capital. The other portion only is paid for the use of the original power of the land.

† Excepting, as has been before observed,[1] the real wages of labour should rise, or a worse system of agriculture be practised.

[1] Above, p. 11.

But the price of corn, and of all other raw produce, has been invariably observed to rise as a nation became wealthy, and was obliged to have recourse to poorer lands for the production of part of its food; and very little consideration will convince us, that such is the effect which would naturally be expected to take place under such circumstances.

The exchangeable value of all commodities, rises as the difficulties of their production increase. If then new difficulties occur in the production of corn, from more labour being necessary, whilst no more labour is required to produce gold, silver, cloth, linen, &c. the exchangeable value of corn will necessarily rise, as compared with those things. On the contrary, facilities in the production of corn, or of any other commodity of whatever kind, which shall afford the same produce with less labour, will lower its exchangeable value.* Thus we see that improvements in agriculture, or in the implements of husbandry, lower the exchangeable value of corn;† improvements in the machinery connected with the manufacture of cotton, lower the exchangeable value of cotton goods; and improvements in mining, or the discovery of new and more abundant mines of the precious metals, lower the value of gold and silver, or which is the same thing, raises the price of all other commodities. Wherever competition can have its full effect, and the pro-

* The low price of corn, caused by improvements in agriculture, would give a stimulus to population, by increasing profits and encouraging accumulation, which would again raise the price of corn and lower profits. But a larger population could be maintained at the same price of corn, the same profits, and the same rents. Improvements in agriculture may then be said to increase profits, and to lower for a time rents.

† The causes, which render the acquisition of an additional quantity of corn more difficult are, in progressive countries, in constant operation, whilst marked improvements in agriculture, or in the implements of husbandry are of less frequent occurrence. If these opposite causes acted with equal effect, corn would be subject only to accidental variation of price, arising from bad seasons, from greater or less real wages of labour, or from an alteration in the value of the precious metals, proceeding from their abundance or scarcity.

duction of the commodity be not limited by nature, as in the case with some wines, the difficulty or facility of their production will ultimately regulate their exchangeable value.* The sole effect then of the progress of wealth on prices, independently of all improvements, either in agriculture or manufactures, appears to be to raise the price of raw produce and of labour, leaving all other commodities at their original prices,[1] and to lower general profits in consequence of the general rise of wages.

This fact is of more importance than at first sight appears, as it relates to the interest of the landlord, and the other parts of the community. Not only is the situation of the landlord improved, (by the increasing difficulty of procuring food, in consequence of accumulation) by obtaining an increased quantity of the produce of the land, but also by the increased exchangeable value of that quantity. If his rent be increased from fourteen to twenty-eight quarters, it would be more than doubled, because he would be able to command more than double the quantity of commodities, in exchange for the twenty-eight quarters. As rents are agreed for, and paid in money, he would, under the circumstances supposed, receive more than double of his former money rent.

In like manner, if rent fell, the landlord would suffer two losses; he would be a loser of that portion of the raw produce which constituted his additional rent; and further, he would

---

* Though the price of all commodities is ultimately regulated by, and is always tending to, the cost of their production, including the general profits of stock, they are all subject, and perhaps corn more than most others, to an accidental price, proceeding from temporary causes.

[1] Shortly after publication Ricardo modified his opinion on this point, and allowed that the prices of other commodities would change owing to 'the altered value of the raw material in all manufactured goods'. See letter to Malthus, 9 March 1815, below, VI, 179, and cp. *Principles*, above, I, 117.

be a loser by the depreciation in the real or exchangeable value of the raw produce in which, or in the value of which, his remaining rent would be paid.*

As the revenue of the farmer is realized in raw produce, or in the value of raw produce, he is interested, as well as the landlord, in its high exchangeable value, but a low price of produce may be compensated to him by a great additional quantity.

It follows then, that the interest of the landlord is always opposed to the interest of every other class in the community. His situation is never so prosperous, as when food is scarce and dear: whereas, all other persons are greatly benefited by procuring food cheap. High rent and low profits, for they invariably accompany each other, ought never to be the subject of complaint, if they are the effect of the natural course of things.

They are the most unequivocal proofs of wealth and prosperity, and of an abundant population, compared with the fertility of the soil. The general profits of stock depend wholly on the profits of the last portion of capital employed on the land; if, therefore, landlords were to relinquish the whole of their rents, they would neither raise the general profits of stock, nor lower the price of corn to the consumer. It would

* It has been thought that the price of corn regulates the prices of all other things.[1] This appears to me to be a mistake. If the price of corn is affected by the rise or fall of the value of the precious metals themselves, then indeed will the price of commodities be also affected, but they vary, because the value of money varies, not because the value of corn is altered. Commodities, I think, cannot materially rise or fall, whilst money and commodities continue in the same proportions, or rather whilst the cost of production of both estimated in corn continues the same. In the case of taxation, a part of the price is paid for the liberty of using the commodity, and does not constitute its real price.

[1] See the quotations from Adam Smith and other writers given in *Principles*, I, 302 ff.

have no other effect, as Mr. Malthus has observed,[1] than to enable those farmers, whose lands now pay a rent, to live like gentlemen, and they would have to expend that portion of the general revenue, which now falls to the share of the landlord.

A nation is rich, not according to the abundance of its money, nor to the high money value at which its commodities circulate, but according to the abundance of its commodities, contributing to its comforts and enjoyments. Although this is a proposition, from which few would dissent, many look with the greatest alarm at the prospect of the diminution of their money revenue, though such reduced revenue should have so improved in exchangeable value, as to procure considerably more of all the necessaries and luxuries of life.

If then, the principles here stated as governing rent and profit be correct, general profits on capital, can only be raised by a fall in the exchangeable value of food, and which fall can only arise from three causes:

1st. The fall of the real wages of labour, which shall enable the farmer to bring a greater excess of produce to market.

2d. Improvements in agriculture, or in the implements of husbandry, which shall also increase the excess of produce.

3dly. The discovery of new markets, from whence corn may be imported at a cheaper price than it can be grown for at home.

The first of these causes is more or less permanent, according as the price from which wages fall, is more or less near that remuneration for labour, which is necessary to the actual subsistence of the labourer.

The rise or fall of wages is common to all states of society, whether it be the stationary, the advancing, or the retrograde state. In the stationary state, it is regulated wholly by the increase or falling off of the population. In the advancing

---

[1] *Inquiry into...Rent,* p. 57.

state, it depends on whether the capital or the population advance, at the more rapid course. In the retrograde state, it depends on whether population or capital decrease with the greater rapidity.

As experience demonstrates that capital and population alternately take the lead, and wages in consequence are liberal or scanty, nothing can be positively laid down, respecting profits, as far as wages are concerned.

But I think it may be most satisfactorily proved, that in every society advancing in wealth and population, independently of the effect produced by liberal or scanty wages, general profits must fall, unless there be improvements in agriculture, or corn can be imported at a cheaper price.

It seems the necessary result of the principles which have been stated to regulate the progress of rent.

This principle will, however, not be readily admitted by those who ascribe to the extension of commerce, and discovery of new markets, where our commodities can be sold dearer, and foreign commodities can be bought cheaper, the progress of profits, without any reference whatever to the state of the land, and the rate of profit obtained on the last portions of capital employed upon it. Nothing is more common than to hear it asserted, that profits on agriculture no more regulate the profits of commerce, than that the profits of commerce regulate the profits on agriculture.[1] It is contended, that they alternately take the lead; and, if the profits of commerce rise, which it is said they do, when new markets are discovered, the profits of agriculture will also rise; for it is admitted, that if they did not do so, capital would be withdrawn from the land to be employed in the more profitable trade. But if the principles respecting the progress of rent be correct, it is evident, that

[1] This was Malthus's reply to Ricardo's theory already in March 1814; see below, VI, 104.

with the same population and capital, whilst none of the agricultural capital is withdrawn from the cultivation of the land, agricultural profits cannot rise, nor can rent fall: either then it must be contended, which is at variance with all the principles of political economy, that the profits on commercial capital will rise considerably, whilst the profits on agricultural capital suffer no alteration, or, that under such circumstances, the profits on commerce will not rise.*

It is this latter opinion which I consider as the true one. I do not deny that the first discoverer of a new and better market may, for a time, before competition operates, obtain unusual profits. He may either sell the commodities he exports at a higher price than those who are ignorant of the new market, or he may purchase the commodities imported at a cheaper price. Whilst he, or a few more exclusively follow this trade, their profits will be above the level of general profits. But it is of the general rate of profit that we are speaking, and not of the profits of a few individuals; and I cannot doubt that, in proportion as such trade shall be generally known and followed, there will be such a fall in the price of the foreign commodity in the importing country, in consequence of its increased abundance, and the greater facility with which it is procured, that its sale will afford only the common rate of profits—that so far from the high profits obtained by the few

* Mr. Malthus has supplied me with a happy illustration—he has correctly compared "the soil to a great number of machines, all susceptible of continued improvement by the application of capital to them, but yet of very different original qualities and powers."[1] How, I would ask, can profits rise whilst we are obliged to make use of that machine which has the worst original qualities and powers? We cannot abandon the use of it; for it is the condition on which we obtain the food necessary for our population, and the demand for food is by the supposition not diminished—but who would consent to use it if he could make greater profits elsewhere?

[1] *Inquiry into...Rent*, p. 37.

who first engaged in the new trade elevating the general rate of profits—those profits will themselves sink to the ordinary level.

The effects are precisely similar to those which follow from the use of improved machinery at home.

Whilst the use of the machine is confined to one, or a very few manufacturers, they may obtain unusual profits, because they are enabled to sell their commodities at a price much above the cost of production—but as soon as the machine becomes general to the whole trade, the price of the commodities will sink to the actual cost of production, leaving only the usual and ordinary profits.

During the period of capital moving from one employment to another, the profits on that to which capital is flowing will be relatively high, but will continue so no longer than till the requisite capital is obtained.

There are two ways in which a country may be benefited by trade—one by the increase of the general rate of profits, which, according to my opinion, can never take place but in consequence of cheap food, which is beneficial only to those who derive a revenue from the employment of their capital, either as farmers, manufacturers, merchants, or capitalists, lending their money at interest—the other by the abundance of commodities, and by a fall in their exchangeable value, in which the whole community participate. In the first case, the revenue of the country is augmented—in the second the same revenue becomes efficient in procuring a greater amount of the necessaries and luxuries of life.

It is in this latter mode only* that nations are benefited by the extension of commerce, by the division of labour in manufactures, and by the discovery of machinery,—they all augment

* Excepting when the extension of commerce enables us to obtain food at really cheaper prices.

the amount of commodities, and contribute very much to the ease and happiness of mankind; but, they have no effect on the rate of profits, because they do not augment the produce compared with the cost of production on the land, and it is impossible that all other profits should rise whilst the profits on land are either stationary, or retrograde.

Profits then depend on the price, or rather on the value of food. Every thing which gives facility to the production of food, however scarce, or however abundant commodities may become, will raise the rate of profits, whilst on the contrary, every thing which shall augment the cost of production without augmenting the quantity of food,* will, under every circumstance, lower the general rate of profits. The facility[1] of obtaining food is[2] beneficial in two ways to the owners of capital, it at the same time raises profits and increases the amount of consumable commodities. The facility in obtaining all other things, only increases the amount of commodities.

If, then, the power of purchasing cheap food be of such great importance, and if the importation of corn will tend to reduce its price, arguments almost unanswerable respecting the danger of dependence on foreign countries for a portion of our food, for in no other view will the question bear an argument, ought to be brought forward to induce us to restrict importation, and thereby forcibly to detain capital in an employment which it would otherwise leave for one much more advantageous.

If the legislature were at once to adopt a decisive policy

---

* If by foreign commerce, or the discovery of machinery, the commodities consumed by the labourer should become much cheaper, wages would fall; and this, as we have before observed, would raise the profits of the farmer, and therefore, all other profits.

[1] Printed 'facilities', here and three lines below. Corrected by Ricardo in his copy at Gatcombe.   [2] Printed 'are'. Corrected by Ricardo in his copy.

with regard to the trade in corn—if it were to allow a permanently free trade, and did not with every variation of price, alternately restrict and encourage importation, we should undoubtedly be a regularly importing country. We should be so in consequence of the superiority of our wealth and population, compared to the fertility of our soil over our neighbours. It is only when a country is comparatively wealthy, when all its fertile land is in a state of high cultivation, and that it is obliged to have recourse to its inferior lands to obtain the food necessary for its population; or when it is originally without the advantages of a fertile soil, that it can become profitable to import corn.*

It is, then, the dangers of dependence on foreign supply for any considerable quantity of our food, which can alone be opposed to the many advantages which, circumstanced as we are, would attend the importation of corn.

These dangers do not admit of being very correctly estimated, they are in some degree, matters of opinion and cannot like the advantages on the other side, be reduced to accurate calculation. They are generally stated to be two—1st, that in the case of war a combination of the continental powers, or the influence of our principal enemy, might deprive us of our accustomed supply—2dly, that when bad seasons occurred abroad, the exporting countries would have, and would exercise, the power of withholding the quantity usually exported to make up for their own deficient supply.†

If we became a regularly importing country, and foreigners could confidently rely on the demand of our market, much

* This principle is most ably stated by Mr. Malthus in page 42 of "An Inquiry," &c.

† It is this latter opinion which is chiefly insisted upon by Mr. Malthus, in his late publication, "The grounds of An Opinion," &c.[1]

[1] pp. 17–20.

more land would be cultivated in the corn countries with a view to exportation. When we consider the value of even a few weeks consumption of corn in England, no interruption could be given to the export trade, if the continent supplied us with any considerable quantity of corn, without the most extensively ruinous commercial distress—distress which no sovereign, or combination of sovereigns, would be willing to inflict on their people; and, if willing, it would be a measure to which probably no people would submit. It was the endeavour of Buonaparte to prevent the exportation of the raw produce of Russia, more than [any][1] other cause which produced the astonishing efforts of the people of that country against the most powerful force perhaps ever assembled to subjugate a nation.

The immense capital which would be employed on the land, could not be withdrawn suddenly, and under such circumstances, without immense loss; besides which, the glut of corn in their markets, which would affect their whole supply, and lower its value beyond calculation; the failure of those returns, which are essential in all commercial adventures, would occasion a scene of wide spreading ruin, which if a country would patiently endure, would render it unfit to wage war with any prospect of success. We have all witnessed the distress in this country, and we have all heard of the still greater distress in Ireland, from a fall in the price of corn, at a time too when it is acknowledged that our own crop has been deficient; when importation has been regulated by price, and when we have not experienced any of the effects of a glut. Of what nature would that distress have been if the price of corn had fallen to a half a quarter, or an eighth part of the present price. For the effects of plenty or scarcity, in the price of corn, are incalculably greater than in proportion to the increase or de-

[1] Omitted by a mistake.

ficiency of quantity. These then, are the inconveniencies which the exporting countries would have to endure.

Ours would not be light. A great diminution in our usual supply, amounting probably to one-eighth of our whole consumption, it must be confessed, would be an evil of considerable magnitude; but we have obtained a supply equal to this, even when the growth of foreign countries was not regulated by the constant demand of our market. We all know the prodigious effects of a high price in procuring a supply. It cannot, I think be doubted, that we should obtain a considerable quantity from those countries with which we were not at war; which, with the most economical use of our own produce, and the quantity in store,* would enable us to subsist till we had bestowed the necessary capital and labour on our own land, with a view to future production. That this would be a most afflicting change, I certainly allow; but I am fully persuaded that we should not be driven to such an alternative, and that notwithstanding the war, we should be freely supplied with the corn, expressly grown in foreign countries for our consumption. Buonaparte, when he was most hostile to us, permitted the exportation of corn to England by licences, when our prices were high from a bad harvest, even when all other commerce was prohibited. Such a state of things could not come upon us suddenly; a danger of this nature would be partly foreseen, and due precautions would be taken. Would it be wise then to legislate with the view of preventing an evil

---

* As London is to be a depot for foreign corn,[1] this store might be very great.

[1] This was to be effected by permitting the free import of foreign corn to be bonded and warehoused. See 'Report from the Select Committee on Petitions relating to the Corn Laws', 1814, pp. 15–16, *Parliamentary Papers*, 1813–14, vol. III; the proposal was subsequently adopted in the Corn Law of 1815.

which might never occur; and to ward off a most improbable danger, sacrifice annually a revenue of some millions?

In contemplating a trade in corn, unshackled by restrictions on importation, and a consequent supply from France, and other countries, where it can be brought to market, at a price not much above half that at which we can ourselves produce it on some of our poorer lands, Mr. Malthus does not sufficiently allow for the greater quantity of corn, which would be grown abroad, if importation was to become the settled policy of this country.[1] There cannot be the least doubt that if the corn countries could depend on the markets of England for a regular demand, if they could be perfectly secure that our laws, respecting the corn trade, would not be repeatedly vacillating between bounties, restrictions, and prohibitions, a much larger supply would be grown, and the danger of a greatly diminished exportation, in consequence of bad seasons, would be less likely to occur. Countries which have never yet supplied us, might, if our policy was fixed, afford us a considerable quantity.

It is at such times that it would be particularly the interest of foreign countries to supply our wants, as the exchangeable value of corn does not rise in proportion only to the deficiency of supply, but two, three, four, times as much, according to the amount of the deficiency.

If the consumption of England is ten million quarters, which, in an average year, would sell for forty millions of money; and, if the supply should be deficient one fourth, the seven million five hundred thousand quarters would not sell for forty millions only, but probably for fifty millions, or more. Under the circumstances then of bad seasons, the exporting country would content itself with the smallest possible quantity necessary for their own consumption, and would take advantage

[1] *Grounds of an Opinion*, pp. 14–15.

of the high price in England, to sell all they could spare, as not only would corn be high, as compared with money, but as compared with all other things; and if the growers of corn adopted any other rule, they would be in a worse situation, as far as regarded wealth, than if they had constantly limited the growth of corn to the wants of their own people.

If one hundred millions of capital were employed on the land, to obtain the quantity necessary to their own subsistence, and twenty millions more, that they might export the produce, they would lose the whole return of the twenty millions in the scarce year, which they would not have done had they not been an exporting country.

At whatever price exportation might be restricted, by foreign countries, the chance of corn rising to that price would be diminished by the greater quantity produced in consequence of our demand.

With respect to the supply of corn, it has been remarked,[1] in reference to a single country, that if the crops are bad in one district, they are generally productive in another; that if the weather is injurious to one soil, or to one situation, it is beneficial to a different soil and different situation; and, by this compensating power, Providence has bountifully secured us from the frequent recurrence of dearths. If this remark be just, as applied to one country, how much more strongly may it be applied to all the countries together which compose our world? Will not the deficiency of one country be made up by the plenty of another? and, after the experience which we have had of the power of high prices to procure a supply, can we have any just reason to fear that we shall be exposed to any particular danger from depending on importation, for so much corn as may be necessary for a few weeks of our consumption.

[1] *Wealth of Nations*, Bk. IV, ch. v; Cannan's ed., vol. II, p. 28.

From all that I can learn, the price of corn in Holland, which country depends almost wholly on foreign supply, has been remarkably steady, even during the convulsed times which Europe has lately experienced—a convincing proof, notwithstanding the smallness of the country, that the effects of bad seasons are not exclusively borne by importing countries.

That great improvements have been made in agriculture, and that much capital has been expended on the land, it is not attempted to deny; but, with all those improvements, we have not overcome the natural impediments resulting from our increasing wealth and prosperity, which obliges us to cultivate at a disadvantage our poor lands, if the importation of corn is restricted or prohibited. If we were left to ourselves, unfettered by legislative enactments, we should gradually withdraw our capital from the cultivation of such lands, and import the produce which is at present raised upon them. The capital withdrawn would be employed in the manufacture of such commodities as would be exported in return for the corn.* Such a distribution of part of the capital of the country, would be more advantageous, or it would not be adopted. This principle is one of the best established in the science of political economy, and by no one is more readily admitted than by Mr. Malthus. It is the foundation of all his arguments, in his comparison of the advantages and disadvantages attending an unrestricted trade in corn, in his "Observations on the Corn Laws."

* If it be true, as Mr. Malthus observes,[1] that in Ireland there are no manufactures in which capital could be profitably employed, capital would not be withdrawn from the land, and then there would be no loss of agricultural capital. Ireland would, in such case, have the same surplus corn produce, although it would be of less exchangeable value. Her revenue might be diminished; but if she would not, or could not manufacture goods, and would not cultivate the ground, she would have no revenue at all.

[1] *Grounds of an Opinion*, pp. 25–26.

In his last publication, however, in one part of it,[1] he dwells with much stress on the losses of agricultural capital, which the country would sustain, by allowing an unrestricted importation. He laments the loss of that which by the course of events has become of no use to us, and by the employment of which we actually lose. We might just as fairly have been told, when the steam-engine, or Mr. Arkwright's cotton-machine, was brought to perfection, that it would be wrong to adopt the use of them, because the value of the old clumsy machinery would be lost to us. That the farmers of the poorer lands would be losers, there can be no doubt, but the public would gain many times the amount of their losses; and, after the exchange of capital from land to manufactures had been effected, the farmers themselves, as well as every other class of the community, except the landholders, would very considerably increase their profits.

It might, however, be desirable, that the farmers, during their current leases, should be protected against the losses which they would undoubtedly suffer from the new value of money, which would result from a cheap price of corn, under their existing money engagements with their landlords.

Although the nation would sacrifice much more than the farmers would save even by a temporary high price of corn, it might be just to lay restrictive duties on importation for three or four years, and to declare that, after that period, the trade in corn should be free, and that imported corn should be subject to no other duty than such as we might find it expedient to impose on corn of our own growth.*

* I by no means agree with Adam Smith,[2] or with Mr. Malthus,[3] respecting the effects of taxation on the necessaries of life. The former can find no term too severe by which to characterize them. Mr. Malthus is

[1] *ib.* p. 30.

[2] Bk. v, ch. ii, pt. ii, art. i; vol. II, pp. 321–2.

[3] *Inquiry into...Rent*, pp. 52–3.

Mr. Malthus is, no doubt, correct, when he says, "If merely the best modes of cultivation now in use, in some parts of Great Britain, were generally extended, and the whole country was brought to a level, in proportion to its natural advantages of soil and situation, by the further accumulation and more equable distribution of capital and skill, the quantity of additional produce would be immense, and would afford the means of subsistence to a very great increase of population.["]*

This reflection is true, and is highly pleasing—it shews that we are yet at a great distance from the end of our resources, and that we may contemplate an increase of prosperity and wealth, far exceeding that of any country which has preceded us. This may take place under either system, that of importation or restriction, though not with an equally accelerated pace, and is no argument why we should not, at every period of our improvement, avail ourselves of the full extent of the advantages offered to our acceptance—it is no reason why we should not make the very best disposition of our capital, so as to ensure the most abundant return. The land has, as I before said,[1] been compared by Mr. Malthus to a great number of machines, all susceptible of continued improvement by the application of capital to them, but yet of very different original qualities and powers. Would it be wise at a great expense to use some of the worst of these machines, when at a less expense we could hire the very best from our neighbours.

more lenient. They both think that such taxes, incalculably more than any other, tend to diminish capital and production. I do not say that they are the best of taxes, but they do not, I think, subject us to any of the disadvantages of which Adam Smith speaks in foreign trade: nor do they produce effects very different from other taxes. Adam Smith thought that such taxes fell exclusively on the landholder; Mr. Malthus thinks they are divided between the landholder and consumer. It appears to me that they are paid wholly by the consumer.

* Page 22, Grounds, &c.

[1] Above, p. 24.

Mr. Malthus thinks that a low money price of corn would not be favourable to the lower classes of society, because the real exchangeable value of labour; that is, its power of commanding the necessaries, conveniences, and luxuries of life, would not be augmented, but diminished by a low money price.[1] Some of his observations on this subject are certainly of great weight, but he does not sufficiently allow for the effects of a better distribution of the national capital on the situation of the lower classes. It would be beneficial to them, because the same capital would employ more hands; besides, that the greater profits would lead to further accumulation; and thus would a stimulus be given to population by really high wages, which could not fail for a long time to ameliorate the condition of the labouring classes.

The effects on the interests of this class, would be nearly the same as the effects of improved machinery, which it is now no longer questioned, has a decided tendency to raise the real wages of labour.[2]

Mr. Malthus also observes, "that of the commercial and manufacturing classes, only those who are directly engaged in foreign trade will feel the benefit of the importing system."[3]

If the view which has been taken of rent be correct,—if it rise as general profits fall, and falls as general profits rise,—and if the effect of importing corn is to lower rent, which has been admitted, and ably exemplified by Mr. Malthus himself,—all who are concerned in trade,—all capitalists whatever, whether they be farmers, manufacturers, or merchants, will have a great augmentation of profits. A fall in the price of corn, in consequence of improvements in agriculture or of importation, will lower the exchangeable value of corn only,—the price of no other commodity will be affected. If, then, the price

[1] *Grounds of an Opinion*, p. 24.
[2] For Ricardo's later views on
machinery see *Principles*, ch. XXXI.
[3] *Grounds of an Opinion*, p. 30.

of labour falls, which it must do when the price of corn is lowered, the real profits of all descriptions must rise; and no person will be so materially benefited as the manufacturing and commercial part of society.

If the demand for home commodities should be diminished, because of the fall of rent on the part of the landlords, it will be increased in a far greater degree by the increased opulence of the commercial classes.

If restrictions on the importation of corn should take place, I do not apprehend, that we shall lose any part of our foreign trade; on this point, I agree with Mr. Malthus.[1] In the case of a free trade in corn, it would be considerably augmented; but the question is not, whether we can retain the same foreign trade—but, whether, in both cases, it will be equally profitable.

Our commodities would not sell abroad for more or for less in consequence of a free trade, and a cheap price of corn; but the cost of production to our manufacturers would be very different if the price of corn was eighty, or was sixty shillings per quarter; and consequently profits would be augmented by all the cost saved in the production of the exported commodities.

Mr. Malthus notices an observation, which was first made by Hume,[2] that a rise of prices, has a magic effect on industry: he states the effects of a fall to be proportionally depressing.* A rise of prices has been stated to be one of the advantages, to counterbalance the many evils attendant on a depreciation of money, from a real fall in the value of the precious metals, from raising the denomination of the coin, or from the over-issue of paper money.

* Grounds, &c. p. 32.

[1] *Grounds of an Opinion*, p. 31.   [2] Essay 'Of Money', in *Political Discourses*, 1752, p. 41.

It is said to be beneficial, because it betters the situation of the commercial classes at the expense of those enjoying fixed incomes;—and that it is chiefly in those classes, that the great accumulations are made, and productive industry encouraged.

A recurrence to a better monetary system, it is said, though highly desirable, tends to give a temporary discouragement to accumulation and industry, by depressing the commercial part of the community, and is the effect of a fall of prices: Mr. Malthus supposes that such an effect will be produced by the fall of the price of corn. If the observation made by Hume were well founded, still it would not apply to the present instance:—for every thing that the manufacturer would have to sell, would be as dear as ever: it is only what he would buy that would be cheap, namely, corn and labour by which his gains would be increased. I must again observe, that a rise in the value of money lowers all things; whereas a fall in the price of corn, only lowers the wages of labour, and therefore raises profits.

If then the prosperity of the commercial classes, will most certainly lead to accumulation of capital, and the encouragement of productive industry; these can by no means be so surely obtained as by a fall in the price of corn.

I cannot agree with Mr. Malthus in his approbation of the opinion of Adam Smith, "that no equal quantity of productive labour employed in manufactures, can *ever* occasion so great a re-production as in agriculture."[1] I suppose that he must have overlooked the term ever in this passage, otherwise the opinion is more consistent with the doctrine of the Economists, than with those which he has maintained; as he has stated, and I think correctly, that in the first settling of a new country, and in every stage of its improvement, there is a portion of its

[1] *Wealth of Nations*, Bk. II, ch. v; vol. I, p. 344. Quoted by Malthus, *Grounds of an Opinion*, p. 35. The italics are Ricardo's.

capital employed on the land, for the profits of stock merely, and which yields no rent whatever. Productive labour employed on such land never does in fact afford so *great* a re-production, as the same productive labour employed in manufactures.

The difference is not indeed great, and is voluntarily relinquished, on account of the security and respectability which attends the employment of capital on land. In the infancy of society, when no rent is paid, is not the re-production of value in the coarse[1] manufactures, and in the implements of husbandry with a given capital, at least as great as the value which the same capital would afford if employed on the land?

This opinion indeed is at variance with all the general doctrines of Mr. Malthus, which he has so ably maintained in this as well as in all his other publications. In the "Inquiry,"[2] speaking of what I consider a similar opinion of Adam Smith, he observes, "I cannot, however, agree with him in thinking that all land which yields food must necessarily yield rent. The land which is successively taken into cultivation in improving countries, may only pay profits and labour. A fair profit on the stock employed, including, of course, the payment of labour, will always be a sufficient inducement to cultivate." The same motives will also induce some to manufacture goods, and the profits of both in the same stages of society will be nearly the same.

In the course of these observations, I have often had occasion to insist, that rent never falls without the profits of stock rising. If it suit us to day to import corn rather than grow it, we are solely influenced by the cheaper price. If we import the portion of capital last employed on the land, and which yielded no rent, will be withdrawn; rent will fall and profits rise, and another portion of capital employed on the land will come

---

[1] Misprinted 'course'.   [2] *Inquiry into...Rent*, p. 3, n.

under the same description of only yielding the usual profits of stock.

If corn can be imported cheaper than it can be grown on this rather better land, rent will again fall and profits rise, and another and better description of land will now be cultivated for profits only. In every step of our progress, profits of stock increase and rents fall, and more land is abandoned: besides which, the country saves all the difference between the price at which corn can be grown, and the price at which it can be imported, on the quantity we receive from abroad.

Mr. Malthus has considered, with the greatest ability, the effect of a cheap price of corn on those who contribute to the interest of our enormous debt.[1] I most fully concur in many of his conclusions on this part of the subject. The wealth of England would, I am persuaded, be considerably augmented by a great reduction in the price of corn, but the whole money value of that wealth would be diminished. It would be diminished by the whole difference of the money value of the corn consumed,—it would be augmented by the increased exchangeable value of all those commodities which would be exported in exchange for the corn imported. The latter would, however, be very unequal to the former; therefore the money value of the commodities of England would, undoubtedly, be considerably lowered.

But, though it is true, that the money value of the mass of our commodities would be diminished, it by no means follows, that our annual revenue would fall in the same degree. The advocates for importation ground their opinion of the advantages of it on the conviction that the revenue would not so fall. And, as it is from our revenue that taxes are paid, the burthen might not be really augmented.

Suppose the revenue of a country to fall from ten to nine

[1] *Grounds of an Opinion*, pp. 38 ff.

millions, whilst the value of money altered in the proportion of ten to eight, such country would have a larger neat revenue, after paying a million from the smaller, than it would have after paying it from the larger sum.

That the stockholder would receive more in real value than what he contracted for, in the loans of the late years, is also true; but, as the stockholders themselves contribute very largely to the public burthens, and therefore to the payment of the interest which they receive, no inconsiderable proportion of the taxes would fall on them; and, if we estimate at its true value the additional profits made by the commercial class, they would still be great gainers, notwithstanding their really augmented contributions.

The landlord would be the only sufferer by paying really more, not only without any adequate compensation, but with lowered rents.

It may indeed be urged, on the part of the stockholder, and those who live on fixed incomes, that they have been by far the greatest sufferers by the war. The value of their revenue has been diminished by the rise in the price of corn, and by the depreciation in the value of paper money, whilst, at the same time, the value of their capital has been very much diminished from the lower price of the funds. They have suffered too from the inroads lately made on the sinking fund, and which, it is supposed, will be still further extended,—a measure of the greatest injustice,—in direct violation of solemn contracts;[1] for the sinking fund is as much a part of the contract as the dividend, and, as a source of revenue, utterly at variance with all sound principles. It is to the growth of that fund that we ought to look for the means of carrying on future wars, unless we are prepared to relinquish the funding system al-

---

[1] The reference is to Vansittart's 'Plan of Finance' of 1813; see below, pp. 159–60.

together. To meddle with the sinking fund, is to obtain a little temporary aid at the sacrifice of a great future advantage. It is reversing the whole system of Mr. Pitt, in the creation of that fund: he proceeded on the conviction, that, for a small present burthen, an immense future advantage would be obtained; and, after witnessing, as we have done, the benefits which have already resulted from his inflexible determination to leave that fund untouched, even when he was pressed by the greatest financial distress, when three per cents. were so low as forty-eight, we cannot, I think, hesitate in pronouncing, that he would not have countenanced, had he still lived, the measures which have been adopted.

To recur, however, to the subject before me, I shall only further observe, that I shall greatly regret that considerations for any particular class, are allowed to check the progress of the wealth and population of the country. If the interests of the landlord be of sufficient consequence, to determine us not to avail ourselves of all the benefits which would follow from importing corn at a cheap price, they should also influence us in rejecting all improvements in agriculture, and in the implements of husbandry; for it is as certain that corn is rendered cheap, rents are lowered, and the ability of the landlord to pay taxes, is for a time, at least, as much impaired by such improvements, as by the importation of corn. To be consistent then, let us by the same act arrest improvement, and prohibit importation.

PROPOSALS

FOR AN

ECONOMICAL AND SECURE

CURRENCY;

WITH

OBSERVATIONS

ON THE

PROFITS OF THE BANK OF ENGLAND,

AS THEY REGARD THE PUBLIC AND THE PROPRIETORS

OF BANK STOCK.

BY DAVID RICARDO, ESQ.

LONDON:

PRINTED FOR JOHN MURRAY, ALBEMARLE-STREET.

1816.

PROPOSALS

FOR AN

ECONOMICAL AND SECURE

CURRENCY;

WITH

OBSERVATIONS

ON THE

PROFITS OF THE BANK OF ENGLAND,

AS THEY REGARD THE PUBLIC AND THE PROPRIETORS
OF BANK STOCK.

BY DAVID RICARDO, ESQ.

SECOND EDITION.

LONDON:

PRINTED FOR JOHN MURRAY, ALBEMARLE-STREET.

1816.

[Title-page to ed. 2]

NOTE ON 'ECONOMICAL AND SECURE CURRENCY'

RICARDO undertook to write the *Proposals for an Economical and Secure Currency* at the suggestion of Pascoe Grenfell in the summer of 1815. The latter, in May and June, had been demanding in the House of Commons measures to limit the profits which the Bank made from their transactions with the Government, and he intended to raise the matter again in the next Session.

In July Ricardo and Grenfell met frequently in London and discussed the subject of the Bank.[1] At the beginning of August, after Ricardo had gone to Gatcomb, Grenfell wrote urging him to overcome his modesty and write, before the Bank Court to be held in September or October, 'a Short Pamphlet on the Subject to which I have lately called the attention of Parliament'.[2] By the end of August Ricardo was at work on the pamphlet, Grenfell supplying him with the relevant Parliamentary Papers and Accounts, with his own calculations and with Allardyce's pamphlets on the Bank; from these sources Ricardo drew most of his facts.

A considerable part of the pamphlet was devoted to the development of the points which Grenfell had raised, namely, the excessive profits made by the Bank from its bargains with the Government, and their failure to distribute them among the proprietors. On these questions Ricardo went 'much further' than Grenfell.[3] Indeed, at one stage of writing it is clear that he intended his main proposal to be that the Government should dispense altogether with the services of the Bank as being 'an unnecessary establishment', by appointing independent Commissioners who would be the sole issuers of paper money, would manage the National Debt and act as bankers to all public departments.[4] There is, however, only an inci-

---

[1] See below, VI, 267–8.
[2] Below, VI, 241–2. The pamphlet was published too late for the Bank Courts both of September and December. It was in time however for the debate on Grenfell's motion in the House of Commons on 13 Feb. 1816.
[3] Below, VI, 268.
[4] Letter to Malthus of 10 Sept. 1815, below, VI, 268. He added, 'I always enjoy any attack upon the

dental allusion to this plan, in the closing paragraph of the pamphlet,[1] and it was not until 1823 that Ricardo developed the idea, in his *Plan for a National Bank*.

Though the writing of the pamphlet was suggested by Grenfell, its most important proposal (to make Bank Notes payable in bullion instead of coin) from which it took its title had nothing to do with Grenfell, and was indeed 'quite new' to him.[2] Ricardo had originally outlined this proposal in the Appendix to the fourth edition of the *High Price of Bullion* (April 1811) and had submitted it to Perceval, the Prime Minister, in July 1811 and to Tierney, one of the leaders of the Opposition, in December of the same year.[3] He now revived it in the expectation that the date for the resumption of cash payments would be fixed in the approaching session of 1816.

Late in September 1815 the MS was finished and sent to Grenfell, who found it excellent.[4] Ricardo was unconvinced, and sought Malthus's opinion of the MS, declaring himself 'too little pleased with it to think of publishing'.[5] Malthus approved the matter but criticised the style and arrangement.[6] Grenfell continued to urge publication,[7] so Ricardo set to work to improve it.[8] Early in November he submitted the revised MS to Mill who, nearly a month later (the MS having gone astray in transit), recommended its publication, but advised him to divide it into sections (for which he suggested the titles), to recast the first section and to write an introduction.[9] Ricardo also appealed to Mill's judgment as to the propriety of his making proposals which might entail repudiation on the

Bank and if I had sufficient courage I would be a party to it.' No doubt Malthus had this remark in mind, when, having read the MS, he wrote, 'I conclude that you have no reason to care much for the resentment of the Bank. The publication will no doubt make the Directors very angry.' (16 Oct. 1815, below, VI, 302.)

[1] Below, p. 114. The wording of the paragraph in question suggests that it was drafted or revised by Mill.

[2] Below, VI, 286. Also unconnected with Grenfell's agitation was the proposal to issue dividend warrants in advance of the date of payment, in order to relieve the periodical pressure on the money market, below, pp. 74–5.

[3] Below, VI, 43 and 67.

[4] *ib.* 285–6.

[5] *ib.* 294–5.

[6] *ib.* 298 and cp. 315.

[7] *ib.* 305.

[8] *ib.* 315.

[9] *ib.* 331.

part of the Government of the bargain made by Perceval with the
Bank in 1808. Mill, while providing legal arguments in defence of
such a course,[1] advised him to dwell upon 'the *moral* part of the
argument against the Bank'; this Ricardo did, using Mill's own
words.[2]

Mill's encouragement was decisive.[3] In January Ricardo saw
Murray in London about publication,[4] which he was anxious should
take place before Parliament met on 1 February 1816. Indeed, a
preliminary advertisement appeared in the press[5] announcing its
publication for 1 February, but some further delay was caused by
Mill's offer to revise the proofs and to improve the expressions and
the punctuation.[6] The pamphlet was eventually published on
6 February 1816,[7] a week before the debate in the House of Commons on Grenfell's Motion concerning the transactions with the Bank.

Although Ricardo had anticipated so little success for his work
that he had offered to Murray to bear the charge in case of loss,[8] it
sold unexpectedly well, and by 23 February a second edition was
being printed.[9] The only changes, apart from minor verbal alterations, were two footnotes,[10] one on the Bank Court held on
8 February and the other qualifying his calculations of the Bank's
profits.

Nearly three years later, when the question of the resumption of
cash payments was about to come before Parliament, McCulloch
again drew the attention of the public to *Economical and Secure
Currency* by a review in the *Edinburgh Review* for December 1818;
and at his suggestion Ricardo quoted in ed. 2 of the *Principles*,
1819, a passage from the pamphlet containing the plan of bullion
payments.[11] The evidence before both the Lords' and Commons'

---

[1] See below, VI, 337–8.

[2] See below, p. 93 and cp. VII, 5.
Mill had also to allay Ricardo's
fears that, 'as a loan contractor, and
a successful one', he was himself
open to the accusation of having
made excessive profits.

[3] Below, VI, 335.

[4] Below, VII, 1.

[5] *The Times*, 22 January; see below, VII, 13, n. 4.

[6] See below, VII, 4.

[7] See below, VII, 16 and 19. Ad-
vertised as 'lately published' in
Monthly Literary Advertiser for 10
Feb. 1816.

[8] Below, VII, 14.

[9] *ib.* 24. It was advertised in *The
Times* of 28 February.

[10] Below, pp. 87–8 and 97.

[11] Above, I, 356–61 and cp. below,
VII, 353.

Committees of 1819 centred largely on Ricardo's plan, which was finally adopted as the basis of Peel's Bill for the Resumption of Cash Payments.

As a result of this new interest a third edition of the pamphlet was published in March 1819.[1] This edition is in every respect identical with the second, except for the punctuation and capitalization which appear to have been arbitrarily changed by the printer, with the addition of some misprints. It is clear that Ricardo had no hand in these alterations, and therefore in the present text the second edition has been followed.

[1] Advt. in *The Times*, 25 March 1819.

CONTENTS[1]

APPENDIX

[1] The original editions have no Table of Contents.

INTRODUCTION

THE following important questions concerning the Bank of England will, next session, come under the discussion of parliament:

1st. Whether the Bank shall be obliged to pay their notes in specie at the demand of the holders?

2dly. Whether any alteration shall be made in the terms agreed upon in 1808, between Government and the Bank, for the management of the national debt?

And, 3dly, what compensation the public shall receive for the large amount of public deposits from which the Bank derive profit?[1]

In point of importance, the first of these questions greatly surpasses the rest:—but so much has already been written on the subject of currency, and on the laws by which it should be regulated, that I should not trouble the reader with any further observations on those topics, did I not think that a more economical mode of effecting our payments might be advantageously adopted; to explain which, it will be necessary to premise briefly some of the general principles which are found to constitute the laws of currency, and to vindicate them from some of the objections which are brought against them.

The other two questions, though inferior in importance, are, at these times of pressure on our finances, when economy is so essential, well deserving of the serious consideration of parlia-

---

[1] The first question came before the House of Commons on Horner's motion for a Committee on the Resumption of Cash Payments, 1 May, which was defeated, and again on the Bill for further continuing the Bank Restriction, 3 May 1816, which was passed; the second and third questions came up for discussion on Grenfell's motion on certain Transactions between the Public and the Bank of England, 13 Feb. 1816.

ment. If, on examination, it should be found that the services performed by the Bank for the public are most prodigally paid; and that this wealthy corporation has been accumulating a treasure of which no example can be brought—much of it at the expense of the public, and owing to the negligence and forbearance of government—a better arrangement, it is hoped, will now be made; which, while it secures to the Bank a just compensation for the responsibility and trouble which the management of the public business may occasion, shall also guard against any wasteful application of the public resources.

It must, I think, be allowed, that the war, which has pressed heavily on most of the classes of the community, has been attended with unlooked for benefits to the Bank; and that in proportion, to the increase of the public burdens and difficulties have been the gains of that body.

The restriction on the cash payments of the Bank, which was the effect of the war, has enabled them to raise the amount of their notes in circulation from twelve millions to twenty-eight millions; whilst, at the same time, it has exonerated them from all necessity of keeping any large deposit of cash and bullion, a part of their assets from which they derive no profit.

The war too has raised the unredeemed public debt, of which the Bank have the management, from 220 to 830 millions; and notwithstanding the reduced rate of charge, they will receive for the management of the debt alone, in the present year, 277,000*l.*,* whereas in 1792 their whole receipt on account of the debt was 99,800*l.*

It is to the war that the Bank are also indebted for the increase in the amount of public deposits. In 1792 these deposits were probably less than four millions. In and since 1806 we know that they have generally exceeded eleven millions.

It cannot, I think, be doubted, that all the services, which

* See Appendix, No. 3.

the Bank perform for the public, could be performed, by public servants and in public offices established for that purpose, at a reduction or saving of expense of nearly half a million per annum.

In 1786 the auditors of public accounts stated it as their opinion, that the public debt, then amounting to 224 millions, could be managed by government for less than 187*l*. 10*s*. per million.[1] On a debt of 830 millions the Bank are paid 340*l*. per million on 600 millions, and 300*l*. per million on 230 millions.

Against the mode in which the public business is managed at the Bank no complaint can be justly made; ability, regularity, and precision, are to be found in every office; and in these particulars it is not probable that any change could be made which would be deemed an improvement.

As far as the public are bound to the Bank by any existing agreement, an objection, on that score, will be urged against any alteration. Inadequate as, in my opinion, was, at that time, and under the circumstances in which it was granted, the compensation which the public received from the Bank, for the renewal of their charter, I shall not plead for a revision of that contract; but permit the Bank to enjoy unmolested all the fruits of so improvident and unequal a bargain.

But the agreement entered into with the Bank in 1808, for the management of the national debt, is not, I think, of the above description, and either party is now at liberty to annul it. The agreement was for no definite period; and has no necessary connexion with the duration of the charter, which was made eight years before it. Applying to the state of things existing at the time of its formation, or such a state as might be expected to occur within a few years, it is not any longer binding. This

[1] See 'Second Report from the Committee on the Public Expenditure, &c. of the United Kingdom. The Bank', 1807, p. 71; in *Parliamentary Papers*, 1807, vol. II.

is declared in the following passage of Mr. Perceval's letter to the Bank, dated the 15th January, 1808, on accepting the scale in respect to the rate for management proposed by the Bank. "Under this impression," says Mr. Perceval, "I am strongly inclined to give way to the suggestion of the Bank in the minor parts of the arrangement, and will therefore accede to the scale of allowances therein proposed for the management of the public debt, *so far as it applies to present circumstances, or to such as can be expected to occur within any short period.*"[1] Eight years having since elapsed, and the unredeemed debt having, in that time, increased 280 millions, can it be justly contended that it is not in the power of either party, now or hereafter, to annul this agreement, or to propose such alterations in it as time and circumstances may render expedient?

To Mr. Grenfell I am very materially indebted; I have done little more, on this part of the subject, than repeat his arguments and statements. I have endeavoured to give my feeble aid to a cause which he has already so ably advocated in parliament, and in which I trust success will crown his future efforts.

SECTION I

In the medium of circulation—cause of uniformity is cause of goodness

ALL writers on the subject of money have agreed that uniformity in the value of the circulating medium is an object greatly to be desired. Every improvement therefore which can promote an approximation to that object, by diminishing the causes of variation, should be adopted. No plan can possibly be devised which will maintain money at an absolutely uniform value, because it will always be subject to those variations to which

---

[1] 'Papers presented to the House of Commons, relating to the Bank; &c.', ordered to be printed 3 Feb. 1808, p. 13; in *Parliamentary Papers*, 1808, vol. x. The italics are Ricardo's.

the commodity itself is subject, which has been fixed upon as the standard.

While the precious metals continue to be the standard of our currency, money must necessarily undergo the same variations in value as those metals. It was the comparative steadiness in the value of the precious metals, for periods of some duration, which probably was the cause of the preference given to them in all countries, as a standard by which to measure the value of other things.

A currency may be considered as perfect, of which the standard is invariable, which always conforms to that standard, and in the use of which the utmost economy is practised.

Amongst the advantages of a paper over a metallic circulation, may be reckoned, as not the least, the facility with which it may be altered in quantity, as the wants of commerce and temporary circumstances may require: enabling the desirable object of keeping money at an uniform value to be, as far as it is otherwise practicable, securely and cheaply attained.

The quantity of metal, employed as money, in effecting the payments of any particular country, using metallic money; or the quantity of metal for which paper money is the substitute, if paper money be partly or wholly used, must depend on three things: first, on its value;—secondly, on the amount or value of the payments to be made;—and, thirdly, on the degree of economy practised in effecting those payments.

A country using gold as its standard would require, at least, fifteen times less of that metal than it would of silver, if using silver, and nine hundred times less than it would of copper, if using that metal,—fifteen to one being about the proportion which gold bears in value to silver, and nine hundred to one the proportion which it bears to copper. If the denomination of a pound were given to any specific weight of these metals, fifteen times more of such pounds would be required in the one case, and nine hundred times more in the other, whether the metals themselves were employed as money, or paper was partly, or entirely, substituted for them. And if a country uniformly employed the same metal as a standard, the quantity of money required would be in an inverse proportion to the value of that metal. Suppose the metal to be silver, and that, from the difficulty of working the mines, silver should be doubled in value,—half the quantity only would then be wanted for money; and if the whole business of circulation were carried on by paper, of which the standard was silver,—to sustain that paper, at its bullion value, it must in like manner be reduced one half. In the same way it might be shewn, that, if silver became as cheap again, compared with all other commodities, double the quantity would be required to circulate the same quantity of goods.—When the number of transactions increase in any country from its increasing opulence and industry— bullion remaining at the same value, and the economy in the use of money also continuing unaltered—the value of money will rise on account of the increased use which will be made of it, and will continue permanently above the value of bullion, unless the quantity be increased, either by the addition of paper, or by procuring bullion to be coined into money. There will be more commodities bought and sold, but at lower prices; so that the same money will still be adequate to the increased number of transactions, by passing in each transaction at a higher value. The value of money then does not wholly depend upon its absolute quantity, but on its quantity relatively to the payments which it has to accomplish; and the same effects would follow from either of two causes—from increasing the uses for money one tenth—or from diminishing its quantity one tenth; for, in either case, its value would rise one tenth.

It is the rise in the value of money above the value of bullion which is always, in a sound state of the currency, the cause of its increase in quantity; for it is at these times that either an opening is made for the issue of more paper money, which is always attended with profit to the issuers; or that a profit is made by carrying bullion to the mint to be coined.

To say that money is more valuable than bullion or the standard, is to say that bullion is selling in the market under the mint price. It can therefore be purchased, coined, and issued as money, with a profit equal to the difference between the market and mint prices. The mint price of gold is 3*l*. 17*s*. 10½*d*. If, from increasing opulence, more commodities came to be bought and sold, the first effect would be that the value of money would rise. Instead of 3*l*. 17*s*. 10½*d*. of coined money being equal in value to an ounce of gold, 3*l*. 15*s*. 0*d*. might be equal to that value; and therefore a profit of 2*s*. 10½*d*. might be made on every ounce of gold that was carried to the mint to be coined. This profit, however, could not long continue; for the quantity of money which, by these means, would be added to the circulation, would sink its value, whilst the diminishing quantity of bullion in the market would also tend to raise the value of bullion to that of coin: from one or both these causes a perfect equality in their value could not fail to be soon restored.

It appears then, that, if the increase in the circulation were supplied by means of coin, the value both of bullion and money would, for a time at least, even after they had found their level, be higher than before; a circumstance which though often unavoidable, is inconvenient, as it affects all former contracts. This inconvenience is wholly got rid of, by the issue of paper money; for, in that case, there will be no additional demand for bullion; consequently its value will continue unaltered; and the new paper money, as well as the old, will conform to that value.

Besides, then, all the other advantages attending the use of paper money; by the judicious management of the quantity, a degree of uniformity, which is by no other means attainable, is secured to the value of the circulating medium in which all payments are made.

The value of money and the amount of payments remaining the same, the quantity of money required must depend on the degree of economy practised in the use of it. If no payments were made by checks on bankers; by means of which money is merely written off one account and added to another, and that to the amount of millions daily, with few or no bank notes or coin passing; it is obvious that considerably more currency would be required, or, which is the same in its effects, the same money would pass at a greatly increased value, and would therefore be adequate to the additional amount of payments.

Whenever merchants, then, have a want of confidence in each other, which disinclines them to deal on credit, or to accept in payment each other's checks, notes, or bills; more money, whether it be paper or metallic money, is in demand; and the advantage of a paper circulation, when established on correct principles, is, that this additional quantity can be presently supplied without occasioning any variation in the value of the whole currency, either as compared with bullion or with any other commodity; whereas, with a system of metallic currency, this additional quantity cannot be so readily supplied, and when it is finally supplied, the whole of the currency, as well as bullion, has acquired an increased value.

SECTION II

Use of a standard commodity—objections to it considered

DURING the late discussions on the bullion question, it was most justly contended, that a currency, to be perfect, should be absolutely invariable in value.

But it was said too, that ours had become such a currency, by the Bank restriction bill; for by that bill we had wisely discarded gold and silver as the standard of our money; and in fact that a pound note did not and ought not to vary with a given quantity of gold, more than with a given quantity of any other commodity. This idea of a currency without a specific standard was, I believe, first advanced by Sir James Steuart,[*][1] but no one has yet been able to offer any test by which we could ascertain the uniformity in the value of a money so constituted. Those who supported this opinion did not see, that such a currency, instead of being invariable, was subject to the greatest variations,—that the only use of a standard is to regulate the quantity, and by the quantity the value of the currency—and that without a standard it would be exposed to all the fluctuations to which the ignorance or the interests of the issuers might subject it.

It has indeed been said that we might judge of its value by its relation, not to one, but to the mass of commodities. If it should be conceded, which it cannot be, that the issuers of paper money would be willing to regulate the amount of their circulation by such a test, they would have no means of so doing; for when we consider that commodities are continually varying in value, as compared with each other; and that when such variation takes place, it is impossible to ascertain which commodity has increased, which diminished in value, it must be allowed that such a test would be of no use whatever.

Some commodities are rising in value, from the effects of

---

* The writings of Sir James Steuart on the subject of coin and money are full of instruction, and it appears surprising that he could have adopted the above opinion, which is so directly at variance with the general principles he endeavoured to establish.

[1] *An Inquiry into the Principles of Political Œconomy*, London, 1767, Book III, ch. i, 'Of Money of Accompt'.

taxation, from the scarcity of the raw material of which they are made, or from any other cause which increases the difficulty of production. Others again are falling, from improvements in machinery, from the better division of labour, and the improved skill of the workman; from the greater abundance of the raw material, and generally from greater facility of production. To determine the value of a currency by the test proposed, it would be necessary to compare it successively with the thousands of commodities which are circulating in the community, allowing to each all the effects which may have been produced upon its value by the above causes. To do this is evidently impossible.

To suppose that such a test would be of use in practice, arises from a misconception of the difference between price and value.

The price of a commodity is its exchangeable value in money only.

The value of a commodity is estimated by the quantity of other things generally for which it will exchange.

The price of a commodity may rise while its value falls, and *vice versa*. A hat may rise from twenty to thirty shillings in price, but thirty shillings may not procure so much tea, sugar, coffee, and all other things, as twenty shillings did before, consequently a hat cannot procure so much. The hat, then, has fallen in value, though it has increased in price.

Nothing is so easy to ascertain as a variation of price, nothing so difficult as a variation of value; indeed, without an invariable measure of value, and none such exists, it is impossible to ascertain it with any certainty or precision.

A hat may exchange for less of tea, sugar, and coffee, than before, but, at the same time, it may exchange for more of hardware, shoes, stockings, &c. and the difference of the comparative value of these commodities may either arise from a stationary value of one, and a rise, though in different degrees, of the other two; or a stationary value in one, and a fall in the value of the other two; or they may have all varied at the same time.

If we say that value should be measured by the enjoyments which the exchange of the commodity can procure for its owner, we are still as much at a loss as ever to estimate value, because two persons may derive very different degrees of enjoyment from the possession of the same commodity. In the above instance, a hat would appear to have fallen in value to him whose enjoyments consisted in tea, coffee and sugar; while it would appear to have risen in value to him who preferred shoes, stockings, and hardware.

Commodities generally, then, can never become a standard to regulate the quantity and value of money; and although some inconveniences attend the standard which we have adopted, namely, gold and silver, from the variations to which they are subject as commodities, these are trivial, indeed, compared to those which we should have to bear, if we adopted the plan recommended.

When gold, silver, and almost all other commodities, were raised in price, during the last twenty years, instead of ascribing any part of this rise to the fall of the paper currency, the supporters of an abstract currency had always some good reason at hand for the alteration in price. Gold and silver rose because they were scarce, and were in great demand to pay the immense armies which were then embodied. All other commodities rose because they were taxed either directly or indirectly, or because from a succession of bad seasons, and the difficulties of importation, corn had risen considerably in value; which, according to their theory, must necessarily raise the price of commodities. According to them, the only things which were unalterable in value were bank notes; which were, therefore, eminently well calculated to measure the value of all other things.

If the rise had been 100 per cent., it might equally have been denied that the currency had any thing to do with it, and it might equally have been ascribed to the same causes. The argument is certainly a safe one, because it cannot be disproved. When two commodities vary in relative value, it is impossible with certainty to say, whether the one rises, or the other falls; so that, if we adopted a currency without a standard, there is no degree of depreciation to which it might not be carried. The depreciation could not admit of proof, as it might always be affirmed that commodities had risen in value, and that money had not fallen.

SECTION III

The standard, its imperfections—Variations below without allowance of the countervailing variations above the standard, their effects— Correspondence with the standard the rule for paper money

WHILE a standard is used, we are subject to only such a variation in the value of money, as the *standard* itself is subject to; but against such variation there is no possible remedy, and late events have proved that, during periods of war, when gold and silver are used for the payment of large armies, distant from home, those variations are much more considerable than has been generally allowed. This admission only proves that gold and silver are not so good a standard as they have been hitherto supposed; that they are themselves subject to greater variations than it is desirable a standard should be subject to. They are, however, the best with which we are acquainted. If any other commodity, less variable, could be found, it might very properly be adopted as the future standard of our money, provided it had all the other qualities which fitted it for that purpose; but, while these metals are the standard, the currency should conform in value to them, and whenever it does not, and the market price of bullion is above the mint price, the currency is depreciated.—This proposition is unanswered, and is unanswerable.

Much inconvenience arises from using two metals as the standard of our money; and it has long been a disputed point whether gold or silver should by law be made the principal or sole standard of money. In favour of gold, it may be said, that its greater value under a smaller bulk eminently qualifies it for the standard in an opulent country; but this very quality subjects it to greater variations of value during periods of war, or extensive commercial discredit, when it is often collected and hoarded, and may be urged as an argument against its use. The only objection to the use of silver, as the standard, is its bulk, which renders it unfit for the large payments required in a wealthy country; but this objection is entirely removed by the substituting[1] of paper money as the general circulation medium of the country. Silver, too, is much more steady in its value, in consequence of its demand and supply being more regular; and as all foreign countries regulate the value of their money by the value of silver, there can be no doubt, that, on the whole, silver is preferable to gold as a standard, and should be permanently adopted for that purpose.[2]

A better system of currency may, perhaps, be *imagined* than that which existed before the late laws made bank notes a legal tender; but while the law recognized a standard, while the mint was open to any person, who chose, to take thither gold and silver to be coined into money, there was no other limit to the fall in the value of money than to the fall in the value of the precious metals. If gold had become as plentiful and as cheap as copper, bank notes would necessarily have partaken of the same depreciation, and all persons the whole of whose posses-

---

[1] Ed. 1 reads 'substitution'.

[2] Ricardo afterwards changed his mind on the merits of silver; see below, V, 390–1 and 427.

sions consisted of money—such as those who hold exchequer bills, who discount merchants' bills, or whose income is derived from annuities, as the holders of the public funds, mortgagees, and many others—would have borne all the evils of such a depreciation. With what justice, then, can it be maintained, that when gold and silver rise, money should be kept by force and by legislative interference at its former value; while no means are, or ever have been, used to prevent the fall of money when gold and silver fall? If the person possessed of money is subject to all the inconveniences of the fall in the value of his property, he ought also to have the benefits of the rise. If a paper currency without a standard be an improvement, let it be proved to be so, and then let the standard be disused; but do not preserve it to the disadvantage solely, never to the advantage, of a class of persons possessed of one out of the thousands of commodities which are circulating in the community, of which no other is subject to any such rule.

The issuers of paper money should regulate their issues solely by the price of bullion, and never by the quantity of their paper in circulation. The quantity can never be too great nor too little, while it preserves the same value as the standard. Money, indeed, should be rather *more* valuable than bullion, to compensate for the trifling delay which takes place before it is returned in exchange for bullion at the mint. This delay is equivalent to a small seignorage; and coined money, or bank notes, which represent coined money, should, in their natural and perfect state, be just so much more valuable than bullion. The Bank of England, by not having paid a due regard to this principle, have, in former times, been considerable losers. They supplied the country with all the coined money for which it had occasion, and, consequently, purchased bullion with their paper, that they might carry it to the mint to be coined. If their paper had been sustained, by limiting its quantity, at a value somewhat greater than bullion, they would, in the cheapness of their purchases, have covered all the expenses of brokerage and refining, including the just equivalent for the delay at the mint.

SECTION IV

An expedient to bring the English currency as near as possible to perfection

IN the next session of parliament, the subject of currency is again to be discussed; and, probably, a time will then be fixed for the resumption of cash payments, which will oblige the Bank to limit the quantity of their paper till it conforms to the value of bullion.[1]

A well regulated paper currency is so great an improvement in commerce, that I should greatly regret, if prejudice should induce us to return to a system of less utility. The introduction of the precious metals for the purposes of money may with truth be considered as one of the most important steps towards the improvement of commerce, and the arts of civilised life; but it is no less true that, with the advancement of knowledge and science, we discover that it would be another improvement to banish them again from the employment to which, during a less enlightened period, they had been so advantageously applied.[2]

If the Bank should be again called upon to pay their notes in specie, the effect would be to lessen greatly the profits of the Bank without a correspondent gain to any other part of the community. If those who use one and two, and even five pounds notes, should have their option of using guineas, there can be little doubt which they would prefer; and thus, to

---

[1] See above, p. 51, n. 1.
[2] Ed. 1 reads 'performed' in place of 'applied'; and accordingly it does not contain 'to' after 'employment', nor 'been' after 'they had'.

indulge a mere caprice, a most expensive medium would be substituted for one of little value.

Besides the loss to the Bank, which must be considered as a loss to the community, general wealth being made up of individual riches, the state would be subjected to the useless expense of coinage, and, on every fall of the exchange, guineas would be melted and exported.

To secure the public against any other variations in the value of the currency than those to which the standard itself is subject, and, at the same time, to carry on the circulation with a medium the least expensive, is to attain the most perfect state to which a currency can be brought, and we should possess all these advantages by subjecting the Bank to the delivery of uncoined gold or silver at the mint standard and price, in exchange for their notes, instead of the delivery of guineas; by which means paper would never fall below the value of bullion without being followed by a reduction of its quantity. To prevent the rise of paper above the value of bullion, the Bank should be also obliged to give their paper in exchange for standard gold at the price of 3*l.* 17*s.* per ounce. Not to give too much trouble to the Bank, the quantity of gold to be demanded in exchange for paper at the mint price of 3*l.* 17*s.* 10½*d.*, or the quantity to be sold to the Bank at 3*l.* 17*s.*, should never be less than twenty ounces. In other words, the Bank should be obliged to purchase any quantity of gold that was offered them, not less than twenty ounces, at 3*l.* 17*s.** per ounce, and to sell any quantity that might be demanded at 3*l.* 17*s.* 10½*d.* While they have the power

---

* The price of 3*l.* 17*s.* here mentioned, is, of course, an arbitrary price. There might be good reason, perhaps, for fixing it either a little above, or a little below. In naming 3*l.* 17*s.* I wish only to elucidate the principle. The price ought to be so fixed as to make it the interest of the seller of gold rather to sell it to the Bank than to carry it to the mint to be coined.

The same remark applies to the specified quantity of twenty ounces. There might be good reason for making it ten or thirty.

of regulating the quantity of their paper, there is no possible inconvenience that could result to them from such a regulation.

The most perfect liberty should be given, at the same time, to export or import every description of bullion. These transactions in bullion would be very few in number, if the Bank regulated their loans and issues of paper by the criterion which I have so often mentioned, namely, the price of standard bullion, without attending to the absolute quantity of paper in circulation*.

The object which I have in view would be in a great measure attained, if the Bank were obliged to deliver uncoined bullion in exchange for their notes at the mint price and standard; though they were not under the necessity of purchasing any quantity of bullion offered them at the prices to be fixed, particularly if the mint were to continue open to the public for the coinage of money: for that regulation is merely suggested to prevent the value of money from varying from the value of bullion more than the trifling difference between the prices at which the Bank should buy and sell, and which would be an approximation to that uniformity in its value which is acknowledged to be so desirable.

If the Bank capriciously limited the quantity of their paper, they would raise its value; and gold might appear to fall below the limits at which I propose the Bank should purchase. Gold, in that case, might be carried to the mint, and the money returned from thence being added to the circulation would have the effect

* I have already observed that silver appears to me to be best adapted for the standard of our money. If it were made so by law, the Bank should be obliged to buy or sell silver bullion only. If gold be exclusively the standard, the Bank should be required to buy or sell gold only; but if both metals be retained as the standard, as they now by law are, the Bank should have the option which of the two metals they would give in exchange for their notes, and a price should be fixed for silver rather under the standard, at which they should not be at liberty to refuse to purchase.

of lowering its value, and making it again conform to the standard; but it would neither be done so safely, so economically, nor so expeditiously, as by the means which I have proposed; against which the Bank can have no objection to offer, as it is for their interest to furnish the circulation with paper, rather than oblige others to furnish it with coin.

Under such a system, and with a currency so regulated, the Bank would never be liable to any embarrassments whatever, excepting on those extraordinary occasions, when a general panic seizes the country, and when every one is desirous of possessing the precious metals as the most convenient mode of realizing or concealing his property. Against such panics, Banks have no security, *on any system*; from their very nature they are subject to them, as at no time can there be in a Bank, or in a country, so much specie or bullion as the monied individuals of such country have a right to demand. Should every man withdraw his balance from his banker on the same day, many times the quantity of bank notes now in circulation would be insufficient to answer such a demand. A panic of this kind was the cause of the crisis in 1797; and not, as has been supposed, the large advances which the Bank had then made to government. Neither the Bank nor government were at that time to blame; it was the contagion of the unfounded fears of the timid part of the community, which occasioned the run on the Bank, and it would equally have taken place if they had not made any advances to government, and had possessed twice their present capital. If the Bank had continued paying in cash, probably the panic would have subsided before their coin had been exhausted.

With the known opinion of the Bank directors, as to the rule for issuing paper money,[1] they may be said to have exercised

[1] 'I think if we discount only for solid persons, and such paper as is for real *bonâ fide* transactions, we cannot materially err.' Evidence of J. Harman, a Director of the Bank of England, before the Bullion Committee, above, III, 375 and cp. 363.

their powers without any great indiscretion. It is evident that they have followed their own principle with extreme caution. In the present state of the law, they have the power, without any control whatever, of increasing or reducing the circulation in any degree they may think proper: a power which should neither be intrusted to the state itself, nor to any body in it; as there can be no security for the uniformity in the value of the currency, when its augmentation or diminution depends solely on the will of the issuers. That the Bank have the power of reducing the circulation to the very narrowest limits will not be denied, even by those who agree in opinion with the directors, that they have not the power of adding indefinitely to its quantity. Though I am fully assured, that it is both against the interest and the wish of the Bank to exercise this power to the detriment of the public, yet when I contemplate the evil consequences which might ensue from a sudden and great reduction of the circulation, as well as from a great addition to it, I cannot but deprecate the facility with which the state has armed the Bank with so formidable a prerogative.

The inconvenience to which country banks were subjected before the restriction on cash payments, must at times have been very great. At all periods of alarm, or of expected alarm, they must have been under the necessity of providing themselves with guineas, that they might be prepared for every exigency which might occur. Guineas, on these occasions, were obtained at the Bank in exchange for the larger notes, and were conveyed by some confidential agent, at expense and risk, to the country bank. After performing the offices to which they were destined, they found their way again to London, and in all probability were again lodged in the Bank, provided they had not suffered such a loss of weight, as to reduce them below the legal standard.

If the plan now proposed, of paying bank notes in bullion,

be adopted, it would be necessary either to extend the same privilege to country banks, or to make bank notes a legal tender, in which latter case there would be no alteration in the law respecting country banks, as they would be required, precisely as they now are, to pay their notes, when demanded, in Bank of England notes.

The saving which would take place, from not submitting the guineas to the loss of weight, from the friction which they must undergo in their repeated journeys, as well as of the expenses of conveyance, would be considerable; but by far the greatest advantage would result from the permanent supply of the country, as well as of the London circulation, as far as the smaller payments are concerned, being provided in the very cheap medium, paper, instead of the very valuable medium, gold; thereby enabling the country to derive all the profit which may be obtained by the productive employment of a capital to that amount. We should surely not be justified in rejecting so decided a benefit, unless some specific inconvenience could be pointed out as likely to follow from adopting the cheaper medium.

Much has been ably written on the benefits resulting to a country from the liberty of trade, leaving every man to employ his talents, and capital, as to him may seem best, unshackled by restrictions of every kind. The reasoning by which the liberty of trade is supported, is so powerful, that it is daily obtaining converts. It is with pleasure, that I see the progress which this great principle is making amongst those whom we should have expected to cling the longest to old prejudices. In the petitions to parliament against the corn bill, the advantages of an un-restricted trade were generally recognised; but by none more ably than by the clothiers of Gloucestershire, who were so convinced of the impolicy of restriction, that they expressed a willingness to relinquish every restraint which might be found to attach to their trade.[1] These are principles which cannot be too widely extended, nor too generally adopted in practice; but if foreign nations are not sufficiently enlightened to adopt this liberal system, and should continue their prohibitions and excessive duties on the importation of our commodities and manufactures, let England set them a good example by benefiting herself; and instead of meeting their prohibitions by similar exclusions, let her get rid, as soon as she can, of every vestige of so absurd and hurtful a policy.

The pecuniary advantage which would be the result of such a system would soon incline other states to adopt the same course, and no long period would elapse before the general prosperity would be seen to be best promoted by each country falling naturally into the most advantageous employment of its capital, talents, and industry.

Advantageous, however, as the liberty of trade would prove, it must be admitted that there are a few, and a very few exceptions to it, where the interference of government may be beneficially exerted. Monsieur Say, in his able work on Political Economy, after shewing the advantages of a free trade, observes*, that the interference of government is justifiable only in two cases; first, to prevent a fraud, and secondly, to certify a fact. In the examinations to which medical practitioners are obliged to submit, there is no improper interference; for it is necessary to the welfare of the people, that the fact of their having acquired a certain portion of knowledge respecting the diseases of the human frame should be ascertained and certified. The same may be said of the stamp which government puts on

* Economie Politique, livre i. chap. 17.[2]

[1] See the extracts from the resolutions of a meeting of the woollen manufacturers of Gloucestershire read to the House of Lords by Lord Grenville on 15 March 1815 (*Hansard*, XXX, 191–2).

[2] The words quoted are from the 'Table analytique', vol. II, p. 386 (2nd ed., 1814).

plate and money; it thereby prevents fraud, and saves the necessity of having recourse on each purchase and sale to a difficult chemical process. In examining the purity of drugs sold by chemists and apothecaries, the same object is had in view. In all these cases, the purchasers are not supposed to have, or to be able to acquire sufficient knowledge to guard them against deception; and government interferes to do that for them which they could not do for themselves.

But if the public require protection against the inferior money which might be imposed upon them by an undue mixture of alloy, and which is obtained by means of the government stamp when metallic money is used; how much more necessary is such protection when paper money forms the whole, or almost the whole, of the circulating medium of the country? Is it not inconsistent, that government should use its power to protect the community from the loss of one shilling in a guinea; but does not interfere to protect them from the loss of the whole twenty shillings in a one pound note? In the case of Bank of England notes, a guarantee is taken by the government for the notes which the Bank issue; and the whole capital of the Bank, amounting to more than eleven millions and a half, must be lost before the holders of their notes can be sufferers from any imprudence they may commit. Why is not the same principle followed with respect to the country banks? What objection can there be against requiring of those who take upon themselves the office of furnishing the public with a circulating medium, to deposit with government an adequate security for the due performance of their engagements? In the use of money, every one is a trader; those whose habits and pursuits are little suited to explore the mechanism of trade are obliged to make use of money, and are no way qualified to ascertain the solidity of the different banks whose paper is in circulation; accordingly we find that men living on limited incomes, women, labourers, and mechanics of all descriptions, are often severe sufferers by the failures of country banks, which have lately become frequent beyond all former example. Though I am by no means disposed to judge uncharitably of those who have occasioned so much ruin and distress to the middle and lower classes of the people, yet, it must be allowed by the most indulgent, that the true business of banking must be very much abused before it can be necessary for any bank, possessing the most moderate funds, to fail in their engagements; and I believe it will be found, in by far the major part of these failures, that the parties can be charged with offences much more grave than those of mere imprudence and want of caution.

Against this inconvenience the public should be protected by requiring of every country bank to deposit with government, or with commissioners appointed for that purpose, funded property or other government security, in some proportion to the amount of their issues.

Into the details of such a plan it is not necessary to enter very minutely. Stamps for the issue of notes might be delivered on the required deposit being made, and certain periods in the year might be fixed upon, when the whole or any part of the security should be returned, on proof being given, either by the return of the cancelled stamps, or by any other satisfactory means, that the notes for which it was given were no longer in circulation.

Against such a regulation no country bank of respectability would object; on the contrary, it would, in all probability, be most acceptable to them, as it would prevent the competition of those, who are at present so little entitled to appear in the market against them.

SECTION V

A practice which creates a great mass of mercantile inconvenience—
Remedy proposed

AFTER all the improvements however that can be made in our system of currency, there will yet be a temporary inconvenience, to which the public will be subject, as they have hitherto been, from the large quarterly payment of dividends to the public creditors;—an inconvenience which is often severely felt; and to which I think an easy remedy might be applied.

The national debt has become so large, and the interest which is paid quarterly upon it is so great a sum, that the mere collecting the money from the receivers general of the taxes, and the consequent reduction of the quantity in circulation, just previously to its being paid to the public creditor, in *January*, *April*, *July*, and *October*, occasions, for a week or more, the most distressing want of circulating medium. The Bank, by judicious management, discounting bills probably very freely, just at the time that these monies are paid into the Exchequer, and arranging for the receipt of large sums, immediately after the payment of the dividends, have, no doubt, considerably lessened the inconvenience to the mercantile part of the community. Nevertheless, it is well known to those who are acquainted with the money market that the distress for money is extreme at the periods I have mentioned. Exchequer bills, which usually sell at a premium of five shillings per 100*l.* are at such times at so great a discount, that by the purchase of them then, and the re-sale when the dividends are paid, a profit may often be made equal to the rate of fifteen to twenty per cent. interest for money. At these times, too, the difference between the price of stock for ready money, and the price for a week or two to come, affords a profit, to those who can advance money, even greater than can be made by employing money in the purchase of exchequer bills. This great distress for money is frequently, after the dividends are paid, followed by as great a plenty, so that little use can for some time be made of it.

The very great perfection to which our system of economizing the use of money has arrived, by the various operations of banking, rather aggravates the peculiar evil of which I am speaking; because, when the quantity of circulation is reduced, in consequence of the improvements which have been adopted in the means of effecting our payments, the abstraction of a million or two from that reduced circulation becomes much more serious in its effects, being so much larger a proportion of the whole circulation.

On the inconvenience to which trade and commerce are exposed by this periodical distress for money, I should think no difference of opinion can possibly exist. The same unanimity may not prevail with respect to the remedy which I shall now propose.

Let the Bank be authorised by government to deliver the dividend warrants to the proprietors of stock a few days *before* the receivers-general are required to pay their balances into the Exchequer.

Let these warrants be payable to the bearer exactly in the same manner as they now are.

Let the day for the payment of these dividend warrants in bank notes be regulated precisely as it now is.

If the day of payment could be named on or before the delivery of the warrants, it would be more convenient.

Finally, let these warrants be receivable into the Exchequer from the receivers general, or from any other person who may have payments to make there, in the same manner as bank notes; the persons paying them allowing the discount for the number of days which will elapse before they become due.

If a plan of this sort were adopted there could never be any particular scarcity of money before the payment of the dividends, nor any particular plenty of it after. The quantity of money in circulation would be neither increased nor diminished by the payment of the dividends. A great part of these warrants would, from the stimulus of private interest, infallibly find their way into the hands of those who had public payments to make, and from them to the Exchequer. Thus then would a great part of the payments to government, and the payments from government to the public creditor, be effected without the intervention of either bank notes or money; and the demands for money for such purposes, which are now so severely felt by the mercantile classes, would be effectually prevented.

Those who are well acquainted with the economical system, now adopted in London, throughout the whole banking concern, will readily understand that the plan here proposed is merely the extension of this economical system to a species of payments to which it has not yet been applied. To them it will be unnecessary to say any thing further in recommendation of a plan, with the advantages of which, in other concerns, they are already so familiar.

SECTION VI

The public services of the Bank excessively overpaid— Remedy proposed

MR. GRENFELL has lately called the attention of parliament to a subject of importance to the financial interests of the community.[1] At a time when taxes bear so heavy on the people, brought upon them by the unexampled difficulties and expenses of the war, a resource so obvious as that which he has pointed out will surely not be neglected.

It appears by the documents which Mr. Grenfell's motions

[1] See Appendix VI, below, pp. 136–7.

have produced,[1] that the Bank have, for many years, on an average, had no less a sum of the public money in their hands, on which they have obtained an interest of five per cent., than eleven millions; and the only compensation which the public have derived for the advantage which the Bank have so long enjoyed is a loan of three millions from 1806 to 1814, a period of eight years, at an interest of three per cent.—and a further loan of three millions, without interest, which the Bank, in 1808, agreed to afford the public till six months after the definitive treaty of peace, and which by an act of last session[2] was continued without interest till April 1816. From 1806 to 1816, a period of ten years, the Bank have gained five per cent. per annum on 11,000,000*l.*, which will amount to   £5,500,000

During the same time the public have received the following compensation: the difference between three per cent. and five per cent. interest; or, two per cent. per annum on 3,000,000*l.* for eight years, or -   -   -   £480,000

From 1808 to 1816, the public will have had the advantage of a loan of three millions without interest, which at five per cent. per ann. would amount, in eight years, to   -   -   -   £1,200,000
                                                                ———————   1,680,000

        Balance gained by the Bank   -   -   -   -   -   3,820,000
                                                                ———————

3,820,000*l.* will have been gained by the Bank in ten years, or 382,000*l.* per ann. for acting as bankers to the public, when, perhaps, the whole expense attending this department of their business does not exceed 10,000*l.* per ann.

In 1807, when these advantages were first noticed by a committee of the house of commons, it was contended, by many persons, in favour of the Bank, and by Mr. Thornton, one of

[1] These documents, printed by order of the House of Commons in May and June 1815, are in *Parliamentary Papers*, 1814–15, vol. x.
[2] 55 Geo. 3. c. 16.

the directors who had been governor, that the gains of the Bank were in proportion to the amount of their notes in circulation, and that no advantage was derived from the public deposits, further than as they enabled the Bank to maintain a larger amount of notes in circulation. This fallacy was completely exposed by the committee.[1]

If Mr. Thornton's argument were correct, no advantage whatever would have resulted to the Bank from the deposits of the public money—for those deposits do not enable them to maintain a larger amount of notes in circulation.

Suppose that before the Bank had any of the public deposits, the amount of their notes in circulation were twenty-five millions, and that they derived a profit by such circulation. Suppose now that government received ten millions for taxes in bank notes, and deposited them permanently with the Bank. The circulation would be immediately reduced to fifteen millions, but the profits of the Bank would be precisely the same as before; though fifteen millions only were then in circulation, the Bank would obtain a profit on twenty-five millions. If now they again raise the circulation to twenty-five millions, by employing the ten millions in discounting bills, purchasing exchequer bills, or advancing the payments on the loan for the year, for the holders of scrip receipts, will they not have added the interest of ten millions to their usual profits, although they should at no time have raised their circulation above the original sum of twenty-five millions?

That the increase in the amount of public deposits should enable the Bank to add to the amount of their notes in circulation is neither supported by theory nor experience. If we attend to the progress of these deposits, we shall observe that at no time did they increase so much as from 1800 to 1806, during

[1] See 'Second Report from the Committee on the Public Expenditure ...', 1807, pp. 104–5 and 77–9.

which time there was no increase in the circulation of notes of
five pounds and upwards; but from 1807 to 1815, when there
was no increase whatever in the amount of public deposits, the
amount of notes of five pounds and upwards had increased five
millions.

Nothing can be more satisfactory on the subject of the profits
of the Bank, from the public deposits, than the report of the
committee on public expenditure, in 1807. It is as follows:

"In the evidence upon this part of the subject, it is admitted
that the notes of the Bank are productive of profit, but it
appears to be assumed that the government balances are only
so in proportion as they tend to augment the amount of notes;
whereas your committee are fully persuaded that both balances
and notes are and must necessarily be productive.

"The funds of the Bank, which are the sources of profit, and
which constitute the measure of the sum which they have to
lend (subject only to a deduction on account of cash and bullion),
may be classed under three heads.

"First. The sum received from their proprietors as capital,
together with the savings which have been added to it.

"Secondly. The sum received from persons keeping cash at
the Bank. This sum consists of the balances of the deposit
accounts, both of government and of individuals. In 1797, this
fund, including all the balances of individuals, was only
5,130,140*l.* The present government balances alone have been
stated already at between eleven and twelve millions, including
bank notes deposited in the Exchequer*.

* By some of my readers the words "including bank notes deposited
in the Exchequer" may not be understood. They are bank notes never
put into circulation; neither are they included in any return made by the
Bank. They are called at the Exchequer special notes, and[1] are mere
vouchers, (not having even the form of bank notes), of the payment to

[1] Ed. 1 reads ', but' in place of '. They are called at the Exchequer
special notes, and'.

"Thirdly. The sum received in return for notes put into circulation. A correspondent value for every note must originally have been given, and the value thus given for notes constitutes one part of the general fund to be lent at interest. A note-holder, indeed, does not differ essentially from a person to whom a balance is due. Both are creditors of the Bank; the one holding a note, which is the evidence of the debt due to him, the other having the evidence of an entry in the ledger of the Bank. *The sum at all times running at interest will be in exact proportion to the amount of these three funds combined, deduction being made for the value of cash and bullion*.*" [1]

Every word of this statement appears to me unanswerable, and the principle laid down by the committee would afford us an infallible clue to ascertain the net profits of the Bank, if we knew the amount of their savings,—their cash and bullion, and their annual expenses, as well as the other particulars, are known to us.

It will be seen by the above extract, that in 1807 the amount

the Bank from the Exchequer of such monies as are daily received at the latter office. They are the record, therefore, of a part of the public deposits lodged with the Bank.

* In 1797 the Bank stated their finances to be as follows: [2]

Bank notes in circulation	-	-	-	-	£8,640,000
Public and private deposits	-	-	-	-	5,130,140
Surplus capital	-	-	-	-	-	3,826,890

17,597,030

On the other side of the account they shewed in what securities these funds were invested, and, with the exception of cash and bullion, and a small sum for stamps, [3] they were all yielding interest and profit to the Bank.

[1] 'Second Report from the Committee on the Public Expenditure...', 1807, p. 77. The italics are Ricardo's.
[2] See 'Report of the Lords' Committee of Secrecy. Order of Council 26th February 1797; Relating to the Bank', Appendix 'Papers and Accounts', p. 75; reprinted in *Parliamentary Papers*, 1810, vol. III.
[3] Ed. 1 does not contain 'and a small sum for stamps,'.

of the public deposits was between eleven and twelve millions, whereas in 1797 the amount of public and private deposits were together only equal to 5,130,140*l.* In consequence of this report, Mr. Perceval applied to the Bank, on the part of the public, for a participation in their additional profits from this source, either in the way of an annual payment or as a loan of money without interest; and, after some negociation, a loan of three millions was obtained without interest, payable six months after a definitive treaty of peace.[1]

The same report also notices the exorbitant allowance which was made to the Bank for the management of the national debt. The public paid the Bank at that time at the rate of 450*l.* per million, for management, and it was stated by the committee that the additional allowance for management in the ten years, ending in 1807, in consequence of the increase of the debt, was more than 155,000*l.* whilst the "whole increase of the officers who actually transact the business, in the last eleven years, is only one hundred and thirty-seven, whose annual expence may be from 18,449*l.* to 23,290*l.*; the addition to the other permanent charges being probably about one half or two thirds of that sum."[2]

After this report a new agreement was made with the Bank for the management of the public debt.

450*l.* per million was to be paid if the unredeemed capital exceeded three hundred millions, but fell below four hundred millions.

340*l.* per million, if the capital exceeded four hundred millions, but fell below six hundred millions.[3]

---

[1] See 'Papers presented to the House of Commons, relating to the Bank...', 3 Feb. 1808, pp. 4–13; in *Parliamentary Papers*, 1808, vol. x.

[2] 'Second Report from the Committee on the Public Expenditure...', 1807, p. 71.

[3] See 'Papers presented to the House of Commons, relating to the Bank...', 1808, p. 15.

300*l.* per million on such part of the public debt as exceeded six hundred millions.

Besides these allowances the Bank are paid 800*l.* per million for receiving contributions on loans; 1000*l.* on each contract for lotteries, and 1250*l.* per million, or one eighth per cent. for receiving contributions on the profits arising from property, professions, and trades. This agreement has been in force ever since.

As the period is now approaching when the affairs of the Bank will undergo the consideration of parliament, and when the agreement which regards the public deposits will expire, by the payment of the three millions borrowed of the Bank without interest, in 1808; no time can be more proper than the present to point out the undue advantages which were given to the Bank in the terms settled between them and Mr. Perceval in 1808. This I apprehend was the chief object of Mr. Grenfell; for it is not alone to the additional advantages which the Bank have obtained since the agreement in 1808 that he wishes to call the attention of parliament; but also to that agreement itself, under which the public are now paying, and have long paid, in one shape or another, enormous sums for very inadequate services.

Mr. Grenfell probably thinks, and, if he does, I most heartily concur with him, that a profit of 382,000*l.* per annum, which is the sum at which the advantages of the public deposits to the Bank, for a period of ten years, may be calculated, as will be seen page [77], very far exceeds the just compensation which the public ought to pay to the Bank, for doing the mere business of bankers; particularly when, in addition to this sum, 300,000*l.* per annum is now also paid for the management of the national debt, loans, &c.; when moreover the Bank have been enjoying, ever since the renewal of their charter, immense additional profits, from the substitution of paper money in lieu of a currency consisting partly of metallic and partly of paper money, which additional profits were not in contemplation, either of parliament which granted, or of the Bank which obtained that charter, when the bargain was made in 1800; and of which they might be in a great measure deprived by the repeal of the bill which restricts them from paying their notes in specie. Under these circumstances it must, I think, be allowed that in 1808 Mr. Perceval by no means obtained for the public what they had a right to expect; and it is to be hoped that, with the known sentiments of the Chancellor of the Exchequer,[1] as to the right of the public to participate in the additional advantages of the Bank, arising from public deposits, terms more consonant with the public interest will now be insisted on.

It is true that the above sums, though paid by the public, are not the net profits of the Bank; from them a deduction must be made for the expences of that part of the Bank establishment which is exclusively appropriated to the public business; but those expences do not probably exceed 150,000l. per annum.

The committee on public expenditure stated in their report to the House of Commons,[2] in 1807, "that the number of clerks employed by the Bank exclusively or principally in the public business was,

In 1786	243
1796	313
1807	450

whose salaries, it is presumed, may be calculated at an average of between 120l. and 170l. for each clerk: taking them at 135l. which exceeds the average of those employed in the South Sea House, the sum is - - - - - - 60,750l.
at 150l. the sum is - - - - - - 67,500l.
at 170l. the sum is - - - - - - 76,500l.
either of which two last sums would be sufficient to provide a superannuation fund.

[1] See below, p. 90.   [2] 'Second Report...', p. 71.

"The very moderate salaries, the report continues, received by the governor, deputy governor, and directors, amount to

	£8,000
Incidental expences may be estimated at about -	15,000
Building additional and repairs, at about - -	10,000
Law expences and loss by frauds, forgeries, at about - - - - - - -	10,000"
	————
	43,000
Add the largest estimate for clerks - - -	76,500
	————
Total	£119,500

Allowing, then, the very highest computation of the committee, the expence of managing the public business in 1807, including the *whole* of the salaries of the directors, incidental expences, additional buildings and repairs, together with law expences and loss by frauds and forgeries, amounted to 119,500*l*.

The committee also stated that the increased expences of the Bank for managing the public business, after a period of eleven years, from 1796 to 1807, were about 35,000*l*. per annum, on an increased debt of two hundred and seventy eight millions, being at the rate of 126*l*. per million. From 1807 to the present time the unredeemed debt managed by the Bank has increased from about five hundred and fifty millions to about eight hundred and thirty millions, or about two hundred and eighty millions—little more than from 1796 to 1807, and therefore at the same rate of 126*l*. per million, would be attended with a similar expence of 35,000*l*.; but, "as the rate of expence diminishes as the scale of business enlarges,"[1] I shall estimate it at 30,500*l*. which added to 119,500*l*., the expences of 1807, will

[1] The Report actually says: 'in proportion as the scale of business becomes enlarged, the rate of commission may be reduced', p. 70.

make the whole expence of managing the public business amount to 150,000*l*. The auditors of public accounts in 1786 estimated that 187*l*. 10*s*. per million was sufficient to pay the expences of managing a debt of two hundred and twenty-four millions.[1] The estimate which I have just made is about 180*l*. per million, on a debt of eight hundred and thirty millions, which will appear an ample allowance when it is considered in what different proportions the debt itself increases, compared with the work which it occasions.

Supposing, then, the expences to be about 150,000*l*. the net profits obtained by the Bank by all its transactions with the public this year will be as follows:

Charge for managing the national debt for one year, ending the 1st *February*[2], 1816*, - -	254,000
For receiving contributions on loans, at 800*l*. per million, on thirty-six millions - - -	28,800
Ditto lotteries - - - - - -	2,000
Average profits on public deposits† - - -	382,000
Allowance for receiving property tax - -	3,480
	670,280
Expences attending the management of the public business - - - - - - -	150,000
Net profits of the Bank paid by the public - -	£520,280

Of this vast sum, 372,000*l*. probably arises from the deposits alone, an expence which might almost wholly be saved to the nation, if government were to take the management of that

---

* This charge is calculated on the debt as it stood in February, 1815: more than seventy-five millions have been added since. See Appendix.

† See page [77].

[1] See above, p. 53.   [2] Ed. 1 reads '5th *April*'.

concern into their own hands, by having a common treasury, on which each department should draw in the same manner as they now do on the Bank of England, investing the eleven millions, which appears to be the average deposits, in Exchequer bills, a part of which might be sold in the market, if any unforeseen circumstances should reduce the deposits below that sum.

The resolutions* proposed by Mr. Grenfell, and on which parliament will decide the next session, after briefly recapitulating the facts contained in the documents which his motions have produced, conclude thus: "That this House will take into early consideration the advantages derived by the Bank, as well from the management of the national debt, as from the amount of balances of public money remaining in their hands, with the view to the adoption of such an arrangement, when the engagements now subsisting shall have expired, as may be consistent with what is due to the interest of the public, and the rights, credit, and stability of the Bank of England."

Mr. Mellish, the governor of the Bank, has also proposed resolutions to be submitted to parliament next session. These resolutions* admit all the facts stated by Mr. Grenfell's; they mention also one or two trifling services which the Bank perform for the public, one without charge,† and another at a less

* See Appendix.

† The one without charge is the calculating the deduction from each dividend warrant for property tax.

The other is receiving contributions from those who pay their property tax into the Bank, for which the Bank receives 1250*l*. per million, or one-eighth per cent.

If the collector had gone from house to house to receive this money, he would have had an allowance of five pence per pound, which would have cost the public 58,007*l*. instead of 3480*l*. paid to the Bank.

Perhaps no part of the business of the Bank is more easily transacted than this which they have pointed out. Instead of being under-paid, it appears to me to be paid most liberally.

The saving to the public is really effected by the money being brought to one focus, instead of being collected from various quarters. The Bank charge than is incurred by employing the ordinary collector of taxes. But the 8th and 9th resolutions advance an extraordinary pretension,—they appear to question whether *on the expiration of the loan of* 3,000,000*l. in* 1816, government will be at liberty before 1833, the time when the charter will expire, to demand any compensation whatever from the Bank for the advantages they derive from the public deposits, or to make any new arrangement respecting the charge for management of the national debt. These resolutions are as follows:

8th. "That by the 39 and 40 *Geo.* 3. *c.* 28. *s.* 13, it is enacted, "That during the continuance of the charter, the Bank shall enjoy all privileges, profits, emoluments, benefits, and advantages whatsoever, which they now possess and enjoy by virtue of any employment by or on behalf of the public.

"That previously to such renewal of their charter, the Bank was employed as the public banker, in keeping the cash of all the principal departments in the receipt of the public revenue, and in issuing and conducting the public expenditure, &c."

9th. "That whenever the engagements now subsisting between the public and the Bank shall expire, it may be proper to consider the advantages derived by the Bank from its transactions with the public, with a view to the adoption of such arrangements as may be consistent with those principles of equity and good faith, which ought to prevail in all transactions between the public and the Bank of England."*

appear to consider the rule, by which they are to measure the moderation of their charges, to be the saving which they effect to their employer, rather than the just compensation for their own trouble and expence. What would they think of an engineer, if in his charge for the construction of a steam engine he should be guided by the value of the labour which the engine was calculated to save, and not by the value of the labour and materials necessary to its construction?

* Since the first edition of this work was published, the first Lord of the Treasury, and the Chancellor of the Exchequer, have proposed to the Bank that they shall continue the advance of three millions, which would have been due in April next, for two years without interest:—and further

That the Bank should now *for the first time* intimate that their charter precludes the public from making any demand on the Bank for a participation in the advantages arising from the public deposits, after all that has passed since 1800 on that subject, does indeed appear surprising.

The charter of the Bank was renewed in 1800 for twenty-one years, from its expiration in 1812; consequently it will not now terminate till 1833. But since 1800, so far from the Bank asserting any such claim of right to the whole advantages of the public deposits, they in 1806 lent government 3,000,000*l.* till 1814, at 3 per cent. interest, and in 1808 they lent 3,000,000*l.* more till the termination of the war, without interest, and in the last session of parliament the loan of 3,000,000*l.* was continued without interest till *April* 1816. These loans were expressly

that the Bank shall advance the sum of six millions at four per cent. for two years certain, and shall continue the same for three years longer from such period, subject to repayment upon six months notice to be given, at any time between the 10th October in any year, and the 5th of April following, either by the Lords of the Treasury to the Bank, or by the Bank to their Lordships. This proposal was agreed to by a General Court of Proprietors of Bank Stock, held, on the 8th of February, for the purpose of considering the same.[1]

At this general court, on asking for some explanation respecting the deposit of the public money at the end of the two years, I noticed with approbation the departure of the Bank from the claim which they had set up in the above resolutions, in which they appeared to me to assert the *right* of the Bank to the custody of the public money without paying any remuneration whatever; to which the Governor of the Bank, Mr. Mellish, replied, that I had totally misconceived the meaning of those resolutions, and he was sure if I read them again with attention, I should be convinced that no such construction could be put on them. I am glad the Bank disclaim having had the intention of depriving the public of the advantage which they have enjoyed since the report of the Committee on Public Expenditure; though I regret, that they have expressed themselves so obscurely, as to have given me and many others a different impression. The resolutions still appear to me to assert that the privilege of being public banker was for a valuable consideration secured to the Bank during the continuance of their charter, and that at the expiration of that engagement, and not before, it might be proper to consider of a new arrangement.

[1] On the General Court held on 8 Feb. 1816, two days after publication of ed. 1, see below, V, 465.

granted, in consideration of the increase in the amount of the public deposits.

The committee on public expenditure, in their report (1807), to which I have already referred, speaking of the loan of 3,000,000*l.* to the public in 1806, at three per cent. interest, observe, "But the transaction is most material in another view, as it evinces that the agreement made in 1800 was not considered either by those who acted on the part of the public, or by the Bank directors themselves, as a bar against further participation, whenever the increase of their profits derived from the public, and the circumstances of public affairs, might, upon similar principles, *make such a claim reasonable and expedient.*"[1] And what is Mr. Perceval's language at the same period, when in consequence of this report he applied for and obtained a loan of 3,000,000*l.* till the end of the war? In his letter to the governor and deputy governor of the Bank, dated the 11th of *January* 1808, he says, "I think it necessary to observe, that the proposal to confine the duration of the advance, by way of loan, or of the annual payment into the Exchequer, to the period of the present war, and twelve months after the termination of it, is by no means to be understood as an admission on my part, that at the expiration of such period, the public will no longer be entitled to look to any advantage from the continuance of such deposits; but simply as a provision, by which the government and the Bank may be respectively enabled, under the change in the state of affairs which will then have taken place, probably affecting the amount of public balances in the hands of the latter, to consider of a new arrangement."[2] On the 19th of *January*, Mr. Perceval's proposals were submitted to the Court of Directors in a more official form,—they conclude thus: "And it is understood that *during the continuance of this advance by the Bank*, no alteration is to be proposed in the general course

[1] p. 83. The italics are Ricardo's.
[2] 'Papers presented to the House of Commons, relating to the Bank...', 3 Feb. 1808, p. 12.

of business, between the Bank and the Exchequer, nor any regulation introduced by which the accounts now by law directed to be kept at the Bank shall be withdrawn from thence."[1] These proposals were recommended for acceptance by the Court of Directors to the Court of Proprietors, and were, without comment, agreed to on the 21st of *January*.

Mr. Vansittart, in his application to the Bank in *November* 1814, relative to continuing the loan of 3,000,000*l.*, which would have become due on the 17th of *December* following, till *April* 1816, uses these words: "But I beg to be distinctly understood as not departing from the reservation made by the late Mr. Perceval, in his letter to the governor and deputy governor of the Bank, of the 11th *January*, 1808, by which he guarded against the possibility of any misconstruction which could preclude the public, after the expiration of the period of the loan then agreed upon, from asserting its title to future advantage from the continuance or increase of such deposits; and as adhering generally to the principles maintained by Mr. Perceval, in the discussion which then took place."[2]

No comment whatever appears to have been made by the Bank on these observations: a general Court of Proprietors was called, and the loan of three millions was continued till *April*, 1816.

It surely will not come with a very good grace now from the Bank, to insist that the agreement of 1800 precludes the public from demanding any compensation for the advantages which the Bank have derived from the increase of the public deposits since that period, when, on so many occasions, the right of participation has been so expressly claimed on the part of government, and acceded to by the Court of Directors.

In addition to these strong facts, by a reference to the basis

---

[1] 'Papers presented to the House of Commons, relating to the Bank...', 3 Feb. 1808, p. 15. The italics are Ricardo's.

[2] 'Correspondence with the Bank', ordered to be printed 10 Feb. 1815, p. 1; in *Parliamentary Papers*, 1814–15, vol. X.

on which the agreement for the renewal of the charter was founded, as detailed by Mr. Thornton in his evidence before the committee of public expenditure in 1807*, it will still further appear, that the Bank have no claim whatever to shelter themselves under their charter, in refusing to let the public participate in the profits which have accrued from the augmentation of the public deposits.

It must be recollected that Mr. Thornton was, in 1800, the governor of the Bank; that he was the negociator, on the part of the Bank, with Mr. Pitt, for the renewal of the charter; and that, in fact, the idea of renewing the charter, so long before its expiration, originated with him. Mr. Thornton told the committee, that the only sums of public money, on which the Bank derived profit, and which were referred to by him and Mr. Pitt, with a view to settle the compensation which the public should receive for prolonging the exclusive privileges of the Bank, were those lodged at the Bank for the payment of the growing dividends, and for the quarterly issues to the commissioners for the redemption of the national debt.

The first of these sums Mr. Thornton estimates to be on an average -   -   -   -   -   -   -   £2,500,000†
And it appears by an account lately produced,[1]
   that the second amounted to -   -   615,842

———————

£3,115,842

———————

* Report, page 104.

† By an account laid before parliament last session,[2] it appears, that the amount of exchequer bills and bank notes deposited with the Exchequer, as cash, amounted, on an average of the year ending *March*, 1800, to 3,690,000*l.*

[1] 'An Account of the Average Amount of the Balances of Cash in the hands of the Bank of England, ...from the 1st of February 1799 to the 5th of January 1800', 26 Jan. 1815; in *Parliamentary Papers*, 1814–15, vol. x.

[2] 'An Account of the Exchequer Bills and Bank Notes deposited in the Chests of the Four Tellers in

Mr. Thornton expressly states, that all other public accounts were of trifling amount, and "the probable augmentation of the balances of public money from the various departments of government was not taken into the account;" "that such augmentation was neither adverted to, nor provided for."

If, then, it is acknowledged by the very negociator on the part of the Bank that the probable augmentation of the public balances formed no part of the consideration in settling the pecuniary remuneration which was given to the public for continuing to the Bank their exclusive privileges, how can it now, with any justice, be contended by the Bank, that the profits derived from those augmented balances, which were "neither adverted to, nor provided for," belong of right exclusively to the Bank, and that the public have no claim either to participate in them, or to withdraw the balances to any use to which they may think proper to apply them.

It is to be observed, that Mr. Thornton, in his evidence before alluded to, represented all the other public accounts, excepting the two before mentioned, as of trifling amount; but, by accounts which were last session presented to parliament, it appears that in 1800, the year to which Mr. Thornton's evidence refers, when the charter was renewed, the public balances of all descriptions deposited with the Bank amounted to 6,200,000*l*.,[1] exceeding the aggregate amount stated by Mr. Thornton, by three millions, which he would, if he had been aware of this fact, hardly have called "a trifling amount."

If, then, the fact of this large additional deposit did not come

His Majesty's Receipt of Exchequer; on the 1st April 1797..., down to the year ending 5th April 1800', 27 June 1815; in *Parliamentary Papers*, 1814–15, vol. x.

[1] The figure is calculated from the accounts referred to above, p. 91, notes 1 and 2 and from 'An Account of the Total Amount of the Balances arising from Unclaimed Dividends...in the hands of the Bank from the 1st of February 1799 to the 1st of January 1800...', 26 June 1815; in *Parliamentary Papers*, 1814–15, vol. x.

under the consideration of Mr. Thornton and Mr. Pitt, at the time of renewing the charter; if no part of the remuneration which the public then received was founded on this fact; the large amount of public deposits in 1800, so far from entitling the Bank to retain the whole profits arising from the still larger deposits at the present period, binds them in justice to be particularly liberal in any new engagement they may now make with the public, as affording a remuneration for a profit so long enjoyed, which, it is to be presumed, they would not have been allowed to enjoy, if the facts had been clearly known and considered, at the time of settling the terms on which the charter was renewed.

But whether known or not known, must have been of little consequence in Mr. Thornton's estimation; whose opinion, that the profits of the Bank were not increased by the augmentation of the public balances, otherwise than as they contributed to increase the amount of bank notes in circulation, is so emphatically given.

Is it not lamentable to view a great and opulent body like the Bank of England, exhibiting a wish to augment their hoards by undue gains wrested from the hands of an overburthened people?[1] Ought it not rather to have been expected that gratitude for their charter, and the unlooked for advantages with which it has been attended; for the bonuses and increased dividends which they have already shared, and for the great undivided treasure which it has further enabled them to accumulate, would have induced the Bank voluntarily to relinquish to the state, the whole benefit which is derived from the employment of eleven millions of the public money, instead of manifesting a wish to deprive them of the small portion of it which they have for a few years enjoyed?

[1] The 'moral' argument against the Bank, and the actual wording of this sentence, were suggested by Mill; see below, VII, 5.

When the rate of charge for the management of the national debt was under discussion, in 1807, Mr. Thornton said, "that in a matter between the public and the Bank, he was sure nothing but a fair compensation for trouble, risk, and actual losses, and the great responsibility that attaches to the office, would be required."[1]

How comes it that the language of the directors of the present day is so much changed? Instead of expecting only a fair compensation for trouble, risk, and actual losses, they endeavour to deprive the public even of the inadequate compensation which they have hitherto received; and appeal, now for the first time, to their charter, for their right to hold the public money, and to enjoy all the profit which can be derived from its use, without allowing the least remuneration to the public.

If the charter were as binding as the Bank contend for, a great public company, possessing so advantageous a monopoly, and so intimately connected with the state, might be expected to act on a more liberal policy towards its generous benefactors.

Till the last session of parliament, the Bank were also particularly favoured in the composition which they paid for stamp duties. In 1791, they paid a composition of 12,000*l.* per annum, in lieu of all stamps either on bills or notes. In 1799, on an increase of the stamp duty, this composition was advanced to 20,000*l.*; and an addition of 4,000*l.*, raising the whole to 24,000*l.*, was made for the duty on notes under 5*l.*, which the Bank had then begun to circulate. In 1804, an addition of not less than 50 per cent. was made to the stamp duty imposed by the act of 1799, on notes under 5*l.*, and a considerable increase on the notes of a higher value; and although the Bank circulation of notes under 5*l.* had increased from one and a half to four and a half millions, and the amount of notes of a higher description

[1] 'Second Report from the Committee on the Public Expenditure...', 1807, p. 106.

had also increased, yet the whole composition of the Bank was only raised from 24,000*l*. to 32,000*l*. In 1808, there was a further increase of 33 per cent. to the stamp duty, at which time the composition was raised from 32,000*l*. to 42,000*l*. In both these instances the increase was not in proportion even to the increase of duty; and no allowance whatever was made for the increase in the amount of the Bank circulation.

In the last session of parliament, on a further increase of the stamp duty, the principle was for the first time established, that the Bank should pay a composition, in some proportion to the amount of their circulation. It is now fixed as follows. Upon the average circulation of the three preceding years, the Bank is to pay at the rate of 3500*l*. per million, without reference to the classes or value of the notes of which the aggregate circulation may consist.

The average of the Bank circulation for three years, ending 5th *April*, 1815, was 25,102,600*l*.; and upon this average they will pay this year about 87,500*l*.

Next year the average will be taken upon the three years, ending in *April* 1816; and if it differs from the last, the duty will vary accordingly.[1]

If the same course had been followed now, as in 1804 and 1808, the Bank would have had to pay, even with the additional duty, only 52,500*l*., so that 35,000*l*. per annum has been saved to the public, by parliament having at last recognized the principle which should have been adopted in 1799; and by the neglect of which, the public have probably been losers and the Bank consequently gainers, of a sum little less than 500,000*l*.

[1] The last three paragraphs are adapted by Ricardo from Grenfell's letter of 8 Sept. 1815, below, VI, 266–7.

SECTION VII

Bank Profits and Savings—Misapplication—Proposed Remedy

I HAVE hitherto been considering the profits of the Bank, as they regard the public, and have endeavoured to shew that they have greatly exceeded what a just consideration for *their* rights and interests could warrant.—I propose now to consider them in relation to the interests of the proprietors of Bank stock, for which purpose I shall endeavour to state a basis on which the profits of the Bank may be calculated, with a view to ascertain what the accumulated savings of the Bank now are.—If we knew accurately the expences of the Bank, and the amount of cash and bullion which they may at different times have had in their hands, we should have the means of making a calculation on this subject, which would be a very near approximation to the truth.

The profits of the Bank are derived from sources which are well known. They arise, as has been already stated, from the interest on public and private deposits,—the interest on the amount of their notes in circulation, after deducting the amount of cash and bullion,—the interest on their capital and savings, —the allowance paid them for the management of the public debt,—the profits from their dealings in bullion, and from the destruction of their notes.—All these form the gross profits of the Bank, from which must be deducted only their expences, the stamp duty, and the property tax, in order to ascertain their net profits.

Under the head of expences must be included all the charges attending the management of the national debt, as well as those incurred by the proper business of the Bank.—In estimating the former of these charges, I have already stated my grounds for believing that it could not exceed 150,000*l*.—In the management of the public business, it was stated by the committee on public expenditure, that four hundred and fifty clerks were employed in 1807;[1] and it is probable that the number may now be increased to between five and six hundred.

It has also I understand been stated from the best authority, in parliament, that the Bank employed in the whole of their establishment about one thousand clerks;[2] consequently if five hundred are employed exclusively on the public business, five hundred more must be engaged in the business of the Bank.— Supposing now the expences to bear some regular proportion to the number of clerks employed; as 150,000*l*. has been calculated to be the expence attending the employment of five hundred clerks in the public business, we may estimate a like expence to be incurred by the employment of the other five hundred, and therefore, the whole expences of the Bank to be at the present time about 300,000*l*., including all charges whatsoever*.

But although this large sum is now expended, it must have been of gradual growth since 1797; when, probably, the whole

---

* It has been remarked that a sufficient allowance is not made in my calculations for the losses of the Bank by bad debts, in consequence of the bad bills which they occasionally discount. Their losses from this source, I am told, are often very large. On the other hand, I have been informed that the profits of the Bank, from private deposits, for which I have taken no credit, must be considerable, as the East India Company, and many other public boards, keep their cash at the Bank.

A deduction from the Bank profits should have been made for their loss by Aslett,[3] and for the expences attending their military corps.[4] My argument will not be affected by their surplus capital being only 12 or 11 instead of 13 millions. *Note to Second Edition.*

---

[1] See above, p. 83.
[2] See Samuel Thornton's speech on Grenfell's Motion respecting the Profits of the Bank of England, 13 June 1815 (*Hansard*, XXXI, 770).
[3] Robert Aslett, a cashier of the Bank of England, had embezzled half a million pounds' worth of securities in 1803. See W. M. Acres, *The Bank of England from Within*, London, 1931, p. 364 ff.
[4] The Bank Volunteer Corps, formed in 1798 for the defence of the Bank. See Acres, *op. cit.*, p. 290 ff.

expences of the establishment were not more than one-half the present amount. In the first place, since 1797, the amount of Bank notes in circulation has increased from about twelve millions to twenty-eight millions, but the expences of their circulation, instead of increasing in the same proportion only, have, at least, increased as one to ten.

The amount of notes of five pounds and upwards has been raised from twelve to eighteen millions, and if the average value of notes, of all descriptions above five pounds, be even so low as fifteen pounds, a circulation of twelve millions would consist of 800,000 notes, and a circulation of 18 millions of 1,200,000 notes, an increase in the proportion, as one to one and one-half; but the nine millions of notes under five pounds, which are now in circulation, have been wholly created since 1797, and if they consist of five millions of notes of one pound, and two millions of notes of two pounds, a number of seven millions of notes has been further added to the circulation, and the whole number of notes has been raised since 1797, from 800,000 to 8,200,000, or as one to ten, and at an expence ten times greater than was incurred at that time, the expence being in proportion to the number, and not to the amount of notes. It is probable too, that the notes of one and two pounds, which are so constantly used in the circulation, are more often renewed than notes of a higher value.

The public debt, too, under the management of the Bank, is more than doubled since 1797, and must have added considerably to the expences of that department. These expences have been already calculated to have risen since 1796, from 84,500*l.* to 150,000*l.* or 65,500*l.**

* The Committee on public expenditure calculated these expences at 119,500*l.* in 1807, and stated the increase from 1796 to 1807 at about 35,000*l.*[1]

[1] See above, p. 84.

The public deposits too are at least double what they were in 1797, from all which I have a right to infer, that the expences of the Bank in 1797, could not have exceeded 150,000*l.*, and that they have been gradually increasing since that period; perhaps at the rate of seven or eight thousand pounds per ann.

The next subject for consideration, is the amount of cash and bullion in the Bank, which at no time has been laid before the public;—that, and the amount of their discounts, were the only material facts which the Bank concealed from the public in the eventful year 1797.—They stated in the account laid before parliament, that their cash and bullion, and their bills and notes discounted, amounted together to 4,176,080*l.* on the 26th of *February* 1797. They gave also a scale of discounts from 1782 to 1797, and a scale of the cash and bullion in the Bank for the same period. By comparing these tables with each other, and with some parts of the evidence delivered before the parliamentary committees, an ingenious calculator[1] discovered the whole secret which the Bank wished to conceal. According to his table the cash and bullion in the Bank, on the 26th of *February* 1797, was reduced as low as 1,272,000*l.*[2],—and four millions was about the sum which the Bank considered as fair cash; to which it never attained after *December* 1795, though previously to that year it was on some occasions more than double that amount.

For the first year or two after the suspension of cash payments, the Bank must have made great efforts to replenish their coffers with cash and bullion, as they were then by no means sure that they should not be again required to pay their notes in specie. We find accordingly, by accounts returned to parliament by the mint,[3] that the amount of gold

[1] William Morgan; see Appendix to this volume.

[2] Eds. 2–3 misprint '1,227,000*l.*'

[3] *Bullion Report*, 1810, 'Appendix of Accounts', No. 19.

coined in 1797 and 1798, was very little less in value than 5,000,000*l.**

Whatever might have been the amount of cash and bullion, which the Bank had acquired in the first two years after the suspension of cash payments, it is probable that their stock has been decreasing since that period, as they could have no motive for keeping a large amount of such unproductive capital, when they must have been quite secure that no call could be made on them by the holders of their notes for guineas, and that before they were again required to pay in specie, they would have ample notice to prepare a due store of the precious metals.—It does not appear possible then, under all the circumstances of the case, that the Bank can have added to their stock of bullion, since the great coinages of 1797 and 1798; but it is highly probable that they have considerably reduced it.[1]

In estimating the profits of the Bank, as far as those profits are influenced by their stock of cash and bullion, I shall be justified in considering them greater since 1797 and 1798, as since those years they would naturally keep a less part of their capital in that unproductive shape, and, consequently, more in Exchequer bills, or in merchants' acceptances, securities which pay interest, and are productive of profit.—On an average of

* The committee of secrecy reported to parliament, that the cash and bullion in the Bank, in *November* 1797, had increased to an amount more than five times the value of that at which they stood on the 25th of *February* 1797. They stated too, that the bankers and traders of London, who had a right, by the act of parliament, to demand three-fourths of any deposit in cash, which they had made in the Bank, of five hundred pounds and upwards, after the 25th of *February* 1797, had only claimed in *November* 1797, about one-sixteenth.[2]

[1] Ricardo's supposition is borne out by the Bank accounts for the period in question, which were first published in the 'Report from the Committee of Secrecy on the Bank of England Charter', 1832, Appendix 5; in *Parliamentary Papers*, 1831–32, vol. VI.

[2] See 'Report from the Committee of Secrecy upon the Restriction on Payments in Cash by The Bank', 17 Nov. 1797, p. 119; reprinted in *Parliamentary Papers*, 1926, vol. III.

the whole eighteen years, from 1797 to 1815, the cash and bullion of the Bank cannot be estimated as amounting to more than three millions, though, probably, for the first year or two, it amounted to four or five millions.

These circumstances being premised, it will not be difficult to calculate the profits of the Bank, from 1797 to the present time, all the facts necessary to such calculation being known to us excepting the two I have just stated, viz. the amount of expences and of cash and bullion, but which cannot differ much from that at which I have calculated them.

Proceeding then on this basis, it appears, as will be seen by the accounts in the Appendix, that the profits and surplus capital of the Bank for a series of years, after paying all dividends and bonuses, have been as follows:

Year commencing in January	Surplus capital	Profits after paying dividend and bonuses	Dividend and bonus together
1797	£3,826,890	£ 89,872	7 per cent.
1798	3,916,762	533,621	7 do.
1799	4,450,383	*	17 do.
1800	3,941,228	611,981	7 do.
1801	4,553,209	116,038	12 do.
1802	4,669,247	460,509	9½ do.
1803	5,129,756	765,859	7 do.
1804	5,895,615	306,794	12 do.
1805	6,202,409	346,335	12 do.
1806	6,548,744	368,008	12 do.
1807	6,916,752	581,274	10 do.
1808	7,498,026	385,865	10 do.
1809	7,883,891	470,760	10 do.
1810	8,354,651	651,483	10 do.
1811	9,006,134	722,188	10 do.
1812	9,728,322	739,867	10 do.
1813	10,468,189	809,786	10 do.
1814	11,279,975	1,081,649	10 do.
1815	12,359,624	1,066,625	
1816	13,426,249		

* There was this year a loss of 509,155*l.*

If in the accounts referred to, it should be thought that I have estimated the expences of the Bank too low, it may on the other hand be remarked that I have not allowed for any profit from the deposits of individuals. Those deposits may not be very large, as the Bank do not afford the same accommodation to individuals as given by other bankers. Some profit must, however, be made from this source, as well as from the loss and destruction of notes, which it may be presumed, after a time, are not included in the amount stated to be in circulation. By the purchase of silver, and coinage of tokens, the Bank must, on the whole, have been gainers; for the value of the token has been generally lower in the market, than it has passed for in circulation at the time of its issue.

In point of fact, too, the Bank receives more than five per cent. interest for their money; for Exchequer bills, paying three pence half-penny per day, pay $5l.$ $6s.$ $5\frac{1}{2}d.$ per cent. per ann.; and, in discounting bills, the interest being immediately deducted, is employed as capital, and is instantly productive of profit; at the same time, it must be observed that during a part of the time for which these calculations are made, Exchequer bills bore an interest of only three pence farthing per day, which amounts to $4l.$ $18s.$ $0\frac{1}{4}d.$ per cent. per ann., rather less than five per cent.

In *March* 1801, when a bonus of five per cent., in navy five per cents., was divided amongst the proprietors of Bank stock, Mr. Tierney said in the house of commons, "that when the affairs of the Bank of England were investigated by the house of commons in 1797, the surplus profits were considered by some as a security for the engagements of the Bank to the public." To which Mr. Samuel Thornton, then governor of the Bank, replied, that "he could assure the honourable member, that the security of the public would not be lessened from what it was in 1797, by the division of the sum of $582,120l.$ voted at the general court, on the 19th instant, as exclusive of that sum, the surplus profits of the Bank were more now than they were in 1797*."

On an inspection of the account[1] in the Appendix, it will be seen, that after paying all the dividends and bonuses to the proprietors, the Bank had accumulated in *April* 1801, savings to the amount of 3,945,109*l.* exceeding the savings of 1797, by 118,219*l.*, an increase not inconsistent with the declaration of Mr. Thornton, and therefore tending to confirm the correctness of the basis on which these calculations are made†.

It will appear on an examination of the accounts in the Appendix for the subsequent years, that the profits of the Bank for every year, since 1801, have exceeded the annual dividend paid to the proprietors, and that in 1815, the surplus for that year only must have amounted to 1,066,625*l.* so that the Bank

---

* Allardyce's Address to the proprietors of the Bank of England, Appendix, No. 11.[2]

† The accounts in the Appendix are made up from *Jan.* to *Jan.* The bonus in question was paid in *April* 1801. The net profits of the Bank for the whole year 1801 were 1,526,019*l.*, consequently for the quarter, ending in *April*, they may be stated at - - - - - £ 381,504

Which, added to the surplus capital of *January*
1801 - - - - - - - 4,553,209

Gives the total of the surplus capital in *April* 1801,
before paying the dividend and bonus - - 4,934,713
Deduct

Dividend three and a half per cent., for half a year   407,484
Bonus five per cent. - - - - - 582,120
                                                       ————— 989,604

Leaving a surplus capital in *April*, 1801, of - 3,945,109
And exceeding that in 1797 of - - - - 3,826,890
                                                   by   £118,219

---

[1] Ed. 1 'accounts'.
[2] *A Second Address to the Proprietors of Bank of England Stock,*
by Alexander Allardyce, M.P.,
London, Richardson, 1801, p. 48.

could have paid a dividend for that year of nineteen per cent., instead of ten per cent.

It will appear too that if the Bank affairs have been only moderately well managed, they must now have an accumulated fund of no less than thirteen millions, which, in defiance of the clearest language of an act of parliament,[1] the directors have hitherto withheld from the proprietors.

With such an accumulated fund, the Bank could make a division of one hundred per cent. bonus, without infringing on their permanent capital: and if they could maintain their present profits, with a deduction only of 523,908*l*. per ann. the interest (less income tax) on the surplus capital proposed to be divided, they would still have an unappropriated income of 542,000*l*. which would enable them to increase their permanent dividend from ten to fourteen and a half per cent., in addition to the bonus[2] of one hundred per cent.

If they divided only a bonus of seventy-five per cent. they would retain a surplus capital, exceeding that of 1797, and might on the above supposition have an unappropriated income of 673,000*l*.—they might therefore raise their permanent dividend from ten to fifteen and a half per cent., in addition to the bonus of seventy-five per cent.

But it cannot be expected that the Bank will, during peace, have the same opportunities of making profit as during war, and the proprietors must prepare themselves for a considerable reduction in their annual income. What that reduction may be will depend on the new agreement now to be entered into with government; on the future amount of public deposits; and on the conditions on which the restoration of metallic payments may be enforced. It is evident that if the plan which I have recommended in the fourth section of this work be adopted, the Bank profits from this last item will not be materially reduced.

[1] See below, p. 106.   [2] Ed. 1 'bonuses'.

Supposing, however, that the reduction of the annual income of the Bank should, from the falling off of their profits in all these departments, be as much as 500,000*l.*, the profits of the Bank would, nevertheless, be equal to the payment of the present permanent dividend of ten per cent., even after a division of one hundred per cent. bonus to the proprietors of Bank stock; for, if my calculations be correct, the profits of the Bank, after the payment of the annual dividend of ten per cent. to the proprietors, were for the year ending *January* 1st, 1816 - - - - - - - - - £1,066,625

Deduct then the interest now made on 11,642,400*l.*
    proposed to be divided, less property tax - 523,908
Loss by a peace arrangement - - - - 500,000   1,023,908

Leaving a surplus of, per ann. - - - - £42,717

If, instead of a hundred per cent., fifty per cent. bonus only were paid to the proprietors, the annual surplus profit of the Bank, after paying ten per cent. dividend, would be 304,671*l.* a sum equal to a permanent increase of dividend of two and a half per cent.

And if no bonus whatever were paid, but the savings were considered as part of the Bank capital, the annual surplus profit of the Bank, after paying ten per cent. dividend, would be 566,625*l.*, very nearly equal to a permanent increase of dividend of five per cent.

These estimates are made on a supposition too, that the property tax should permanently continue, which is calculated to be an annual charge of more than 200,000*l.* to the Bank, and consequently more than equal to a dividend of one and three quarters per cent.

But the Directors are bound, in my opinion, under every case, to divide the surplus profits amongst the proprietors, the law imperatively enjoining such a division, and policy being no wise opposed to it.

Well was it urged by the Hon. Mr. Bouverie, who moved in the last Bank court[1] that an account of the surplus capital of the Bank be laid before the proprietors, that this law respecting the division of profits was probably enacted by the legislature, on a consideration of the powers of accumulation at compound interest, and the dangers which might arise to the constitution or the country, from any corporation becoming possessed of millions of treasure. If the profits of the Bank were to continue at the present rate, and no addition were to be made to the dividend now paid of ten per cent., the accumulation of the surplus profits in forty years would give to the Bank a disposable fund of more than one hundred and twenty millions. Wisely then did the legislature enact, that "All the profits, benefits, and advantage from time to time arising out of the management of the said corporation, shall (the charges of managing the business of the said governor and company *only excepted*) be applied from time to time to the uses of all the members of the said corporation for the time being, rateably and in proportion to each member's part, share, and interest, in the common capital, and principal stock, of the said governor and company of the Bank of England."[2]

Those who vindicated the directors at the last general court for their departure from the line of conduct prescribed by the law, recommended the increase of the capital of the Bank,—and they thought that the accumulated savings might be advantageously employed for such purpose.

It is said that the Bank directors are favourable to such a plan.

If the measure should be a good one, the sum of capital to

[1] On 21 Dec. 1815; see below, V, 463.
[2] Act of 1708, prolonging the Bank Charter (7th Anne, chap. 7, Sect. 63); quoted by Allardyce, *An Address to the Proprietors of the Bank of England*, 3rd ed., London, Richardson, 1798, Appendix, p. 124.

be added should be at once defined,—the proprietors should have accounts laid before them of the amount of their accumulated fund, and should be consulted on the expediency of such a disposition of it,—and lastly the sanction of Parliament should be obtained.

The Bank, however, have waited for none of these conditions, —they have been, in fact, for years adding the annual surplus profits to their capital, without defining the amount added, or to be added; they do it without laying any accounts before the proprietors—without consulting them; and not only without the sanction of Parliament, but in defiance of an express law on the subject.

But if the Bank complied with all these conditions, would the measure itself be expedient, and are the reasons given in support of it, namely the enlarged business of the Bank, and that it would tend to the security both of the Bank and the public, of sufficient weight to justify its adoption?

The business and income of the Bank depend, as before stated, on the amount of the aggregate fund which they have to employ, and this fund is derived from the three following sources: The amount of Bank notes in circulation, deducting only the cash and bullion: The amount of public and private deposits: And the amount of that part of the capital of the Bank which is not lent to government. But it is only the two former of these funds which contribute to the real profit of the Bank; for the interest, received for surplus capital, being only five per cent., might be made with as much facility by each individual proprietor, on his share of such capital, if under his own management, as by combining the whole into one fund. If the proprietors were to add from their own individual property ten millions to the capital of the Bank, the income of the Bank would indeed be increased 500,000*l.* or five per cent. on ten millions; but the proprietors would not be gainers by such an arrangement. If, however, ten millions were added to the amount of notes, and could be permanently maintained in circulation,—or if the public and private deposits were to be increased ten millions, the *income* of the Bank would not only be increased 500,000*l.*, but their *real profits* also, and this advantage would arise wholly from their acting as a joint company, and could not be otherwise obtained.

There is this material difference between a Bank and all other trades: A Bank would never be established, if it obtained no other profits but those from the employment of its own capital: its real advantage commences only when it employs the capital of others. Other trades, on the contrary, often make enormous profits by the employment of their own capital only.

But if this argument be correct, with respect to an additional capital to be actually raised from amongst the proprietors, it is equally so to one withheld from them.

To increase the *profits* of the Bank proprietors, then, an increase of capital would be neither necessary nor desirable.

Neither would such an addition contribute towards the *security* of the Bank; for the Bank can never be called upon for more than the payment of their notes, and the public and private deposits; these constituting, at all times, the whole of their debts. After paying away their cash and bullion, their remaining securities, consisting of merchants acceptances and Exchequer bills, must be at least equal to the value of their debts ; and in no case can these securities be deficient, even without *any* surplus capital, excepting the Bank should lose all that which constitutes their growing dividend; and even then they could not be distressed, unless we suppose that at the same time payment were demanded for every note in circulation, and for the whole of their deposits, both public and private.

Is it against such a contingency that the proprietors are called upon to provide; when even under these, almost impossible circumstances, the Bank would have an untouched fund of 11,686,000*l.*, which Government owe them?

Would the security of the public be increased? In one respect it would. If the Bank have no other capital but that which they lend to Government, they must lose all that capital by their trade, or more than eleven millions and a half, before the public can be sufferers; but if the capital of the Bank were doubled, the Bank might lose twenty-three millions, before any creditor of theirs could suffer loss. Are the friends to an increase of the capital of the Bank prepared to say, that it is against the consequences of the loss of the whole Bank capital that they are desirous of protecting the public?

It remains to be considered, whether the ability of the Bank to pay their notes in specie would be increased by an increase of their capital. The ability of the Bank, to pay their notes in specie, must depend upon the proportion of specie which they may keep, to meet the probable demand for payment of their notes; and in this respect their power cannot be increased, for they may now, *if they please*, have a stock of specie, not only equal to all their notes in circulation, but to the whole of the public and private deposits, and under no possible circumstances can more be demanded of them. But the profits of the Bank essentially depend on the smallness of the stock of cash and bullion; and the whole dexterity of the business consists in maintaining the largest possible circulation, with the least possible amount of their funds in the unprofitable shape of cash and bullion. The amount of notes in circulation depends in no degree on the amount of capital possessed by the issuers of notes, but on the amount required for the circulation of the country; which is regulated, as I have before attempted to shew, by the value of the standard, the amount of payments, and the economy practised in effecting them.

The only effect then of the increase of the capital of the Bank would be to enable them to lend to government or to merchants those funds, which would otherwise have been lent by individuals of the community. The Bank would have more business to do—they would accumulate more merchants acceptances and Exchequer bills: they would even increase the income of the Bank; but the profits of the proprietors would be neither more nor less, if the market rate of interest for money were at five per cent., and the business of the Bank were carried on with the same economy. The proprietors would be positive losers, if they could individually have employed their shares of this capital in trade, or otherwise, at a greater profit.

But not only do the Bank refuse, in direct contradiction to an act of parliament, to make a division of their accumulated profits, but they are equally determined not to communicate to the proprietors what those profits are, notwithstanding their bye-law enjoins, "that twice in every year a general court shall be called, and held for considering *the general state and condition of this corporation*, and for the making of dividends, *out of all and singular* the produce and profit of the capital stock and fund of this corporation and the trade thereof, amongst the several owners and proprietors therein, according to their several shares and proportions."[1]

If the law had been silent on the subject, the Bank Directors would, I think, be bound to shew some specific evil which would result from publicity, before they refused to shew a statement of their affairs to the proprietors.

It is in fact the only security which the proprietors have, against the abuse of the trust reposed in the Directors.

The affairs of the Bank may not always be managed by such men as are now in the Direction, against whom not a shadow of suspicion any where exists.

[1] Quoted by Allardyce in *An Address to the Proprietors of the Bank of England*, 3rd ed. 1798; Appendix, p. 120. The italics are Ricardo's.

Without accounts; without a division of profits; and without any other proof of the accumulated fund of the Bank, but the notoriety of the increase of the sources from which the Bank profits are made—and that for a period of more than ten years; what security have the proprietors, against a corrupt administration of their affairs? It is not consistent with the delicacy of the situation of those who are entrusted with the management of millions to demand such unbounded confidence—so much reliance on their own personal character, without stating some grounds for such a demand. Yet the only answer which the Directors made to a motion for a statement of profits, in the last general court,[1] was, that they should consider the passing of such a resolution as betraying a want of confidence in them, and as a censure on their proceedings.

On all sides, such an intention was disclaimed; yet, strange to say, no other reply could be obtained from the Directors.

The publication of accounts, besides being necessary as a check against the *corrupt* administration of the Directors, is also necessary to give assurance to the proprietors, that their affairs are *ably* administered. Since 1797, no statement has been made of the condition of the Bank; and, even in that year, it was made to Parliament, on a particular exigence, and not to the proprietors of Bank stock. How then, can the proprietors know whether, in the favourable circumstances in which the Bank have been placed, the directors have availed themselves of all the opportunities which have offered, of employing the funds entrusted to their charge to the best advantage? Would it not be desirable, that from time to time the proprietors should be able to ascertain whether their just expectations had been realised, and whether their affairs had been ably as well as honourably administered? If the practice of laying all accounts before the proprietors had been always followed, perhaps the

[1] 21 Dec. 1815.

Directors of 1793, 1794, and 1795, might have been admonished for so badly managing the affairs of the Bank, as to keep permanently in their coffers a sum of cash and bullion, generally more than three-fourths, and seldom less than one-half the whole amount of their notes in circulation. They might possibly have been told, that such a waste of the resources of the Bank shewed a very limited knowledge of the principles by which a paper currency should be regulated*.

These irregularities in the proceedings of the Bank excited the attention of an independent proprietor, Mr. Allardyce, in 1797 and 1801. In his excellent publication on Bank affairs,[1] he has pointed out with great force and ability the illegal conduct of the Bank. His opinion was confirmed by Mr., now Sir James, Mansfield, who was consulted by him as to the course, necessary to be pursued, to compel the directors to lay an account before the proprietors of the state of the company. Sir James Mansfield's opinion was given as follows:

"I am of opinion, that *every* proprietor, at a general half yearly court, has a *right* to require from the directors, and it is the *duty* of the latter to produce, all such accounts, books and papers, as are necessary to enable the proprietors to judge of the state and condition of the corporation and its funds, and to determine what dividend ought to be paid. The proper method to be pursued by those who consult me in order to obtain such a production is, that a number of respectable proprietors should immediately give notice to the governor and other directors, that they shall require at the next general court a production of all the necessary books, accounts and papers; and at the general

* For the account of cash and bullion in the Bank in the above years I trust to the calculations to which I have already alluded, page [99][2]. I can see no reason to doubt their general accuracy.

[1] See above, pp. 103 and 106; what follows in the text is taken from Allardyce's *Second Address*, p. 31 ff.

[2] Ed. 1 '74' (*i.e.* p. 99 above); eds. 2–3 '74' (*i.e.* p. 98 above).

court, when it shall be held, to attend and require such a production. If it shall not be obtained, I then advise them immediately, or within a few days after the holding of the general court, to make an application to the governor to call a general court, which application must be made by nine members at least, having each 500*l.* stock. If the governor shall refuse to call such general court, then the nine members who shall have applied to him to have a court called, may themselves call one in the manner prescribed by the charter; and whether the governor calls such court, or it is called by the nine members, I advise them, as soon as it is called, to apply to the court of King's Bench for a mandamus to the governor and directors, to produce at such court all the necessary books, accounts and papers.

J. MANSFIELD."

"Temple, March 9, 1801."

In consequence of this opinion, Mr. Allardyce delivered a demand in writing at the next general court, held the 19th March, 1801, that the accounts should be produced, and no doubt intended to follow up this proceeding in the way recommended by Sir James Mansfield,—but he soon after died; and since that time no proprietor has made any demand for accounts, till at the last general court in December. It is remarkable that, very unexpectedly to the proprietors, a bonus of 5 per cent., in navy 5 per Cents., was voted in the general court of the 19th March, 1801, the day on which Mr. Allardyce's demand was made and refused. The first motion for accounts made by Mr. Allardyce was in the general court, held 14th Dec. 1797; and in March 1799, there was a bonus of 10 per cent. in 5 per Cents. 1797. Mr. Allardyce did not, I believe, make any motion in the Bank court between December, 1797, and March, 1801.

Since 1797, then, the proprietors have remained in utter ignorance of the affairs of the Bank. During eighteen years the directors have been silently enjoying their lucrative trade, and may now possibly think that the same course is best adapted to the interests of the Bank, particularly as negociations are about to take place with government, when it might be as well that the amount of their accumulated fund should not be known. But the public attention has been lately called to the affairs of the Bank; and the subject of their profits is generally canvassed and understood. Publicity would now probably be more beneficial than hurtful to the Bank; for exaggerated accounts of their profits have been published which may raise extravagant expectations, and which may be best corrected by official statements. Besides which, the Bank are secure of their charter for seventeen years to come; and the public cannot, during that time, deprive them of the most profitable part of their trade. If indeed the charter were about to expire, the public might question the policy of permitting a company of merchants to enjoy all the advantages which attend the supplying of a great country with paper money; and although they would naturally look with jealousy, after the experience furnished by other states, to allowing that power to be in the hands of government, they might probably think that in a free country means might be found by which so considerable an advantage might be obtained for the state, independently of all control of ministers. Paper money may be considered as affording a seignorage equal to its whole exchangeable value,—but seignorage in all countries belongs to the state, and with the security of convertibility as proposed in the former part of this work, and the appointment of commissioners responsible to parliament only, the state, by becoming the sole issuer of paper money, in town as well as in the country, might secure a net revenue to the public of no less than two millions sterling. Against this danger, however, the Bank is secure till 1833, and therefore on every ground publicity is expedient.

APPENDIX

No. I*

Table shewing the Amount annually[1] paid by the Public, from 1797 to 1815, for Management of the British, Irish, German, and Portuguese Debt.

Year commencing 5th January				L.	s.	d.
1797	.	.	.	162,431	5	3
1798	.	.	.	212,592	1	5
1799	.	.	.	218,190	17	0
1800	.	.	.	238,294	3	8
1801	.	.	.	236,772	15	8
1802	.	.	.	263,105	14	6
1803	.	.	.	247,538	11	0
1804	.	.	.	267,786	19	7
1805	.	.	.	271,911	11	9
1806	.	.	.	292,127	9	10
1807	.	.	.	297,757	16	1
1808	.	.	.	210,549	2	7
1809	.	.	.	222,775	2	4
1810	.	.	.	217,825	13	5
1811	.	.	.	228,349	16	0
1812	.	.	.	223,705	12	5
1813	.	.	.	238,827	17	7
1814	.	.	.	242,263	14	7

* The particulars in the above table are taken from the annual finance book, printed by order of the house of commons. They include not only what is paid to the Bank, but to the Exchequer and South Sea company. The annual charge of the South Sea company is now about 14,560l. In 1797 it was 14,657l. The Exchequer charge was as high as 6760l. 6s. 8d., in 1807 it fell gradually to 2485l. and has now, I believe, ceased.

The Bank have also been paid for management of life annuities since 1810,—and since 1812, about 1200l. or 1300l. per ann. for management of a loan of two and half millions, raised for the East India Company, which are not included in this table.

[1] Ed. 1 does not contain 'annually' here or in the heading of the next table (No. II).

No. II

Table shewing the Amount annually received by the Bank from 1797 to 1815, for receiving Contributions on Loans.*

Year commencing Michaelmas	L.	s.	d.
1796	20,506	3	4
1797	27,410	0	4

Year commencing 5th January	L.	s.	d.
1799	16,115	6	8
1800	12,489	15	5
1801	39,080	17	11
1802	22,538	12	3
1803	9,669	10	0
1804			
1805	11,683	19	7
1806	18,130	16	3
1807	16,115	16	8
1808	12,650	18	7
1809	8,400	0	0
1810	11,680	0	0
1811	14,705	0	0
1812	19,031	14	0
1813	21,639	8	9
1814	42,200	0	0

* This table is taken from an account laid before parliament, on the 19th of June 1815.

No. III

The total Amount[1] of the Unredeemed Funded Debt of Great Britain and Ireland, including Loans to the Emperor of Germany and Prince Regent of Portugal, payable in Great Britain, was on the first of February 1815, according to accounts laid before parliament   *L*.727,767,421 2 $5\frac{3}{4}$

Do. for East India Company   -   -   -   3,929,561 0 0

731,696,982 2 $5\frac{3}{4}$

Debt contracted from Feb. 1 to }
Aug. 1, 1815   -   -   - } 87,448,402 16

Redeemed from Feb. 1 to Aug. 1, }
1815   -   -   -   - } 11,099,166 0

76,349,236 16 0

Total of unredeemed funded debt on Aug. 1, 1815   *L*.808,046,218 18 $5\frac{3}{4}$

The charge for Management on which is as follows:

L.15,233,484 13 11   South Sea stock and annuities, for the management of which the South Sea Co. is paid -   - *L*. 14,560 4 11

11,686,000 0 0   due to the Bank of England   -   5,898 3 5

600,000,000 0 0   at 340*l*. per million   -   -   204,000 0 0

181,126,734 4 $6\frac{3}{4}$ at 300*l*. do.   -   -   -   54,338 0 5

808,046,218 18 $5\frac{3}{4}$

2,795,340 0 0   life annuities   -   -   -   899 5 0

39,735,898 6 8   for 1,589,435*l*. 6s. 8d. anns. at } 25 years purchase   - }   11,920 15 4

L.850,577,457 5 $1\frac{3}{4}$

291,616 9 7

Deduct the first sum paid to the South Sea Company   14,560 4 11

Management paid to the Bank of England on the Debt } as it stood Aug. 1, 1815   -   -   -   - }   277,056 4 8

[1] Ed. 1 does not contain 'Amount'.

No. IV

Average Amount of Bank of England Notes, including Bank Post Bills, in circulation in each of the following years.

	Notes of five pounds and upwards, including Bank post bills.	Notes under five pounds.	Total.
1797	10,095,620	1,096,100	11,191,720
1798	11,527,250	1,807,502	13,334,752
1799	12,408,522	1,653,805	14,062,327
1800	13,598,666	2,243,266	15,841,932
1801	13,454,367	2,715,182	16,169,594
1802	13,917,977	3,136,477	17,054,454
1803	12,983,477	3,864,045	16,847,522
1804	12,621,348	4,723,672	17,345,020
1805	12,697,352	4,544,580	17,241,932
1806	12,844,170	4,291,230	17,135,400
1807	13,221,988	4,183,013	17,405,001
1808	13,402,160	4,132,420	17,534,580
1809	14,133,615	4,868,275	19,001,890
1810	16,085,522	6,644,763	22,730,285*
1811	16,286,950	7,260,575	23,547,525
1812	15,862,120	7,600,000	23,462,120
1813	16,057,000	8,030,000	24,087,000
1814	18,540,780	9,300,000	27,840,780
1815	18,157,956	9,161,454	27,319,410

* Till 1811, the above are extracted from the report of the bullion committee; since that year from returns made to parliament.

No. V

AN ESTIMATE OF THE PROFITS OF THE BANK OF ENGLAND, FOR THE
YEAR COMMENCING JAN. 5, 1797.

Bank notes in circulation - - -	*L*.11,191,720	
Public deposits - - - -	5,000,000	
Surplus above permanent capital* -	3,826,890	
	20,018,610	
Deduct cash and bullion - - -	5,000,000	
Funds yielding interest - - -	15,018,610 at 5 p.c.	750,930
Charge for management of national debt - - - -		143,800
Do. do. Loan - - - - -		20,506
Do. do. Lottery - - - - -		1,000
Interest on 11,686,000*l.* lent to government at three per cent		350,604
		L.1,266,840

Deduct

Expences - - - - - - -	*L*.150,000	
Stamps - - - - - - -	12,000	
Voluntary contribution - - - - -	200,000	
		362,000
		904,840
Dividend seven per cent. on *L*.11,642,400 - - -		814,968
Profit -		*L*.89,872

ESTIMATE FOR THE YEAR COMMENCING JANUARY 1798.

Surplus before 1797 - - -	*L*.3,826,890	
Do. of 1797 - - -	89,872	
	3,916,762	
Bank notes in circulation - - -	13,334,752	
Public deposits - - -	5,700,000	
	22,951,514	
Deduct cash and bullion - - -	4,000,000	
Funds yielding interest - - -	18,951,514 at 5 p.c.	947,575

* This sum was returned by the Bank to parliament as their surplus
capital, February 26, 1797.[1]

[1] 'Report of the Lords' Committee of Secrecy...', 26 Feb. 1797.
Appendix (Reprint 1810, p. 75).

Brought over - - - - - -				*L.*947,575
Charge for management of national debt -		-	192,000	
Do. Loans - - - - -		-	27,410	
Do. Lottery - - - - -		-	1,000	
				220,410
Interest on 11,686,800*l.* capital at 3 p. c.	-	-	-	350,604
				1,518,589
Deduct				
Expences - - - - - -		-	158,000	
Stamps - - - - - -		-	12,000	
Seven per cent. dividend - - - -		-	814,968	
				984,968
		Profit	-	533,621

Year commencing January 5, 1799.

Former savings - - - -				*L.*3,916,762
Do. for 1798 - - - -				533,621
				4,450,383
Bank notes - - - -				14,062,300
Public deposits - - - -				6,400,000
				24,912,683
Deduct cash and bullion -		-		3,000,000
Funds yielding interest -		-	21,912,683	5 p. c. 1,095,634
Charge for management of national debt		-	196,700	
Do. Loans - - - -		-	16,115	
Do. Lotteries - - - -		-	1,000	
				213,815
Interest on 11,686,800*l.* - - -		-		350,604
				1,660,053
Deduct				
Expences - - - - - -		-	166,000	
Stamps* - - - - - -		-	24,000	
Dividend seven per cent. - - -		-	814,968	
Bonus ten per cent. - - - -		-	1,164,240	
				2,169,208
		Loss	-	509,155

* The composition for stamps was raised this year to 24,000*l.*—in 1803–4, to 32,000*l.*—in 1806–7, to 42,000*l.*—and in 1815–16, to 87,500*l.*

YEAR COMMENCING JANUARY 5, 1800.

Former savings - - - -	*L.*4,450,383	
Loss of 1799 - - - - -	509,155	
	3,941,228	
Bank notes - - - -	15,841,900	
Deposits - - - -	7,100,000	
	26,883,128	

Deduct cash and bullion	3,000,000	
Loan to government	3,000,000*	
	6,000,000	

Funds yielding interest - - -	*L.*20,883,128 at 5 p. c.	1,044,156
Management of national debt - - - -	216,700	
Do. Loans - - - -	12,489	
Do. Lottery - - - -	1,000	
		230,189
Interest on 11,686,800*l.* - - - -		350,604
		1,624,949

Deduct

Expences - - - - - -	174,000	
Stamps - - - - - -	24,000	
Dividend seven per cent. - - -	814,968	
		1,013,968
Profit -		£611,981

YEAR COMMENCING JANUARY 5, 1801.

Former savings - - - -	*L.*3,941,228	
Surplus, 1800 - - - -	611,981	
	4,553,209	
Bank notes - - -	16,169,500	
Deposits - - - -	7,800,000	
	28,522,709	

Loan to government -	3,000,000	
Cash and bullion -	3,000,000	
	6,000,000	

Funds yielding interest - -	22,522,709 at five p. c.	1,126,135

* The Bank lent to government, this year, three millions, without interest, for six years, and afterwards continued the same loan for eight years at three per cent. interest.

Brought over - - - - - - -			L.1,126,135
Charge for management of national debt -		215,200	
Do. do. Loans - - - - - -		39,080	
Do. do. Lottery - - - - -		1,000	
			255,280
Interest on capital - - - - - - -			350,604
			1,732,019
Deduct			
Expences - - - - - - -		182,000	
Stamps - - - - - - -		24,000	
			206,000
			1,526,019
Dividend seven per cent. - - - -		814,968	
Bonus five per cent. - - - - -		582,120	
			1,397,088
			128,931
Property-tax* -			12,893
Profit - - -			116,038

―――――――

Year commencing January, 1802.

Former savings - - - -			L.4,553,209
Profits, 1801 - - - -			116,038
			4,669,247
Bank notes - - - - -			17,050,000
Deposits - - - - -			8,600,000
			30,319,247
Deduct			
Loan to Government -		3,000,000	
Cash and bullion - -		3,000,000	
			6,000,000
Funds yielding interest - - -		24,319,247 at 5 p. c.	1,215,962

* The property-tax was paid by the proprietors till 1806, when the Bank agreed to pay, on their whole profits to Government, and not to make any deduction from the dividend warrant.

Brought over - - - - - - -	*L.* 1,215,962	
Charge for management of national debt - -	241,600	
Do. do. Loans - - - - - -	22,538	
Do. do. Lottery - - - -	1,000	
		265,138
Interest on capital - - - - - - -		350,604
		1,831,704
Deduct		
Expences - - - - - - -	190,000	
Stamps - - - - - - -	24,000	
Dividend seven per cent. - - -	814,968	
Bonus two and half per cent. - - - -	291,060	
		1,320,028
		511,676
Property tax -		51,167
Profit - -		460,509

Year commencing January, 1803.

Former savings - - - -	*L.* 4,669,247		
Profits, 1802 - - - -	460,509		
	5,129,756		
Bank notes - - - - -	16,847,500		
Deposits - - - -	9,300,000		
	31,277,256		
Loan to Government -	3,000,000		
Cash and bullion - -	3,000,000		
	6,000,000		
	25,277,256		1,263,862
Management of the national debt - - -		226,000	
Do. do. Loans - - - -		9,669	
Do. do. Lottery - - - -		1,000	
		236,669	
Interest on[1] capital - - - - - - -			350,604
			1,851,135

[1] Ed. 1 does not contain 'on'.

Brought over - - - - - - - - *L*.1,851,135

    Deduct

Expences - - - - - - - 198,000
Stamps - - - - - - - 32,000
Dividend seven per cent. - - - - 814,968
                                     1,044,968

                                       806,167
Property tax on net profit, five per cent. - - - - 40,308

                          Profit - 765,859

Year commencing January, 1804.

Former savings - - - - *L.* 5,129,756
Profits, 1803 - - - - 765,859

                     5,895,615
Bank notes - - - - - 17,345,020
Deposits - - - - - 10,000,000

                     33,240,635
            Deduct
Loan to Government - 3,000,000
Cash and bullion - - 3,000,000
                         6,000,000

Funds yielding interest - - - 27,240,635 five p. c. 1,362,030
Charge for management of national debt - - 246,700
Do. do.   Loans - - - - - ——
Do. do.   Lottery - - - - - 3,000
                                   249,700
Interest of capital - - - - - - - - 350,604

                                   1,962,334
            Deduct
Expences - - - - - - - 206,000
Stamps - - - - - - - 32,000
Dividend seven per cent. - - - - 814,968
Bonus five per cent. - - - - - 582,120
                                   1,635,088

                                   327,246
Property tax six and a quarter per cent. - - - - 20,452

                          Profit - 306,794

Year commencing 1805.

Former savings	-	-	-	-	*L.* 5,895,615		
Profit, 1814	-	-	-	-	306,794		
					6,202,409		
Bank notes -	-	-	-	-	17,241,932		
Deposits	-	-	-	-	10,700,000		
					34,144,341		
Loan to Government	-	3,000,000					
Cash and bullion -	-	3,000,000					
					6,000,000		
					28,144,341	5 p. c.	1,407,217
Charge for management of national debt -		-			254,400		
Do. do. Loan -	-	-	-	-	11,683		
Do. do. Lotteries	-	-	-	-	4,000		
							270,083
Interest on capital	-	-	-	-	-	-	350,604
							2,027,904
Deduct							
Expences	-	-	-	-	-	214,000	
Stamps	-	-	-	-	-	32,000	
Dividend seven per cent.	-	-	-	-	814,968		
Bonus five per cent.	-	-	-	-	582,120		
							1,643,088
							384,816
Property tax ten per cent.	-	-	-	-	-	-	38,481
							346,335

Year commencing 1806.

Former savings	-	-	-	-	*L.* 6,202,409
Savings, 1805	-	-	-	-	346,335
					6,548,744
Bank notes -	-	-	-	-	17,135,400
Public deposits	-	-	-	-	11,000,000
					34,684,144

Brought over - - - *L.* 34,684,144				
Loan to Government -	3,000,000		at 3 p. c.*	90,000
Cash and bullion - -	3,000,000			
		6,000,000		
		28,684,144 at 5 p. c.[1]		1,434,207
Charge for management of national debt - -			275,000	
Do. do. Loan - - - - - -			18,130	
Do. do. Lotteries - - - - -			2,000	
				295,130
Interest on capital - - - - - - -				350,604
				2,169,941
Deduct				
Expences - - - - - - -			222,000	
Stamps - - - - - - -			32,000	
Dividend of seven per cent. - - - -			814,968	
Bonus of five per cent. - - - - -			582,120	
				1,651,088
				518,853
Property tax ten per cent. on surplus - -			51,885	
†Do. ten per cent. on bonus and Oct. dividend			98,960	
				150,845
			Profit -	368,008

═══════════

Year commencing January, 1807.

Former savings - - - - *L.* 6,548,744				
Profit, 1806 - - - -				368,008
				6,916,752
Bank notes - - - - -				17,405,000
Deposits - - - - -				11,000,000
				35,321,752

* See note, p. [121].[2]   † See note, p. [120].

[1] Ed. 1 does not contain 'at 5 p. c.'   [2] Ed. 1 does not contain this foot-note.

Brought over - - - -		35,321,752	
Loan to Government -	3,000,000		at 3 p. c. 90,000
Cash and bullion - -	3,000,000		
		6,000,000	
		29,321,752	1,466,087
			1,556,087
Management of national debt - - - -		280,500	
Do. do. Loans - - - - -		16,115	
Do. do. Lotteries - - - - -		5,000	
Commission for receiving [1] property tax - -		3,154	
			304,769
Interest on capital - - - - - - -			350,604
			2,211,460

Deduct			
Expences - - - - - - -		230,000	
Stamps - - - - - - -		42,000	
			272,000
Dividend ten per cent. - - - - -		1,164,240	1,939,460
Property tax - - - - -		193,946	
			1,358,186
Profit - 581,274			

===

Year commencing 1808.

Former savings - - - -		6,916,752	
Profit, 1807 - - - -		581,274	
		7,498,026	
Bank notes - - - - -		17,534,580	
Deposits - - - - -		11,000,000	
		36,032,606	
Loan to Government -	3,000,000		at 3 per c. 90,000
Ditto - - - -	3,000,000		
Cash and bullion - -	3,000,000		
		9,000,000	
		27,032,606	1,351,630
			1,441,630

[1] Ed. 1 does not contain 'Commission for receiving' here or in the corresponding item for the subsequent years.

Brought over - - - - - - -	*L.*	1,441,630
Management of national debt - - - -	193,300	
Loan - - -	12,650	
Lotteries - - -	2,000	
Commission for receiving property duty - -	3,154	
		211,104
Interest on capital - - - - - - -		350,604
		2,003,338
Expences - - - - - - -	239,000	
Stamps - - - - - - -	42,000	
		281,000
		1,722,338
Dividend, 10 per cent. - - -	1,164,240	
Property tax, ditto - - -	172,233	
		1,336,473
Profit -		385,865

YEAR COMMENCING JANUARY, 1809.

Former savings - - - -	7,498,026		
Profit, 1808 - - - -	385,865		
	7,883,891		
Bank notes - - - - -	19,000,000		
Deposits - - - - -	11,000,000		
	37,883,891		
Loan to Government - 3,000,000		at 3 per cent.	90,000
Ditto without interest - 3,000,000			
Cash and bullion - - 3,000,000			
	9,000,000		
	28,883,891		1,444,194
Management of national debt - - - -	205,500		
Loan - - -	8,400		
Lotteries - - -	3,000		
Commission for receiving property duty - -	3,154		
			220,054
Interest on capital - - - - - - -			350,604
			2,104,852

Brought over   -   -   -   -   -   -   -   _L._2,104,852
Expences   -   -   -   -   -   -   -   246,000
Stamps   -   -   -   -   -   -   -   42,000
————————
288,000

1,816,852
Dividend 10 per cent.   -   -   -   -   -   1,164,240
Property tax   -   -   -   -   -   181,852
————————
1,346,092

Profit   -   470,760

YEAR COMMENCING JANUARY 1810.

Former savings   -   -   -   -   _L._7,883,891
Profit   -   -   -   -   -   470,760

8,354,651
Bank notes   -   -   -   -   22,730,000
Deposits   -   -   -   -   11,000,000

42,084,651
Loan to Government   -   3,000,000   at 3 per cent.   90,00
Ditto without interest   -   3,000,000
Cash and Bullion -   -   3,000,000
————————
9,000,000

33,084,651   1,654,232

1,744,232
Management of national debt -   -   -   -   200,800
Loan   -   -   -   11,680
Lotteries   -   -   -   3,000
Commission for receiving property tax   -   -   3,154
————————
218,634
Interest on capital   -   -   -   -   -   -   -   350,604

2,313,470

Brought over	-	-	-	-	-	-	L. 2,313,470
Deduct							

Expences	-	-	-	-	-	-	254,000
Stamps	-	-	-	-	-	-	42,000
							296,000

	2,017,470
Dividend, 10 per cent. - - - - - 1,164,240	
Property duty - - - - - 201,747	
	1,365,987
Profit -	651,483

▬▬▬▬

YEAR COMMENCING JANUARY 1811.

Former savings	-	-	-	-	L.8,354,651	
1810 -	-	-	-	-	651,483	
					9,006,134	
Bank notes -	-	-	-	-	23,547,000	
Deposits -	-	-	-	-	11,000,000	
					43,553,134	
Loan to Government	-	3,000,000			at 3 per cent.	90,000
Ditto without interest	-	3,000,000				
Cash and bullion -	-	3,000,000				
			9,000,000			
			34,553,134			1,727,765
						1,817,765

Management of national debt -	-	-	-	211,300	
Loan	-	-	-	14,705	
Lotteries	-	-	-	4,000	
Life annuities	-	-	206		
Commission for receiving property duty -	-	3,451[1]			
					233,662
Interest on capital	- - - - - - -				350,604
					2,402,031

[1] Eds. 2–3 misprint '3,454'. Although the sum requires 3451 as given in ed. 1, the correct figure is clearly 3154 as for all the other years.

Brought over - - - - - - -			*L.*2,402,031
Expences - - - - - - -		264,000	
Stamps - - - - - - -		42,000	
			306,000
			2,096,031
Dividend, 10 per cent. - - - - -		1,164,240	
Property tax - - - - -		209,603	
			1,373,843
Profit -			722,188

───

Year commencing January 1812.

Former savings - - - -		*L.*9,006,134		
1811 - - - - - -		722,188		
		9,728,322		
Bank notes - - - - -		23,462,000		
Deposits - - - - -		11,000,000		
		44,190,322		
Loan to Government -	3,000,000		at 3 per cent.	90,000
Ditto without interest -	3,000,000			
Cash and bullion - -	3,000,000			
		9,000,000		
		35,190,322		1,759,516
Management of national debt - - - -		208,000		
Loans - - -		19,031		
Life annuities - -		369		
Commission for receiving property duty - -		3,154		
				230,554
Interest on capital - - - - - - - -				350,604
				2,430,674

Brought over - - - - - - -			*L*.2,430,674
Expences - - - - - - -		273,000	
Stamps - - - - -		42,000	
			315,000
			2,115,674
Dividend, 10 per cent. - - - - -		1,164,240	
Property duty - - - - - -		211,567	
			1,375,807
	Profit -		739,867

―――――――

Year commencing January 1813.

Former savings - - - -		*L*.9,728,322		
1812 - - - - -		739,867		
		10,468,189		
Bank notes - - - - -		24,080,000		
Deposits - - - - -		11,000,000		
		45,548,189		
Loan to Government -	3,000,000		at 3 per cent.	90,000
Ditto without interest -	3,000,000			
Cash and bullion - -	3,000,000			
		9,000,000		
				1,827,400
		36,548,189		
				1,917,400
Management of national debt - - - -		223,100		
Loan - - - - -		21,639		
Ditto - - - - -		2,000		
Life annuities - - -		462		
Commission for receiving property duty - -		3,154		
				250,355
				2,167,755

Brought over	-	-	-	-	-	-	-		*L.*2,167,755
Interest of capital -	-	-	-	-	-	-			350,604
									2,518,359
Expences	-	-	-	-	-	-	-	283,000	
Stamps	-	-	-	-	-	·	-	42,000	
									325,000
									2,193,359
Dividend, 10 per cent.	-	-	-	-	-	-	1,164,240	
Property duty[1]	-	-	-	-	-	-	219,333	
									1,383,573
					Profit	-			809,786

═══════

Year commencing January 1814.

Former savings	-	-	-	-	*L.*10,468,189	
1813 -	-	-	-	-	809,786	
					11,277,975	
Bank notes -	-	-	··	-	27,840,000	
Deposits	-	-	-	-	11,000,000	
					50,117,975	
Loan to Government with- out interest }		-	-	3,000,000		
Cash and bullion -	-	3,000,000				
				6,000,000		
				44,117,975		2,205,898
Management of national debt -	-	-	-		227,000	
Loan	-	-	-	-	42,200	
Life annuities	-	-	-		576	
Commission for receiving property duty -	-			3,154		
					272,930	
Interest of capital -	-	-	-	-	-	350,604
						2,829,432

[1] Eds. 2–3 erroneously alter this into 'Commission for receiving property duty', by a false analogy with the correction mentioned above, p. 127 n.

Brought over - - - - - .. -		*L*.2,829,432
Expences - - - - - - .	292,000	
Stamps - - - - - - ..	42,000	
		334,000
		2,495,432
Dividend, 10 per cent. - - - - -	1,164,240	
Property tax - - - - - -	249,543	
		1,413,783
Profit -		1,081,649

Year commencing January 1815.

Former savings - - - -	11,277,975		
1814 - - - - - -	1,081,649		
	12,359,624		
Bank notes - - - - -	27,300,000		
Deposits - - - - -	11,000,000		
	50,659,624		
Loan to Government -	3,000,000		
Cash and Bullion - -	3,000,000		
	6,000,000		
	44,659,624		2,232,980
Management of national debt - - - -		250,000	
Loan - - - -		28,800	
Life annuities - - -		700	
Commission for receiving property tax - -		3,154	
		282,654	
Interest on capital - - - - - - -			350,604
			2,866,238
Expences - - - - - - -		300,000	
Stamps - - - - - - -		87,500	
		387,500	
			2,478,738

Brought over	-	-	-	-	-	-	-	*L.* 2,478,738
Dividend, 10 per cent.	-	-	-	-	-	1,164,240	
Property tax	-	-	-	-	-	247,873	
							1,412,113
					Profit	-	1,066,625

———

JANUARY 1816.

Former savings	-	-	-	-	-	-	-	12,359,624
Savings, 1815	-	-	-	-	-	-	-	1,066,625
							*L.*13,426,249

No. VI

Resolutions proposed concerning the Bank of England,
by Mr. Grenfell

1. That it appears, that there was paid by the public to the Bank of England, for managing the national debt, including the charge for contributions on loans and lotteries, in the year ending 5th of July 1792, the sum of 99,803*l*. 12*s*. 5*d*.; and that there was paid for the like service, in the year ending 5th April 1815, the sum of 281,568*l*. 6*s*. 11¼*d*.; being an increase of 181,764*l*. 14*s*. 6¾*d*. In addition to which, the Bank of England have charged at the rate of 1250*l*. per million on the amount of property duty received at the Bank on profits arising from professions, trades, and offices.

2. That the total amount of Bank notes and Bank post bills, in circulation in the years 1795 and 1796 (the latter being the year previous to the restriction on cash payments,) and in the year 1814, was as follows:

1795, 1st Feb. £12,735,520; and 1st Aug. £11,214,000.
1796, 1st Feb. 10,784,740; and 1st Aug. 9,856,110.
1814, 1st Feb. 25,154,950; and 1st Aug. 28,802,450.

3. That at present, and during many years past, more particularly since the year 1806, considerable sums of public money, forming together an average stationary balance amounting to many millions, have been deposited with, or otherwise placed in the custody of the Bank of England, acting in this respect as the bankers of the public.

4. That it appears, from a report ordered to be printed 10th of August 1807, from "the committee on the public expenditure of the united kingdom," that the aggregate amount of balances and deposits of public money in the hands of the Bank of England, including Bank notes deposited in the Exchequer, made up in four different periods of the quarter ending 5th January 1807, fluctuated betwixt the sums

Vide Report p. 74 & 75.

of £11,461,200 and 12,198,236 including Bank notes deposited in the chests of the Exchequer.

or,

8,178,536 and 9,948,400 excluding Bank notes deposited at the Exchequer.

5. That the aggregate amount of such deposits, together with the Exchequer bills and Bank notes deposited in the chests of the four tellers of the Exchequer, was, on an average, in the year 1814,

£11,966,371; including Bank notes deposited at the Exchequer, amounting to 642,264*l*.

or,

11,324,107; excluding Bank notes deposited at the Exchequer.

6. That it appears, that this aggregate amount of deposits, together with such portions of the amount of Bank notes and Bank post bills in circulation as may have been invested by the Bank in securities bearing interest, was productive, during the same period, of interest and profit to the Bank of England.

7. That the only participation hitherto enjoyed by the public, since the year 1806, in the profits thus made on such deposits by the Bank, has consisted in a loan of three millions, advanced to the public by the Bank, by the 46 Geo. III. cap. 41., bearing 3 per cent. interest; which loan was discharged in December 1814: And in another loan of three millions, advanced to the public by the Bank, by the 48 Geo. III. cap. 3, free of any charge of interest; which loan became payable in December 1814, but has, by an act of the present session of parliament, cap. 16, been continued to the 5th of April 1816.

8. That this house will take into early consideration the advantages derived by the Bank, as well from the management of the national debt, as from the amount of balances of public money remaining in their hands, with the view to the adoption of such an arrangement, when the engagements now subsisting shall have expired, as may be consistent with what is due to the interests of the public, and to the rights, credit and stability, of the Bank of England.

13 *June* 1815.

No. VII

Resolutions proposed concerning the Bank of England, by Mr. Mellish

1. That by the act of 31 Geo. III. cap. 33, there was allowed to the Bank of England, for the management of the public debt, 450*l.* per million on the capital stock transferrable at the Bank, amounting in the year ending 5th July 1792, to 98,803*l.* 12*s.* 5*d.* on about 219,596,000*l.* then so transferrable; and that by the act 48 Geo. III. cap. 4, the said allowance was reduced to the rate of 340*l.* per million on all sums not exceeding 600 millions, and to 300*l.* per million on all sums exceeding that amount, whereby the Bank was entitled, in the year ending 5th April 1815, to the sum of 241,971*l.* 4*s.* 2¼*d.* on about 726,570,700*l.* capital stock, and 798*l.* 3*s.* 7*d.* on 2,347,588*l.*, 3 per cents. transferred for life annuities, being an increase of 143,965*l.* 15*s.* 4¾*d.* for management, and an increase of about 509,322,000*l.* capital stock: Also the Bank was allowed 1,000*l.* for taking in contributions, amounting to 812,500*l.* on a lottery in the year ending 5th July 1792; and 38,798*l.* 19*s.* 2*d.* for taking in contributions, amounting to 46,585,533*l.* 6*s.* 8*d.* on loans and lotteries in the year ending 5th April 1815.

2. That it appears, that the Bank, in pursuance of the act 46 Geo. III. cap. 65, has, from the year 1806 to the present time, made the assessments of the duty on profits arising from property, on the proprietors of the whole of the funded debt, transferrable at the Bank of England, and has deducted the said duty from each of the several dividend warrants,which in one year, ending 5th April 1815, amounted in number to 565,600; and that this part of the business has been done without any expense to, or charge on, the public.

That in pursuance of the abovementioned act, the duties so deducted have from time to time been placed to the "account of the commissioners of the treasury, on account of the said duties," together with other sums received from the public by virtue of the said act: part of this money is applied to the payment of certificates of allowances, and the remainder is paid into the Exchequer.

That by virtue of the said act, the lords commissioners of the treasury have made annual allowances, at the rate of 1,250*l.* per million, upon the amount so placed to the account of the commissioners of the treasury at the Bank of England, as a compensation for receiving, paying, and accounting for the same; which allowances, however, have not in any one year exceeded the sum of 3,480*l.*, and upon an average of eight years have amounted annually to 3,154*l.* only.

The amount of duties received for the year ending 5th April 1814, was 2,784,343*l.*, which, if it had been collected in the usual manner, at an allowance of 5*d.* per pound, would have cost the public 58,007*l.*; and the cost for collecting 20,188,293*l.*, being the whole of the duty received from 1806 to 1814, on which allowances have been made, would at the same rate have amounted to 420,589*l.*

That all monies received by the Bank on account of duties on property, are paid into the Exchequer immediately after the receipt thereof: when this circumstance is contrasted with the ordinary progress of monies into the exchequer, the advantage resulting to the public may be fairly estimated at 2*l.* per cent; which on the amount of duties for the year ending 5th April 1814, would be 55,686*l.*, and on the total amount from 1806 to 1814, would be 403,765*l.*

3. That the total amount of Bank notes and Bank post bills in circulation in the years 1795 and 1796, (the latter being the year previous to the restriction on cash payments) and in the year 1814, was as follows:

> 1795, 1st Feb. £12,735,520; . 1st Aug. £11,214,000.
> 1796, 1st Feb. 10,784,740; . 1st Aug. 9,856,110.
> 1814, 1st Feb. 25,154,950; . 1st Aug. 28,802,450.

4. That at present, and during many years past, both before and since the renewal of the charter of the Bank, considerable sums of the public money have been deposited with, or otherwise placed in the custody of the governor and company of the Bank of England, who act in this respect as the banker of the public. The average balances of these deposits, both before and after the renewal of the charter, were as follows:—

Public balances on an average of one year ending the
15th January 1800 . . . . . . 1,724,747.
Unclaimed dividends for the average of one year
ending 1 Jan. 1800 . . . . . . 837,966.

£2,562,713.

Public balances on an average of eight years, from
1807 to 1815 . . . . 4,375,405.
Unclaimed dividends.   do. . . . 634,614.

£5,010,019.

5. That it appears, from a report ordered to be printed 10th August 1807, from "the committee on public expenditure of the united kingdom," that the aggregate amount of balances and deposits of public money in the Bank of England, including Bank notes deposited in the Exchequer, made up in four different periods of the quarter ending 5th January 1807, fluctuated between the sums of 11,461,200*l.* and 12,198,236*l.*; or, excluding Bank notes deposited at the Exchequer, the amount fluctuated between 8,178,536*l.* and 9,948,400*l.*; the reason for which exclusion is not obvious, as by the act of 48 Geo. III. cap. 3, the tellers of the Exchequer are authorized to take as securities on monies lodged, either Exchequer bills,

or notes of the governor and company of the Bank of England. And it also appears, according to accounts laid before this house in the present session of parliament, that the aggregate amount of such deposits, together with the Exchequer bills and Bank notes deposited in the chests of the four tellers of the Exchequer, was, on an average, in the year 1814,

£.11,966,371. Including Bank notes deposited at the Exchequer, amounting to 642,264*l.*

11,324,107. Excluding Bank notes deposited at the Exchequer.

6. That it appears, according to accounts before this house, that the average of the aggregate amount of balances of public money in the hands of the Bank of England, from February 1807 to February 1815, was 5,010,019*l.*; and that the average of bills and Bank notes deposited in the chests of the four tellers of the Exchequer, from August 1807 to April 1815, was 5,968,793*l.*; making together 10,978,812*l.*, being 850,906*l.* less than the average of the said accounts for one year ending 5th January 1807, as stated in the report of the committee on the public expenditure.

7. That by the 39 & 40 Geo. III. cap. 28, extending the charter of the Bank for twenty-one years, the Bank advanced to the public 3,000,000*l.* for six years without interest, and extended the loan of 11,686,800*l.* for twenty-one years at an interest of 3*l.* per cent. per annum, as a consideration for the privileges, profits, emoluments, benefits and advantages, granted to the Bank by such extension of its charter.

That the interest of 3,000,000*l.* for six years, at 5*l.* per cent. per annum, is .   .   .   .   .   £ 900,000.

That the difference between 3*l.* per cent. and 5*l.* per cent. on 11,686,800*l.* is 233,736*l.*; which in twenty-one years amounts to   .   .   .   .   4,908,456.

That the above loan of 3,000,000*l.* was continued to the public from 1806, when it became payable, until 1814, at an interest of 3*l.* per cent. making an advantage in favour of the public of 2*l.* per cent. or 60,000*l.* per annum; which in eight years and eight months amounts to .   .   .   .   .   520,000.

That in 1808 the Bank advanced to the public 3,000,000*l.* without interest, which by an act of the present session is to remain without interest until the 5th of April 1816; the interest on this advance, at 5*l.* per cent. will for eight years amount to .   .   .   .   1,200,000.

8. That by the 39 and 40 Geo. III. cap. 28, sec. 13, it is enacted, That during the continuance of the charter, the Bank shall enjoy all privileges, profits, emoluments, benefits and advantages whatsoever, which they now possess and enjoy by virtue of any employment by or on behalf of the public.

That previously to such renewal of their charter, the Bank was employed as the public banker, in keeping the cash of all the principal departments in the receipt of the public revenue, and in issuing and conducting the public expenditure.

> That the average amount of the public balances in the hands of the Bank, between the 1st February 1814, and the 15th January 1815, upon accounts opened at the Bank previously to the renewal of the charter on the 28th March 1800, was . . . . 4,337,025.
>
> Unclaimed dividends, for the average of one year ending 1st January 1815 . . . . . 779,794.
>
> L.5,116,819

> That the average public balances in the hands of the Bank during the same period, upon accounts opened at the Bank between the 28th March 1800 and the 27th Feb. 1808, was . . . . . . L.370,018.
>
> That the average public balances in the hands of the Bank, during the same period, upon accounts opened at the Bank subsequent to the 27th February 1808, was . . . . 261,162.

9. That whenever the engagements now subsisting between the public and the Bank shall expire, it may be proper to consider the advantages derived by the Bank from its transactions with the public, with a view to the adoption of such arrangements as may be consistent with those principles of equity and good faith, which ought to prevail in all transactions between the public and the Bank of England.

26 June, 1815.

FUNDING SYSTEM

AN ARTICLE IN THE *SUPPLEMENT TO THE FOURTH, FIFTH AND SIXTH EDITIONS OF THE ENCYCLOPÆDIA BRITANNICA*

1820

THE article 'Funding System' was written by Ricardo for the *Supplement to the Fourth, Fifth and Sixth Editions of the Encyclopædia Britannica*, edited by Macvey Napier, which was published in parts between 1814 and 1824 by Constable of Edinburgh.[1] The half volume containing Ricardo's article (Part II of vol. IV) was published early in September 1820.[2] It was the practice of the *Supplement* to have all articles signed with letters, the key to which was given in a Table in vol. I. In Ricardo's case the signature was '(E.E.E.)'.

At the beginning of September 1819 Napier had asked Mill, who was one of his chief contributors, to induce Ricardo to write the article on the Sinking Fund. After much persuasion Ricardo agreed to put down his thoughts but warned Napier that eventually he would have to write the article himself.[3]

At Mill's request, Francis Place, who had been agitating against the Sinking Fund for many years,[4] sent him at Gatcomb a parcel of books on the subject.[5]

By 21 September Ricardo was 'very hard at work', as he wrote to Malthus, although still protesting that he was not competent.[6] On 25 September he wrote to Trower that he had made the attempt but had not succeeded and would probably abandon it. 'The truth is that Dr Hamilton's book on the Sinking Fund is so good that very little of original observations can be made on the subject. It would be unjust not to refer to him on all occasions, and if you do so it may be asked whether you have done any thing yourself?' He added that the only point on which he thought he was entitled to attention was his plan for paying off the national debt by a tax on property,[7] which he had incorporated in the article.[8] He had already

---

[1] The 5th ed. (1815) and the 6th ed. (1823) were virtual reprints of the 4th ed., which had been published at intervals between 1801 and 1810. All the new matter was contained in the*Supplement*.

[2] Advertised in *Scotsman*, 9 Sept. 1820; cp. below, VIII, 240.

[3] Below, VIII, 54 and 60.

[4] See Graham Wallas, *Life of Francis Place*, p. 159 ff.

[5] See below, VIII, 66.

[6] *ib.* 72.

[7] *ib.* 78–9.

[8] Below, pp. 196–7.

outlined this proposal in the *Principles*, in 1817,[1] and had mentioned it casually in a speech on 9 June 1819;[2] before the article was published, more deliberate references to the proposal in his speeches on 16 and 24 December 1819 gave rise to considerable discussion.[3]

By 28 September 1819 Mill and Place had received Ricardo's manuscript in London. Mill thought it excellent[4] and after a second reading had nothing but a few verbal corrections to suggest.[5] Place, however, sent a long commentary, and this led to a correspondence with Ricardo which continued till November, turning on the question whether in effect there was or was not a Sinking Fund.[6]

On 9 November Ricardo wrote to Malthus: 'I finished in my hasty way the article I had undertaken to do on the Sinking Fund, and then became so disgusted with it, that I was glad to get rid of it.—I have given so many injunctions not to regard my supposed feelings in deciding whether it shall or shall not be published, that I much doubt whether it will ever see the light.'[7]

When, a month earlier, McCulloch had written to Ricardo that he had heard he was to write the article Funding System,[8] Ricardo apparently replied that he was not writing on the Funding System in general but only on the Sinking Fund.[9] Nevertheless, in December, Napier having shown the article to McCulloch, the latter wrote to Ricardo: 'You have in fact written an article on the Funding System in general, and not on the Sinking fund; and all that is necessary to give it this shape is to transpose a few of the pages'.[10] But Ricardo replied that he would 'make it worse rather than better, by further meddling with it.' 'You' he added 'can transpose passages, and new model the productions of your pen with great facility—I with the greatest difficulty. To compose is to you an easy task, with me it is a laborious effort.'[11]

It thus appears that the article remained much the same as it had

---

[1] Above, I, 247–8.
[2] Below, V, 21.
[3] Below, V, 34–5 and 38–9; cp. VIII, 147.
[4] Below, VIII, 83.
[5] *ib.* 105.
[6] *ib.* 105 and 118 ff.

[7] *ib.* 131. Mill had forwarded the article to Napier in October; see *ib.* 141 and 144.
[8] *ib.* 81.
[9] *ib.* 127.
[10] *ib.* 137–8.
[11] *ib.* 141.

first been written, except that a Table originally attached at the end was omitted.[1]

Publication of the article was delayed as it was found that Part I of vol. IV of the *Supplement to the Encyclopædia Britannica*, in which it should have been included, was becoming too bulky; it was therefore included in Part II of the Volume, which was published in September 1820.[2]

When the question of payment arose, Ricardo regarded himself as not entitled to any, on the ground that, as Mill reported to Napier, the article was 'not worth payment' and in any case payment had formed no part of the motive which induced him to write it. He appears eventually to have accepted 20 guineas, being the ordinary rate of 10 guineas per sheet.[3]

Trower, to whom Ricardo sent an offprint of the article, suggested that he should publish it also as a pamphlet, enlarging more on his plan for paying off the National Debt. Ricardo replied that he might try to do so at some future time. The article however was never published separately.

The article was retained in the 7th and 8th editions of the *Encyclopædia Britannica*. In the 8th edition the following note was prefixed to it by the Editor: 'The article on The Funding System, by the late David Ricardo, Esq., has always been reputed so excellent that it has been considered advisable to retain it entire, and the supplement to it by his son will bring down the information on the subject to the present time.' The supplement, signed 'J.L.R.', was written by John Lewis Ricardo, who was not the son, but the nephew of Ricardo.

This was the only article that Ricardo contributed to the *Supplement*.[4] At one time Napier appears to have intended asking Ricardo to write the article Lottery and he consulted Mill. But the matter

---

[1] See below, VIII, 188.
[2] See above, p. 145, n. 2.
[3] See below, VIII, 240–1.
[4] John McVickar, in his *Outlines of Political Economy*, New York, 1825, p. 76, n., says that the article Trading System in the *Supplement* to the *Encyclopædia Britannica* over the signature E.E.E. is by Ricardo. As Professor Viner, to whom I owe this reference, suggests, Trading System must be an error for Funding System. There is no article Trading System in the *Supplement*.

was dropped when, on 15 March 1821, Mill replied: 'Till this moment I have overlooked what you say about Lottery. I see not however any thing in that for which Ricardo is particularly qualified. The question is one of morals, rather than political Economy, and I think you should reserve him for the important questions in his own science.'[1]

[1] Unpublished, in British Museum Add. MSS 34612, fol. 414.

FUNDING SYSTEM

UNDER this head we propose, first, to give an account of the rise, progress, and modifications of the SINKING FUND, accompanied with some observations as to the probability of its accomplishing the object for which it was instituted; and, next, briefly to consider the best mode of providing for our annual expenditure both in war and peace,—an inquiry necessarily involving the policy of that SYSTEM OF FUNDING of which the Sinking Fund has long been considered as one of the principal recommendations and props.

I. On the subject of the Sinking Fund, we shall have frequent occasion to refer to the statements of Professor Hamilton, in his very valuable publication, entitled, *An Inquiry concerning the Rise and Progress, the Redemption, and Present State of the National Debt of Great Britain.*[1] "The first plan for the discharge of the national debt, formed on a regular system, and conducted with a considerable degree of firmness," says this able writer, "was that of the Sinking Fund, established in 1716. The author of this plan was the Earl of Stanhope; but as it was adopted under the administration of Sir Robert Walpole, it is commonly denominated from him. The taxes which had before been laid on for limited periods, being rendered perpetual, and distributed among the *South Sea*, *Aggregate*, and *General Funds*, and the produce of these funds being greater than the charges upon them, the surpluses, together with such farther surpluses as might afterwards accrue, were united under the name of the *Sinking Fund*, being appropriated for the discharge of the national debt, and expressly ordained to

[1] The quotations are from the 'Third Edition, Enlarged', Edinburgh, Oliphant, 1818, p. 135 ff.

be applicable to no other purpose whatever. The legal interest had been reduced from six to five per cent. about two years before; and as that reduction was conformable[1] to the commercial state of the country, government was now able to obtain the same reduction on the interest of the public debt, and apply the savings in aid of the Sinking Fund. In 1727, a further reduction of the interest of the public debt, from five to four per cent. was obtained, by which nearly 400,000*l*. was added to the sinking fund. And, in the year 1749, the interest of part of the debt was again reduced to $3\frac{1}{2}$ per cent. for seven years, and to 3 per cent. thereafter; and, in 1750, the interest of the remainder was reduced to $3\frac{1}{2}$ per cent. for five years, and to 3 per cent. thereafter, by which a further saving of about 600,000*l*. was added to the sinking fund."

This sinking fund was for some time regularly applied to the discharge of debt. The sums applied, from 1716 to 1728, amounted to 6,648,000*l*., being nearly equal to the additional debt contracted in that time. From 1728 to 1733, 5,000,000*l*. more were paid. The interest of several loans, contracted between 1727 and 1732, was charged upon surplus duties, which, according to the original plan, ought to have been appropriated to the sinking fund.

"Soon after, the principle of preserving the sinking fund inviolable was abandoned. In 1733, 500,000*l*. was taken from that fund, and applied to the services of the year."—"In 1734, 1,200,000*l*. was taken from the sinking fund for current services; and, in 1735, it was anticipated and mortgaged." The produce of the sinking fund, at its commencement in 1717, was 323,437*l*. In 1776, it was at its highest amount, being then 3,166,517*l*.; in 1780, it had sunk to 2,403,017*l*.

"The sinking fund would have risen higher, had it not been depressed, especially in the latter period, by various encroach-

[1] Misprinted 'unfavourable'; Hamilton says 'conformable'.

ments. It was charged with the interest of several loans, for which no provision was made; and, in 1772, it was charged with an annuity of 100,000*l.*, granted in addition to the civil list. During the three wars which were waged while it subsisted, the whole of its produce was applied to the expence of the war; and even in time of peace, large sums were abstracted from it for current services. According to Dr. Price, the amount of public debt paid off by the sinking fund, since its first alienation in 1733, was only three millions, paid off in 1736 and 1737; three millions in the peace between 1748 and 1756; two millions and a half in the peace between 1763 and 1775; in all, eight millions and a half.

"The additional debt discharged during these periods of peace was effected, not by the sinking fund, but from other sources.

"On the whole, this fund did little in time of peace, and nothing in time of war, to the discharge of the national debt. The purpose of its inviolable application was abandoned, and the hopes entertained of its powerful efficacy entirely disappointed. At this time, the nation had no other free revenue, except the land and malt-tax granted annually; and as the land-tax during peace was then granted at a low rate, their produce was inadequate to the expence of a peace establishment, on the most moderate scale. This gave occasion to encroachments on the sinking fund. Had the land-tax been always continued at 4*s*. in the pound, it would have gone far to keep the sinking fund, during peace, inviolate."

This fund terminated in 1786, when Mr. Pitt's sinking fund was established.

To constitute this new fund, one million per annum was appropriated to it by Parliament, the capital stock of the national debt then amounting to 238,231,248*l.*

This million was to be allowed to accumulate at compound

interest, by the addition of the dividends on the stock which it purchased, till it amounted to four millions, from which time it was not further to increase. The four millions were then annually to be invested in the public funds as before, but the dividends arising from the stock purchased were no longer to be added to the sinking fund for the purpose of being invested in stock; they were to be applied to the diminution of taxes, or to any other object that Parliament might direct.

A further addition to this fund was proposed by Mr. Pitt, and readily adopted, in 1792, consisting of a grant of 400,000*l.* arising from the surplus of the revenue, and a further *annual* grant of 200,000*l.*; but it was expressly stipulated, that no relief from taxation should be given to the public, as far as this fund was concerned, till the original million, with its accumulations, amounted to four millions. The addition made to the fund, by the grant of 400,000*l.*, and of 200,000*l.* per annum, together with the interest on the stock those sums might purchase, were not to be taken or considered as forming any part of the four millions. At the same time (in 1792), a sinking fund of a new character was constituted. It was enacted, that, besides a provision for the interest of any loan which should thenceforward be contracted, taxes should also be imposed for a one per cent. sinking fund on the capital stock created by it, which should be exclusively employed in the liquidation of such particular loan; and that no relief should be afforded to the public from the taxes which constituted the one per cent. sinking fund, until a sum of capital stock, equal in amount to that created by the loan, had been purchased by it. That being accomplished, both the interest and sinking fund were to be applicable to the public service. It was calculated, that, under the most unfavourable circumstances, each loan would be redeemed in 45 years from the period of contracting for it. If made in the 3 per cent., and the price of that stock should continue uniformly at 60, the redemption would be effected in 29 years.

In the years 1798, 1799, and 1800, a deviation was made from Mr. Pitt's plan, of providing a sinking fund of one per cent. on the capital stock created by every loan, for the loans of those years had no sinking fund attached to them. The interest was charged on the war-taxes; and, in lieu of a one per cent. sinking fund, it was provided, that the war-taxes should continue during peace, to be then employed in their redemption, till they were all redeemed.

In 1802, Lord Sidmouth, then Mr. Addington, was Chancellor of the Exchequer. He being desirous of liberating the war-taxes from the charges with which they were encumbered, proposed to raise new annual permanent taxes for the interest of the loans of which we have just spoken, as well as for that which he was under the necessity of raising for the service of the year 1802; but he wished to avoid loading the public with additional taxes for a one per cent. sinking fund on the capitals created by those loans, and which capitals together amounted to 86,796,375*l*. To reconcile the stockholder to this arrangement, he proposed to rescind the provision, which limited the fund of 1786, to four millions, and to consolidate the old and the new sinking funds, i.e. that which arose from the original million per annum, with the addition made to it of 200,000*l*. per annum subsequently granted, and that which arose from the one per cent. on the capital of every loan that had been contracted since 1792. These combined funds he proposed should from that time be applied to the redemption of the whole debt without distinction; that the dividends arising from the stock purchased by the commissioners for the reduction of the national debt should be applied in the same manner; and that this arrangement should not be interfered with till the redemption of the whole debt was effected.

In February 1803 the debt amounted to 480,572,470*l.*, and the produce of the joint sinking fund to 6,311,626*l.* In 1786 the proportion of the sinking fund to the debt was as 1 to 238, in 1792 as 1 to 160, and in 1803 as 1 to 77.

This was the first deviation of importance from Mr. Pitt's plan; and this alteration made by Lord Sidmouth was not, perhaps, on the whole, injurious to the stockholder. He lost, indeed, the immediate advantage of an additional sinking fund of 867,963*l.*, the amount of 1 per cent. on the capitals created by the loans of 1798, 1799, 1800, and 1802; "but, in lieu," says Mr. Huskisson, "of this sinking fund, a reversionary sinking fund was created to commence, indeed, in about twelve to fifteen years from that time; but to be of such efficacy when it should commence, and to be so greatly accelerated by subsequent additions in its progress, as, under the most unfavourable supposition, to be certain of reducing the whole of this debt within 45 years. This reversionary sinking fund was to arise in the following manner; by continuing the *old* sinking fund at *compound* interest, *after* it should have reached its *maximum* of four millions; and by continuing also the *new* sinking fund or aggregate of the one per cents of the loans since 1792, after such one per cents should have liquidated the several loans, in respect of which they are originally issued. There is nothing, therefore, in the act of 1802, which is a departure from the spirit of the act of 1792."*

The next alteration that was proposed to be made in the sinking fund was in 1807 by Lord Henry Petty, then Chancellor of the Exchequer. His plan was extremely complicated; and had for its object, that which ministers are too much disposed at

* Mr. Huskisson's *Speech on the State of the Finance and Sinking Fund*, 25th March 1813.[1]

[1] See *Substance of the Speech of W. Huskisson...*, London, Murray, 1813, pp. 29–30.

all times to view with complacency, namely, to lessen the burthen of taxation at the present, with the certainty of aggravating its pressure at a future day.

It was estimated by Lord Henry Petty that the expences of the country during war would exceed its permanent annual revenue by thirty-two millions. For twenty-one millions of this deficiency, provision was made by the war-taxes, the property-tax amounting to 11,500,000*l.*, and the other war-taxes to 9,500,000*l.* The object then was to provide eleven millions per annum. If this sum had been raised by a loan in the three per cents, when their price was 60, provision must have been made by taxes for the interest and sinking fund, so that each year we should have required additional taxes to the amount of 733,333*l.* But Government wished to raise the money without imposing these additional taxes, or by the imposition of as few as circumstances would permit. For this purpose, they proposed to raise the money required, by loan, in the usual way, but to provide, out of the war-taxes, for the interest and redemption of the stock created. They proposed to increase the sinking fund of every such loan, by taking from the war-taxes 10 per cent. on its amount for interest and sinking fund, so that if the interest and management absorbed only 5 per cent.; the sinking fund would also amount to 5 per cent., if the interest amounted to 4 per cent., the sinking fund would be 6 per cent. The sums proposed to be borrowed, in this manner, were twelve millions for the first three years, fourteen millions for the fourth, and sixteen millions for each succeeding year, making together, in fourteen years, 210 millions, for which, at the rate of 10 per cent., the whole of the war-taxes would be mortgaged. It was calculated, that, by the operation of the sinking fund, each loan would be paid off in fourteen years from the time of contracting for it; and, therefore, the 1,200,000*l.* set apart for the interest and sinking fund of the first loan would be liberated and available for the loan of the fifteenth year. At the end of fifteen years a like sum would be set free, and so on each succeeding year, and thus loans might be continued on this system, without any limitation of time.

But these successive sums could not be withdrawn from the war-taxes, for interest and sinking fund on loans, and be at the same time applied to expenditure; and, therefore, the deficiency of eleven millions, for which provision was to be made, would, from year to year, increase as the war-taxes became absorbed, and at the end of fourteen years, when the whole twenty-one millions of the war-taxes would be absorbed, instead of eleven millions, the deficiency would be thirty-two millions.

To provide for this growing deficiency, it was proposed to raise supplementary loans, increasing in amount from year to year; and for the interest and sinking fund on such loans, provision was to be made in the usual way by annual permanent taxes; on these loans the sinking fund was not to be more than 1 per cent.

By the plan proposed, in fifteen years from its commencement, on the supposition of the war continuing so long, the regular loan would have been twelve millions, and the supplementary loan twenty millions.

If the expences of the war should *have exceeded* the estimate then made, provision for such excess was to *have been* made by other means.

The ministry who proposed this plan, not continuing in office, the plan was acted upon only for one year. "In comparing the merit of different systems," says Dr. Hamilton,[1] "the only points necessary to be attended to are the amount of

----

[1] p. 216.

the loans contracted—the part of these loans redeemed—the interest incurred—and the sums raised by taxes. The arrangements of the loan[1] under different branches, and the appropriation of particular funds for payment of their respective interests, are matters of official regulation; and the state of the public finance is neither the better nor the worse, whether they be conducted one way or other. A complicated system may perplex and mislead, but it can never ameliorate." Accordingly, Dr. Hamilton has shown,[2] that the whole amount of taxes that would have been paid in twenty years, for an annual loan of eleven millions on the old plan of a sinking fund of 1 per cent., would be 154 millions. On Lord Henry Petty's plan, these taxes would, in the same time, have been ninety-three millions, —a difference in favour of Lord Henry Petty's plan of fifty-one millions; but to obtain this exemption we should have been encumbered with an additional debt of 119,489,788*l.* of money capital, which, if raised in a 3 per cent. stock at 60, would be equal to a nominal capital of 199,149,646*l.*

The sinking fund was established with a view to diminish the national debt during peace, and to prevent its rapid increase during war. The only wise and good object of war-taxes is also to prevent the accumulation of debt. A sinking fund and war-taxes are only useful while they are strictly applied to the objects for which they are raised; they become instruments of mischief and delusion when they are made use of for the purpose of providing the interest on a new debt.

In 1809, Mr. Perceval, who was then Chancellor of the Exchequer, mortgaged 1,040,000*l.* of the war-taxes for the interest and sinking fund of the stock he funded in that year.

By taking more than a million from the war-taxes, not for

---

[1] Hamilton actually says 'The arrangement of the loans'.   [2] p. 214.

the annual expenditure, but for the interest of a loan, Mr. Perceval rendered it necessary to add one million to the loan of the next and all following years; so that the real effect of this measure differed in no respect from one which should have taken the same sum annually from the sinking fund.

In 1813, the next, and most important alteration was made in the sinking fund. Mr. Vansittart was then Chancellor of the Exchequer. It has been already observed, that the national debt amounted to 238,231,248*l*. in 1786, when Mr. Pitt established his sinking fund of one million. By the act of 1786, as soon as the sum of one million amounted, by the aid of the dividends on the stock, which was to be purchased by it, to four millions, its accumulation was to cease, and the dividends on the stock purchased were to be available for the public service. If the 3 per cents. were at 60, when this million had accumulated to four millions, the public would have had a disposable fund of 20,000*l*. per annum; if at 80, of 15,000*l*. per annum; and no other relief was to be given to the public till the four millions had purchased the whole sum of 238 millions, the then amount of the debt. In 1792 Mr. Pitt added 200,000*l*. per annum to the sinking fund, and accompanied it by the following observations: "When the sum of four millions was originally fixed as the limit for the sinking fund, it was not in contemplation to issue more annually from the surplus revenue than one million; consequently, the fund would not rise to four millions, till a proportion of debt was paid off, the interest of which, together with the annuities which might fall in, in the interval, should amount to three millions. But, as on the present supposition, additional sums beyond the original million are to be annually issued from the revenue, and applied to the aid of the sinking fund, the consequence would be, that, if that fund, with these additions carried to it, were still to be limited to four millions, it would reach that amount, and cease to accumulate, before as great a portion of the debt is reduced as was originally in contemplation." "In order to avoid this consequence, which would, as far as it went, be a relaxation in our system, I should propose, that whatever may be the additional annual sums applied to the reduction of debt, the fund should not cease to accumulate till the interest of the capital discharged, and the amount of the expired annuities should, together with the annual million only, and exclusive of any additional sums, amount to four millions."*

It will be recollected, that, in 1792, a provision was made for attaching a sinking fund of 1 per cent. to each loan separately, which was to be exclusively employed in the discharge of the debt contracted by that loan, but no part of these one per cents. were to be employed in the reduction of the original debt of 238,000,000*l.* The act of 1802 consolidated all these sinking funds, and the public were not to be exempted from the payment of the sinking fund itself, nor of the dividends on the stock to be purchased by the commissioners, till the whole debt existing in 1802 was paid off. Mr. Vansittart proposed to repeal the act of 1802, and to restore the spirit of Mr. Pitt's act of 1792. He acknowledged, that it would be a breach of faith to the national creditor if the fair construction of that act, the act of 1792, were not adhered to.[1] It was, in Mr. Vansittart's opinion, no breach of faith to do away the conditions of the act of 1802. Supposing, however, that the act of 1802 had been really more favourable to the stockholder than that of 1792, it is not easy to comprehend by what arguments it can be proved

* Mr. Pitt's Speech, 17th February 1792.[2]

[1] See *Outlines of a Plan of Finance: proposed to be submitted to Parliament*, 1813, p. 7; and Vansittart's speech, 3 March 1813 (*Hansard*, XXIV, 1086).

[2] On the State of the Public Revenue and Expenditure, in *The Speeches of William Pitt*, London, 1806, vol. II, pp. 36-7.

not to be a breach of faith, to repeal the one and enact the other. Were not all the loans from 1802 to 1813 negotiated on the faith of that act? Were not all bargains made between the buyer and seller of stock made on the same understanding? Government had no more right to repeal the act of 1802, and substitute another less favourable to the stockholder, and acknowledged to be so by the minister himself, than it would have had to get rid of the sinking fund altogether. But what we are at present to inquire into is, whether Mr. Vansittart did as he professed to do? Did he restore the stockholder to all the advantages of the act of 1792? In the first place, it was declared by the new act,[1] that as the sinking fund consolidated in 1802, had redeemed 238,350,143*l*. 18*s*. 1*d*. exceeding the amount of the debt in 1786 by 118,895*l*. 12*s*. 10½*d*., a sum of capital stock equal to the total capital of the public debt, existing on the 5th January 1786, viz. 238,231,248*l*. 5*s*. 2¾*d*. had been satisfied and discharged; "and that, in like manner, an amount of public debt equal to the capital and charge of every loan contracted since the said 5th January 1786, shall successively and in its proper order, be deemed and declared to be wholly satisfied and discharged, when and as soon as a further amount of capital stock, not less than the capital of such loan, and producing an interest equal to the dividends thereupon, shall be so redeemed or transferred."

It was also resolved, "that after such declaration as aforesaid, the capital stock purchased by the commissioners for the reduction of the national debt, shall from time to time be cancelled; at such times, and in such proportions, as shall be directed by any act of Parliament to be passed for such purpose, in order to

---

[1] An Act relating to the Redemption of the National Debt (53 Geo. III. c. 35). The quotations that follow are from the resolutions moved by Vansittart, 3 March 1813, and adopted by the House of Commons, 26 March 1813 (*Hansard*, XXIV, 1091–3).

make provision for the charge of any loan or loans thereafter to be contracted."

It was also resolved, ["] that, in order to carry into effect the provisions of the acts of the 32d and 42d of the King, for redeeming every part of the national debt within the period of 45 years from the time of its creation, it is also expedient that, in future, whenever the amount of the sum to be raised by loan, or by any other addition to the public funded debt, shall in any year exceed the sum estimated, to be applicable in the same year to the reduction of the public debt, an annual sum equal to one-half of the interest of the excess of the said loan or other addition, beyond the sum so estimated to be applicable, shall be set apart out of the monies composing the consolidated fund of Great Britain; and shall be issued at the receipt of the Exchequer to the Governor and Company of the Bank of England, to be by them placed to the account of the commissioners for the reduction of the national debt;* and upon the remainder of such loan or other addition, the annual sum of 1 per cent. on the capital thereof, according to the provisions of the said act of the 32d year of his present Majesty. ["]

A provision was also made, for the first time, for 1 per cent. sinking fund on the unfunded debt then existing, or which might thereafter be contracted.

In 1802, it has been already observed, it was deemed expedient that no provision should be made for a sinking fund of 1 per cent. on a capital of 86,796,300l.; and as it was considered by the proposer of the new regulation in 1813, that he was reverting to the principle of Mr. Pitt's act of 1792, he provided that 867,963l. should be added to the sinking fund for the 1 per

---

* The effect of this clause was to give a sinking fund of 1½ instead of 1 per cent. on such excess of loan above the sinking fund, if the loan were raised in a 3 per cent. stock, and of 2¼ per cent. if raised in a 5 per cent. stock.

cent. on the capital stock created, and which was omitted to be provided for in 1802.*

This was the substance of Mr. Vansittart's new plan, and which he contended was not injurious to the stockholder, as it strictly conformed to the spirit of Mr. Pitt's act of 1792.

1st, By Mr. Pitt's act, no relief could be afforded to the public from the burthens of taxation, till the stock redeemed by the original sinking fund of one million amounted to such a sum as that the dividends on the capital stock redeemed should amount to three millions, making the whole sinking fund four millions; from thenceforth the four millions were to discharge debt as before, but the interest of debt so discharged was to be available for the public service, and the public was not to be relieved from the charge on the remainder of the debt of 238 millions till the four millions, at simple interest, and the further sinking fund which might arise from the falling in of terminable annuities, together with the additional sum of 200,000*l.* per annum, voted in 1792, with their accumulations, had redeemed the capital of 238 millions. The sinking fund arising from the 1 per cent. on

---

* Mr. Vansittart's plan has added to the sinking fund

1 per cent. on a capital of 86,796,300*l.* . . .	867,963*l.*
On fifty-six millions of Exchequer bills outstanding, 5th January 1818, 1 per cent.	560,000
By attaching a sinking fund of one-half the interest, instead of 1 per cent. on a part of the capital created by loans, *he has added to the sinking fund* . .	793,343
Total added	2,221,311*l.*
From stock, cancelled and available for public service	7,632,969
Total deduction from sinking fund, on 5th January 1819	5,411,658*l.*

On the 3d of February 1819, the Commissioners certified, that there had been transferred to them 378,519,969*l.* 5*s.* 3¾*d.* capital stock, the interest on which was 11,448,564*l.* 10*s.* 6¼*d.*, and that the debt created prior to, and by the 37th Geo. III amounted to 348,684,197*l.* 1*s.* 5¾*d.*, with a yearly interest of 11,446,736*l.* 3*s.* 4¾*d.*; and, consequently, the excess redeemed was 29,835,772*l.* 3*s.* 9¼*d.*, with a yearly interest of 1828*l.* 7*s.* 1¼*d.* Of the above sum of 11,448,564*l.*, 7,632,969*l.* only has been cancelled.

each loan, was directed, by the act of 1792, to be applied to each separate loan for which it was raised. Mr. Vansittart thought himself justified and free from any breach of faith to the stock-holder, in taking for the public service, not the interest of four millions, which is all that Mr. Pitt's bill would allow him to take, but the interest on 238 millions: And on what plea? because the whole consolidated sinking funds, comprising the 1 per cent. on every loan raised since 1793, had purchased 238 millions of stock. On Mr. Pitt's plan, he might have taken 20,000*l.* per annum from the sinking fund; on his own construction of that act, he took from it more than seven millions per annum.

2*dly*, Mr. Vansittart acknowledged, that the stockholder, in 1802, was deprived of the advantage of 1 per cent. sinking fund on a capital of 86,796,300*l.*, and therefore to be very just, he gives, in 1813, 1 per cent. on that capital; but should he not have added the accumulation which would have been made in the eleven years, from 1802 to 1813, on 867,963*l.*, at compound interest, and which would have given a further addition to the sinking fund of more than 360,000*l.* per annum;

3*dly*, On Mr. Pitt's plan, every loan was to be redeemed by its sinking fund, under the most unfavourable circumstances, in 45 years. If the loan was raised in a 3 per cent. fund at 60, and the stock was uniformly to continue at that price, a 1 per cent. sinking fund would redeem the loan to which it was attached in 29 years; but then no relief would be given to the public from taxation till the end of 29 years; and, if there had been loans of ten millions every year for that period, when the first loan was paid off, the second would require only one year for its final liquidation; the third two years, and so on. On Mr. Vansittart's plan, under the same circumstances, the sinking fund of each and every loan was to be applied, in the first instance, to the redemption of the first loan; and when that was redeemed and cancelled, the whole of the sinking funds were to be applied to the payment of the second; and so on successively. The first loan of ten millions would be cancelled in less than 13 years, the second in less than six years after the first, the third in a less time, and so on. At the end of the 13th year, the public would be relieved from the interest on the first loan, or, which is the same thing, from the necessity of finding fresh taxes for a new loan at the end of 13 years, for two new loans at the end of 19 years; but what would be the state of its debt at either of these periods, or at the end of 29 years? Could this advantage be obtained without a corresponding disadvantage? No; the excess of debt on Mr. Vansittart's plan would be exactly equal to these various sums, thus prematurely released by cancelled stock, accumulated at compound interest. How could it be otherwise? Is it possible that we could obtain a present relief from the charge of debt without either directly or indirectly borrowing the fund necessary to provide that relief at compound interest? "By this means," says Mr. Vansittart,[1] "the loan first contracted would be discharged at an earlier period, and the funds charged with the payment of its interest would become applicable to the public service. Thus, in the event of a long war, a considerable resource might accrue during the course of the war itself, as every successive loan would contribute to accelerate the redemption of those previously existing; and the total amount of charge to be borne by the public, in respect of the public debt, would be reduced to a narrower compass than in the other mode, in which a greater number of loans would be co-existing. At the same time, the ultimate discharge of the whole debt would be rather accelerated than retarded." "It is now only necessary to declare, that an amount of stock equal to the whole of the debt existing in 1786 has been redeemed; and that, in like manner, whenever an amount of stock

[1] Speech on the New Plan of Finance, 3 March 1813 (*Hansard*, XXIV, 1088–9). The italics are Ricardo's.

equal to the capital and charge of any loan raised since 1792 shall be redeemed, in its proper order of succession, such loan shall be deemed and taken to be redeemed and satisfied. Every part of the system will then fall at once into its proper place; and we shall proceed with the future redemption with all the advantages which would have been derived from the original adoption of the mode of successive instead of simultaneous redemption. Instead of waiting till the purchase of the whole of the debt consolidated in 1802 shall be completed, that part of it which existed previously to 1792 will be considered as already redeemed, and the subsequent loans will follow in succession, whenever equal portions of stock shall have been purchased. *It is satisfactory to observe, that, by a gradual and equable progress, we shall still have the power of effecting the complete repayment of the debt more speedily than by the present course.*" Is it possible that Mr. Vansittart could so deceive himself as to believe that, by taking five millions from the sinking fund, which would not have been taken by the provisions of the act of 1802, which would not have been taken by the act of 1792, and other sums successively, in shorter times than could have been effected by the provisions of those two acts, he would be enabled to complete the repayment of the debt more speedily? Is it possible that he could believe that, by diminishing the sinking fund, that is, the amount of revenue as compared with expenditure, he would effect the payment of our debt more speedily? It is impossible to believe this. How then are his words to be accounted for? In one way he might have a meaning. It might be this,—I know we shall be more in debt in 10, 20, and 30 years, on my plan, than we should have been on that of Lord Sidmouth, or on that of Mr. Pitt; but we shall have effected a greater payment, in that time, of *the stock now existing*; as the sinking funds attached to future loans will be employed in paying our present debt. On Mr. Pitt's plan, those sinking funds would be used for the payment of the new debt to be created; that is to say, of the loans to which they are respectively attached. We shall be more in debt at every subsequent period, it is true; but, as our debt may be divided into old stock and new stock, I am correct when I say, that we shall have the power of completing the repayment of the debt, meaning by the debt the stock now existing, sooner than by the present course.

This plan of Mr. Vansittart was opposed with great ability, both by Mr. Huskisson and Mr. Tierney.[1] The former gentleman said, "The very foundation of the assumption that the old debt has been paid off, is laid in the circumstance of our having incurred a new debt, of a much larger amount; and, even allowing that assumption, Mr. Vansittart would not have been able to erect his present scheme upon it, if the credit of the country had not been, for the last twenty years, materially impaired by the pressure of that new debt. On the one hand, had the sinking fund been operating at 3 per cent. during that period, he would not have touched it, even under his own construction of the act of 1792. On the other hand, had the price of the stocks been still lower than it has been, he would have taken from that sinking fund still more largely than he is now, according to his own rule, enabled to take. This, then, is the new doctrine of the sinking fund;—that, having been originally established "to prevent the inconvenient and dangerous accumulation of debt hereafter" (to borrow the very words of the act), and for the support and improvement of public credit, it is in the accumulation of new debt that Mr. Vansittart finds at once the means and the pretence for invading that sinking fund; and the degree of depression of public credit is, with him, the measure of the extent to which that invasion may be carried. And this is the system of which it is gravely predicated,

[1] See Tierney's speech on Vansittart's New Plan, 3 March 1813 (*Hansard*, XXIV, 1095–8).

that it is no departure from the letter, and no violation of the spirit, of the act of 1792; and of which we are desired seriously to believe, that it is only the following up and improving upon the original measure of Mr. Pitt!—of which measure the clear and governing intention was, that every future loan should, from *the moment of its creation*, carry with it the seeds of its destruction; and that the course of its reimbursement should, *from that moment*, be placed beyond the discretion and control of parliament."—Mr. Huskisson's *Speech*, 25th March 1813.[1]

This is the last alteration that has taken place in the *machinery* of the sinking fund. Inroads more fatal than this which we have just recorded have been made on the fund itself; but they have been made silently and indirectly, while the machinery has been left unaltered.

It has been shown by Dr. Hamilton,[2] that no fund can be efficient for the reduction of debt but such as arises from an excess of revenue above expenditure.

Suppose a country at peace, and its expenditure, including the interest of its debt, to be forty millions, its revenue to be forty-one millions, it would possess one million of sinking fund. This million would accumulate at compound interest; for stock would be purchased with it in the market, and placed in the names of the commissioners for paying off the debt. These commissioners would be entitled to the dividends before received by private stock-holders, which would be added to the capital of the sinking fund. The fund thus increased would make additional purchases the following year; and would be entitled to a larger amount of dividends; and thus would go on accumulating, till in time the whole debt would be discharged.

Suppose such a country to increase its expenditure one million, without adding to its taxes, and to keep up the machi-

[1] See *Substance of the Speech of W. Huskisson...*, pp. 20-2.

[2] pp. 44-58.

nery of the sinking fund; it is evident, that it would make no progress in the reduction of its debt, for, though it would accumulate a fund in the same manner as before in the hands of the commissioners, it would, by means of adding to its funded or unfunded debt, and by constantly borrowing, in the same way, the sum necessary to pay the interest on such loans, accumulate its million of debt annually, at compound interest, in the same manner as it accumulated its million annually of sinking fund.

But suppose that it continued its operations of investing the sinking fund in the purchase of stock, and made a loan for the million which it was deficient in its expenditure, and that, in order to defray the interest and sinking fund of such loan, it imposed new taxes on the people to the amount of 60,000*l.*, the real and efficient sinking fund would, in that case, be 60,000*l.* per annum and no more, for there would be 1,060,000*l.* and no more to invest in the purchase of stock, while one million was raised by the sale of stock, or, in other words, the revenue would exceed the expenditure by 60,000*l.*

Suppose a war to take place, and the expenditure to be increased to sixty millions, while its revenue continued as before forty-one millions, still keeping on the operation of the commissioners, with respect to the investment of one million. If it were to raise war-taxes for the payment of the twenty millions additional expence, the million of sinking fund would operate to the reduction of the national debt at compound interest as it did before. If it raised twenty millions by loan in the stocks or in exchequer bills, and did not provide for the interest by new taxes, but obtained it by an addition to the loan of the following year, it would be accumulating a debt of twenty millions at compound interest, and while the war lasted, and the same expenditure continued, it would not only be accumulating a debt of twenty millions at compound interest, but a debt of twenty millions per annum, and, consequently, the real increase of its debt, after allowing for the operation of the million of sinking fund, would be at the rate of nineteen millions per annum at compound interest. But if it provided by new taxes 5 per cent. interest for this annual loan of twenty millions, it would, on one hand, simply increase the debt twenty millions per annum; on the other, it would diminish it by one million per annum, with its compound interest. If we suppose that, in addition to the 5 per cent. interest, it raised also by annual taxes 200,000*l.* per annum, as a sinking fund, for each loan of twenty millions, it would, the first year of the war, add 200,000*l.* to the sinking fund; the second year 400,000*l.*; the third year 600,000*l.*, and so on, 200,000*l.* for every loan of twenty millions. Every year it would add, by means of the additional taxes, to its annual revenue, without increasing its expenditure. Every year too that part of this revenue which was devoted to the purpose of purchasing debt, would increase by the amount of the dividends on the stock purchased, and thus would its revenue still farther increase, till at last the revenue would overtake the expenditure, and then once again it would have an efficient sinking fund for the reduction of debt.

It is evident, that the result of these operations would be the same, the rate of interest being supposed to be always at 5 per cent. or any other rate, if, during the excess of expenditure above revenue, the operation of the commissioners in the purchase of stock were to cease. The real increase of the national debt must depend upon the excess of expenditure above revenue, and that would be no ways altered by a different arrangement. Suppose that, instead of raising twenty millions the first year, and paying off one million, only nineteen millions had been raised by loan, and the same taxes had been raised, namely, 1,200,000*l.* As 5 per cent. would be paid on nineteen millions only, instead of on twenty millions, or 950,000*l.* for interest instead of one million, there would remain, in addition to the original million,

250,000*l*. towards the loan of the following year, consequently, the loan of the second year would be only for 18,750,000*l*.,—but as 1,200,000*l*. would be again raised by additional taxes, or 2,400,000*l*. in the whole the second year, besides the original million, there would be a surplus, after paying the interest of both loans, of 1,512,500*l*., and therefore the loan of the third year would be for 18,487,500*l*. The progress during five years is shown in the following table:

	Loan each Year	Amount of Loans	Amount of Interest	Amount of Taxes	Surplus
1st year	19,000,000*l*.	19,000,000	950,000	2,200,000	1,250,000
2d year	18,750,000	37,750,000	1,887,500	3,400,000	1,512,500
3d year	18,487,500	56,237,500	2,811,875	4,600,000	1,788,125
4th year	18,211,875	74,449,375	3,722,469	5,800,000	2,077,531
5th year	17,922,469	92,371,844	4,618,592	7,000,000	2,381,408

If, instead of thus diminishing the loan each year, the same amount of taxes precisely had been raised, and the sinking fund had been applied in the usual manner, the amount of debt would have been exactly the same at any one of these periods. In the third column of the above table it will be seen that, in the 5th year, the debt had increased to 92,371,844*l*. On the supposition that 200,000*l*. per annum had each year been added to the sinking fund, and invested in stock by the commissioners, the amount of unredeemed debt would have been the same sum of 92,371,844*l*., as will be seen by the last column of the following table:

	Loan each Year	Amount of Loans	Debt redeemed each Year	Amount Debt Redeemed	Interest on Debt Redeemed	Debt remaining Unredeemed
1st year	20,000,000*l*.	20,000,000	1,000,000	1,000,000	50,000	19,000,000
2d year	20,000,000	40,000,000	1,250,000	2,250,000	112,500	37,750,000
3d year	20,000,000	60,000,000	1,512,500	3,762,500	188,125	56,237,500
4th year	20,000,000	80,000,000	1,788,125	5,550,625	277,531	74,449,375
5th year	20,000,000	100,000,000	2,077,531	7,628,156	381,408	92,371,844

A full consideration of this subject, in all its details, has led Dr. Hamilton to the conclusion, that this first mode of raising the supplies during war, viz. by diminishing the amount of the annual loans, and stopping the purchases of the commissioners in the market, would be more economical, and that it ought therefore to be adopted. In the first place, all the expences of agency would be saved. In the second, the premium usually obtained by the contractor for the loan would be saved, on that part of it which is repurchased by the commissioners in the open market. It is true that the stocks may fall as well as rise between the time of contracting for the loan, and the time of the purchases made by the commissioners; and, therefore, in some cases, the public may gain by the present arrangement; but as these chances are equal, and a certain advantage is given to the loan contractor to induce him to advance his money, independently of all contingency of future price, the public now give this advantage on the larger sum instead of on the smaller. On an average of years this cannot fail to amount to a very considerable sum. But both these objections would be obviated, if the clause in the original sinking fund bill, authorizing the commissioners to subscribe to any loan for the public service, to the amount of the annual fund which they have to invest, were uniformly complied with. This is the mode which has, for several years, been strongly urged on ministers by Mr. Grenfell,[1] and is far preferable to that which Dr. Hamilton recommends. Dr. Hamilton and Mr. Grenfell both agree, that, in time of war, when the expenditure exceeds the revenue, and when, therefore, we are annually increasing our debt, it is a useless operation to buy a comparatively small quantity of stock in the market, while we are at the same time under the necessity of making large sales; but Dr. Hamilton would not keep the sinking fund

---

[1] See Grenfell's motions respecting the Sinking Fund in 1814 (*Hansard*, XXVII, 578–82 and 651) and cp. below, V, 4.

as a separate fund, Mr. Grenfell would, and would have it increased with our debt by some known and fixed rules. We agree with Mr. Grenfell. If a loan of twenty millions is to be raised annually, while there is in the hands of the commissioners ten millions which they annually receive, the obvious and simple operation should be really to raise only ten millions by loan; but there is a convenience in calling it twenty millions, and allowing the commissioners to subscribe ten millions. All the objections of Dr. Hamilton are by these means removed; there will be no expence for agency; there will be no loss on account of any difference of price at which the public sell and buy. By calling the loan twenty millions, the public will be induced more easily to bear the taxes which are necessary for the interest and sinking fund of twenty millions. Call the loan only ten millions, abolish, during the war, the very name of the sinking fund in all your public accounts, and it would be difficult to show to the people the expediency of providing 1,200,000*l.* per annum by additional taxation, for the interest of a loan of ten millions. The sinking fund is, therefore, useful as an engine of taxation; and, if the country could depend on ministers, that it would be faithfully devoted to the purposes for which it was established, namely, to afford at the termination of war a clear additional surplus revenue beyond expenditure, in proportion to the addition made to the debt, it would be wise and expedient to keep it as a separate fund, subject to fixed rules and regulations.

We shall presently inquire, whether there can be any such dependence; and, therefore, whether the sinking fund is not an instrument of mischief and delusion, and really tending rather to increase our debt and burthens than to diminish them.

It is objected both to Dr. Hamilton's and Mr. Grenfell's projects, that the disadvantages which they mention are trifling in degree, and are more than compensated by the steadiness which is given to the market by the daily purchases of the commissioners,—that the money which those purchases throw into the market is a resource on which bankers and others, who may suddenly want money, with certainty rely.

Those who make this objection forget, that, if by the adoption of this plan, a daily purchaser is withdrawn from the market, so also is a daily seller. The minister gives now to one party ten millions of money to invest in stock, and to another party as much stock as ten millions costs to sell; and as the instalments on the loan are paid monthly, it may fairly be said that the supply is as regular as the demand. It cannot be doubted, too, that a loan of twenty millions is negotiated on worse terms than one of ten; it is true that no more stock will remain in the market at the end of the year, whether the one or the other sum be raised by loan; but for a time the contractor must make a large purchase, and he must wait before he can make his sale of ten millions to the commissioners. He is induced then to sell much more largely before the contract, which cannot fail to affect the market price; and it must be recollected, that it is the market price on the day of bidding for the loan which governs the terms on which the loan is negotiated. It is looked to both by the minister who sells, and the contractor who purchases. The experiment on Mr. Grenfell's suggestion was tried for the first time in the present year, 1819; the sum required by Government was twenty-four millions, to which the commissioners subscribed twelve millions. In lieu of a loan of twenty-four millions from the contractor, there was one only of twelve millions; and as soon as this arrangement was known, previous to the contract, the stocks rose 4 or 5 per cent., and influenced the terms of the loan in that degree. The reason was, that a preparation had been made for twenty-four or thirty millions loan, and as soon as it was known that it would be for twelve millions only, a part of the stock sold was repurchased. Another advantage attending the smaller loan is that 800 per million which is paid to the bank for management of the loan is saved on the sum subscribed by the commissioners.

Dr Hamilton, in another part of his work, observes, "If the sinking fund could be conducted without loss to the public, or even if it were attended with a moderate loss,[1] it would not be wise to propose an alteration of a system which has gained the confidence of the public, and which points out a rule of taxation that has the advantage at least of being steady. If that rule be laid aside, our measures of taxation might become entirely loose.[2]

"The means, and the only means, of restraining the progress of national debt are, saving of expenditure, and increase of revenue. Neither of these has a necessary connection with a sinking fund. But, if they have an eventual connection; and, if the nation, impressed with a conviction of the importance of a system established by a popular minister, has, in order to adhere to it, adopted measures, either of frugality in expenditure, or exertion in raising taxes, which it would not otherwise have done, the sinking fund ought not to be considered as inefficient, and its effects may be of great importance."[3]

It will not, we think, admit of a doubt, that if Mr. Pitt's sinking fund, as established in 1792, had been always fairly acted upon, if, for every loan, in addition to the war-taxes, the interest, and a 1 per cent. sinking fund, had been invariably supplied by annual taxes, we should now be making rapid progress in the extinction of debt. The alteration in principle which was made in the sinking fund by the act of 1802 was, in our opinion, a judicious one; it provided, that no part of the sinking fund, neither that which arose from the original million, with its addition of 200,000*l.* per annum, nor that which arose from the 1 per cent. raised for the loans since 1792,

---

[1] The clause beginning 'or even' is not in Hamilton.
[2] Hamilton, p. 206.
[3] *ib.* p. 205.

should be applicable to the public service, till the whole of the debt then existing was redeemed. We should have been disposed to have extended this principle further, and to have made a provision, that no part of the sinking fund should be applicable to the public service, until the whole of the debt then existing, *and subsequently to be created*, should be redeemed. We do not think that there is much weight in the objection to this clause, which was made to it by Lord Henry Petty in 1807, and referred to, and more strongly urged by Mr. Vansittart[1] in 1813. The noble Lord said,[2] "I need hardly press upon the consideration of the committee, all the evils likely to result from allowing the sinking fund to accumulate without any limit; for the nation would be exposed, by that accumulation, to the mischief of having a large portion of capital taken at once out of the market, without any adequate means of applying it, which would, of course, be deprived of its value.

"This evil must appear so serious to any man who contemplates its character, that I have no doubt it will be felt, however paradoxical it may seem, that the redemption of the whole national debt at once would be productive of something like national bankruptcy, for the capital would be equivalent almost to nothing, while the interest he had before derived from it would be altogether extinguished. The other evils which would arise from, and which must serve to demonstrate the mischievous consequence of a prompt discharge of the national debt, I will show presently. Different arrangements were adopted in the further provisions made on the subject of the sinking fund in 1792 and in 1802. By the first the sinking fund of 1 per cent., which was thenceforward to be provided for every new loan, was made to accumulate at compound interest

[1] Speech on the New Plan of Finance, 3 March 1813 (*Hansard*, XXIV, 1083).

[2] Speech on a Plan of Finance, 29 Jan. 1807 (*Hansard*, VIII, 585–7).

until the whole of the debt created by such new loan should be extinguished. And, by the second arrangement, all the various sinking funds existing in 1802 were consolidated, and the whole were appropriated to accumulate at compound interest until the discharge of the whole of the debt also existing in 1802. But the debt, created since 1802, amounting to about one hundred millions of nominal capital, is still left subject to the acts of 1792, which provides for each separate loan a sinking fund of only 1 per cent. on the nominal capital. The plan of 1802, engrafted on the former acts of 1786 and 1792, provided for the still more speedy extinction of the debt to which it applied. But it would postpone all relief from the public burthens to a very distant period (computed, in 1802, to be from 1834 to 1844); and it would throw such large and disproportionate sums into the money market in the latter years of its operation, as might produce a very dangerous depreciation of the value of money. Many inconveniences might also arise from the sudden stop which would be put to the application of those sums when the whole debt should have been redeemed, and from the no less sudden change in the price of all commodities, which must follow from taking off at one and the same moment taxes to an extent probably then much exceeding thirty millions. The fate of merchants, manufacturers, mechanics, and every description of dealers, in such an event, must be contemplated by every thinking man with alarm; and this applies to my observation respecting a national bankruptcy, for, should the national debt be discharged, and such a weight of taxation taken off at once, all the goods remaining on hand would be, comparatively speaking, of no value to the holders, because, having been purchased or manufactured while such taxation prevailed, they must be undersold by all those who might manufacture the same kind of goods after such taxation had ceased. These objections were foreseen, and to a certain degree acknowledged, at the time when the act of 1802 was passed: and it was then answered, that, whenever the danger approached, it might be obviated by subsequent arrangements." A great many of these objections appear to us to be chimerical, but, if well founded, we agree with the latter part of the extract, "whenever the danger approached, it might be obviated by subsequent arrangements." It was not necessary to legislate in 1807, or in 1813, for a danger which could not happen till between 1834 and 1844. It was not necessary to provide against the evils which would arise from a plethora of wealth at a remote period, when our real difficulty was how to supply our immediate and pressing wants.

What are the evils apprehended from the extravagant growth of the sinking fund, towards the latter years of its existence? Not that taxation will be increased, because the growth of the sinking fund is occasioned by dividends on stock purchased; but first, that capital will be returned too suddenly into the hands of the stockholder, without his having any means of deriving a revenue from it; and, secondly, that the remission of taxes, to the amount probably of thirty millions, will have a great effect on the prices of particular commodities, and will be very pernicious to the interest of those who may deal in or manufacture such commodities.

It is obvious that the commissioners have no capital. They receive quarterly, or daily, certain sums arising from the taxes, which they employ in the redemption of debt. One portion of the people pay what another portion receive. If the payers employed the sums paid as capital, that is to say, in the production of raw produce, or manufactured commodities, and the receivers, when they received it, employed it in the same manner, there would be little variation in the annual produce. A part of that produce might be produced by A instead of by B; not that even this is a necessary consequence, for A, when he received the money for his debt, might lend it to B, and might receive from him a portion of the produce for interest, in which case B would continue to employ the capital as before. On the supposition, then, that the sinking fund is furnished by capital and not by revenue, no injury would result to the community, however large that fund might be,—there might or might not be a transfer of employments, but the annual produce, the real wealth of the country, would undergo no deterioration, and the actual amount of capital employed would neither be increased nor diminished. But if the payers of taxes, for the interest and sinking fund of the national debt, paid them from revenue, then they would retain the same capital as before in active employment, and as this revenue, when received by the stockholder, would be by him employed as capital, there would be, in consequence of this operation, a great increase of capital,—every year an additional portion of revenue would be turned into capital, which could be employed only in furnishing new commodities to the market. Now the doubts of those who speak of the mischievous effects of the great accumulation of the sinking fund, proceed from an opinion they entertain that a country may possess more capital than it can beneficially employ, and that there may be such a glut of commodities, that it would be impossible to dispose of them on such terms as to secure to the producers any profits on their capitals. The error of this reasoning has been made manifest by M. Say, in his able work *Economie Politique*,[1] and afterwards by Mr. Mill, in his excellent reply to Mr. Spence, the advocate of the doctrine of the Economistes.[2] They show that demand is only limited by production; whoever can produce has a right to consume, and

---

[1] *Traité d'Économie politique*, Paris, Deterville, 1st ed., 1803; see Bk. I, ch. XXII, 'Des Débouchés'.
[2] *Commerce Defended. An Answer to the Arguments by which Mr.* Spence, Mr. Cobbett, and Others, have Attempted to Prove that Commerce is not a Source of National Wealth, by James Mill, London, Baldwin, 1808.

he will exercise his privilege to the greatest extent. They do not deny that the demand for particular commodities is limited, and therefore they say, there may be a glut of such commodities, but in a great and civilized country, wants, either for objects of necessity or of luxury, are unlimited, and the employment of capital is of equal extent with our ability of supplying food and necessaries for the increasing population, which a continually augmenting capital would employ. With every increased difficulty of producing additional supplies of raw produce from the land, corn, and the other necessaries of the labourer, would rise. Hence wages would rise. A real rise of wages is necessarily followed by a real fall of profits, and, therefore, when the land of a country is brought to the highest state of cultivation,— when more labour employed upon it will not yield in return more food than what is necessary to support the labourer so employed, that country is come to the limit of its increase both of capital and population.

The richest country in Europe is yet far distant from that degree of improvement, but if any had arrived at it, by the aid of foreign commerce, even such a country could go on for an indefinite time increasing in wealth and population, for the only obstacle to this increase would be the scarcity, and consequent high value, of food and other raw produce. Let these be supplied from abroad in exchange for manufactured goods, and it is difficult to say where the limit is at which you would cease to accumulate wealth and to derive profit from its employment. This is a question of the utmost importance in political economy. We hope that the little we have said on the subject will be sufficient to induce those who wish clearly to understand the principle, to consult the works of the able authors whom we have named, to which we acknowledge ourselves so much indebted. If these views are correct, there is then no danger that the accumulated capital which a sinking fund, under particular circumstances, might occasion, would not find employment, or that the commodities which it might be made to produce would not be beneficially sold, so as to afford an adequate profit to the producers. On this part of the subject it is only necessary to add, that there would be no necessity for stockholders to become farmers or manufacturers. There are always to be found in a great country, a sufficient number of responsible persons, with the requisite skill, ready to employ the accumulated capital of others, and to pay to them a share of the profits, and which, in all countries, is known by the name of interest for borrowed money.

The second objection to the indefinite increase of the sinking fund remains now to be noticed. By the remission of taxes suddenly to the amount probably of thirty millions per annum, a great effect would be produced on the price of goods. "The fate of merchants, manufacturers, mechanics, and every description of dealers, in such an event, must be contemplated by every thinking man with alarm; for should the national debt be discharged, and such a weight of taxation taken off at once, all the goods remaining on hand would be, comparatively speaking, of no value to the holders, because having been purchased or manufactured while such taxation prevailed, they must be undersold by all those who might manufacture the same kind of goods after such taxation had ceased."[1] It is only then on the supposition that merchants, manufacturers, and dealers, would be affected as above described, that any evil would result from the largest remission of taxes. It would not of course be said, that, by remitting a tax of 5l. to A, 10l. to B, 100l. to C, and so on, any injury would be done to them. If they added these different sums to their respective capitals they would augment their permanent annual revenue, and would be contributing to the increase of the mass of commodities, thereby adding to the

[1] Lord Henry Petty, quoted above, p. 176.

general abundance. We have already, we hope, successfully shown, that an augmentation of capital is neither injurious to the individual by whom it is saved, nor to the community at large, —its tendency is to increase the demand for labour, and consequently the population, and to add to the power and strength of the country. But they will not add these respective sums to their capitals,—they will expend them as revenue! The measure cannot be said to be either injurious to themselves or to the community on that account. They annually contributed a portion of their produce to the stockholder in payment of debt, who immediately employed it as capital; that portion of produce is now at their own disposal; they may consume it themselves if they please. A farmer who used to sell a portion of his corn for the particular purpose of furnishing this tax, may consume this corn himself,—he may get the distiller to make gin of it, or the brewer to turn it into beer, or he may exchange it for a portion of the cloth which the clothier, who is now released from the tax, as well as the farmer, is at liberty to dispose of for any commodity which he may desire. It may indeed be said, where is all this cloth, beer, gin, &c. to come from; there were no more than necessary for the general demand before this remission of taxes; if every man is now to consume more, from whence is this supply to be obtained? This is an objection of quite an opposite nature to that which was before urged. Now it is said there would be too much demand and no additional supply; before, it was contended that the supply would be so great that no demand would exist for the quantity supplied. One objection is no better founded than the other. The stockholders, by previously receiving the payment of their debt, and employing the funds they received productively, or lending them to some other persons who would so employ them, would produce the very additional commodities which the society at large would have it in their power to consume. There would be a general augmentation of revenue, and a general augmentation of enjoyment, and it must not, for a moment, be supposed that the increased consumption of one part of the people would be at the expence of another part. The good would be unmixed, and without alloy. It remains then only to consider the injury to traders from the fall in the price of goods, and the remedy against this appears to be so very simple, that it surprises us that it should ever have been urged as an objection. In laying on a new tax, the stock in hand of the article taxed is commonly ascertained, and, as a measure of justice, the dealer in such article is required to pay the imposed tax on his stock. Why may not the reverse of this be done? Why may not the tax be returned to each individual on his stock in hand, whenever it shall be thought expedient to take off the tax from the article which he manufactures, or in which he deals? It would only be necessary to continue the taxes for a very short time for this purpose. On no view of this question can we see any validity in the arguments which we have quoted,[1] and which have been so particularly insisted on by Mr. Vansittart.

There are some persons who think that a sinking fund, even when strictly applied to its object, is of no national benefit whatever. The money which is contributed, they say, would be more productively employed by the payers of the taxes, than by the Commissioners of the Sinking Fund. The latter purchase stock with it, which probably does not yield 5 per cent. the former would obtain from the employment of the same capital much more than 5 per cent. consequently the country would be enriched by the difference. There would be in the latter case a larger nett supply of the produce of our land and labour, and that is the fund from which ultimately all our expenditure must be drawn. Those who maintain this opinion, do

[1] Above, pp. 175–7.

not see that the commissioners merely receive money from one class of the community and pay it to another class, and that the real question is, Which of these two classes will employ it most productively? Forty millions per annum are raised by taxes, of which twenty millions, we will suppose, is paid for sinking fund, and twenty millions for interest of debt. After a year's purchase is made by the commissioners, this forty millions will be divided differently, nineteen millions will be paid for interest, and twenty-one millions for sinking fund, and so from year to year, though forty millions is always paid on the whole, a less and less portion of it will be paid for interest, and a larger portion for sinking fund, till the commissioners have purchased the whole amount of stock, and then the whole forty millions will be in the hands of the commissioners. The sole question then with regard to profits is, Whether those who pay this forty millions, or those who receive it, will employ it most productively?—the commissioners, in fact, never employing it at all, their business being to transfer it to those who will employ it. Now, of this we are quite certain, that all the money received by the stockholder, in return for his stock, must be employed as capital, for if it were not so employed, he would be deprived of his revenue on which he had habitually depended. If then the taxes which are paid towards the sinking fund be derived from the revenue of the country, and not from its capital, by this operation a portion of revenue is yearly realized into capital, and consequently the whole revenue of the society is increased; but it might have been realized into capital by the payer of the tax, if there had been no sinking fund, and he had been allowed to retain the money to his own use! It might so, and if it had been so disposed of, there can be no advantage in respect to the accumulation of the wealth of the whole society by the establishment of the sinking fund, but it is not so probable that the payer of the tax would make this use of it as the receiver. The receiver when he gets paid for his stock, only substitutes one capital for another,—and he is accustomed to look to his capital for all his yearly income. The payer will have all that he paid in addition to his former revenue; if the sinking fund be discontinued he may indeed realize it into capital, but he may also use it as revenue, increasing his expenditure on wine, houses, horses, clothes, &c. The payer might too have paid it from his capital, and, therefore, the employment of one capital might be substituted for another. In this case too, no advantage arises from the sinking fund, as the national wealth would accumulate as rapidly without it as with it, but if any portion of the taxes paid expressly for the sinking fund be paid from revenue, and which, if not so paid, would have been expended as revenue, then there is a manifest advantage in the sinking fund, as it tends to increase the annual produce of our land and labour, and as we cannot but think that this would be its operation, we are clearly of opinion that a sinking fund, honestly applied, is favourable to the accumulation of wealth.

Dr. Hamilton has followed Dr. Price in insisting much on the disadvantage of raising loans during war in a 3 per cent. stock, and not in a 5 per cent. stock. In the former, a great addition is made to the nominal capital, which is generally redeemed, during peace, at a greatly advanced price. Three per cents. which were sold at 60, will probably be repurchased at 80, and may come to be bought at 100. Whereas in 5 per cents. there would be little or no increase of nominal capital, and as all the stocks are redeemable at par, they would be paid off with very little loss. The correctness of this observation must depend on the relative prices of these two stocks. During the war in 1798, the 3 per cents. were at 50, while the 5 per cents. were at 73, and at all times the 5 per cents. bear a very low relative price to the 3 per cents. Here then is one advantage to be put against another, and it must depend upon the degree in which the prices of the 3 per cents. and 5 per cents. differ, whether it be more desirable to raise the loan in the one or in the other. We have little doubt that, during many periods of the war, there would have been a decided disadvantage in making the loan in 5 per cent. stock in preference to a 3 per cent. stock. The market in 5 per cent. stock, too, is limited, a sale cannot be forced in it without causing a considerable fall, a circumstance known to the contractors, and against which they would naturally take some security in the price which they bid for a large loan if in that stock. A premium of 2 per cent. on the market price, may appear to them sufficient to compensate them for their risk in a loan in 3 per cent. stock;—they may require one of 5 per cent. to protect them against the dangers they apprehend from taking the same loan in a 5 per cent. stock.

II. After having duly considered the operation of a sinking fund, derived from annual taxes, we come now to the consideration of the best mode of providing for our annual expenditure, both in war and peace; and, further, to examine whether a country can have any security, that a fund raised for the purpose of paying debt will not be misapplied by ministers, and be really made the instrument for creating new debt, so as never to afford a rational hope that any progress whatever will permanently be made in the reduction of debt.

Suppose a country to be free from debt, and a war to take place, which should involve it in an annual additional expenditure of twenty millions, there are three modes by which this expenditure may be provided; first, taxes may be raised to the amount of twenty millions per annum, from which the country would be totally freed on the return of peace; or, secondly, the money might be annually borrowed and funded; in which case, if the interest agreed upon was 5 per cent., a perpetual charge of one million per annum taxes would be incurred for the first year's expence, from which there would be no relief during peace, or in any future war; of an additional million for the second year's expence, and so on for every year that the war might last. At the end of twenty years, if the war lasted so long, the country would be perpetually encumbered with taxes of twenty millions per annum, and would have to repeat the same course on the recurrence of any new war. The third mode of providing for the expences of the war would be to borrow annually the twenty millions required as before, but to provide, by taxes, a fund, in addition to the interest, which, accumulating at compound interest, should finally be equal to the debt. In the case supposed, if money was raised at 5 per cent., and a sum of 200,000*l*. per annum, in addition to the million for interest, were provided, it would accumulate to twenty millions in 45 years; and, by consenting to raise 1,200,000*l*. per annum by taxes, for every loan of twenty millions, each loan would be paid off in 45 years from the time of its creation; and in 45 years from the termination of the war, if no new debt were created, the whole would be redeemed, and the whole of the taxes would be repealed.

Of these three modes, we are decidedly of opinion that the preference should be given to the first. The burthens of the war are undoubtedly great during its continuance, but at its termination they cease altogether. When the pressure of the war is felt at once, without mitigation, we shall be less disposed wantonly to engage in an expensive contest, and if engaged in it, we shall be sooner disposed to get out of it, unless it be a contest for some great national interest. In point of economy, there is no real difference in either of the modes; for twenty millions in one payment, one million per annum for ever, or 1,200,000*l*. for 45 years, are precisely of the same value; but the people who pay the taxes never so estimate them, and therefore do not manage their private affairs accordingly. We are too apt to

think, that the war is burdensome only in proportion to what we
are at the moment called to pay for it in taxes, without reflecting
on the probable duration of such taxes. It would be difficult to
convince a man possessed of 20,000*l.*, or any other sum, that a
perpetual payment of 50*l.* per annum was equally burdensome
with a single tax of 1000*l.* He would have some vague notion
that the 50*l.* per annum would be paid by posterity, and would
not be paid by him; but if he leaves his fortune to his son, and
leaves it charged with this perpetual tax, where is the difference
whether he leaves him 20,000*l.*, with the tax, or 19,000*l.*
without it? This argument of charging posterity with the interest of our debt, or of relieving them from a portion of such
interest, is often used by otherwise well informed people, but
we confess we see no weight in it. It may, indeed, be said, that
the wealth of the country may increase; and as a portion of the
increased wealth will have to contribute to the taxes, the proportion falling on the present amount of wealth will be less,
and thus posterity will contribute to our present expenditure.
That this may be so is true; but it may also be otherwise—the
wealth of the country may diminish—individuals may withdraw from a country heavily taxed; and therefore the property
retained in the country may pay more than the just equivalent,
which would at the present time be received from it. That an
annual tax of 50*l.* is not deemed the same in amount as 1000*l.*
ready money, must have been observed by every body. If an
individual were called upon to pay 1000*l.* to the income-tax, he
would probably endeavour to save the whole of it from his
income; he would do no more if, in lieu of this war-tax, a loan
had been raised, for the interest of which he would have been
called upon to pay only 50*l.* income-tax. The war-taxes, then,
are more economical; for when they are paid, an effort is made
to save to the amount of the whole expenditure of the war,
leaving the national capital undiminished. In the other case, an

effort is only made to save to the amount of the interest of such expenditure, and therefore the national capital is diminished in amount. The usual objection made to the payment of the larger tax is, that it could not be conveniently paid by manufacturers and landholders, for they have not large sums of money at their command. We think that great efforts would be made to save the tax out of their income, in which case they could obtain the money from this source; but suppose they could not, what should hinder them from selling a part of their property for money, or of borrowing it at interest? That there are persons disposed to lend, is evident from the facility with which government raises its loans. Withdraw this great borrower from the market, and private borrowers would be readily accommodated. By wise regulations, and good laws, the greatest facilities and security might be afforded to individuals in such transactions. In the case of a loan, A advances the money, and B pays the interest, and every thing else remains as before. In the case of war-taxes, A would still advance the money, and B pay the interest, only with this difference, he would pay it directly to A; now he pays it to government, and government pays it to A.

These large taxes, it may be said, must fall on property, which the smaller taxes now do not exclusively do. Those who are in professions, as well as those who live from salaries and wages, and who now contribute annually to the taxes, could not make a large ready money payment; and they would, therefore, be benefited at the expence of the capitalist and landholder. We believe that they would be very little, if at all benefited by the system of war-taxes. Fees to professional men, salaries, and wages, are regulated by the prices of commodities, and by the relative situation of those who pay, and of those who receive them. A tax of the nature proposed, if it did not disturb prices, would, however, change the relation between these classes, and a new arrangement of fees, salaries, and wages, would take place, so that the usual level would be restored.

The reward that is paid to professors, &c. is regulated, like every thing else, by demand and supply. What produces the supply of men, with certain qualifications, is not any particular sum of money, but a certain relative position in society. If you diminished, by additional taxes, the incomes of landlords and capitalists, leaving the pay of professions the same, the relative position of professions would be raised; an additional number of persons would, therefore, be enticed into those lines, and the competition would reduce the pay.

The greatest advantage that would attend war-taxes would be, the little permanent derangement that they would cause to the industry of the country. The prices of our commodities would not be disturbed by taxation, or if they were, they would only be so during a period when every thing is disturbed by other causes, during war. At the commencement of peace, every thing would be at its natural price again, and no inducement would be afforded to us by the direct effect, and still less by the indirect effect of taxes on various commodities, to desert employments in which we have peculiar skill and facilities, and engage in others in which the same skill and facilities are wanting. In a state of freedom every man naturally engages himself in that employment for which he is best fitted, and the greatest abundance of products is the result. An injudicious tax may induce us to import what we should otherwise have produced at home, or to export what we should otherwise have received from abroad; and in both cases, we shall receive, besides the inconvenience of paying the tax, a less return for a given quantity of our labour, than what that labour would, if unfettered, have produced. Under a complicated system of taxation, it is impossible for the wisest legislature to discover all the effects, direct and indirect, of its taxes; and if it cannot do this, the industry of the country will not be exerted to the greatest advantage. By war-taxes, we should save many millions in the collection of taxes. We might get rid of at least some of the expensive establishments, and the army of officers which they employ would be dispensed with. There would be no charges for the management of debt. Loans would not be raised at the rate of 50*l.* or 60*l.* for a nominal capital of 100*l.*, to be repaid at 70*l.*, 80*l.*, or possibly at 100*l.*; and perhaps, what is of more importance than all these together, we might get rid of those great sources of the demoralization of the people, the customs and excise. In every view of this question, we come to the same conclusion, that it would be a great improvement in our system for ever to get rid of the practice of funding. Let us meet our difficulties as they arise, and keep our estates free from permanent incumbrances, of the weight of which we are never truly sensible, till we are involved in them past remedy.

We are now to compare the other two modes of defraying the expences of a war, one by borrowing the capital expended, and providing annual taxes permanently for the payment of the interest, the other by borrowing the capital expended, and besides providing the interest by annual taxes, raising, by the same mode, an additional revenue (and which is called the sinking fund), with a view, within a certain determinate time, to redeem the original debt, and get rid entirely of the taxes.

Under the firm conviction that nations will at last adopt the plan of defraying their expences, ordinary and extraordinary, at the time they are incurred, we are favourable to every plan which shall soonest redeem us from debt; but then we must be convinced that the plan is effective for the object. This then is the place to examine whether we have, or can have, any security for the due application of the sinking fund to the payment of debt.

When Mr. Pitt, in 1786, established the sinking fund, he was aware of the danger of entrusting it to ministers and parliament; and, therefore, provided that the sums applicable to the sinking fund should be paid by the Exchequer into the hands of commissioners, by quarterly payments, who should be required to invest equal sums of money in the purchase of stock, on four days in each week, or about fifty days in each quarter. The commissioners named were, the Speaker of the House of Commons, the Chancellor of the Exchequer, the Master of the Rolls, the Accountant General of the Court of Chancery, and the Governor and Deputy-Governor of the Bank. He thought, that, under such management, there could be no misapplication of the funds, and he thought correctly, for the commissioners have faithfully fulfilled the trust reposed in them. In proposing the establishment of a sinking fund to Parliament in 1786, Mr. Pitt said, "With regard to preserving the fund to be invariably applied to the diminution of the debt inalienable, it was the essence of his plan to keep that sacred, and most effectually so in time of war. He must contend, that to suffer the fund at any time, or on any pretence, to be diverted from its proper object, would be to ruin, defeat, and overturn his plan. He hoped, therefore, when the bill he should introduce should pass into a law, that House would hold itself solemnly pledged, not to listen to a proposal for its repeal on any pretence whatever."[1]

"If this million, to be so applied, is laid out with its growing interest, it will amount to a very great sum in a period that is not very long in the life of an individual, and but an hour in the existence of a great nation; and this will diminish the debt of this country so much, as to prevent the exigencies of war from raising it to the enormous height it has hitherto done. In the period of twenty-eight years, the sum of a million, annually

[1] In the debate on his own Plan for the Reduction of the National Debt, 29 March 1786 (*Hansard's* *Parliamentary History*, XXV, 1321-2).

improved, would amount to four millions per annum, but care must be taken that this fund be not broken in upon; *this has hitherto been the bane of this country*; for if the original sinking fund had been properly preserved, it is easy to be proved that our debts, at this moment, would not have been very burthensome; *this has hitherto been, in vain, endeavoured to be prevented by acts of Parliament*; the minister has uniformly, when it suited his convenience, gotten hold of this sum, which ought to have been regarded as most sacred. What then is the way of preventing this? The plan I mean to propose is this, that this sum be vested in certain commissioners, to be by them applied quarterly to buy up stock; by this means, no sum so great will ever be ready to be seized upon on any occasion, and the fund will go on without interruption. Long and very long has this country struggled under its heavy load, without any prospect of being relieved; but it may now look forward to an object upon which the existence of this country depends; it is, therefore, proper it should be fortified as much as possible against alienation. By this manner of paying 250,000*l.* quarterly into the hands of commissioners, it would make it impossible to take it by stealth; and the advantage would be too well felt ever to suffer a public act for that purpose. A minister could not have the confidence to come to this House, and desire the repeal of so beneficial a law, which tended so directly to relieve the people from burthen."[1]

Mr. Pitt flattered himself most strangely, that he had found a remedy for the difficulty which "had hitherto been the bane of this country"; he thought he had discovered means for preventing "ministers, when it suited their convenience, from getting hold of this sum, which ought to be regarded as most sacred." With the knowledge of Parliament which he had, it is surprising that he should have relied so firmly on the resistance

[1] *ib.* 1309. The italics are Ricardo's.

which the House of Commons would offer to any plan of ministers for violating the sinking fund. Ministers have never desired the partial repeal of this law, without obtaining a ready compliance from Parliament.

We have already shown,[1] that, in 1807, one Chancellor of the Exchequer proposed to relieve the country from taxation, with a very slight exception, for several years together, while we were, during war, keeping up, if not increasing our expenditure, and supplying it by means of annual loans. What is this but disposing of a fund which ought to have been regarded as most sacred?

In 1809, another Chancellor of the Exchequer raised a loan, without raising any additional taxes to pay the interest of it, but pledged a portion of the war-taxes for that purpose, thereby rendering an addition to that amount, necessary to the loan of the following and every succeeding year. Was not this disposing of the sinking fund by stealth, and accumulating debt at compound interest? Another Chancellor of the Exchequer, in 1813, proposed a partial repeal of the law, by which seven millions per annum of the sinking fund was placed at his disposal, and which he has employed in providing for the interest of new debt. This was done with the sanction of Parliament, and, as we apprehend, in direct violation of all the laws which had before been passed regarding the sinking fund. But what has become of the remainder of this fund, after deducting the seven millions taken from it by the act of 1813? It should now be sixteen millions, and at that amount it was returned in the annual finance accounts last laid before Parliament. The finance committee appointed by the House of Commons[2] did not fail to see that nothing can be deemed an efficient fund for the redemption of debt in time of peace, but such as arises from an

[1] Above, pp. 154–5.
[2] In their 'First Report', 1819 (reprinted in *Hansard*, Appendix to vol. XL).

excess of revenue above expenditure, and as that excess, under the most favourable view, was not quite two millions, they considered that sum as the real efficient sinking fund, which was now applicable to the discharge of debt. If the act of 1802 had been complied with, if the intentions of Mr. Pitt had been fulfilled, we should now have had a clear excess of revenue of above twenty millions, applicable to the payment of the debt; as it is, we have two millions only, and if we ask ministers what has become of the remaining eighteen millions, they show us an expensive peace establishment, which they have no other means of defraying but by drafts on this fund, or several hundred millions of 3 per cents. on which it is employed in discharging the interest. If ministers had not had such an amount of taxes to depend on, would they have ventured, year after year, to encounter a deficiency of revenue below expenditure, for several years together, of more than twelve millions? It is true that the measures of Mr. Pitt locked it up from their immediate seizure, but they knew it was in the hands of the commissioners, and presumed as much upon it, and justly, with the knowledge they had of Parliament, as if it had been in their own. They considered the commissioners as their trustees, accumulating money for their benefit, and of which they knew that they might dispose whenever they should consider that the urgency of the case required it. They seem to have made a tacit agreement with the commissioners, that they should accumulate twelve millions per annum at compound interest, while they themselves accumulated an equal amount of debt, also at compound interest. The facts are indeed no longer denied. In the last session of Parliament, for the first time the delusion was acknowledged by ministers,[1] after it had become manifest to every other person;

[1] The acknowledgement was implied in the proposal of the Budget of 1819 to borrow £12,000,000 from the Sinking Fund for the service of the year; see below, V, 20.

but yet it is avowed to be their intention, to go on with this nominal sinking fund, raising a loan every year for the difference between its real and nominal amount, and letting the commissioners subscribe to it. On what principle this can be done, it would be difficult to give any rational account. Perhaps it may be said, that it would be a breach of faith to the stockholder to take away the sinking fund, but is it not equally a breach of faith if the Government itself sells to the commissioners the greatest part of the stock which they buy? The stockholder wants something substantial and real to be done for him, and not any thing deceitful and delusive. Disguise it as you will, if of fourteen millions to be invested by the commissioners in time of peace, the stock which twelve millions will purchase is sold by the Government itself, which creates it for the very purpose of obtaining these twelve millions, and only stock for two millions is purchased in the market, and no taxes for sinking fund or interest are provided for the twelve millions which Government takes; the result is precisely the same to the stockholder, and to every one concerned, as if the sinking fund was reduced to two millions. It is utterly unworthy of a great country to countenance such pitiful shifts and evasions.

The sinking fund, then, has, instead of diminishing the debt, greatly increased it. The sinking fund has encouraged expenditure. If, during war, a country spends twenty millions per annum, in addition to its ordinary expenditure, and raises taxes only for the interest, it will, in twenty years, accumulate a debt of four hundred millions; and its taxes will increase to twenty millions per annum. If, in addition to the million per annum, taxes of 200,000*l.* were raised for a sinking fund, and regularly applied to the purchase of stock, the taxes, at the end of twenty years, would be twenty-four millions, and its debt only 342 millions; for fifty-eight millions will have been paid off by the sinking fund; but if, at the end of this period, new debt shall be contracted, and the sinking fund itself, with all its accumulations, amounting to 6,940,000*l.*, be absorbed in the payment of interest on such debt, the whole amount of debt will be 538 millions, exceeding that which would have existed if there had been no sinking fund by 138 millions. If such an additional expenditure were necessary, provision should be made for it without any interference with the sinking fund. If, at the end of the war, there is not a clear surplus of revenue above expenditure of 6,940,000*l.*, on the above supposition, there is no use whatever in persevering in a system which is so little adequate to its object. After all our experience, however, we are again toiling to raise a sinking fund; and, in the last session of Parliament, three millions of new taxes were voted, with the avowed object of raising the remnant of our sinking fund, now reduced to two millions, to five millions.[1] Is it rash to prognosticate that this sinking fund will share the fate of all those which have preceded it? Probably it will accumulate for a few years, till we are engaged in some new contest, when ministers, finding it difficult to raise taxes for the interest of loans, will silently encroach on this fund, and we shall be fortunate if, in their next arrangement, we shall be able to preserve out of its wreck an amount so large as two millions.

It is, we think, sufficiently proved, that no securities can be given by ministers that the sinking fund shall be faithfully devoted to the payment of debt, and without such securities we should be much better without such a fund. To pay off the whole, or a great portion of our debt, is, in our estimation, a most desirable object; if, at the same time, we acknowledged the evils of the funding system, and resolutely determined to carry on our future contests without having recourse to it. This cannot, or rather will not, be done by a sinking fund as at present constituted, nor by any other that we can suggest; but

[1] See below, V, 20.

if, without raising any fund, the debt were paid by a tax on property, once for all, it would effect its object. Its operation might be completed in two or three years during peace; and, if we mean honestly to discharge the debt, we do not see any other mode of accomplishing it. The objections to this plan are the same as those which we have already attempted to answer[1] in speaking of war-taxes. The stockholders being paid off, would have a large mass of property, for which they would be eagerly seeking employment. Manufacturers and landholders would want large sums for their payments into the Exchequer. These two parties would not fail to make an arrangement with each other, by which one party would employ their money, and the other raise it. They might do this by loan, or by sale and purchase, as they might think it most conducive to their respective interests; with this the state would have nothing to do. Thus, by one great effort, we should get rid of one of the most terrible scourges which was ever invented to afflict a nation; and our commerce would be extended without being subject to all the vexatious delays and interruptions which our present artificial system imposes upon it.

There cannot be a greater security for the continuance of peace than the imposing on ministers the necessity of applying to the people for taxes to support a war. Suffer the sinking fund to accumulate during peace to any considerable sum, and very little provocation would induce them to enter into a new contest. They would know that, by a little management, they could make the sinking fund available to the raising of a new supply, instead of being available to the payment of the debt. The argument is now common in the mouths of ministers when they wish to lay on new taxes, for the purpose of creating a new sinking fund, in lieu of one which they have just spent, to say, "It will make foreign countries respect us; they will be

[1] Above, pp. 186–90.

afraid to insult or provoke us, when they know that we are possessed of so powerful a resource." What do they mean by this argument, if the sinking fund be not considered by them as a war fund, on which they can draw in support of the contest? It cannot, at one and the same time, be employed in the annoyance of an enemy, and in the payment of debt. If taxes are, as they ought to be, raised for the expences of a war, what facility will a sinking fund give to the raising of them? none whatever. It is not because the possession of a sinking fund will enable them to raise new and additional taxes that ministers prize it; for they know it will have no such effect; but because they know that they will be enabled to substitute the sinking fund in lieu of taxes, and employ it, as they have always done, in war, and providing interest for fresh debt. Their argument means this, or it means nothing; for a sinking fund does not necessarily add to the wealth and prosperity of a country; and it is on that wealth and prosperity that it must depend whether new burthens can be borne by the people. What did Mr. Vansittart mean in 1813, when he said[1] that "the advantage which his new plan of finance would hereafter give, in furnishing 100 millions in time of peace, as a fund against the return of hostilities, was one of great moment. This would place an instrument of force in the hands of parliament which might lead to the most important results." "It might be objected by some, that, keeping in reserve a large fund to meet the expences of a new war, might be likely to make the government of this country arrogant and ambitious; and therefore have a tendency unnecessarily to plunge us in new contests;"—not a very unreasonable objection, we should think! How does Mr. Vansittart answer it? "On this subject he would say from long experience and observation, that it would be better for our

---

[1] In the debate on the state of the finances of Great Britain, 25 March 1813 (*Hansard*, XXV, 333–4).

neighbours to depend on the moderation of this country, than for this country to depend on them[1]. He should not think the plan objectionable on this account. If the sums treasured up were misapplied by the arrogant or ambitious conduct of our government, the blame must fall on the heads of those who misused it, not on those who put it into their hands for purposes of defence. They did their duty in furnishing the means of preserving the greatness and glory of the country, though those means might be used for the purposes of ambition, rapine, and desolation." These are very natural observations from the mouth of a minister; but we are of opinion that such a treasure would be more safe in the custody of the people, and that Parliament have something more to do than to furnish ministers with the means of preserving the greatness and glory of the country. It is their duty to take every security that the resources of the country are not misapplied "by the arrogant and ambitious conduct of our government," or "used for the purposes of ambition, rapine, and desolation."

If we had no other reason for our opinion, this speech would convince us that, in the present constitution of Parliament, the superintending authority, the sinking fund is pernicious, and that it cannot be too soon abolished.

On the extraordinary assumption that there was any thing in Mr. Vansittart's plan that would, more effectually than the old plan, allow 100 millions hereafter to be appropriated to the public service, Dr. Hamilton has the following observations:

"We are altogether at a loss to form a distinct conception of the *valuable treasure* here held forth. So soon as any stock is purchased by the commissioners, and stands invested in their name, a like amount of the public debt is in fact discharged. Whether a Parliamentary declaration to the effect be made or not, is only a matter of form. If the money remain invested in

[1] 'theirs' in *Hansard*.

the name of the commissioners, no doubt it may be transferred again to purchasers in the stock exchange, when war broke out anew; and money may be raised for the public in this manner. It is an application to the public to invest their capital in the purchase of this dormant stock."[1] "It is true, that, if the taxes imposed during war, for the purpose of a sinking fund, be continued after peace is restored, till a large sum (suppose 100,000,000*l*.) be vested in the hands of the Commissioners, the public, upon the renewal of the war, may spend to that amount without imposing fresh taxes ["]², ["]an advantage," observes Mr. Huskisson, "not only not exclusively belonging to this plan, but unavoidable under any plan of a sinking fund in time of peace."[3] Mr. Vansittart ought to have said, "if our sinking fund should accumulate, in time of peace, to so large a sum that I can take five millions per annum from it; I can spend 100,000,000*l*. in a new war without coming to you for fresh taxes; the disadvantages of my plan are, that by now taking 7,000,000*l*. per annum from it, and making a provision for speedily, and at regular intervals, appropriating more of this fund to present objects, the sinking fund will be so much diminished, that I cannot so soon, by a great many years, avail myself of the five millions for the purpose which I have stated."

(E.E.E.)

---

[1] p. 233.
[2] This part of the quotation is from Hamilton, pp. 234-5, not from Huskisson.

[3] *Substance of the Speech of W. Huskisson...25 March 1813*, p. 40.

ON

PROTECTION

TO

AGRICULTURE.

BY

DAVID RICARDO, Esq. M.P.

––––––––––

LONDON:

JOHN MURRAY, ALBEMARLE-STREET.

MDCCCXXII.

ON

PROTECTION

TO

AGRICULTURE.

BY

DAVID RICARDO, Esq. M.P.

FOURTH EDITION.

LONDON:

JOHN MURRAY, ALBEMARLE-STREET.

MDCCCXXII.

[Title-page to ed. 4]

NOTE ON 'PROTECTION TO AGRICULTURE'

On Protection to Agriculture was published on 18 April 1822,[1] the day after the reassembly of Parliament following the Easter recess. A few days later the debate on the Report of the Agricultural Committee of 1822 was due to begin. Even less than Ricardo's other writings can this pamphlet be detached from the circumstances in which it was written; it is in effect, no less than his speeches, one of Ricardo's contributions to the debate on the agricultural distress, and as Professor Hollander has observed 'is a manner of minority report of the Committee'.[2]

The proposals made in the pamphlet[3] for an unlimited importation of corn to be permanently permitted once the price of wheat had risen to 70s., with an import duty of 20s. a quarter, which should be reduced by 1s. a year till it reached its final level of 10s., and for a drawback of 7s. on exportation, were embodied in the Resolutions which Ricardo moved in the House of Commons on 29 April 1822.[4] His resolutions were lost by 25 votes to 218 on 9 May.

A Select Committee had been appointed in the previous year (on 7 March 1821) to consider the depressed state of agriculture: T. Gooch was the Chairman and Ricardo was one of its members. They took evidence from 42 witnesses and drew up their Report on 18 June 1821, too late in the Session for consideration by Parliament.

Early in the following Session, it was agreed to revive the Agricultural Committee and to refer back to them the Report of 1821. The composition of the revived Committee was almost identical with that of 1821, except that Lord Londonderry (as Castlereagh had now become) was Chairman in place of Gooch. The Report of 1821, having been originally drafted by Huskisson, supported in

---

[1] It was first advertised in the *Morning Chronicle* of 16 April 1822 among 'Books published this day', but as no price was stated this may have been only a preliminary announcement: on 18 April it was again advertised, this time with the price, 3s.

[2] *David Ricardo, A Centenary Estimate*, 1910, p. 54.
[3] See below, p. 263. These proposals had been outlined already in Ricardo's *Principles*, 1817, above, I, 266–7.
[4] Below, V, 158–9.

principle a free trade in corn, but the landlords on the committee had succeeded in adding a number of protectionist recommendations. The Report of 1822 was much more definitely protectionist. It was read by the Chairman to the Committee on 25 March[1] and presented to the House of Commons on 1 April, when it was agreed to postpone its consideration till after the Easter recess. However, on 3 April the presentation of a petition on the agricultural distress provided an opportunity for anticipating the debate on the Report; Ricardo's speech on this occasion, attacking the Report, contained many of the points which he made shortly after in *Protection to Agriculture*. Lord Londonderry was perhaps aware that Ricardo was already engaged upon his pamphlet, when, referring in the same debate to the evils of abundance, he said, 'if the hon. member for Portarlington turned his intelligent mind to it, he could make the House understand this part of the subject.'[2] On the same day the House adjourned until 17 April.

Ricardo remained in London during the recess,[3] occupied in completing and seeing through the press his *Protection to Agriculture*. As he had become acquainted with the contents of the Report only on 25 March, it cannot have taken him much more than three weeks to write and publish the pamphlet.

On 19 April Ricardo wrote to McCulloch that he had sent him an early copy of the pamphlet which he had just published, and McCulloch reviewed it in the *Scotsman* for 27 April.

Whishaw wrote to Thomas Smith on 20 April: 'I have not seen Ricardo's pamphlet, but hear a good account of it from Warburton and the adepts. He did not send me a copy, as he had done of his former works, considering me perhaps as a heretic.' And on 27 April: 'I have not yet read Ricardo's pamphlet, but hear it much praised. The ministerialists, in particular, are much pleased with his doctrines, evidently because he says little against taxation.'[4]

Opening the debate on the Report on 29 April Lord Londonderry declared that in repeating his opinion that the necessary relief for agriculture could not come from the remission of taxation, he was

[1] See below, IX, 180.
[2] Below, V, 154.
[3] See below, IX, 179.

[4] *The 'Pope' of Holland House*, ed. by Lady Seymour, London, 1906, pp. 248–9. Cp. below, V, 127, n.

'fortified considerably' by the sanction and confirmation received from 'the able work which has recently been published by the hon. member for Portarlington (Mr. Ricardo), than whom it is impossible for the House on such questions to have higher authority'.[1]

Within a few days of its publication new editions of the pamphlet were called for; on 29 April *The Times* advertised the second edition, and on the same day the *Morning Chronicle* advertised the third; the fourth edition followed soon after.[2] In each successive edition Ricardo introduced small alterations, mainly verbal.

The text of the present edition follows that of the fourth edition, while the variants of the earlier editions are given in footnotes.

[1] Below, V, 155.
[2] In some copies of the fourth edition there is attached Murray's list of 'Works Recently Published' dated June 1822.

CONTENTS

INTRODUCTION

It cannot, I think, be denied, that, within these few years, great progress has been made in diffusing correct opinions on the impolicy of imposing restrictions on the importation of foreign corn; but, unhappily, much prejudice yet exists on this subject, and it is to be feared that the generally-prevailing errors in the minds of those who are suffering from the distressed state of our agriculture, may lead to measures of increased restriction, rather than to the only effectual remedy for those distresses, the gradual approach to a system of free trade. It is to the present corn-law that much of the distress is to be attributed, and I hope to make it appear, that the occupation of a farmer will be exposed to continual hazard, and will be placed under peculiar disadvantages, as compared with all other occupations, while any system of restriction on the importation of foreign corn is continued, which shall have the effect of keeping the price of corn in this country habitually and considerably above the prices of other countries.

Before I proceed, however, to this, which is the main object that I have in view, I wish to notice some of the prevailing opinions which are daily advanced on the subject of the causes of the present distress; on the doctrine of remunerating price; on taxation; on currency, &c.: after disposing of these, we shall be better able to examine the important question of what ought to be the permanent regulations of this country, respecting the trade in corn, in order to afford the greatest security to the people, for a cheap and steady price, with an abundant supply of that essential article.

SECTION I

On Remunerating Price

THE words Remunerative Price are meant to denote the price at which corn can be raised, paying all charges, including rent, and leaving to the grower a fair profit on his capital. It follows from this definition, that in proportion as a country is driven to the cultivation of poorer lands for the support of an increasing population, the price of corn, to be remunerative, must rise; for even if no rent is paid for such poorer land—as the charges on its cultivation must, for the same quantity of produce, be greater than on any other land previously cultivated,[1] those charges can only be returned to the grower by an increase of price. "I know districts of the country*," says Mr. Iveson, "taking the very best qualities in them, that will produce from four to five quarters by the acre. I know there are farms that have averaged in the wheat crop, four quarters to the acre, or 32 bushels." "In what part of the kingdom? In Wiltshire." "What would you estimate the second quality of land at? I think the middling, or second, what I should call the middling quality of lands under good cultivation, may be taken at two quarters and a half." "And the inferior lands? From 12 to 15 bushels an acre." Mr. Harvey was asked, "What is the lowest rent you have ever known to be paid for the worst land on which corn is raised? Eighteen-pence an acre." Mr. Harvey further stated, that on[2] an average of the last ten years he had obtained 30 bushels of wheat per acre

* Report, Agricultural Committee, 1821, page 338.[3]

[1] Eds. 1-2 contain here in addition 'yielding the same,'.
[2] Eds. 1-2 'in' instead of 'on'.
[3] 'Report from the Select Committee, to whom the Several Petitions Complaining of the Depressed State of the Agriculture of the United Kingdom, were Referred', 18 June 1821; in *Parliamentary Papers*, 1821, vol. IX.

from his land.[1] Mr. Wakefield's evidence was to the same effect as Mr. Iveson's; but the difference according to him between the produce of wheat per acre on the best and worst land in cultivation was as much as 32 bushels; for he said "that on the sea coast of Norfolk, Suffolk, Essex, and Kent, the crop is thought a bad one, if it be not 40 bushels per acre;" and he added, "I do not believe, that the very poor lands produce above eight bushels per acre."[2]

Suppose now, that the population of England had only been one half its present amount, and that it had not been necessary to take any other quality of land into cultivation than that which yielded 32 bushels of wheat per acre; what would have been the remunerative price? Can any one doubt of its being so low, that, if the prices on the Continent had been at the same average at which they have been for the last five or ten years, we should have been an exporting instead of an importing country? It is true, that this land now yields 32 bushels, and would have yielded no more on the supposition that I have made; but is it not true, that the value of the 32 bushels now raised, is regulated by the cost of producing the 12 or 15 bushels on the inferior lands of which Mr. Iveson speaks? If the cost of raising 15 bushels of wheat is as great now, as the cost was of raising 30 bushels formerly, the price must be doubled to be remunerative, for the degree in which the price must rise to compensate the producer for the charges which he has to pay, does not depend on the quantity produced, nor on the quantity consumed, but on the cost of its production. The difference in the value of the quantity raised on the good land, and on the inferior land, will always constitute rent; so that the profits of the occupiers of the good and bad land will be the same, but the rent of the best land will exceed the rent of the worst by the difference in the quantity of produce, which

[1] ib. p. 37.   [2] ib. pp. 219–20.

with the same expense, it can be made to yield. It is now universally admitted, that rent is the effect of the rise in the price of corn, and not the cause; it is also admitted, that the only permanent cause of rise in the value of corn, is an increased charge on its production, caused by the necessity of cultivating poorer lands; on which, by the expenditure of the same quantity of labour, the same quantity of produce cannot be obtained.

Is it not true that the rent on the better land is regulated by the lesser quantity of 15 bushels, with which we are now obliged to be contented on our poorer lands? The rent which is now a charge on cultivating the land which yields the 32 bushels, and which is equal to the value of 17 bushels, the difference between 15 and 32 bushels, could not have existed, if no land was cultivated but such as yielded 32 bushels. If, then, with the charge of rent, the cost of raising 15 bushels on the rich land—and without the payment of rent, the cost of raising the same quantity on the poor land, is now[1] as great as the cost of raising 30 bushels was formerly on the rich land, when no rent was paid, the price must be doubled.

It appears then that, in the progress of society, when no importation takes place, we are obliged constantly to have recourse to worse soils to feed an augmenting population, and with every step of our progress the price of corn must rise, and with such rise, the rent of the better land which had been previously cultivated, will necessarily be increased. A higher price becomes necessary to compensate for the smaller quantity which is obtained; but this higher price must never be considered as a good,—it would not have existed if the same return had been obtained with less labour,—it would not have existed if, by the application of labour to manufactures, we had indirectly obtained the corn by the exportation of those manufactures in exchange for corn. A high price, if the effect of a

---

[1] Eds. 1-2 'now is'.

high cost, is an evil, and not a good; the price is high, because a great deal of labour is bestowed in obtaining the corn. If only a little labour was bestowed upon it, more of the labour of the country, which constitutes its only real source of wealth, would have been at its disposal to procure other enjoyments which are desirable.

SECTION II

On the Influence of a Rise of Wages on the price of Corn

Much of what has been said in the foregoing section, would probably be allowed by some of those who are the advocates for a restricted trade in corn; they would however add, that though it could be shewn that no protecting duties on the importation of corn could be justifiable, merely on account of the increased expenditure of labour necessary to obtain a given quantity in this country, yet such duties were necessary to protect the farmer against the effects of high wages in this country, caused by the taxation which falls on the labouring classes, and which must be repaid to them by their employers, by means of high wages. This argument proceeds on the assumption, that high wages tend to raise the price of the commodities on which labour is bestowed. If the farmer, they say, could, before taxation, and the high wages which are the effect of it, compete with the foreign grower of corn, he can no longer do so now he is exposed to a burthen from which his competitor is free.

This whole argument is fallacious,—the farmer is placed under no comparative disadvantage, in consequence of a rise of wages. If, in consequence of taxes paid by the labouring class, wages should[1] rise, which they, in all probability, would do, they would equally affect all classes of producers. If it be deemed necessary, that corn should rise in order to remunerate

[1] Eds. 1-2 do not contain 'should'.

the growers, it is also necessary that cloth, hats, shoes, and every other commodity should rise, in order to remunerate the producers of those articles. Either then corn ought not to rise, or all other commodities should rise along with it.

If neither corn, nor any other commodity, rise, they will of course be all of the same relative value as before; and if they do all rise, the same will be true. All must require protecting duties, or none. To impose protecting duties on all commodities would be absurd, because nothing would be gained by it; it would in no way alter the relative value of commodities; and it is only by altering the relative value of commodities that any particular trade is protected; not merely by an alteration of price. If England gave a yard of superfine cloth to Germany for a quarter of wheat, she would neither be more nor less disposed to carry on this trade, if both cloth and corn were raised 20 per cent. in price. All foreign trade finally resolves itself into an interchange of commodities; money is but the measure by which the respective quantities are[1] ascertained. No commodity can be imported unless another commodity is exported; and the exported commodity must be equally raised in price by the rise of wages. It is essential that a drawback should be allowed on the exported article, if the one imported be protected by a duty. But it comes to the same thing, if no drawback be allowed on the one, nor protection granted to the other, because, in either case, precisely the same quantity of the foreign commodity will be obtained for a given quantity of the home-made commodity.

If a quarter of corn be raised from 60s. to 75s., or 25 per cent. by a rise of wages, and a certain quantity of hats or cloth be raised in the same proportion by the same cause, the importer of corn into England would lose just as much by the commodity which he exports, as he would gain by the corn

---

[1] Eds. 1-2 'is' in place of 'are'.

which he imports. If trade were left free, corn would not rise
from 60 to 75, notwithstanding the rise of wages; nor would
cloth, or hats, or shoes rise from this cause. But, if I should
allow that they would rise, it would make no difference to my
argument; we should then export money in exchange for corn,
because no commodity could be so profitably employed in
paying for it; for, by the supposition, every other commodity
is raised in price. The exportation of money would gradually
lessen the quantity, and raise its value in this country, while
the importation of it into other countries would have a contrary
effect in them; it would increase the quantity, and sink its value,
and thus the price of corn, of cloth, of hats, and of all other
things in England, would bear the same relation to the prices
of the same commodities in other countries, as they bore before
wages were raised. In all cases, the rise of wages, when general,
diminishes profits, and does not raise the prices of commodities.
If the prices of commodities rose, no producer would be
benefited; for of what consequence could it be to him to sell
his commodity at an advance of 25 per cent., if he, in his turn,
were obliged to give 25 per cent. more for every commodity
which he purchased? He would be precisely in the same condition, whether he sold his corn for 25 per cent. advance, and
gave an additional 25 per cent. in the price of his hats, shoes,
clothes, &c. &c., as if he sold his corn at the usual price, and
bought all the commodities which he consumed at the prices
which he had before given for them. No one class of producers, then, is entitled to protection on account of a rise of
wages, because a rise of wages equally affects all producers;
it does not raise the prices of commodities because it diminishes
profits; and, if it did raise the price of commodities, it would
raise them all in the same proportion, and would not therefore
alter their exchangeable value. It is only when commodities
are altered in relative value, by the interference of Govern-

ment, that any tax, which shall act as a protection against the importation of a foreign commodity, can be justifiable.

It is by many supposed, that a rise in the price of corn will raise the price of all other things; this opinion is founded on the erroneous view which they take of the effect of a general rise of wages. Corn rises because it is more difficult to produce, and its cost is raised; it would be no rise at all, if all other things rose with it. It is a real rise to the hatter and clothier, if they are obliged one to give more hats, the other more cloth for their corn; it would be no rise at all to them, and it would be impossible to shew who paid for the increased cost, if their commodities also rose, and exchanged for the same quantity of corn.

It may be laid down as a principle, that any cause which operates in a country to affect equally all commodities, does not alter their relative value, and can give no advantage to foreign competitors, but that any cause which operates partially on one, does alter its value[1] to others, if not countervailed by an adequate duty; it will give advantage to the foreign competitor, and tend to deprive us of a beneficial branch of trade.

SECTION III

On the Effects of Taxes imposed on a particular Commodity

FOR the same reasons that protecting duties are not justifiable on account of the rise of wages generally, from whatever cause it may proceed, it is evident that they are not to be defended when taxation is general, and equally affects all classes of producers. An income tax is of this description; it affects equally all who employ capital, and it has never yet been suggested by those most favourable to protecting duties that any would be necessary on account of an income tax. But a tax affecting

[1] Eds. 1-2 'its relative value'.

equally all productions is precisely of the same description as an income tax, because it leaves them, after the tax, of the same relative value to each other as before it was imposed. The rise of wages, a tax on income, or a proportional tax on all commodities, all operate in the same way; they do not alter the relative value of goods, and therefore they do not subject us to any disadvantage in our commerce with foreign countries. We suffer indeed the inconvenience of paying the tax, but from that burthen we have no means of freeing ourselves.

A tax, however, which falls exclusively on the producers of a particular commodity tends to raise the price of that commodity, and if it did not so raise it the producer would be under a disadvantage as compared with all other producers; he would no longer gain the general and ordinary profits by his trade. By rising in price, the value of this commodity is altered as compared with other commodities. If no protecting duty is imposed on the importation of a similar commodity from other countries, injustice is done to the producer at home, and not only to the producer but to the country to which he belongs. It is for the interest of the public that he should not be driven from a trade which, under a system of free competition, he would have chosen, and to which he would adhere if every other commodity were taxed equally with that which he produces. A tax affecting him exclusively is, in fact, a bounty to that amount on the importation of the same commodity from abroad; and to restore competition to its just level, it would be necessary not only to subject the imported commodity to an equal tax, but to allow a drawback of equal amount,[1] on the exportation of the home-made commodity.

The growers of corn are subject to some of these peculiar taxes, such as tithes, a portion of the poors' rate, and, perhaps, one or two other taxes, all of which tend to raise the price of

[1] Eds. 1-2 'also, equal to the tax' in place of 'of equal amount,'.

corn, and other raw produce, equal to these peculiar burthens. In the degree then in which these taxes raise the price of corn, a duty should be imposed on its importation. If from this cause it be raised ten shillings per quarter, a duty of ten shillings should be imposed on the importation of foreign corn, and a drawback of the same amount should be allowed on the exportation of corn. By means of this duty and this drawback, the trade would be placed on the same footing as if it had never been taxed, and we should be quite sure that capital would neither be injuriously for the interests of the country, attracted towards, nor repelled from it.

The greatest benefit results to a country when its Government forbears to give encouragement, or oppose obstacles, to[1] any disposition of capital which the proprietor may think most advantageous to him. By imposing tithes, &c. on the farmer exclusively, no obstacle would be opposed to him, if there were no foreign competition, because he would be able to raise the price of his produce, and if he could not do so he would quit a trade which no longer afforded him the usual and ordinary profits of all other trades. But if importation was allowed, an undue encouragement would be given to the importation of foreign corn, unless the foreign commodity were subject to a[2] duty, equal to tithes or any other exclusive tax[3] imposed on the home-grower.

But the home-grower would still have to complain, if he was refused a drawback on exportation, because he might then say, "Before your duty, and before the price of my produce was raised in consequence of it, I could compete with the foreign grower in foreign markets; by making the remunerating price of my corn higher, you have deprived me of that advantage,

---

[1] Eds. 1-2 'in the way of' in place of 'to'.

[2] Eds. 1-2 'the same' in place of 'a'.

[3] Eds. 1-2 contain here in addition ', as that'.

therefore give me a drawback equal to the duty, and you, in
every respect, restore me to the position,[1] as it regards both
my own countrymen, as producers of other commodities, and
foreign growers of raw produce, in which I was before placed."
On every principle of justice, and consistently with the best
interests of the country his demand should be acceded to.

SECTION IV

On the effect of Abundant Crops on the Price of Corn

IN a former section I[2] have endeavoured to shew, that the price
of corn, to be remunerative, must pay all the charges of its
production, including in those charges the ordinary profits of
the stock employed. It is, in fact, by these conditions being
fulfilled, that the supply, on an average of years, is regulated.
If the price obtained be less than remunerative, profits will be
depressed, or will entirely disappear. If it be more than remunerative, profits will be high. In the first case, capital will
be withdrawn from the land, and the supply will gradually conform to the demand. In the second case, capital will be attracted
to the land, and the supply will be increased. But, notwithstanding this tendency of the supply of corn to conform itself
to the demand, at prices which shall be remunerative, it is
impossible to calculate accurately on the effects of the seasons.
Sometimes, for a few years successively, crops will be abundant;
at other times they will, for an equal period, be scanty and insufficient. When the quantity of corn at market, from a succession of good crops, is abundant, it falls in price, not in the
same proportion as the quantity exceeds the ordinary demand,
but very considerably more. The demand for corn, with a given

---

[1] Eds. 1-2 have 'both' here, in-
stead of four words later.   [2] Eds. 1-2 'we' in place of 'I'.

population, must necessarily be limited; and, although it may be, and undoubtedly is, true, that when it is abundant and cheap, the quantity consumed will be increased, yet it is equally certain, that its aggregate value will be diminished. Suppose 14 millions of quarters of wheat to be the ordinary demand of England, and that, from a very abundant season, 21 millions is produced. If the remunerative price were 3*l*. per quarter, and the value of the 14 millions of quarters 42,000,000*l*., there cannot be the least doubt, that the 21 millions of quarters would be of very considerably less value than 42,000,000*l*. No principle can be better established, than that a small excess of quantity operates very powerfully on price. This is true of all commodities; but of none can it be so certainly asserted as of corn, which forms the principal article of the food of the people. The principle, I believe, has never been denied by those who have turned their attention to this subject. Some, indeed, have attempted to estimate the fall of price which would take place, under the supposition of the surplus bearing different proportions to the average quantity. Such calculations, however, must be very deceptious, as no general rule can be laid down for the variations of price in proportion to quantity. It would be different in different countries; it must essentially depend on the wealth or poverty of the country, and on its means of holding over the superfluous quantity to a future season. It must depend, too, on the opinions formed of the probability of the future supply being adequate or otherwise to the future demand. This, however, is, I think, certain, that the aggregate value of an abundant crop will always be considerably less than the aggregate value of an average one; and that the aggregate value of a very limited crop will be considerably greater than that of an average crop. If 100,000 loaves were sold every day in London, and the supply should all at once be reduced to 50,000 per day, can any one doubt but that the price of each loaf would be considerably more than doubled? The rich would continue to consume precisely the same number of loaves, although the price was tripled or quadrupled. If, on the other hand, 200,000 loaves, instead of 100,000, were daily exposed for sale, could they be disposed of without a fall of price, far exceeding the proportion of the excess of quantity? Why is water without value, but because of its abundance? If corn were equally plenty, it would have no greater value, whatever quantity of labour might have been bestowed on its production.

In proof of the correctness of this view, I may refer to the prices of wheat in this country in different seasons of plenty, when it will be seen that, notwithstanding we were in a degree relieved by exportation, yet, from the abundance of crops, corn has been known to fall 50 per cent. in three years. Now to what can this be imputed but to excess of quantity? The document which follows is copied from Mr. Tooke's evidence before the committee of 1821.

		s.	d.	Quarters.
In 1728 the price of wheat was	48	5½	with an excess of import of	70,757
1732	„	„	23	8¼	with an excess of export of	202,058
1740	„	„	45	0½	„	„	46,822
1743	„	„	22	1	„	„	371,429
1750	„	„	28	10¾	„	„	947,323
1757	„	„	53	4	excess of import	130,017
1761	„	„	26	10¾	excess of export	441,956

Page 229 *Agricultural Report.*

Because it has been said, that abundance may be prejudicial to the interests of the producers, it has been objected that the new doctrine on this subject is, that the bounty of Providence may become a curse to a country; but this is essentially changing the proposition. No one has said that abundance is injurious to a country, but that it frequently is so to the producers of the abundant commodity. If what they raised was all destined for their own consumption, abundance never could be hurtful to them; but if, in consequence of the plenty of corn, the quantity with which they go to market to furnish themselves with other things is very much reduced in value, they are deprived of the means of obtaining their usual enjoyments; they have, in fact, an abundance of a commodity of little exchangeable value. If we lived in one of Mr. Owen's parallelograms, and enjoyed all our productions in common, then no one could suffer in consequence of abundance, but as long as society is constituted as it now is, abundance will often be injurious to producers, and scarcity beneficial to them.

SECTION V

On the effect produced on the Price of Corn by Mr. Peel's Bill for restoring the ancient standard

MUCH difference of opinion prevails on the effect produced on the price of corn by Mr. Peel's bill for restoring the ancient standard. On this subject there is a great want of candour in one of the disputing parties; and I believe it will be found, that many of those who contended during the war, that our money was not depreciated at all, now endeavour to shew that the depreciation was then enormous, and that all the distresses which we are now suffering, have arisen from restoring our currency from a depreciated state to par.

It is also forgotten, that from 1797 to 1819 we had no standard whatever, by which to regulate the quantity or value of our money. Its quantity and its value depended entirely on the Bank of England, the directors of which establishment, however desirous they might have been to act with fairness and justice to the public, avowed that they were guided in their issues by principles which, it is no longer disputed, exposed the country to the greatest embarrassment. Accordingly we find that the currency varied in value considerably during the period of 22 years, when there was no other rule for regulating its quantity and value but the will of the Bank.

In 1813 and 1814, the depreciation of our currency was probably at its highest point, gold being then 5*l*. 10*s*. and 5*l*. 8*s*. per ounce; but in 1819, the value of paper was only 5 per cent. below its ancient standard, gold being then 4*l*. 2*s*. or 4*l*. 3*s*. per ounce. It was in 1819 that Mr. Peel's bill passed into a law. At the time of passing that bill, Parliament had to deal with the question as it then presented itself. It was thought expedient that an end should be put to a state of things which allowed a company of merchants to regulate the value of money as they might think proper; and the only point which could then come under consideration was, whether the standard should be fixed at 4*l*. 2*s*., which was the price of gold not only at the time when Parliament was legislating, but its price for nearly the whole of the four preceding years; or the ancient standard of 3*l*. 17*s*. 10½*d*. should be restored. Between these two prices Parliament was constrained to determine, and I think, in choosing to go back to the ancient standard, it pursued a wise course. But when it is now said that money has been forcibly raised in value—25 per cent., according to some; 50, and even 60 per cent., according to others, they do not refer to 1819, the period at which that bill passed, but to the period of the greatest depression; and they charge the whole increase in the value of the currency to Mr. Peel's bill. Now, it is to the system which allowed of such variations in the value of money that Mr. Peel's bill put an end. If, indeed, in 1819, or immediately preceding 1819, gold had been at 5*l*. 10*s*. an ounce, no measure could have been more inexpedient than to make so violent a change in all subsisting engagements, as would have been made by restoring the ancient standard; but the

price of gold, as I have already said, was then, and had been
for four years, about 4*l.* 2*s.*, never above, and frequently rather
under, that price; and no measure could have been so mon-
strous as that which some reproach the House of Commons
for not having adopted, namely, of fixing the standard at
5*l.* 10*s.*; that is, in other words, after the currency had regained
its value within 5 per cent. of gold, under the operation of the
bad system, again to have degraded it to 30 per cent. below
the value of gold.

It will be remembered, that a plan was by me submitted to
the country, for the restoration of a fixed standard, which would
have rendered the employment of any greater quantity of gold
than the Bank then possessed wholly unnecessary.

That plan was to make the Bank liable to the payment of a
certain large and fixed amount of their notes in gold bullion,
at the Mint price of 3*l.* 17*s.* 10½*d.* an ounce, instead of payment
in gold coin. If that plan had been adopted, not a particle of
gold would have been used in the circulation,—all our money
must have consisted of paper, excepting the silver coin necessary for payments under the value of a pound. In that case
it is demonstrable, that the value of money could only have
been raised 5 per cent, by reverting to the fixed ancient standard,
for that was the whole difference between the value of gold
and paper. There was nothing in the plan which could cause
a rise in the value of gold, for no additional quantity of gold
would have been required, and therefore 5 per cent. would
have been the full extent of the rise in the value of money*.
Mr. Peel's bill adopted this plan for four years, after which

---

* With 4*l.* 2*s.* in bank notes any one could purchase precisely the same
quantity of commodities as with the gold in 3*l.* 17*s.* 10½*d.*; the object
of the plan was to make 3*l.* 17*s.* 10½*d.* in bank notes, as valuable as
3*l.* 17*s.* 10½*d.* in gold. To effect this object, could it have been necessary,
could it indeed have been possible, to lower the value of goods more
than 5 per cent., if the value of gold had not been raised?

payments in coin were to be established. If for the time specified by the bill, the Bank Directors had managed their affairs with the skill which the public interest required, they would have been satisfied with so regulating their issues, after Mr. Peel's bill passed, that the exchange should continue at par, and consequently no importation of gold could have taken place; but the Bank, who always expressed a decided aversion to[1] the plan of bullion payments, immediately commenced preparations for specie payments. Their issues were so regulated, that the exchange became extremely favourable to this country, gold flowed into it in a continued stream, and all that came the Bank eagerly purchased at 3*l.* 17*s.* 10½*d.* per ounce. Such a demand for gold could not fail to elevate its value, compared with the value of all commodities. Not only, then, had we to elevate the value of our currency 5 per cent., the amount of the difference between the value of paper and of gold before these operations commenced, but we had still further to elevate it to the new value to which gold itself was raised, by the injudicious purchases which the Bank made of that metal. It cannot, I think, be doubted, that if bullion payments had been fairly tried for three out of the four years, between 1819 and 1823, and had been found fully to answer all the objects of a currency regulated by gold at a fixed value; the same system would have been continued, and we should have escaped the further pressure which the country has undoubtedly undergone, from the effects of the great demand for gold which specie payments have[2] entailed upon us.

The Bank Directors urge in defence of the measures which they have pursued, the complaints which were made against them, on account of the frequent executions for forgery, which rendered it indispensable that they should withdraw the one-pound notes from circulation, for the purpose of replacing

---

[1] Eds. 1-2 'against' in place of 'to'.   [2] Eds. 1-2 'has'.

them with coin. If they could not substitute a note better calculated to prevent forgery, than the one which they have hitherto used, this plea is a valid one; for the sacrifice of a small pecuniary interest could not be thought too great, if it took away the temptation to the crime of forgery, for which so many unfortunate persons were annually executed; but this excuse comes with a bad grace from the Bank of England, who did not discover the importance of preventing forgery by the issue of coin till 1821, after they had made such large purchases of gold, that they were under the necessity of applying to Parliament for a bill, to enable them to issue coin in payment of their notes, which, by Mr. Peel's bill, they were prevented from doing till 1823. How comes it that they did not make this discovery in 1819, when the Committees of the Lords and Commons were sitting on Bank payments? Instead of being eager at that period to commence specie payments, they remonstrated, in a manner which many thought unbecoming, against any plan of metallic payments, which did not leave the uncontrolled power of increasing or diminishing the amount of the currency in their hands. It surely is not forgotten, that on an application by the Lords' Committee to the Bank, dated the 24th March, 1819, asking if "the Bank had any, and what objections to urge against the passing a law to require it should pay its notes in bullion on demand, but in sums not less in amount than 100*l.*, 200*l.*, or 300*l.*, at 3*l.* 17*s.* 10½*d.*, and to buy gold bullion at 3*l.* 17*s.* 6*d.* by an issue of its notes; the said plan to commence after a period to be fixed for that purpose;" the Directors answered, "The Bank has taken into consideration the question sent by the Committee of the House of Lords, under date of the 24th March, and is not aware of any difficulty in exchanging, for a fixed amount of bank notes, gold bullion of a certain weight, provided it be melted, assayed, and stamped by his Majesty's mint.

"The attainment of bullion by the Bank at 3*l.* 17*s.* 6*d.* is in the estimation of the Court so uncertain, that the Directors, in duty to their proprietors, do not feel themselves competent to engage to issue bullion at the price of 3*l.* 17*s.* 10½*d.*; but the Court beg leave to suggest, as an alternative, the expediency of its furnishing bullion of a fixed weight to the extent stated at the market price as taken on the preceding foreign post day, in exchange for its notes; provided a reasonable time be allowed for the Bank to prepare itself to try the effect of such a measure."[1]

If this proposal had been acceded to, the Bank would itself have determined the price at which it should have sold gold from time to time to the public, because by extending or curtailing their issues, they had the power to make the price of gold just what they pleased, 4*l.* or 10*l.* an ounce, and at that price to which they might choose to elevate it, they graciously proposed to sell it, "provided a reasonable time be allowed to prepare itself to try the effect of such a measure."

After this proposal, after the representation made to the Chancellor of the Exchequer by the Directors of the Bank of England on the 20th May, 1819*, it will not be said that the question of forgery appeared so urgent to the Directors that they were eager to substitute coin for their small notes in 1819, however important the question became in their view in 1820.

It is a question exceedingly difficult to determine what the effect has been on the value of gold, and consequently on the value of money produced by the purchases of bullion made by the Bank. When two commodities vary, it is impossible

* See Appendix, A.

[1] 'Second Report' from the Lords' Committee on the Resumption of Cash Payments, 12 May 1819, Appendix A. 8, p. 314; in *Parliamentary Papers*, 1819, vol. III.

to be certain whether one has risen, or the other fallen. There are no means of even approximating to the knowledge of this fact, but by a careful comparison of the value of the two commodities, during the period of their variation, with the value of many other commodities.

Even this comparison does not afford a certain test, because one half of the commodities to which they are compared, may have varied in one direction, while the other half may have varied in another: by which half shall the variation of gold be tried? If by one it appears to have risen, if by the other to have fallen. From observations, however, on the price of silver, and of various other commodities, making due allowance for the particular causes which may have specially operated on the value of each, Mr. Tooke, one of the most intelligent witnesses examined by the Agricultural Committee, came to the conclusion that the eager demand for gold made by the Bank in order to substitute coin for their small notes, had raised the value of currency about five per cent.[1] In this conclusion, I quite concur with Mr. Tooke. If it be well founded, the whole increased value of our currency since the passing of Mr. Peel's bill in 1819, may be estimated at about ten per cent. To that amount, taxation has been increased by the measure for restoring specie payment; to that amount the fall of grain, and with it of all other commodities has taken place as far as this cause alone has operated on them; but all above that amount, all the further depression which the price of corn has sustained, must be accounted for by the supply having exceeded the demand; a depression, which would have equally occurred, if no alteration whatever had been made in the value of the currency.

It is, indeed, alleged by many of the landed interest, that

[1] Tooke actually said 'About six per cent.', according to the 'Minutes of Evidence' before the Agricultural Committee of 1821, p. 296.

to one cause alone, all the distress in agriculture is to be ascribed. They go so far as to say, that there is now no surplus produce on the land, but what is paid to the Government for taxes; that there is nothing whatever left for rent or profit; that what-ever rent is paid, is derived from the capital of the farmer, and all these effects they charge on the alteration in the value of the currency.

It is evident that those who advance this most extravagant proposition, do not know how the alteration in the value of the currency affects the different interests of a country. If it injures the debtor, it in the same degree benefits the creditor; if its pressure is felt by the tenant, it must be advantageous to the landlord, and to the receivers of taxes. They, then, who maintain this doctrine, must be prepared to contend that all that fund, which formerly constituted the rent of the landlord, and the profits of the farmer, are, by the alteration in the value of money, transferred to the State, and are now paid to the receivers of taxes, and, among them, the stock-holders. That the situation of the stock-holder is improved, by his dividends being paid in a currency increased in value, there can be no doubt; but what evidence is there to shew that his situation is so much improved, that he has now at his disposal, in addition to his former means of enjoyment, all those which were before at the disposal of the whole of the tenantry, and of the land-lords of the country? So wild an assertion cannot be for a moment entertained; we have not heard of splendid equipages and superb mansions having been built by the stock-holders since, and in consequence of, the Bill of 1819. Besides, if this were true, how comes it that the profits of the merchant and manufacturer have escaped the fund-holder, this devouring monster, as he has been called?[1] Are not their profits governed

[1] The 'all-devouring monster' is Cobbett's description of the fund-holder. (*Cobbett's Weekly Political Register*, 2 March 1822, p. 517.)

by the same principle, and by the same law, as the profits of the farmer? How have they contrived to exempt themselves from this desolating storm? The answer is plain, there is no truth in the allegation. Agriculture has been depressed by causes of which the currency forms only a little part. The peculiar hardships which the landed interest are suffering, are of a temporary character, and will continue only while the supply of produce exceeds the demand. A remunerative price is impossible while this cause of low value continues; but the situation of things which we now witness cannot have any permanence.

Is it not quite certain, that if the pressure on the farmers, from the alteration in the value of currency, and the increased taxation consequent upon it, has been so great as to take from them all the profits of their capital, it must also have taken away the profits of all other persons employing capital? for it is quite impossible that one set of capitalists should be permanently without any profit at all, whilst others are making reasonable profits.

On the part of the landlords it may be said, that they are encumbered with fixed charges on their estates, such as dowers, provision for daughters, and younger children, mortgages, &c. It cannot be denied that an alteration in the value of currency must greatly affect such engagements, and must be very burdensome to landlords; but they should remember that they or their fathers benefited by the depreciation of the value of the currency. All their fixed engagements, their taxes included, were for many years paid in the depreciated medium. If they suffer injustice now, they profited by injustice at a former period; and if the account were fairly made up, it would, I believe, be found that, as far as alteration in the value of currency is concerned, they have little just cause for complaint.

But, on the score of money engagements, which are now

affected by the increased value of currency, have the commercial interest no cause for complaint? Are they not debtors in as large an amount as the landed interest? How many persons have retired from business, whose capitals are, directly or indirectly, still employed by their successors? What vast sums are employed by bankers and others in discounting bills? For the whole of this value there must be debtors, and the increased value of money could not have failed very much to aggravate the pressure of their debts.

I mention these circumstances to shew that if the real efficient cause of the distress of the landed gentlemen was the increased value of money, it ought to have produced similar distress in other quarters;—it has not done so, and therefore I have a right to infer, that the cause of the distress has been mistaken.

The profits of the farmer must bear some uniform proportion to the profits of the other classes of capitalists; they are subject to temporary fluctuations, perhaps, in a greater degree than the profits of others; but the circumstances of which they complain, though severe and aggravated at the present time by other causes, yet are by no means new or uncommon.

Mr. Tooke, in his evidence before the Agricultural Committee, in pages 230 and 231, has furnished us with extracts from publications in the last century, in which the ruin of the landed interest was foretold in terms not very unlike those used in the present day. Those difficulties have passed, and the present ones will, with a little good legislation, soon only be matter of history.

At a late Court of Proprietors of Bank Stock, the Directors said that, so far from having reduced the amount of the circulation since 1819, they had considerably increased it, and that it was this year actually more by 3,000,000*l.* than the amount of the circulation at the same period last year, or the year preceding.[1] If the Directors were quite correct in this statement, it is no answer to the charge of their having kept the circulation too low, and thereby caused the great influx of gold. My question to them is, "Was your circulation so high as to keep the exchange at par?" To this they must answer in the negative; and therefore I say, that if in consequence of the importation of gold, that metal is enhanced in value, and the pressure on the country is thereby increased, it is because the Bank did not issue a sufficient quantity of notes to keep the exchange at par. This charge is of the same force whether the amount of bank-notes has, in point of fact, been stationary, increasing, or diminishing.

But I dispute the fact of the circulation having been even half a million higher in amount in 1822, than in 1821 and 1820. The mode of proving the proposition, adopted by the Bank, is not satisfactory; they say, in 1821 we had 23,800,000*l.* in circulation, and now the notes in circulation, with the sovereigns we have since issued, amount to 3,000,000*l.* more. But as sovereigns are circulated in Ireland, and in other districts of the United Kingdom, how can they affirm, that in the same channel in which 23,800,000*l.* bank-notes circulated in 1821, 26,800,000 bank-notes and sovereigns together, are now in circulation? I believe the contrary to be the fact, for I find

[1] At the Bank Court of Proprietors held on 21 March 1822, in reply to criticisms of the Bank by Alderman Heygate, 'The Governor remarked, that he happened accidentally to have a paper in his hand, which would, he trusted, convince the hon. alderman, that if the Bank had erred, it was not on the side of a reduction of the circulating medium; for upon looking at the amount of their issues, he found, that on the 9th of March, 1822, their issues exceeded, by the sum of 3,859,000 l., those of the same date in the preceding year (March 9, 1821), and that the latter exceeded the issues of the 9th of March, 1820, by the sum of 3,444,000 l. (Hear.) It was therefore quite clear, that the repayment of the Government debt called for in July, 1819, did not induce the Bank to diminish their issues, for they had been increasing them in the years which had since followed.' (*The Times*, 22 March 1822.)

that the amount of notes of five pounds and above, which have been in circulation for several years past, in the month of February is as follows:—

Years	£.
1815 —	16,394,359
1816 —	15,307,228
1817 —	17,538,656
1818 —	19,077,951
1819 —	16,148,098
1820 —	15,393,770
1821 —	15,766,270
1822 —	15,784,770

And as the notes of five pounds and upwards have not increased 400,000*l.* since 1820, I find it impossible to believe that the circulation of a smaller denomination can have increased in any much larger proportion.

Before I conclude this section I must observe that the complaints made against the Bank for refusing to lend money on discount at four per cent. are without any good foundation. The reason for such complaints is, that by lending at four per cent. they would lower the rate of interest generally, and the landed interest would be benefited by being able to raise money on mortgage on cheaper terms than they now pay for it. I believe, however, that no amount of loans which the Bank might make, and no degree of lowness of interest at which they might choose to lend, would alter the permanent rate of interest in the market. Interest is regulated chiefly by the profits that may be made by the use of capital, it cannot be controlled by any bank, nor by any assemblage of banks. During the last war the market rate of interest for money was, for years together, fluctuating between seven and ten per cent.; yet the Bank never lent at a rate above five per cent. In Ireland the Bank by its charter is obliged to lend, at a rate of interest not exceeding five per cent., yet all other persons lend at six per cent.

A Bank has fulfilled all its useful functions when it has

substituted paper in the circulation for gold; when it has enabled us to carry on our commerce with a cheap currency, and to employ the valuable one which it supplants productively: provided it fulfils this object it is of little importance at what rate of interest it lends its money.

One argument used by a very enlightened member of Parliament, during a late discussion on the rate of interest charged by the Bank, was rather a singular one; he said that the Bank of France, and other Banks on the Continent, lent at a low rate, and therefore, the Bank of England should do so.[1] I can see no connexion between his premises and conclusion. The Bank of France ought to be[2] governed by the market rate of interest and the rate of profits in France; the Bank of England by the market rate of interest and the rate of profit in England. One may be very different from the other. From the whole of his argument, I should infer that he considered a low rate of interest, in itself, beneficial to a country. The very contrary, I imagine, is the truth. A low rate of interest is a symptom of a great accumulation of capital; but it is also a symptom of a low rate of profits, and of an advancement to a stationary state; at which the wealth and resources of a country will not admit of increase. As[3] all savings are made from profits, as a country is most happy when it is in a rapidly progressive state, profits and interest cannot be too high. It would be a poor consolation indeed to a country for low profits and low interest, that landlords were enabled to raise money on mort-

[1] This argument was used by J. A. Stuart Wortley, M.P. for Yorkshire, in presenting a petition for the relief of agricultural distress on 1 April 1822 (*Hansard*, N.S., VI, 1402). Huskisson supported him with a similar argument (*ib.* 1405).

[2] Ed. 1 'is' in place of 'ought to be'.

[3] In place of the last four lines ed. 1 reads 'A low rate of interest is a symptom of a low rate of profits. But, as' etc. Eds. 2–3 are uniform with ed. 4, except that they open the second sentence with 'But, as' in place of 'As'.

gage with diminished sacrifices. Nothing contributes so much to the prosperity and happiness of a country as high profits.

This complaint against the Bank, which comes, I think, with an ill grace from a Member of Parliament, as representing the public interest, might be consistently urged by a Bank proprietor at a general meeting of their body, for it is difficult to account on what principle of advantage to the concern which they manage, the Directors can think it right to lend their proprietors['] money at three per cent. to Government* when they could obtain four per cent. from other borrowers; but with this the public have no concern, and they and their proprietors should be left to settle this matter as they please.

SECTION VI

On the Effects of a Low Value of Corn on the Rate of Profits

WHEN I use the term—a low value of corn, I wish to be clearly understood. I consider the value of corn to be low, when a large quantity is the result of a moderate quantity of labour. In proportion, as for a given quantity of labour a smaller quantity of corn is obtained, corn will rise in value. In the progress of society there are two opposite causes operating on the value of corn; one, the increase of population, and the necessity of cultivating, at an increased charge, land of an inferior quality, which always occasions a rise in the value of corn; the other, improvements in agriculture, or the discovery of new and abundant foreign markets, which always tend to lower the value. Sometimes one predominates, sometimes the other, and the value of corn rises or falls accordingly.

* The Bank are now in advance[1] many millions to the Government on Exchequer Bills at three per cent., besides the fixed advance of their capital, also at three per cent.; which latter they are, by their charter, obliged to lend at that rate of interest.
[1] Should be 'to advance'; see, for the proposed advance, below, V, 129, 133.

In speaking of the value of corn, I mean something rather different from its price;—when its value rises, its price generally rises, and would always do so, if money, in which price is uniformly estimated, were invariable in value. But corn may not vary as compared with all other things—it may not be the result of either more or less labour, and yet it may rise or fall in price, because money may become more plentiful and cheap, or more scarce and dear. Nothing is of so little importance to the community collectively, as an alteration in the *price* of corn, caused by an alteration in the value of money merely; nothing of greater importance, as far as its profits and its wealth are concerned, than a rise or fall in the price of corn, when money continues of a fixed and invariable value. We will suppose money to continue at a fixed and invariable value, that we may ascertain the effects of a rise or fall in the value of corn; which on this supposition will be synonymous with a rise or fall in its price.

Corn being one of the chief articles on which the wages of labour are expended, its value, to a great degree, regulates wages. Labour itself is subject to a fluctuation of value, in the same manner as every thing which is the subject of demand and supply, but it is also particularly affected by the price of the necessaries of the labourer; and corn, as I have already observed, is amongst the principal of those necessaries. In a former section[1] I have endeavoured to shew, that a general rise of wages will not raise the prices of commodities on which labour is expended. If wages rose in one trade, the commodity produced in that trade must rise, to place the producer of it on a par with all other trades; but when wages affect all producers alike, a rise in the value of all their commodities must, as I have on a former occasion remarked, be a matter of great indifference to them, as whether they were all at a high price

[1] Section II.

or all at a low price, their relative values would be the same, and it is the alteration of their relative values only which gives to the holders of them a greater or less command of goods. Every man exchanges his goods, finally, for other goods, or for labour, and he cares little whether he sells his own goods at a high price if he is obliged to give a high price for the goods he purchases, or sells them at a low price, if, at the same time, he can also procure the goods he wants at a low price. In either case his enjoyments are the same.

With a permanently high price of corn, caused by increased labour on the land, wages would be high; and, as commodities would not rise on account of the rise of wages, profits would necessarily fall. If goods worth 1000*l.* require at one time labour which cost 800*l.*, and at another the price of the same quantity of labour is raised to 900*l.*, profits will fall from 200*l.* to 100*l.* Profits would not fall in one trade only, but in all. High wages, when general, equally affect the profits of the farmer, the manufacturer, and the merchant. There is no other way of keeping profits up but by keeping wages down. In this view of the law of profits, it will at once be seen how important it is that so essential a necessary as corn, which so powerfully affects wages, should be at a low price; and how injurious it must be to the community generally, that, by prohibitions against importation, we should be driven to the cultivation of our poorer lands to feed our augmenting population.

Besides the impolicy of devoting a greater portion of our labour to the production of food than would otherwise be necessary, thereby diminishing the sum of our enjoyments and the power of saving,[1] by lowering profits, we offer an irresistible temptation to capitalists to quit this country, that they may take their capitals to places where wages are low and profits high. If landlords could be sure of the prices of corn remaining

[1] Ed. 1 'saving;'.

steadily high, which happily they cannot be, they would have an interest opposed to every other class in the community; for a high price, proceeding from difficulty of production, is the main cause of the rise of rent: not that the rise of rent, the advantage gained by the landlord, is an equivalent for the disadvantage imposed on the other classes of the community, in being prevented from importing cheap corn; we have not that consolation: for to give a moderate advantage to one class, a most oppressive burthen must be laid on all the other classes.

This advantage to the landlords themselves would be more apparent than real; for, to complete the advantage, they should be able to calculate on steady as well as high prices. Nothing is so injurious to tenants as constantly fluctuating prices, and under a system of protection to the landlord, and prohibition against the importation of foreign corn, tenants must be exposed to the most injurious fluctuations of profits, as I shall attempt to shew in the next Section. When the profits of a farmer are high, he is induced to live more profusely, and to make his arrangements as if his good fortune were always to continue; but a reverse is sure to come: he has then to suffer from his former improvidence, and he finds himself entangled in expenses, which render him utterly unable to fulfil his engagements with his landlord.

The landlord's rent is, indeed, nominally high, but he is frequently in the situation of not being able to realize it; and little doubt can exist, that a more moderate and steady price of corn, with regular profits to the tenant, would afford to the landlord the best security for his happiness and comfort, if not for the receipt of the largest amount of rent.

It appears, then, that a high but steady price of corn is most advantageous to the landlord; but, as steadiness in a country situated as ours, is nearly incompatible with a price high in this country, as compared with other countries, a more moderate price is really for his interest. Nothing can be more clearly established, than that low prices of corn are for the interest of the farmer, and of every other class of society; high prices are incompatible with low wages, and high wages cannot exist with high profits.

I must here notice an error, which has been supported by one of those, whose talents give them great authority in the place where the opinion was delivered;[1] it is, that though the manufacturer has it in his power to raise the price of his commodity when it is taxed, and even, on some occasions, to profit by its being taxed, yet the farmer cannot so indemnify himself, and that, consequently at the end of his lease, if not before, the whole weight of the tax must fall on his landlord. This is an error of long standing, for it is supported by no less an authority than Adam Smith.[2] The subject of rent, and the laws by which its fall and rise are regulated, have been explained since the time of Adam Smith; and all those men who are acquainted with this explanation, are incapable of falling into the error. I am not now going into the question of rent; that subject has been well elucidated by several able writers. But I would ask those who still adhere to Adam Smith's doctrine, on whom the tax on land could fall when it was equal to three shillings per acre, if the land cultivated were of the description mentioned by Mr. Harvey in his evidence, and to which I have already referred;[3] land for which eighteen-pence only is paid as rent? The farmer must either get lower profits than other farmers who pay higher rents, or he must be able to transfer this charge to the consumer. But why should he remain in an occupation in which his profits are below the

---

[1] See Brougham's speech on the distressed state of the country, 11 Feb. 1822 (*Hansard*, N.S., VI, 240 and 243-4); and cp. Ricardo's speech on the same occasion, below, V, 124-5.

[2] See quotations given in *Principles*, above, I, 183-4.

[3] Above, p. 210.

profits of all other capitalists in the community? He might require time to remove himself from an unprofitable employment; but he would not perseveringly continue in it, more than any other person similarly circumstanced in other occupations.

I have taken the instance mentioned by Mr. Harvey, because, as he is a practical man, weight will be given to his information; but I am myself fully persuaded that a large quantity of corn is raised in every country, for the privilege of raising which, no rent whatever is paid. Every farmer is at liberty to employ an additional portion of capital on his land after all that which is necessary for affording his rent, has already been employed. The corn raised with this capital, can only afford the usual profits if no rent is paid out of it. Impose a tax on producing it, without admitting a compensation by a rise of price, and that moment you offer an inducement to the withdrawing of that portion of capital from the land, thereby diminishing the supply. No point is more satisfactorily established in my opinion, than that every tax imposed on the production of raw produce falls ultimately on the consumer, in the same way as taxes on the production of manufactured commodities fall on the consumers of those articles.

SECTION VII

Under a system of Protecting Duties established with a view to give the Monopoly of the Home Market to the Home Grower of Corn, Prices cannot be otherwise than fluctuating

PROTECTING duties on the importation of corn must always be imposed on the supposition that corn is cheaper in foreign countries, by the amount of such duties; and that if they were not imposed[1], foreign corn would be imported. If foreign

[1] Ed. 1 misprints 'imported' for 'imposed'.

corn were not cheaper, no protecting duty would be necessary, for, under a system of free trade, it would not be imported. To the amount, then, of the protecting duty, the ordinary and average price of corn must be supposed to be[1] higher in the country imposing it than in others, and when abundant harvests occur, before any corn can be exported from a country so circumstanced, corn must fall from its usual and average price, not only by the amount of the duty, but also by the further amount of the expenses of exporting the corn. Under a system of free trade, the price of corn in two countries could not materially differ more than the expenses attending the exportation of it from one country to the other; and therefore, if an abundant harvest occurred in either, and was not common to both, after an inconsiderable fall of price, a vent for the superfluous produce would be immediately found in exportation. But under a system of protecting duties, or of prohibitory laws, the fall in the price of corn from an abundant crop, or from a succession of abundant crops, must be ruinous to the grower, before he can relieve himself by exportation. If we could listen to Mr. Webb Hall's recommendation of a fixed duty of 40s., on the importation of foreign corn;[2] and if he be right in supposing that 40s. is the difference of the natural price of corn in England and in the corn countries, on every occasion of abundant harvests, corn must actually fall 40s., before it can be the interest of any party to export it to the Continent; a fall so great that, if the farmers were subjected to it, they would be totally unable to pay their rents in abundant seasons, without a great sacrifice of capital.

---

[1] From here ed. 1 reads 'higher in the importing, than in the exporting, country; and before any corn can be exported from the country which imposes the protecting duty, corn must fall from its usual' etc.

[2] See the evidence of George Webb Hall, Secretary of the Board of Agriculture, before the Agricultural Committee of 1821, 'Minutes of Evidence', pp. 164–5.

The same observation is applicable to the present corn law, which prohibits importation till the price rises to 80s. The effect of this law is to make the price of corn in this country habitually and considerably above the price in other countries; and therefore, on occasion of abundant crops, it must fall below the price of those other countries, before any relief can be afforded to the grower by exportation. Its effect, indeed, in this view, is precisely the same as that of the high-fixed duty which we have been already considering.

But the present law has another capital defect, from which the system of fixed duties is free. When the average price of wheat reaches 80s. per quarter, the ports are now open for three months, for an unlimited importation of foreign wheat, duty free. With prices somewhat about 40s. per quarter on the Continent, in average years, the temptation to import into this country, during the three months that the ports are open, must operate to the introduction of an enormous quantity.

During these three months, and for a very considerable time afterwards, for the effect cannot cease with the shutting of the ports, the home grower and the foreign grower are placed in a state of free competition, to the ruin of the former. By prohibitory duties he is encouraged to employ his capital on the poorer lands of this country, which require a great expense for a small produce; and when he has an unusually short crop, and most stands in need of a high price, he is all at once exposed to the free competition of the grower of corn on the Continent, to whom a price of 40s. would be amply sufficient to compensate him for the whole cost of production. A system of fixed duties protects the farmer against this particular danger, but it leaves him exposed, in the same degree as on the present system, to all the evils which arise from abundant crops, and which can never fail to accompany every plan of a corn law, which shall elevate the price of corn in the country in which they prevail, considerably above the level of the prices of other countries.

It must not be supposed, however, that to obviate this difficulty, the importation of corn should be at all times allowed without the payment of any duty whatever; that is not under our circumstances, the course which I should recommend. I have already shewn in Section 3, that with a view to the real interest of the consumer, in which the interests of the whole community are, and ever must be, included, whenever any peculiar tax falls on the produce of any one commodity, from the effects of which all other producers are exempted, a counter-vailing duty to that amount, but no more, should on every just principle be imposed on the importation of such commodity; and further, that a drawback should be allowed, to the same amount also on the exportation of the like commodity. If, before any taxation, the remunerating price of wheat was 60s. per quarter, both in England and on the Continent, and in consequence of the imposition of a tax, such as tithes, falling exclusively on the farmer, and not on any other producer, wheat was raised in England to 70s., a duty of 10s. should be also imposed on the importation of foreign corn. This tax on foreign corn, and on home corn also, should be drawn back on exportation. However large the aggregate amount might be of the drawback given to the exporter it would only be returning to him a tax which he had before paid, and which he must have to place him in a fair state of competition in the foreign markets, not only with the foreign producer, but with his own countrymen who are producing other commodities. It is essentially different from a bounty on exportation, in the sense that the word bounty is usually understood; for by a bounty is generally meant a tax levied on the people for the purpose of rendering corn unnaturally cheap to the foreign consumer, whereas, what I propose, is to sell our corn at the price at which we can really afford to produce it, and not to add to its price a tax which shall induce the foreigner rather to purchase it from some other country, and deprive us of a trade, which, under a system of free competition, we might have selected.

The duty which I have here proposed, is the only legitimate countervailing duty, which neither offers inducements to capital to quit a trade, in which for us it is the most beneficially employed, nor holds out any temptations to employ an undue proportion of capital in a trade to which it would not otherwise have been destined. The course of trade would be left precisely on the same footing as if we were wholly an untaxed country, and every person was at liberty to employ his capital and skill in the way he should think most beneficial to himself. We cannot now help living under a system of heavy taxation, but to make our industry as productive to us as possible, we should offer no temptations to capitalists, to employ their funds and their skill in any other way than they would have employed them, if we had had the good fortune to be untaxed, and had been permitted to give the greatest development to our talents and industry.

The Report of the Committee on Agricultural Distress in 1821, contains some excellent statements and reasonings on this subject.

To that important document I can with confidence refer, in support of the principles which I am endeavouring to lay down on the impolicy of protecting corn laws. The arguments in it in favour of freedom of trade, appear to me unanswerable; but it must be confessed, that in that same Report, recommendations are made utterly inconsistent with those principles.[1]

After condemning restrictions on trade, it recommends

[1] On the contradiction between the arguments and recommendations of this Report, see Ricardo's speech of 3 April 1822, below, V, 151–2.

measures of permanent restriction; after shewing the evils resulting from prematurely taking poor lands into cultivation, it countenances a system, which, at all sacrifices, is to keep them in tillage. In principle, nothing so odious as monopoly and restriction; in practice, nothing so salutary and desirable.

The Committee on Agriculture this year avoid taking any notice of the sound doctrines entertained by the last Committee, but have founded their whole Report on the erroneous ones; and conclude their recommendations to the House in the following words:—"If the circumstances of this country should hereafter allow the trade in corn to be permanently settled upon a footing constantly open to all the world, *but subject to such a fixed and uniform duty as might compensate to the British grower the difference of expense at which his corn can be raised and brought to market, together with the fair rate of profit upon the capital employed, compared with the expense of production, and other charges attending corn grown and imported from abroad, such a* system would, in many respects, be preferable to any modification of regulations depending upon average prices, with an ascending and descending scale of duties; because it would prevent the effects of combination and speculation, in endeavouring to raise or depress those averages, and render immaterial those inaccuracies which from management or negligence have occasionally produced, and may again produce such mischievous effects upon our market; but your Committee rather look forward to such a system as fit to be kept in view for the ultimate tendency of our law, than as practicable within any short or definite period."[1]

---

[1] '1822. Report from the Select Committee appointed to inquire into the allegations of the Several Petitions presented to the House in the last and present Sessions of Parliament, complaining of the distressed State of the Agriculture of the United Kingdom', 1 April 1822, p. 8; in *Parliamentary Papers*, 1822, vol. v. The italics are Ricardo's.

The system which we are to keep in view for the ultimate tendency of our law, we are told, is one of a fixed duty; but on what principle is the fixed duty to be calculated? not on that which I have endeavoured to shew is the only sound one, namely, that the duty should accurately countervail the peculiar burthens to which the grower of corn is subject, but a fixed duty which should compensate to the British grower the difference of expense at which his corn can be raised and brought to market, compared with the expense of production, and other charges, attending corn grown and imported from abroad. Instead of holding out any hope to the consumer, that we shall at any future time legislate on a principle which shall enable him to purchase corn at as cheap a price as British industry shall be enabled to obtain it for him; instead of giving any security to the British capitalist, that wages shall not be unnaturally raised in this country, by obliging the labourer to purchase corn at a dear, and not at a cheap rate, a security so essential to the keeping up the rate of profits; instead of bidding the farmer look forward to a time when he will be spared from the fluctuations in the price of the commodity which he raises, and which are so destructive to his interests; we are told that the present mode in which the price of corn is kept in this country habitually and considerably above its price in other countries, is not, perhaps, the best mode of effecting that object, as it may be more conveniently done, by means of a fixed duty, instead of a varying duty; but at any rate, corn is to be rendered habitually and considerably dearer in this country, than in others. A duty calculated upon the principle of the Committee cannot fail to perpetuate a difference of price between this and other countries, equal to the difference of expense of growing corn in this country beyond the expense of growing it in others. If we had not already pushed the endeavour of providing food for ourselves too far,—if we had not by our own acts made the expense of growing corn in this country greater than in others, such a law would be nugatory, because no difference of expense would exist. Is it not then in the highest degree absurd, first to pass a law under the operation of which the necessity is created of cultivating poor lands, and then having so cultivated them at a great expense, make that additional expense the ground for refusing ever to purchase corn from those who can afford to produce it at a cheaper price? I can produce a quantity of cloth which affords me a remunerating price at sixty pounds, which I can sell to a foreign country, if I will lay out the proceeds in the purchase of thirty quarters of wheat at two pounds per quarter, but I am refused permission to do so, and am obliged, by the operation of a law, to employ the capital which yielded me sixty pounds in cloth, in raising fifteen quarters of wheat at four pounds per quarter.

The exchange of the cloth for wheat, the production of the cloth[1] is wholly prevented by the countervailing duty of two pounds per quarter on the importation of wheat, which obliges me to raise the corn, and prevents me from employing my capital in the making of cloth for the purpose of exchanging it for wheat.

It is true, indeed, that in both cases I raise a commodity worth sixty pounds, and to those who look only at money, and not money's worth, either of these employments of my capital appears equally productive, but a moment's reflection will convince us that there is the greatest difference imaginable between obtaining (with the same quantity of labour, mind) thirty quarters of wheat, and fifteen quarters, although either should, under the circumstances supposed, be worth sixty pounds.

If the principle recommended by the Committee were con-

[1] Eds. 1-2 'of the cloth even,'.

sistently followed, there is no commodity whatever which we can raise at home, which we should ever import from abroad; we should cultivate beet-root and make our own sugar, and impose a duty on the importation of sugar equal to the difference of expense of growing sugar here, and growing it in the East or West Indies. We should erect hot-houses, and raise our own grapes for the purpose of making wine, and protect the maker of wine by the same course of policy. Either the doctrine is untenable in the case of corn, or it is to be justified in all other cases. Does the purchaser of a commodity ever inquire concerning the terms on which the producer can afford to raise or make it? His only consideration is the price at which he can purchase it. When he knows that, he knows the cheapest mode of obtaining it; if he can himself produce it cheaper than he can purchase it, he will devote himself to its production rather than to the production of the commodity with which he, in fact, must otherwise purchase it.

But there are persons, and of the number of those too who are considered of authority on these matters, who say this reasoning would be correct if we were about to employ capital on the land with a view to obtain more corn; that then it would, undoubtedly, be wise to consider whether we could purchase it from abroad cheaper than we could grow it at home, and govern our proceedings accordingly, but that when capital has been expended on the land, it is quite another question; since much of that capital would be lost if we then resolved rather to import cheap corn from abroad than grow it at a dear price at home. That some capital would be lost cannot be disputed, but is the possession or preservation of capital the end, or the means? The means, undoubtedly. What we want is an abundance of commodities, and if it could be proved that by the sacrifice of a part of our capital we should augment the annual produce of those objects which contribute to our enjoyment and happiness, we ought not, I should think, to repine at the loss of a part of our capital.

Mr. Leslie has invented an ingenious apparatus, by the use of which we might fill our ice-houses with ice.[1] Suppose a capital of half a million were expended on these machines, would it not nevertheless be wise in us, to get our ice, without any expense, from the frozen ponds in our neighbourhoods, rather than employ the labour, and waste the acid or other ingredients in the manufacture of ice, although, by so doing, we should for ever sacrifice the 500,000*l.* which we had expended on air-pumps?

In this recommendation, which must have the effect of perpetuating the difference between the price of corn here and its price in other countries, we should naturally conclude that the Committee did not admit the evils which, from time to time, must thence inevitably arise in this country. Quite the contrary; they admit them to the fullest extent, and they refer to the statements made on that subject in a former report, for the purpose of expressing their approbation of the reasoning which is founded on them. They say,[2] "the excessive inconvenience and impolicy of our present system have been so fully treated, and so satisfactorily exposed in the Report already alluded to[3] (p. 10 and 12,) that it is unnecessary to do more than to refer to it; adding only, that every thing which has happened subsequent to the presentation of that Report, as well as all our experience since 1815, has more and more tended to demonstrate how little reliance can be placed upon a regulation which contains an absolute prohibition up to a certain price, and an unlimited competition beyond that price; which, so far from affording steadiness to our market, *may at one time reduce*

---

[1] Professor John Leslie described his 'process of artificial congelation' in the *Supplement to the Encyclopædia Britannica*, vol. III (article 'Cold') published in 1818.

[2] Agricultural Report of 1822, p. 6. The italics are Ricardo's.

[3] The Agricultural Report of 1821.

prices, already too low, still lower than they might have been even under a free trade; and at another, unnecessarily enhance the prices already too high, which tends to aggravate the evils of scarcity, *and render more severe the depression of profits[1] from abundance.*"

Here the two evils of our corn law are very fairly stated; and against one of them, that of unlimited competition beyond the price of 80s., a remedy, though by no means the best which might have been temporarily established, is recommended; but, instead of suggesting any means of alleviating or remedying the other evil, proceeding from abundance, which is so fully acknowledged, measures are recommended for immediate and temporary adoption; and others are suggested as desirable to be at a future time permanently adopted, which cannot fail to perpetuate this evil, because they cannot fail to make the price of corn constantly and considerably higher in this than in any other neighbouring country.

One of the grounds advanced for high duties on the importation of corn is, that the manufacturer is protected by high duties against the competition of the foreign manufacturer, and that the cultivator of the soil should have a similar protection against the foreign grower of corn. To this it is impossible to give an answer in language more satisfactory than has been done by Lord Grenville.

"If the measures which had formerly been adopted for the protection of trade and manufactures were right, let them be continued; if wrong, let them be abrogated; not suddenly, but with that caution with which all policy, however erroneous, so engrafted into our usage by time, should be changed; but let it be consecrated as a principle of legislation, that in no case should the grounds for advising the Legislature to afford any particular protection, rest on the protection which might have

---

[1] The Report reads 'prices'.

been afforded in any other quarter. In fact, he could not well conceive how the noble earl[1] could argue[2], that measures which he admitted to have been wrong with respect to manufactures, would nevertheless be right with respect to Agriculture.

"It would be an extraordinary mode of doing justice, thus to declare that, because a large, the largest, part of the community were already oppressed by favours shewn to one particular class, they should be still farther oppressed by favours shewn to another particular class."—*Speech*, March 15, 1815.[3]

If any thing more is required against this pretension of protection for the land, it is furnished in the following passage of the Report of the Agricultural Committee of last year:[4]

"They, (the Committee), observe, that one of the witnesses, in order to illustrate his ideas and the wishes of the petitioners, has furnished a table of the duties payable on foreign manufactured articles, of which several are subject to duties of excise in this country; and upon which the importation duty, as, for instance, upon the article of glass, is imposed in a great measure to countervail the duty upon that article manufactured in this kingdom.

"But the main ground upon which your Committee are disposed to think that the House will look with some mistrust to the soundness of this principle, is—first, that it may be well doubted, whether (with the exception of silk) any of our considerable manufactures derive benefit from this assumed protection in the markets of this country: for how could the foreign manufactures of cotton, of woollens, of hardware, compete with our own in this country, when it is notorious that we can afford to undersell them in the products of those great branches of our manufacturing industry, even in their own

---

[1] The Earl of Liverpool.
[2] Ed. 1 misprints 'agree'.

[3] In the Lords' debate on the Corn Bill (*Hansard*, XXX, 190–1).
[4] Agricultural Report, 1821, p. 23.

markets, notwithstanding that cotton and wool are subject to a direct duty on importation, not drawn back upon their export in a manufactured state, as well as to all the indirect taxation, which affects capital in these branches, in common with that capital which is employed in raising the productions of the soil?"

This is followed by other passages which are excellent, and all[1] tend to shew, that the protection which manufactures are said to possess, is not really afforded them; though, if it were, Lord Grenville's argument is conclusive against that being a ground for extending protection to agriculture.

It is to be hoped that we shall, even in the present Session of Parliament, get rid of many of these injurious laws; a better spirit of legislation appears likely to prevail in the present day; and that absurd jealousy which influenced our forefathers, will give way to the pleasing conviction, that we can never, by freedom of commerce, promote the welfare of other countries without also promoting our own.

The passage from the Report is useful in another respect: it shews us that the writer of it understood well what a countervailing duty is, and should be; for he states that the duty on the importation of glass "is imposed in a great measure to countervail the duty upon that article manufactured in this kingdom." How is this passage to be reconciled with the recommendation in both Reports, that, in imposing a duty on the importation of corn, "it should be calculated fairly to countervail the difference of expense, including the ordinary rate of profit, at which corn, in the present state of this country, *can be grown and brought to market*[2] within the United Kingdom, compared with the expense, including also the ordinary rate of profit, of producing it in any of those countries from whence

[1] Eds. 1-2 'the whole' in place of 'all'.   [2] Ricardo's italics.

our principal supplies of foreign corn have usually been drawn, joined to the ordinary charge of conveying it from thence to our markets"?[1]

SECTION VIII

On the Project of advancing Money on Loan, to Speculators in Corn, at a low Interest

IT is allowed by the Report, that "the universal rule of allowing all articles, as much as possible, to find their own natural level, by leaving the supply to adjust itself to the demand," discouraged the Committee from recommending that government should employ money, in making purchases of corn, with a view to sell it when the price rose; but the Committee do not appear to have seen that the same universal rule, of which they speak with approbation, ought to have discouraged them also from recommending that government should advance money, at a low rate of interest, to persons who should purchase wheat, to deposit it in the King's warehouses, while it was under 60s. per quarter.[2]

Will not such an advance of money at a low rate of interest, and for twelve months certain, if the parties desire it, prevent the article from "finding its own level," and "will the supply be left to adjust itself to the demand?"

If the cause of the low price of corn be owing to an abundant quantity in the country, and not to an abundant quantity hurried prematurely to market by the distress of the farmers, the proposed remedy will be really mischievous, as in that case we must go through the ordeal of low prices, and increased consumption, which is always in a degree consequent on low

---

[1] This quotation is from the Agricultural Report of 1821, p. 16; for the corresponding recommendation in the Agricultural Report of 1822, see above, p. 245.

[2] Agricultural Report, 1822, p. 4.

price, before the supply will adjust itself to the demand, and prices become again remunerative. By the encouragement thus given to storing corn for a twelvemonth, the period of glut may be retarded, but it must come at last. On the other supposition, that from alarm or distress more than a due portion of corn is prematurely sent to market, and that before the next harvest the whole supply will, in consequence, prove deficient, and the price will rise; I must observe, that sharp-sighted individuals, prompted by a regard to their interest, can discover this, if it be so, with more certainty than Government. Money is not wanted to purchase the wheat thus unduly brought to market; nothing is required but a conviction of the probability of a diminished supply, or an increased demand, and a probable rise of price, to awaken the spirit of speculation. If there were any well-founded opinion of such a rise, we should soon witness a more than usual activity among the corn-dealers. When there was a prospect of continued wet weather, just before the harvest of last year, did we not see an immediate spring in the price of corn? On what was such rise founded, but on an anticipation of probable scarcity, and an increased price? If, then, there be any good foundation for a probable deficiency before the wheat of the next harvest comes into use, individuals will be found to speculate without any encouragement from Government; the difference between a rate of interest of 3 per cent. and of 5 per cent. must be of little importance in such a transaction, and as far as the public is concerned may be wholly neglected, when we are considering the advantages of such a measure.

It has been said that similar advances have been made to the commercial interest on more than one occasion, why then should the agricultural interest be excluded from a similar benefit? In the first place, I doubt whether the measure be justifiable in any case whatever; but it cannot be disputed that the commercial class made their application for this indulgence under very different circumstances from the agricultural class.

The commercial class are liable to stagnation of business; a market for which they have prepared their goods may, during war, (and it is only during war that such advances have been made,) be shut against them. On the probability of selling their goods, they have given bills which are becoming due, and their character and fortune depend on fulfilling their engagements. All they want is time; by forbearing to produce more of the commodity for which there is a diminished demand, they are sure, though probably with great loss, to dispose of their articles. Is the situation of the farmer any thing like this? Has he any bills becoming due? Do all his future transactions depend on his momentarily sustaining his credit? Are markets ever wholly shut against him? Is it a mere supply of money to meet his bills that he requires? The cases are most widely different, and the analogy which is attempted to be set up between them fails in every particular.

SECTION IX

Can the present State of Agricultural Distress be attributed to Taxation?

THE present distress is caused by an insufficient price for the produce of the land, which it appears impossible, with any degree of fairness, to ascribe to taxation. Taxation is of two kinds, it either falls on the producer of a commodity in his character of producer, or it falls on him as a consumer. When a farmer has to pay an agricultural horse-tax, tithes, land-tax, he is taxed as a producer, and he seeks to repay himself, as all other producers do, by imposing an additional price, equivalent to the tax, on the commodity which he produces. It is the consumer, then, that finally pays the tax, and not the producer, as nothing can prevent the latter from transferring the tax to the consumer,[1] but the production of too great a quantity of the commodity for the demand. Whenever the price of a commodity does not repay to the producer all the charges of every description which he is obliged to incur, it fails to give him a remunerating price; it places him under a disadvantage, as compared with the producers of other commodities; he no longer gets the usual and ordinary profits of capital, and there are only two remedies by which he can be relieved: one, the diminution of the quantity of the commodity, which will not fail to raise its price, if the demand do not at the same time diminish; the other, the relieving him from the taxes which he pays as a producer. The first remedy is certain and efficacious; the second is of a more doubtful description, because, if the price of the commodity did once remunerate the producer, after the tax was imposed, it could only fall afterwards from increased supply, or diminished demand.

The repeal of the tax will not diminish quantity; and if it does not further lower the price, it will not increase demand. If the price falls still lower, then the repeal of the tax will not afford relief to the producer. It is only in the case of the commodity falling no lower, although the producer is relieved from one of the charges of production, that he can be said to be benefited by the repeal of a tax on production; and a very reasonable doubt may be entertained, whether the competition of the sellers may not further diminish the price of the commodity in consequence of the repeal of the tax. That taxes on production may be the cause of an excess of the supply above the demand, is true, when the tax is a new one, and when the consumers are unwilling to re-pay, in the additional price, the additional charge imposed on the producer. But this is not the case in this country at the present moment; the taxes are

[1] Ed. 1 'producer,' clearly an error.

not new ones; the prices of raw produce were sufficiently high, notwithstanding the taxes, to afford a remunerating price to the producer; and no doubt can exist, that if there had been no such taxes, raw produce would have been considerably lower than it now is. The same cause which made wheat fall from 80s. to 60s., or 25 per cent., would have made it fall from 60s. to 45s., if, in consequence of fewer taxes on the land, 60s. and not 80s. had been the ordinary average price. Some of the charges of production have actually been diminished, while there is every reason to conclude, that the quantity consumed by the people has been increasing.

The alteration in the value of money has been generally supposed to be favourable to the working classes, as their money wages are said not to have fallen in proportion to the increased value of money, and the fall in the price of necessaries. Their condition is then bettered, and their power of consuming increased; but prices can never stand against a great augmentation of quantity, and therefore there is no other rational solution of the cause of the fall of agricultural produce but abundance.

Taxes on consumers affect consumers generally, and will in no way account for the distress of a particular class, or for an insufficient price of the commodity which they grow or manufacture. The taxes on candles, soap, salt, &c. &c., are not only paid by farmers, but by all persons who consume those commodities. The repeal of those taxes would afford relief to all, and not to the agricultural class particularly.

Those who maintai hat on no reasonable grounds can it be shewn, that taxation is the cause of agricultural distress and of the low price of corn, are sometimes represented as maintaining that a repeal of taxes will afford no relief; such a conclusion shews a want of candour, or of intelligence, for it is perfectly consistent to maintain, that taxation is not the cause of some particular distress, and at the same time insist that a repeal of taxes would afford relief. When Lord John Russell's horse falls because he trips over a stone, and is enabled to get up again when relieved from the burthen of his harness, it would surely be incorrect to say that the horse fell because he was burthened with harness; though it would be right to assert, that the tripping over the stone threw him down, while the relief from the confinement of the harness enabled him to get up again.[1]

For my own part then, being of opinion that almost all taxes on production fall finally on the consumer, I think that no repeal of taxes could take place which would have any other effect than to relieve consumers generally of a part of the burthens which they now bear. Although I am at all times a friend to the most rigid economy in the public expenditure, yet I am also convinced, that there are causes of distress, to the producers of a particular commodity, arising from abundant quantity, from which no practicable repeal of taxes could materially relieve, particularly if the commodity be agricultural

[1] The allusion is to Lord John Russell's speech in the House of Commons, on 21 February 1822, advocating a reduction of taxes as the only means of relieving the distress: 'It was idle to say that heavy taxes were not a cause of distress. There was a manifest absurdity in the assertion. With just as much reason might it be said, that if a carriage broke down with the horses under it, it would be wrong to disengage them from the harness. If such a case occurred, and, as might happen, if the persons who came to assist were beginning to remove the harness by which the horses were kept down, some philosopher were to come up and say, "Oh, the removal of the harness is not the way to relieve them; they have been thrown down by a stone in the road, or some such cause; but the removal of the harness will do no good"—if such language were addressed to the by-standers, they would, he had no doubt, treat the advice with contempt, and proceed in the only effectual way by taking off the harness. So it was with taxation: it pressed and weighted down the people in every part of the country, and the only way in which they could be effectually assisted was, by a removal of part, at least, of the weight.' (*Hansard*, N.S., VI, 574-5.)

produce, and if its ordinary price be kept above the level of the prices of other countries by restrictions on importation.

Against such distress no country, and more particularly no country having a bad system of corn laws, is exempted. If we were absolutely without any taxes whatever; if the public expenditure was the most economical possible, and was supported by a revenue drawn from lands appropriated for that purpose; if we had no national debt, no sinking fund, we yet should be exposed to a destructive fall of price from occasional abundance. It is impossible to read Mr. Tooke's able evidence before the Agricultural Committee of 1821,[1] without being struck with the surprising effects which an excess of supply produces on price, and for which there is in fact, no effectual remedy but a reduction of quantity. If there be any other remedy, why do not those who complain of the distress, and who have been in situations so favourable to make themselves heard, state it? With the exception of a reduction of taxation, new and additional protection against the competition of foreigners for every description of agricultural produce, direct purchases to be made by Government, or encouragements to others to make them, I have heard no remedies suggested; and as to the efficacy of these remedies, I must leave that to the reader's judgment; my own opinion of them having been already most decidedly expressed.

On the causes which have produced the degree of abundance to which I attribute all that part of the fall of raw produce since 1819, which cannot fairly be ascribed to the alteration in the value of the currency*, it will not be necessary for me to say much; we are, I think, justified in ascribing it to a succession of good crops, to an increasing importation from Ireland, and to the increase of tillage which the high prices and the obstacles

* To that cause it will have been seen I ascribe a fall of 10 per cent.[2]

[1] 'Minutes of Evidence', pp. 224–32.   [2] Above, p. 228.

opposed to importation during the war occasioned? Many of the gentlemen who gave evidence before the Committee concurred in describing the harvests of 1819 and 1820 as unusually abundant. Mr. Wakefield said on the 5th April, 1821, "I think there is a wonderful quantity of corn in the country; I now think that there is as much corn left in the country, as generally, in common years, there is after harvest." "I think, that if you were to have for the next two or three years, fair average crops, it would leave you with a great stock in hand."[1]

Mr. Iveson. "I think, the last crop was abundant; the crop of 1820 was considerably beyond an average." p. 338.

Mr. J. Brodie. "The crop in Scotland was very abundant last year."

"The crop of the year before was above an average crop too." p. 327.

Besides this abundant crop at home, the importations from Ireland were unusually great, as will be seen by the following account of the importation of oats, wheat, and wheat-flour, the production of Ireland imported into Great Britain, which was laid before the Agricultural Committee of 1821.[2]

Years Ending 5th Jan.	Oats. Qrs.	Wheat. Qrs.	Wheat flour. Cwt.
5th Jan. 1818	594,337	50,842	16,238
1819	1,001,247	95,677	33,258
1820	759,608	127,308	92,893
1821	892,605	351,871	180,375
For three months From 5th Jan. 1821 to 5th April 1821	437,245	218,764	99,062

It will be seen by the above account, how greatly the importation from Ireland has increased, which, coming in addition to the abundant quantity yielded by the harvests of 1819

[1] Agricultural Report, 1821, 'Minutes of Evidence', p. 217.
[2] The table is based on accounts Nos. 17 and 19, of the Appendix to the Agricultural Report of 1821.

and 1820 will, I think, sufficiently account for the depression of price.

To trace this abundance to its source is not, however, necessary in this case; it is sufficient to shew that the low price cannot have arisen from any other cause but an increased supply, or a diminished demand, to be convinced that the evil admits of no other effectual remedy but a reduction of quantity or an increased demand.

That an abundant quantity has been exposed to sale, will be shewn by the account[1] of the sales in Mark Lane*. It will be found, too, that an unusually large quantity has arrived in the port of London from ports in Great Britain and Ireland.

It must, indeed, not be forgotten, that the fall of price is attributed to the abundant quantity actually in the market, and the reasoning founded on the doctrine of abundance being the cause of low price, would in no degree be invalidated, if, before the next harvest, our supply should be found to be below the demand, and there should be a great increase of price. We can have no unequivocal proof of abundance but by its effects. I believe in the existence of an abundant quantity, but I should not think my argument in the least weakened if corn should, before next harvest, rise to eighty shillings per quarter.

CONCLUSION

HAVING disposed of most of the subjects which are intimately connected with the question of the policy which it would be

---

* See Appendix B.

[1] From here to the end of the paragraph ed. 1 reads 'of the quantity sold in Mark Lane, in the Appendix*, which I have every reason to believe correct.' Cp. the corresponding changes made in Appendix B in eds. 2–4.

wise for this country to adopt, respecting the trade in corn, I shall briefly recapitulate the opinions which will be found more at large in various parts of this inquiry.

The cause of the present low price of agricultural produce is partly the alteration in the value of the currency, and mainly an excess of supply above the demand. To Mr. Peel's bill, even in conjunction with the operation of the Bank, no greater effect on the price of corn can, with any fairness, be attributed than 10 per cent., and to that amount the far greatest part of the taxation of the country has been increased: but this increased taxation does not fall on the landed interest only; it falls equally on the funded interest, and every other interest in the country. Suppose the land to pay one half of the whole taxation of the country, after deducting that part of the expenditure which depends on the value of money, and which would therefore be augmented in proportion as money fell in value, the whole increase of taxation which, since 1819, has fallen upon the landed interest, taking tenants and landlords together, cannot have exceeded two millions; but suppose it four millions per annum*; is four millions per annum the amount of the whole loss sustained by landlords and tenants together, by the fall in the price of agricultural produce? Impossible, because, by the allegations of the landed interest, all rent is now paid from capital, leaving nothing for profit; and therefore, if the only cause of distress be the alteration in the value of the currency, four millions must have constituted all the net income both of landlords and tenants before such alteration, a proposition which no man would venture to sustain. To what other cause

---

* The whole amount of taxes paid to the public creditor and sinking fund, is 36 millions; suppose the other fixed charges to be four millions, then the whole taxation on which the altered value of money has operated, is 40 millions. I estimate the increase 10 per cent, or four millions, which falls on all classes,—landlords, merchants, manufacturers, labourers, and, though last not least,—stockholders.

then is the distress to be attributed? To what other cause are we to ascribe the extreme depression of all agricultural produce? The answer is, I think, plain, intelligible, and satisfactory; to the general prevalence of abundance arising from good crops, and large importations from Ireland.

This fall has been increased by the operation of the present corn laws, which have had the effect of driving capital to the cultivation of poor lands, and of making the price of corn in average years in this country greatly to exceed the price in other countries. The price, under such circumstances, must be high, but in proportion as it is raised, so is it liable to a greater fall; for, in abundant seasons, the whole increased quantity gluts our own market, and if it be above the quantity which we can consume, rapidly depresses the price, without our having any vent from exportation, till the fall of price is ruinous to the interests of farmers, who are never so secure as when the resource of exportation can be easily had recourse to.

To obviate, as far as is practicable, this enormous evil, all undue protection to agriculture should be gradually withdrawn. The policy which we ought, at this moment of distress to adopt, is to give the monopoly of the home-market to the British grower till corn reaches seventy shillings per quarter. When it has reached seventy shillings, all fixed price and system of averages should be got rid of, and a duty of twenty shillings per quarter on the importation of wheat, and other grain in proportion, might be imposed.

This change would do but little in protecting us from the effects of abundant crops, but it would be greatly beneficial in preventing an unlimited importation of corn when the ports were opened. Under the payment of a fixed duty corn would be imported only in such quantities as it might be required, and as no one would fear the shutting of the ports, no one would hurry corn to this country till we really wanted it.

Against the effects of glut, caused by an unlimited supply from abroad, we should be then amply protected.

This measure however, although a great improvement on the present corn law, would be very deficient if we proceeded no farther. To establish measures which should at once drive capital from the land would under the present circumstances of the country be rash and hazardous, and therefore I should propose that the duty of twenty shillings should every year be reduced one shilling, until it reached ten shillings. We should also allow a drawback of seven shillings per quarter on the exportation of wheat; and these should be considered as permanent measures.

A duty of 10s. per quarter, on importation, to which I wish to approach, is, I am sure, rather too high as a countervailing duty for the peculiar taxes which are imposed on the corn grower, over and above those which are imposed on the other classes of producers in the country; but I would rather err on the side of a liberal allowance than of a scanty one; and it is for this reason that I do not propose to allow a drawback quite equal to the duty. As far as the producer of corn was concerned, when the duty had fallen to 10s., the trade would, to him, have all the advantages of a free trade, within the trifling amount of 3s. per quarter. Whenever his crops were abundant, he could be relieved by exportation, after a very moderate fall of price, unless, indeed, the abundance and fall were general in all countries; but, at any rate, the price of his corn would be nearer the general rate of prices of the rest of the world by 20s. or 25s., than it is under the existing regulations, and this alteration would be invaluable to him.

Before I conclude, it will be proper to notice an objection which is frequently made against freedom of trade in corn, *viz.*, the dependence in which it would place us for an essential article of subsistence on foreign countries. This objection is founded on the supposition that we should be importers of a considerable portion of the quantity which we annually consume.

In the first place, I differ with those who think that the quantity which we should import would be immense; and, in the second, if it were as large as the objection requires, I can see no danger as likely to arise from it.

From all the evidence given to the Agricultural Committee, it appears that no very great quantity could be obtained from abroad, without causing[1] a considerable increase in the remunerating[2] price of corn in foreign countries. In proportion as the quantity required came from the interior of Poland and Germany, the cost would be greatly increased by the expenses of land carriage. To raise a larger supply, too, those countries would be obliged to have recourse to an inferior quality of land, and as it is the cost of raising corn on the worst soils in cultivation requiring the heaviest charges, which regulates the price of all the corn of a country, there could not be a great additional quantity produced, without a rise in the price necessary to remunerate the foreign grower. In proportion as the price rose abroad, it would become advantageous to cultivate poorer lands at home; and, therefore, there[3] is every probability that, under the freest state of demand, we should not be importers of any very large quantity.

But suppose the case to be otherwise, what danger should we incur from our dependence, as it is called, on foreign countries for a considerable portion of our food? If our demand was constant and uniform, which, under such a system, it would undoubtedly be, a considerable quantity of corn must be grown abroad expressly for our market. It would be more

[1] Ed. 1 does not contain 'causing'.   [3] Misprinted 'here' in eds. 3–4.
[2] Ed. 1 reads 'growing' in place of 'remunerating'.

the interest, if possible, of the countries so growing corn for our use, to oppose no obstacles to its reaching us, than it would be ours to receive it.

Let us look attentively at what is passing in this country before our eyes. Do we not see the effects of a small excess of quantity on the price of corn? What would be the glut, if England habitually raised a considerable additional quantity for foreign consumption? Should we be willing to expose our farmers and landlords to the ruin which would overwhelm them if we voluntarily deprived them of the foreign market, even in case of war? I am sure we should not. Whatever allowance we may make for the feelings of enmity, and for the desire which we might have to inflict suffering on our foe, by depriving him of part of his usual supply of food, I am sure that at such a price as it must be inflicted, in the case which I am supposing, we should forbear to exercise such a power. If such would be our policy, so would it also be that of other countries in the same circumstances; and I am fully persuaded that we should never suffer from being deprived of the quantity of food for which we uniformly depended on importation.

All our reasoning on this subject leads to the same conclusion, that we should, with as little delay as possible, consistently with a due regard to temporary interests, establish what may be called a substantially free trade in corn. The interests of the farmer, consumer, and capitalist, would all be promoted by such a measure; and as far as steady prices and the regular receipt of rents is more advantageous to the landlord than fluctuating prices and irregular receipt of rents, I am sure his interest well understood would lead to the same conclusion; although I am willing to admit, that the average money-rents, to which he would be entitled if his tenants could fulfil their contracts, would be higher under a system of restricted trade.

APPENDIX

(A.)

Representation, agreed upon the 20th day of May, 1819, by The Directors of the Bank of England, and laid before The Chancellor of the Exchequer.

Ordered, by The House of Commons, to be Printed,
21 May 1819.

AT A COURT OF DIRECTORS AT THE BANK.

On Thursday 20th May 1819.

THE DIRECTORS of the Bank of *England,* having taken into their most serious consideration the Reports of the Secret Committees of the two Houses of Parliament, appointed to inquire into the State of the Bank of England, with reference to the expediency of the Resumption of Cash Payments at the period now fixed,—have thought it their duty to lay before HIS MAJESTY'S Ministers, as early as possible, their sentiments, with regard to the measures suggested by these Committees for the approbation of Parliament.

IN the first place it appears, that, in the view of the Committees, the measure of the Bank recommencing Cash Payments on the 5th of July next, the time prescribed by the existing law, "is utterly impracticable, and would be entirely inefficient, if not ruinous."

Secondly, it appears, that the two Committees have come to their conclusion at a period, when the outstanding Notes of the Bank of England do not much exceed 25,000,000*l.*; when the price of Gold is about 4*l.* 1*s.* per ounce; and when there is great distress, from the stagnation of Commerce, and the fall of prices of imported Articles.

IT must be obvious to His Majesty's Ministers, that, as long as such a state of things shall last, or one in any degree similar, without either considerable improvement on one side, or growing worse on the other, the Bank, acting as it does at present, and keeping its Issues nearly at the present level, could not venture to return to Cash Payments, with any probability of benefit to the Public, or safety to the Establishment.

The two Committees of Parliament, apparently actuated by this consideration, have advised that the Bank shall not open payments in Coin for a period of four years, but shall be obliged, from the 1st of May, 1821, to discharge their notes in standard Gold Bullion, at mint price, when demanded in sums not amounting to less than thirty ounces. And, as it appears to the Committees expedient, that this return to payments at mint price should be made gradually, they propose that on the first day of February next, the Bank should pay their Notes in Bullion, if demanded in sums not less than sixty ounces, at the rate of 4*l*. 1*s*. an ounce, and from the 1st of October, 1820, to the 1st of May following, at 3*l*. 19*s*. 6*d*. an ounce.

If the Directors of the Bank have a true comprehension of the views of the Committees in submitting this scheme to Parliament, they are obliged to infer, that the object of the Committees is to secure, at every hazard, and under every possible variation of circumstances, the return of payments in Gold at mint price for Bank Notes, at the expiration of two years; and that this measure is so to be managed, that the mint price denominations shall ever afterwards be preserved, leaving the market or exchange price of Gold to be controlled by the Bank, solely by the amount of their issues of Notes.

It further appears to the Directors, with regard to the final execution of this plan, and the payment of Bank Notes in Gold at mint price, that discretionary power is to be taken away from the Bank; and that it is merely to regulate its Issues, and make purchases of Gold, so as to be enabled to answer all possible demands, whenever its Treasury shall be again open for the payment of its Notes.

Under these impressions, the Directors of the Bank think it right to observe to His Majesty's Ministers, that being engaged to pay on demand their Notes in statutable Coin, at the mint price of 3*l*. 17*s*. 10½*d*. an ounce, they ought to be the last persons who should object to any measure calculated to effect that end; but as it is incumbent on them to consider the effect of any measure to be adopted, as operating upon the general issue of their Notes, by which all the private Banks are regulated, and of which the whole Currency, exclusive of the Notes of private Bankers, is composed, they feel themselves obliged, by the new situation in which they have been placed by the Restriction Act of 1797, to bear in mind, not less their duties to the Community at large, whose interest in a pecuniary and commercial relation, have in a great degree been confided to their discretion.

The Directors being thus obliged to extend their views, and embrace the interests of the whole Community, in their consideration of this measure, cannot but feel a repugnance, however involuntary, to pledge themselves in approbation of a system, which, in their opinion, in all its great tendencies and operations, concerns the Country in general more than the immediate interests of the Bank alone.

It is not certainly a part of the regular duty of the Bank, under its original institution, to enter into the general views of policy, by which this great empire is to be governed, in all its commercial and pecuniary transactions, which exclusively belong to the Administration, to Parliament, and to the Community at large; nor is it the province of the Bank to expound the principles by which these views ought to be regulated. Its peculiar and appropriate duty is the management of the concerns of the Banking Establishment, as connected with the payment of the Interest of the National Debt, the lodgments consigned to its care, and the ordinary Advances it has been accustomed to make to Government.

But when the Directors are now to be called upon, in the new situation in which they are placed by the Restriction Act, to procure a Fund for supporting the whole National Currency, either in Bullion or in Coin, and when it is proposed that they should effect this measure within a given period, by regulating the market price of Gold by a limitation of the amount of the Issue of Bank Notes, with whatever distress such limitation may be attended to individuals, or the Community at large; they feel it their bounden and imperious duty to state their sentiments thus explicitly, in the first instance to His Majesty's Ministers, on this subject, that a tacit consent and concurrence at this juncture may not, at some future period, be construed into a previous implied sanction on their part, of a system, which they cannot but consider fraught with very great uncertainty and risk.

It is impossible for them to decide beforehand what shall be the course of events for the next two, much less for the next four, years; they have no right to hazard a flattering conjecture, for which they have not real grounds, in which they may be disappointed, and for which they may be considered responsible. They cannot venture to advise an unrelenting continuance of pecuniary pressures upon the Commercial world, of which it is impossible for them either to foresee or estimate the consequences.

The Directors have already submitted to the House of Lords, the expediency of the Bank paying its Notes in Bullion at the market price of the day, with a view of seeing how far favourable Commercial balances may operate in restoring the former order of things, of which they might take advantage: And with a similar view they have proposed, that Government should repay the Bank a considerable part of the sums that have been advanced upon Exchequer Bills.

These two measures would allow time for a correct judgment to be formed upon the state of the Bullion market, and upon the real result of those changes, which the late war may have produced, in all its consequences, of increased public Debt, increased Taxes, increased Prices, and altered relations, as to Interest, Capital, and Commercial dealings with the Continent; and how far the alterations thus produced are temporary or permanent; and to what extent, and in what degree, they operate.

It was the design of the Directors, in pursuance of the before mentioned two measures, to take advantage of every circumstance which could enable the Bank to extend its purchases of Bullion, as far as a legitimate consideration of the ordinary wants of the Nation, for a sufficient Currency, could possibly warrant. Beyond this point, they do not consider themselves justified in going, upon any opinion, conjecture, or speculation, merely their own; and when a system is recommended, which seems to take away from the Bank any thing like a discretionary consideration of the necessities and distresses of the Commercial world; if the Directors withhold their previous consent, it is not from a want of deference to His Majesty's Government, or to the opinions of the Committees of the two Houses of Parliament, but solely from a serious feeling, that they have no right whatever to invest themselves, of their own accord, with the responsibility of countenancing a Measure, in which the whole Community is so deeply involved; and possibly to compromise the universal Interests of the Empire, in all the relations of Agriculture, Manufacture, Commerce, and Revenue, by a seeming acquiescence, or declared approbation, on the part of the Directors of the Bank of England.

The consideration of these great questions, and of the degree in which all these leading and commanding interests may be affected by the measure proposed, rests with the Legislature; and it is for them, after solemn deliberation, and not for the Bank, to determine and decide upon the course to be adopted.

Whatever reflections may have from time to time been cast upon the Bank, whatever invidious representations of its conduct may have been made, the cautious conduct it adopted, in so measuring the amount of currency, as to make it adequate to the wants both of the Nation and of the Government; at the same time keeping it within reasonable bounds, when compared with what existed before the war, as is shown in the Lords' Reports, pages 10, 11, 12 and 13; the recent effort to return to a system of Cash Payments, which commenced with the fairest prospects (but which was afterwards frustrated by events that could not be foreseen nor controlled by the Bank;) are of themselves a sufficient refutation of all the obloquy, which has been so undeservedly heaped upon the Establishment.

The Directors of the Bank of England, in submitting these considerations to His Majesty's Ministers, request that they may be allowed to assure them, that it is always their anxious desire, as far as depends upon them, to aid, by every consistent means, the measures of the Legislature, for furthering the prosperity of the Empire.

ROBERT BEST, Sec.

PLAN

FOR THE ESTABLISHMENT

OF A

NATIONAL BANK.

BY (THE LATE) DAVID RICARDO, ESQ. M.P.

LONDON:

JOHN MURRAY, ALBEMARLE-STREET.

MDCCCXXIV.

NOTE ON 'PLAN FOR A NATIONAL BANK'

THE *Plan for the Establishment of a National Bank* was published in February 1824[1] six months after Ricardo's death.

Ricardo started writing it at Gatcomb, where he had gone in the middle of July 1823, and it was completed by the beginning of August.

On 3 August he wrote to Malthus: 'I have been writing a few pages in favor of my project of a National Bank, with a view to prove that the nation would lose nothing in profits by abolishing the Bank of England, and that the sole effect of the change would be to transfer a part of the profits of the Bank to the national Treasury.'[2]

His plan had first taken shape in 1815 while he was writing the *Economical and Secure Currency*. In a letter to Malthus of 10 September 1815 he had outlined a scheme for transferring the power to issue paper money from the Bank to independent commissioners who would also manage the National Debt and act as bankers to the Government, but he did not develop the idea at that time.[3]

A similar proposal appears to have been made by Say in 1814 in an unpublished paper which he had submitted to Ricardo. At that time Ricardo, while agreeing that the profits arising from the issue of paper currency ought to belong to the public rather than to a company of Bankers, doubted whether the Government if entrusted with the power of issue would not abuse it.[4]

In 1817, in the *Principles*, Ricardo put his scheme before the public for the first time.[5]

In April and May 1822, when the Government intended to renew in advance the Bank Charter which was due to expire only in 1833, Ricardo in the House of Commons, opposing the renewal, suggested that the paper currency should be issued without the assistance of

---

[1] Advertised 'Tomorrow will be published', in *Courier* 23 Feb. 1824.
[2] Below, IX, 325–6. A few days later he wrote of it to Mill (*ib.* 329) and to McCulloch (*ib.* 331.)

[3] See below, VI, 268, and cp. above, pp. 45–6.
[4] Below, VI, 165–6.
[5] Above, I, 361–3.

the Bank of England and said that the profits ought to belong to the public.[1]

The preface to the published pamphlet says that Ricardo showed the MS to 'a member of his own family' who was staying with him. This was no doubt his brother Moses Ricardo, who was on a visit to Gatcomb at the time of Ricardo's last illness.[2] That Moses Ricardo was also the writer of the preface and was responsible for the publication is suggested by his later interest in the matter. When the question of the renewal of the Bank Charter came up for discussion in 1832, he suggested to John Murray, the publisher, that if he had in stock any considerable number of copies of his brother's *Plan for a National Bank* they might be re-issued with a new title-page and with 'a concise account of his plan for a secure and economical currency, together with a few preliminary observations', which he offered to furnish.[3] Nothing came of this suggestion. Shortly after, on 3 May 1832, Moses Ricardo proposed the following question for discussion to the Political Economy Club: 'Would not the establishment of a National Bank for the issue of Notes be advantageous to the country?'[4]

The *Plan for a National Bank* was republished in 1838 as an appendix to a pamphlet by another brother, Samson Ricardo, entitled *A National Bank, the Remedy for the Evils Attendant upon our Present System of Paper Currency* (London, Pelham Richardson).

There are among Ricardo's Papers three MSS in his own handwriting connected with the *Plan for a National Bank*:

(1) A fragment of a draft, covering three quarto pages. This is printed in full below, pp. 298–300.

(2) A sketch of the Regulations for the establishment of a National Bank, covering two quarto pages. This also is printed in full below, p. 300.

(3) A complete draft of the pamphlet, covering fifteen quarto pages (together with three revised passages, undoubtedly belonging

---

[1] Below, V, 156 and 193.
[2] See *Annual Biography and Obituary for 1824*, p. 376.
[3] Letter from Moses Ricardo, 27 March 1832, MS in possession of Sir John Murray.
[4] *Political Economy Club, Minutes of Proceedings, 1821–1882*, p. 110.

to this draft,[1] which are written on the back of a sheet of the fragment denoted as 1). This draft is not printed here as a separate item, since to a large extent it agrees with the text of the posthumous edition of 1824, which is reprinted below. The chief variants are given in footnotes.[2]

The MS from which the edition of 1824 was printed (and which, as the Preface states, was committed to the press 'in the state precisely in which it was found') is not extant.

Since the above Note and the text below were in page-proof the MS from which the edition of 1824 had been printed came to light with the Mill-Ricardo papers. This consists of 14 leaves, written on both sides in Ricardo's handwriting (with eight corrections in Mill's handwriting, referring to changes of phrasing)[3] and bears obvious signs of having been handled by a printer.

A conjecture made in footnote 4 on p. 286 below is confirmed by this MS: a regulation numbered 6, substantially the same as is given in that footnote, is deleted by Ricardo, whilst an equivalent sentence is inserted at the end of regulation 4; but by an oversight the subsequent regulations are not renumbered.

It has not been thought necessary to recast the footnotes attached to the text below; and consequently the 'MS' referred to there is the complete draft described above as (3), *and not* the final copy used by the printer.

---

[1] The location of these three passages is given at the end of the relevant footnotes, *viz*., p. 286 n. 1, p. 289 n. 4, p. 291 n. 1.

[2] These three MSS have been published in Ricardo's *Minor Papers on the Currency Question*, ed. by J. H. Hollander, Baltimore, 1932. There the grouping of the MSS is somewhat different from that adopted here. The MSS here denoted as 1 and 2 are there printed as a single item under A. The draft here denoted as 3 is there printed in full under B. And the revised passages, here included in item 3, are there printed as a separate item under C.

[3] For example, Mill corrects 'because, if it be not, the merchants will suffer' to 'for this reason—that if it be not, the merchants will suffer' (below, p. 278, lines 5–6); and again 'is estimated to amount to about 10 millions' is altered to 'is estimated at about 10 millions' (below, p. 292, lines 16–18).

PREFACE

It was the intention of Mr. Ricardo, on retiring into the country, after the last Session of Parliament, to employ part of his leisure in committing to paper, with a view to publication, a scheme by which, in his opinion, the profit derived from the supply of Paper Currency might be afforded to the public without any diminution of security against the inconveniencies to which such a Currency is liable. It was known, previous to his last illness, that he had carried his design into execution; and the following pages were found among his papers after his decease. It is not known that Mr. Ricardo thought any alteration or addition necessary, unless it be in one point. Having communicated his MS. to a member of his own family,[1] who was near him at the time of its completion; and it being suggested to him that difficulty might be experienced in the country, as the notes of one district were not to be payable in another, in obtaining currency for the purposes of travelling; he admitted that something to obviate this inconvenience might be required, but thought that some very simple arrangement would answer the end. It does not appear that he had committed to writing any expedient which might have occurred to him for that purpose; and his friends have deemed it most proper to commit his manuscript to the press, with this explanation, in the state precisely in which it was found.

[1] Probably his brother Moses Ricardo.

PLAN, &c.

THE Bank of England performs two operations of banking, which are quite distinct, and have no necessary connection with each other: it issues a paper currency as a substitute for a metallic one; and it advances money in the way of loan, to merchants and others.

That these two operations of banking have no necessary connection, will appear obvious from this,—that they might be carried on by two separate bodies, without the slightest loss of advantage, either to the country, or to the merchants who receive accommodation from such loans.[1]

Suppose the privilege of issuing paper money were taken away from the Bank, and were in future to be exercised by the State only, subject to the same regulation to which the Bank is now liable, of paying its notes, on demand, in specie; in what way would the national wealth be in the least impaired? We should then, as now, carry on all the traffic and commerce of the country, with the cheap medium, paper money, instead of the dear medium, metallic money; and all the advantages which now flow from making this part of the national capital productive, in the form of raw material, food, clothing, machinery, and implements, instead of retaining it useless, in the form of metallic money, would be equally secured.[2]

The public, or the Government on behalf of the public, is indebted to the Bank in a sum of money larger than the whole amount of bank notes in circulation; for the Government not

---

[1] In MS the end of the paragraph reads 'without the slightest loss of advantage to the country that is to say without any diminution of the aggregate of profits.'

[2] Cp. the more extensive discussion of the advantages of paper money in the fragment, below, p. 298.

only owes the Bank fifteen millions, its original capital, which is lent at three per cent. interest, but also many more millions, which are advanced on Exchequer bills, on half-pay and pension annuities, and on other securities. It is evident, therefore, that if the Government itself were to be the sole issuer of paper money, instead of borrowing it of the Bank,[1] the only difference would be with respect to the interest;—the Bank would no longer receive interest, and the Government would no longer pay it: but all other classes in the community would be exactly in the same position in which they now stand. It is evident too, that there would be just as much money in circulation; for it could make no difference, in that respect, whether the sixteen millions of paper money now circulating in London, were issued by Government, or by a banking corporation. The merchants could suffer no inconvenience from any want of facility in getting the usual advances made to them, in the way of discount, or in any other manner; for, first, the amount of those advances must essentially depend upon the amount of money in circulation, and that would be just the same as before: and, secondly, of the amount in circulation, the Bank would have precisely the same proportion, neither less nor more,[2] to lend to the merchants.[3]

If it be true, as I think I have clearly proved, that the advances made by the Bank to the Government, exceed the whole amount of the notes of the Bank in circulation, it is evident that part of its advances to Government, as well as the whole of its loans to other persons, must be made from other funds, pos-

[1] MS 'instead of allowing the Bank to issue it and borrowing it of them at interest'.
[2] In the fragment Ricardo says 'the Bank might greatly increase the amount of the particular fund which they now devote to such purposes. See below, p. 299.

[3] MS, in place of the last six lines beginning 'for, first', reads 'because there would be just the same quantity of money in the country, and of that quantity the Bank would have precisely the same proportion as before to lend to them.'

sessed, or at the disposal of the Bank;[1] and which it would continue to possess after Government had discharged its debt to it, and after all its notes were withdrawn from circulation.[2] Let it not then be said that the Bank Charter, as far as regards the issuing of paper money,[3] ought to be renewed, for this reason—that if it be not, the merchants will suffer inconvenience, from being deprived of the usual facilities of borrowing; as I trust I have shown that their means of borrowing would be just as ample as before.[4]

It may however be said, that, if the Bank were deprived of that part of its business which consists in issuing paper money, it would have no motive to continue a joint stock company, and would agree on a dissolution of its partnership. I believe no such thing; it would still have profitable means of employing its own funds: but suppose I am wrong, and that the company were dissolved, what inconvenience would commerce sustain from it?[5] If the joint stock of the company be managed by a few directors, chosen by the general body of proprietors; or if it be divided amongst the proprietors themselves, and each share be managed by the individual to whom it belongs, will that make any difference in its real amount, or in the efficacy with which it may be employed for commercial purposes? It is probable that[6] in no case would it be managed by the individual proprietors, but that it would be collected in a mass or masses, and[7] managed with much more economy and skill than it is now managed by the Bank. A great deal too much stress

---

[1] MS 'it is evident that all their loans to other parties must be made from other funds possessed by the Bank'.
[2] MS does not contain the last nine words.
[3] MS does not contain the last nine words.

[4] MS does not contain the last clause, beginning 'as I trust'.
[5] MS, in place of the passage beginning 'I believe', reads simply 'But suppose this to take place, what inconvenience would commerce sustain by it?'
[6] MS 'The fact however is that'
[7] In MS 'probably' is ins. here.

has always been laid on the benefits which commerce derives from the accommodation afforded to merchants by the Bank. I believe it to be quite insignificant compared with that which is afforded by the private funds of individuals. We know that at the present moment the advances by the Bank to merchants, on discount, are of a very trifling amount; and we have abundant evidence to prove, that at no time have they been great. The whole fund at the disposal of the Bank, for the last thirty years, is well known.[1] It[2] consisted of its own capital and savings—[3] of the amount of deposits left with it by Government and by individuals, who employed it as a banker. From this aggregate fund must be deducted the amount of cash and bullion in the coffers of the Bank; the amount of advances to the holders of receipts, for[4] the loans contracted for during each year; and the amount of advances to Government in every way. After making these deductions, the remainder only could have been devoted to commercial objects; and if it were ascertained, would, I am sure, be comparatively of a small amount.

From papers laid before Parliament in 1797, in which the Bank gave a number, as unit, and a scale of its discounts for different years, it was calculated, by some ingenious individual,[5] after comparing this scale with other documents,[6] also laid before Parliament, that the amount of money advanced in the way of discount to the merchants, for a period of three years and a half previous to 1797, varied from two millions to 3,700,000*l*.

---

[1] In MS the last three lines read ', and we have the best evidence to prove that they never could have been very great. It is not a difficult matter to ascertain what the whole fund at the disposal of the Bank has been during the last 30 years.'

[2] MS has in addition 'necessarily'.

[3] MS, in place of the dash, has ', of the amount of their notes, and'.

This was no doubt omitted in the printed version by an oversight.

[4] MS has not 'receipts, for'.

[5] William Morgan; see Appendix to this volume.

[6] MS, in place of the last two lines has 'for different years without mentioning the actual amount it was calculated on data furnished by other documents'.

These are trifling amounts in such a country as this, and must bear a small proportion to the sum lent by individuals for similar purposes. In 1797, the advances to Government alone, by the Bank, exclusive of its capital, which was also lent to Government, were more than three times the amount of the advances to the whole body of merchants.[1]

A committee of the House of Commons was appointed last session of Parliament, to inquire into the law of pledges, and into the relation of consignors of goods from abroad, to consignees. This committee called before it Mr. Richardson, of the house of Richardson, Overend, and Co., eminent discount brokers in the city. This gentleman was asked—[2]

"*Q.* Are you not in the habit occasionally of discounting to a large extent bills of brokers and other persons, given upon the security of goods deposited in their hands?

"*A.* Very large.

"*Q.* Have you not carried on the business of a bill broker and money agent to a very large extent, much beyond that of any other individual in this town?

"*A.* I should think very much beyond.

"*Q.* To the extent of some millions annually?

"*A.* A great many; about twenty millions annually;—sometimes more."[3]

---

[1] MS, in place of the last two sentences, reads 'In such a country as this 3 or 4 millions is a trifling amount and bears a small proportion to what is lent on discount by bankers and individuals. The advances to Gov.ᵗ in 1797 were more than 3 times greater than the advances to merchants.'

[2] In MS this paragraph reads 'Mr. Richardson an eminent discount broker was lately examined before a committee of the House of Commons on occasion of an enquiry into the state of the law as it regarded consignors and consignees of goods, and he was asked'; blank spaces are left for questions and answers.

[3] 'Report from the Select Committee on the Law Relating to Goods, Wares, Merchandize, intrusted to Merchants, Agents, or Factors and the Effects of the Law upon the Interests of Commerce', 13 June 1823, 'Minutes of Evi-

The evidence of Mr. Richardson satisfactorily proves, I think, the extent of transactions of this kind, in which the Bank has no kind of concern. Can any one doubt, that, if the Bank were to break up its establishment, and divide its funds among the individual proprietors, the business of Mr. Richardson, and of others who are in the same line, would considerably increase? On the one hand, they would have more applications made to them for money on discount: on the other, many who would have money to dispose of, would apply to them to obtain employment for it.[1] The same amount of money, and no more, would be employed in this branch of business; and if not employed by the Bank, or by the individual proprietors, if they had the management of their own funds, it would inevitably find its way, either by a direct or circuitous channel, to Mr. Richardson, or to some other money agent, to be employed by him in promoting the commerce, and upholding the trade of the country; for in no other way could these funds be made so productive to the parties to whom they would belong.

If the view which I have taken of this subject be a correct one, it appears that the commerce of the country would not be in the least impeded by depriving the Bank of England of the power of issuing paper money, provided an amount of such money, equal to the Bank circulation, was issued by Government: and that the sole effect of depriving the Bank of this privilege, would be to transfer the profit which accrues from the interest of the money so issued from the Bank, to Government.

dence', p. 79; in *Parliamentary Papers*, 1823, vol. IV. Ricardo was a member of this Committee.

[1] MS, in place of the last two sentences, reads 'Can it be doubted that the number of individuals applying to Mr. Richardson and to others who carry on the same business as he does for money on their bills, would be increased if the Bank were to break up their establishment and divide their funds amongst the individual proprietors, and can it be less doubted that those same individual proprietors then having their funds consigned to their own care would apply to Mr. Richardson for the means of employing them.'

There remains, however, one other objection, to which the reader's attention is requested.[1]

It is said that Government could not be safely entrusted with the power of issuing paper money; that it would most certainly[2] abuse it; and that, on any occasion when it was pressed for money to carry on a war, it would cease to pay coin, on demand, for its notes; and from that moment the currency would become a forced government paper. There would, I confess, be great danger[3] of this, if Government—that is to say, the ministers—[4] were themselves to be entrusted with the power of issuing paper money. But I propose to place this trust in the hands of Commissioners, not removable from their official situation but by a vote of one or both Houses of Parliament.[5] I propose also to prevent all intercourse between these Commissioners and ministers, by forbidding every species of money transaction between them. The Commissioners should never, on any pretence, lend money to Government, nor be in the slightest degree under its controul or influence. Over Commissioners so entirely independent of them, the ministers would have much less power than they now possess over the Bank Directors. Experience shows how little this latter body have been able to withstand the cajolings of ministers; and how frequently they have been induced to increase their advances on Exchequer bills and Treasury bills, at the very moment they were themselves declaring that it would be attended with the greatest risk to the stability of their establishment, and to the public interest.[6] From a perusal of the correspondence between

[1] MS 'one other objection to notice which will not require much time to answer.'
[2] MS 'would be sure to'.
[3] MS 'some danger'.
[4] MS 'if ['Gover' is del. here] Ministers'.
[5] MS 'by a vote of Parliament.'

[6] MS, in place of the last four sentences, reads: 'I propose also that these Commissioners should have no transactions whatever with ministers, excepting that of laying from time to time a statement of their accounts before them, that they should never lend money to them

Government and the Bank, previous to the stoppage of Bank payments, in 1797,[1] it will be seen, that the Bank attributes the necessity of that measure (erroneously in this instance, I think),[2] to the frequent and urgent demands for an increase of advances on the part of Government. I ask then, whether the country would not possess a greater security against all such influence, over the minds of the issuers of paper, as would induce them to swerve from the strict line of their duty, if the paper money of the country were issued by Commissioners, on the plan I have proposed, rather than by the Bank of England, as at present constituted?[3] If Government wanted money, it should be obliged to raise it in the legitimate way; by taxing the people;[4] by the issue and sale of exchequer bills, by funded loans,[5] or by borrowing from any of the numerous banks which might exist in the country;[6] but in no case should it be allowed to borrow from those, who have the power of creating money.

nor be in the slightest degree bound by their instructions. I should think Ministers would under these circumstances have much less controul over the issues of Commissioners so independent of them than they now possess over those of the Bank of England. The Bank of England as is well known have been in the habit of making advances to Government on Treasury bills and on Exchequer bills, and have frequently been called upon to increase the amount of such advances at times when it was extremely inconvenient to the Bank and highly dangerous to the public interest that they should do so.'

[1] 'Report of the Lords' Committee of Secrecy. Order of Council 26th February 1797; Relating to the Bank'; Appendix 'Papers and Accounts', No. 5, pp. 81–94; reprinted in *Parliamentary Papers*, 1810, vol. III.

[2] MS does not contain the words in brackets.

[3] MS, in place of the last four lines, beginning 'as would induce', reads 'to make them swerve from their duty if so powerful a body as the Government were precluded from having any transaction or holding any correspondence [the last four words are ins.] with them.'

[4] MS does not contain the last eight words.

[5] MS 'public loans'.

[6] MS, in place of the remainder of this paragraph and the first two sentences of the next, reads '. It should be a part of the constitution of the board which I propose to establish that they should at no time and under no circumstances lend money to Govern.ᵗ, but that if

If the funds of the Commissioners became so ample as to leave them a surplus which might be advantageously disposed of, let them go into the market and purchase publicly government securities with it. If on the contrary it should become necessary for them to contract their issues, without diminishing their stock of gold, let them sell their securities, in the same way, in the open market. By this regulation a trifling[1] sacrifice would be made, amounting to the turn of the market, which may be supposed to be gained by those whose business it is to employ their capital and skill in dealing in these securities; but in a question of this importance such a sacrifice is not worth considering. It must be recollected that, from the great competition in this particular business, the turn of the market is reduced to a very small fraction, and that the amount of such transactions could never be great, as the circulation would be kept at its just level, by allowing for a small contraction or extension of the treasure in coin and bullion, in the coffers of the commissioners. It would be only when, from the increasing wealth and prosperity of the country, the country required a permanently increased amount of circulation, that it would be expedient to invest money in the purchase of securities paying interest, and only in a contrary case, that a part of such securities would be required to be sold. Thus, then, we see that[2] the

their funds were so ample as to permit them to dispose of money they should purchase govern! securities in open market, and if on the contrary they had occasion to reduce their ['circulation' is del. here] floating securities they should in like manner sell them in open market.'

[1] MS 'a very trifling'.

[2] MS, in place of the last two sentences and the opening of this sentence, reads: 'It must be recollected that these transactions would be few in amount, as the circulation would be kept at its just level by being exchanged for coin and bullion when it exceeded its proper proportion, and by the sale of gold bullion or of coin to the commissioners when the amount of paper money was below that proportion. It would only be in the case of the stock of coin and bullion in the coffers of the Commissioners being too low that they would be under

most complete security could be obtained against the influence, which, on a first and superficial[1] view, it might be supposed Government would have over the issues of a National Bank; and that, by organizing such an establishment, all the interest, which is now annually paid by Government to the Bank, would become a part of the national resources.

I would propose, then, some such plan as the following, for the establishment of a National Bank.

I.

Five Commissioners shall be appointed, in whom the full power of issuing all the paper money of the country shall be exclusively vested.[2]

2.

On the expiration of the charter of the Bank of England, in 1833, the Commissioners shall issue fifteen millions of paper money, the amount of the capital of the Bank, lent to government, with which that debt shall be discharged. From that time the annual interest of 3 per cent. shall cease and determine.[3]

---

the necessity of selling some of their securities in the market in order to purchase with the paper money which they obtained by such sale the gold which they might deem necessary. On the other hand if the gold came into their coffers too fast, and accumulated in too great a degree, by the issue of more of their paper in the purchase of these securities such a tendency would be checked. By a very trifling sacrifice then'.

[1] MS does not contain 'and superficial'.

[2] In MS the first regulation is ins. and reads: 'Let   Commissioners be appointed for the man-agement of the paper circulation of the country.' Later in the same MS the number of Commissioners is fixed at three; see below, p. 290, n. 1.

[3] In MS this regulation reads: 'On the   1833, the day on which the Bank charter expires, let the Commissioners issue 15 [first written '20', corrected to '15', then restored to '20', and finally written '15'] millions of paper money and pay it to the Bank of England, supposing that sum or more to be due from the Government to the company in discharge of its debt for the Bank Capital for which it is now paying 3 pc.t interest.'

3.

On the same day, ten millions of paper money shall be employed by the Commissioners in the following manner. With such parts of that sum as they may think expedient, they shall purchase gold bullion of the Bank, or of other persons; and with the remainder, within six months from the day above mentioned, they shall redeem a part of the government debt to the Bank, on exchequer bills. The exchequer bills, so redeemed, shall thereafter remain at the disposal of the Commissioners.[1]

4.

The Bank shall be obliged,[2] with as little delay as convenient after[3] the expiration of its charter, to redeem all its notes in circulation, by the payment of them in the new notes issued by government.[4] It shall not pay them in gold, but shall

[1] In MS this regulation was first written: 'Let the Government [replaced by 'Commissioners'] with 5 ['or 10' is ins. here] millions more of paper money purchase gold and silver bullion to that amount.' The last three words were then del. and the following was added: 'and pay the Bank for as many Exchequer bills as they may think proper to take. If the debt of Gov.ᵗ to the Bank exceed the 15 millions and the money paid for Exch.ʳ bills provision must be made for it if the Bank require it by the issue of Exch.ʳ bills or by loan'. A later version, which is much nearer to the printed one, was written at the back of another sheet.

[2] In MS 'to use its best effort' is ins. here.

[3] MS reads 'within 6 months of' in place of 'with as little delay as convenient after'.

[4] In MS regulation 4 ends here. To the remainder of the printed regulation 4 there corresponds in MS a separate regulation 6 which reads: 'The Bank shall not be exempted from the obligation of paying their notes in specie till 6 months after the expiration of their charter after which they shall be bound to pay them only in Government notes and shall be obliged to keep by them a sum of Govern.ᵗ notes equal in amount to the notes which they may have in circulation.' Since there is no regulation 6 in the printed version, it is possible that, in the copy sent to the printer, what was originally a separate regulation 6 was embodied in regulation 4, whilst the numbering was left unadjusted by an oversight.

be obliged to keep always a reserve of the new notes, equal in amount to its own notes which may remain in circulation.

5.

The notes of the Bank of England shall be current for six months after the expiration of the Bank charter, after which they shall no longer be received by government in payment of the revenue.

7.[1]

Within six[2] months after the expiration of the Bank charter, the notes of the country banks shall cease to circulate, and the different banks, which shall have issued them, shall be under the same obligation as the Bank of England[3] to pay them in government notes. They shall have the privilege of paying their notes in gold coin, if they prefer so to do.

8.

For the greater security of the holders of government notes, residing in the country, there shall be agents in the different[4] towns,[5] who shall be obliged, on demand, to verify the genuineness of the notes, by affixing their signatures to them, after which, such notes shall be exchangeable only in the district where they are so signed.

[1] On the absence of a regulation 6, see above, p. 286, n. 4.
[2] In MS first written '6', altered to '12', finally revised to '8'.
[3] MS, from here to the end of this regulation, reads 'to replace their notes by Gover.ᵗ notes or Gold coin.'
[4] MS has in addition 'large'.
[5] In MS the remainder of this regulation was first written: 'who shall be obliged on demand to pay the notes presented to them in coin, to verify their being genuine by their signature, or by the issue of a local note, at the option of the party presenting them.' Three main alterations were then made: (1) 'for the first twelve months' was ins. after 'obliged'; (2) 'to pay the notes presented to them in coin' was del.; (3) 'at the option of the party presenting them' was replaced by 'as may hereafter be judged most expedient'.

9.

Notes issued in one district,[1] or bearing the signature of an agent in one district, shall not be payable in any other; but on the deposit of any number of notes, in the office of the district where they were originally issued, or where they were signed, agreeably to the last regulation, a bill may be obtained, on any other district, payable in the notes of that district.

10.

Notes issued in the country shall not be payable in coin in the country; but for such notes a bill may be obtained on London, which will be paid in coin, or in London notes, at the option of the party presenting the bill in London.

11.[2]

Any one depositing coin, or London notes, in the London office, may obtain a bill payable in the notes of any other district, to be named at the time of obtaining the bill. And any one depositing[3] coin in the London office may obtain London notes to an equal amount.[4]

12.[5]

The Commissioners in London shall be obliged to buy any quantity of gold of standard fineness, and exceeding one hundred ounces in weight, that may be offered them,[6] at a price not less than £3: 17s. 6d. per oz.

---

[1] The 'issue of a local note' had been previously mentioned in the MS (cp. the preceding footnote) but not in the printed version.

[2] In MS regulation 11 originally concluded the Plan; what corresponds to the subsequent regulations was ins.

[3] In MS 'gold' is ins. here.

[4] In MS this sentence is ins. and forms a separate regulation numbered 12.

[5] Numbered 13 in MS.

[6] In MS the remainder of this regulation reads 'at £3.17.6—they shall be at liberty to give a price as high as £3.17.10¼ if they think proper to do so.'

13.

From the moment of the establishment of the National Bank, the Commissioners shall be obliged to pay their notes and bills, on demand, in gold coin.[1]

14.

Notes of one pound shall be issued at the first establishment of the National Bank, and shall be given to any one requiring them in exchange for notes of a larger amount, if the person presenting them prefer such notes to coin. This regulation to continue in force only for one year, as far as regards London, but to be a permanent one in all the country districts.[2]

15.[3]

It must be well understood, that in country districts the agents will neither be liable to give notes for coin, nor coin for notes.

16.[4]

The Commissioners shall act as the general banker to all the public departments, in the same manner as the Bank of England now acts; but they shall be precluded from fulfilling the same office, either to any corporation, or to any individual whatever.[5]

---

[1] In MS the corresponding regulation reads 'The Commissioners shall be obliged to give gold coin of the standard weight on demand for any notes issued in London or for any bill drawn from the country.'

[2] MS does not contain this sentence.

[3] MS does not contain this regulation.

[4] A corresponding regulation is ins. in MS after regulation 6 (on which see above, p. 286, n. 4) and it reads 'The commiss⁵ should act as the Banker of the public, in the same way that the Bᵏ of England now does.' A later draft of this regulation, corresponding more closely to the printed one, was written at the back of another sheet.

[5] In MS an additional regulation is ins. which reads: 'An account specifying the amount of notes in circulation, the prices of gold and silver for each month, the amount and description of Govᵗ securities which

On the subject of the first regulation I have already spoken. The Commissioners should be, I think, five[1] in number—they should have an adequate salary for the business which they would have to perform and superintend—they should be appointed by government, but not removable by government.[2]

The second regulation refers to the mode in which the new paper circulation should be substituted for the old. By the provision here made, twenty-five millions of paper money will be issued; that sum will not be too large for the circulation of the whole country, but if it should be, the excess may be exchanged for gold coin,[3] or the Commissioners may sell a portion of their exchequer bills, and thus diminish the amount of the paper circulation. There are other modes by which the substitution of the new notes for the old might be made, if the Bank of England co-operated with the Commissioners:[4] but the one here proposed would be effectual. It might be desirable that Government[5] should purchase from the Bank, at a fair valuation, the whole of its buildings, if the Bank were willing to part with them;[6] and also take all its clerks and servants into pay. It would be but just to the clerks and servants of the Bank to provide employment and support for them, and would be useful to the public to have the services of so many tried and experienced officers to conduct their affairs. It is a part of my plan, too, that the payment to the Bank for the management of

the commiss[rs] have bought and sold since the last return shall be laid quarterly before the Lords commissioners of the Treasury who shall transmit a copy of such accounts within one week to the House of Commons, if Parliam[t] be sitting, and if they be not sitting within one week after the commencement of the Session.'

[1] MS '3'.

[2] MS reads 'but should not be removable but in consequence of an address to his majesty by the House of Commons, or by both Houses of Parliament.'

[3] MS does not contain the remainder of the sentence.

[4] MS, from here to the end of the sentence reads 'but which it will not be necessary here to state.'

[5] MS 'the Commissioners'.

[6] MS does not contain the last nine words.

the national debt should wholly cease at the expiration of the Bank charter; and that this department of the public business should be put under the superintendence and controul of the Commissioners.

The third regulation provides for a proper deposit of gold coin and bullion, without which the new establishment could not act. In fact, there would be fourteen millions instead of ten, at the disposal of the Commissioners. It has been seen, by one of the subsequent regulations, that the Commissioners would act as Banker to the public departments; and as it is found by experience, that, on the average, these departments have four millions in their Banker's hands, the Commissioners would have these four millions in addition to the ten millions. If five millions were devoted to the purchase of coin and bullion, nine millions would be invested in floating securities. If eight millions were invested in gold, six millions would remain for the purchase of exchequer bills. Whatever debt remained due to the Bank, after this second payment made by the Commissioners, must be provided for by loan, or made the subject of a special agreement between the Government and the Bank of England.[1]

---

[1] In MS this paragraph reads: 'The third regulation provides for a store of gold coin and bullion without which the new establishment could not act. If it were thought necessary to purchase 10 millions of gold in bullion and coin there would be nothing left for the purchase of Excheq.[r] bills.—In that case Gov.[t] must make some other provision for the payment of the Bank Debt. If 5 mill. of gold should be thought enough 5 millions might be paid for Exch.[r] bills. It must be recollected that as by a subsequent regulation the Commiss.[s] are to act as Bankers to all the public departments this alone would furnish them with four millions of coin and bullion besides that which they should purchase, four millions being the average amount of those deposits even now after the reduction which has taken place in consequence of the cessation of the war. Whatever debt remained due to the Bank after the paym.[t] of the commissioners must be provided for by loan or made the subject of a special agreement between the Gov.[t] and the Bank[;] with this the Commissioners would have no concern.' The last sentence is ins. and the latter part of it is written at the back of another sheet.

The fourth and fifth regulations provide for the substitution of the new paper money for the old;[1] and protect the Bank from the payment in specie of the notes which it may have outstanding. This cannot be attended with any inconvenience to the holders of those notes, because the Bank is bound to give them Government notes, which are exchangeable, on demand, for gold coin.

The seventh regulation provides for the substitution of the new notes for the old Country Bank notes. The country Banks could have no difficulty in providing themselves with the new notes for that purpose. All their transactions finally settle in London, and their circulation is raised upon securities deposited there. By disposing of these securities, they would furnish themselves with the requisite quantity of money to provide for the payment of their notes, consequently the country would at no time be in want of an adequate circulation. The circulation of the country Banks is estimated at about ten millions.[2]

The eighth regulation provides against fraud and forgery. In the first instance, paper money cannot be issued from each district, but must all be sent from London. It is just, therefore, that some public agent, should, in as many places as convenient, be prepared to verify the genuineness of the notes. After a time, the circulation of each district would be carried on by

---

[1] In MS the comment on the 4th and 5th regulations ends here. It is followed by the comment on the 6th regulation of the MS (which corresponds to the last sentence of the 4th regulation of the printed version) reading: 'The 6th resolution preserves to the country the right to obtain gold coin for whatever notes may be in circulation. While any Bank notes are in circulation the Bank will be liable to pay them in specie and this cannot be injurious to the Bank even if they sold all their gold to Gov^t because as they would have an amount of Gov^t notes equal to their own in circulation, they would have the means of providing themselves with gold by demanding it from the Commiss^s in exchange for their notes.'

[2] MS does not contain this sentence.

notes issued in that district, in forms sent for that purpose from London.[1]

The ninth regulation provides every possible facility for making remittances and payments to any district in the country. If a man at York wishes to make a payment of £1000 to a person at Canterbury[2], by the payment of £1000 in notes, issued at York, to the agent in that town, he may receive a bill for £1000, payable at Canterbury, in the notes of that district.[3]

The tenth regulation provides for the payment of the notes of every district, in coin, in London. If a man in York wants £1000 in coin, government should not be at the expense of sending it to him: he ought to be at that expense himself.[4] This is a sacrifice that must be made for the use[5] of paper money; and if the inhabitants of the country are not contented to submit to it, they may use gold instead of paper; they must, nevertheless, be at the expense of procuring it.

The eleventh regulation, as well as the ninth, provides for making remittances and payments to all parts of the country.[6]

The twelfth regulation provides against the amount of the paper currency being too much limited in quantity, by obliging the Commissioners to issue it at all times in exchange for gold, at the price of 3*l*. 17*s*. 6*d*. per *oz*. Regulating their issues by the price of gold, the commissioners could never err. It might be expedient to oblige them to sell gold bullion at 3*l*. 17*s*. 9*d*.; in which case the coin would probably never be exported, because that can never be obtained under 3*l*. 17*s*. 10½*d*. per *oz*. Under

---

[1] MS does not contain the last eight words.

[2] MS 'Brighton'.

[3] MS reads 'he may receive £1000 from the agent at Brighton in notes of that district.'

[4] In MS 'or must impose it upon his debtor' is del. here.

[5] MS 'for the conveniences'.

[6] MS (in which the last sentence of regulation 11 of the printed version stands as a separate regulation 12; cp. above, p. 288, n. 4) has in addition: 'The 12 Regulation gives the option to every man in London to use paper money or the coin of the realm.'

such a system, the only variations that could take place in the price of gold, would be between the prices of 3*l*. 17*s*. 6*d*. and 3*l*. 17*s*. 9*d*.; and by watching the market price, and increasing their issues of paper, when the price inclined to 3*l*. 17*s*. 6*d*., or under; and limiting them, or withdrawing a small portion, when the price inclined to 3*l*. 17*s*. 9*d*., or more; there would not probably be a dozen transactions in the year by the Commissioners in the purchase and sale of gold; and if there were, they would always be advantageous, and leave a small profit to the establishment.[1] As it is, however, desirable to be on the safe side, in managing the important business of a paper money in a great country, it would be proper to make a liberal provision of gold, as suggested in a former regulation, in case it should be thought expedient occasionally to correct the exchanges with foreign countries, by the exportation of gold, as well as by the reduction of the amount of paper.

The thirteenth regulation obliges the Commissioners to pay their notes, on demand, in gold coin.[2]

The fourteenth regulation provides for a supply of one-pound notes for the country circulation. On the first establishment of the National Bank, but not afterwards, these are to be issued in London, to be subsequently counter-signed in the

---

[1] Up to this point the corresponding comment in MS reads: 'The 13ᵗʰ Regulation provides for a due issue of paper money by obliging the Commissⁱˢ to issue more paper when its low value as compared with gold shews that it [replaces 'when the low value of gold as compared with paper shews that the latter'; Ricardo neglected to replace 'low' with 'high'] is not in sufficient quantity. This is the case when 3. 17. 10¹ in paper will purchase more than an ounce of gold for by law an ounce of gold is coined into £3. 17. 10½

and therefore it is of less value than paper money if an ounce of it will not sell for £3. 17. 10½ in paper money. If the commissioners regulate their issues by the comparative value of gold and paper they cannot err and they might carry on the whole business of currency with a very small quantity of gold by merely increasing or diminishing the quantity of paper according as its value was high or low compared with gold.'

[2] MS does not contain this paragraph.

country.[1] As a check on the country agents, every description of note[2] might be sent to them from London, numbered and signed. After receiving them, the agent should countersign them before they were issued to the public; and he should be held strictly responsible for the whole amount sent to him, in the same manner as the distributors of stamps are responsible for the whole amount of stamps sent to them. It is hardly necessary to observe that the country agents ought to be in constant correspondence with the London district, for the purpose of giving information of all their proceedings. Suppose a country agent has given one hundred notes of one pound, for a note of one hundred pounds, he must give information of that fact, sending at the same time the larger note for which he has given them. His account in London would be credited and debited accordingly. If he receive one hundred pounds in notes, and give a bill on another district, he must give advice, both to the London district and to the district on which the bill is given, sending up the note, as in the former instance. His account will be credited for this one hundred pounds, and the agent of the other district will be charged with it. It is not requisite to go any further into details; I may already have said too much; but my object has been to show that the security for the detection of fraud is nearly perfect, as vouchers for every transaction would all be originally issued in London, and must be returned to London, or be in the possession of the country agent.

The fifteenth regulation is only explanatory of some of the former regulations.

The sixteenth regulation directs that the Commissioners shall

---

[1] MS has here in addition 'and may ever after if it be thought right to banish that species of circulation from London be issued in the country only'. In MS two passages corresponding to the remainder of this paragraph are ins., the second on another page.

[2] MS 'the one pound notes'.

act as banker to the public departments, and to the public departments only.[1]

If the plan now proposed should be adopted, the country would, probably, on the most moderate computation, save 750,000*l.* per annum. Suppose the circulation of paper money to amount to twenty-five millions, and the Government deposits to four millions; these together make twenty-nine millions. On all this sum interest would be saved, with the exception of six millions, perhaps, which it might be thought necessary to retain as deposits, in gold coin and bullion; and which would consequently be unproductive. Reckoning interest then at three per cent. only, on twenty-three millions, the public would be gainers of 690,000*l.* To this must be added 248,000*l.* which is now paid for the management of the public debt,—making together 938,000*l.* Now, supposing the expenses to amount to 188,000*l.*, there would remain for the public an annual saving or gain of 750,000*l.*

It will be remarked that the plan provides against any party but the Commissioners in London, making an original issue of notes. Agents in other districts in the country, connected with the Commissioners, may give one description of notes for another; they may give bills for notes, or notes for bills drawn on them; but, in the first instance, every one of these notes must be issued by the Commissioners in London, and consequently the whole is strictly under their cognizance. If, from any circumstances, the circulation in any particular district should become redundant, provision is made for the transfer of such redundancy to London; and if it should be deficient, a fresh supply is obtained from London. If the circulation of London should be redundant, it will show itself by the increased price of bullion, and the fall in the foreign exchanges, precisely as a redundancy is now shown; and the remedy is also the same as

---

[1] MS does not contain this or the preceding paragraph.

that now in operation; *viz.* a reduction of circulation, which is brought about by a reduction of the paper circulation. That reduction may take place two ways; either by the sale of Exchequer bills in the market, and the cancelling of the paper money which is obtained for them,—or by giving gold in exchange for the paper, cancelling the paper as before, and exporting the gold. The exporting the gold will not be done by the Commissioners; that will be effected by the commercial operation of the merchants, who never fail to find gold the most profitable remittance when the paper money is redundant and excessive. If, on the contrary, the circulation of London were too low, there would be two ways of increasing it—by the purchase of Government securities in the market, and the creation of new paper money for the purpose; or by the importation, and purchase, by the Commissioners, of gold bullion; for the purchase of which new paper money would be created. The importation would take place through commercial operations, as gold never fails to be a profitable article of import, when the amount of currency is deficient.[1]

[1] MS, in place of the last paragraph of the printed version, reads: 'It will be seen that the plan provides against any party but the Commiss^{s} in London making an original issue of notes. In the first instance they are all issued in London and a part must find its way into the country and be substituted for the country circulation. If from any circumstances the circulation in any particular country district should become redundant it could only be reduced by the return of notes to the country agent and the demand of a bill on the London Bank or on some other district. If the circulation of London or any of the other districts could not bear an increase the redundant circulation of the particular district would be finally exchanged for gold coin in London which would be melted or exported. If on the contrary the circulation of any particular district were too low it could only be increased by a transfer from London or from some other district where the circulation might be redundant. In London the circulation can always be increased either by means of the sale of gold bullion to the commissioners for paper money to be issued on the demand of the seller of the bullion or by the issue of notes by the commissioners in payment of gov^{t} securities which they are authorised to purchase in the market. ['This

The Bank of England, as well as every other Bank in this country is only of use as it substitutes a cheap currency for a dear one, a paper currency for a metallic one.

The advantages of a paper money provided security be taken to fix its value on a basis as permanent as the metals themselves have been so often and so satisfactorily, stated that it will not be necessary to dwell upon them here;—it will be sufficient simply and briefly to advert to them. The establishment of a paper money enables you to dispense with the use of a great quantity of a very valuable metal which as money produces nothing, but which being exchanged for raw material, machinery, food &cᵃ is made a productive capital and adds annually to the revenue of the country. The whole of such revenue is clear gain. Another advantage attending the use of paper money is the extreme facility with which payments are made by its means;—it is easily counted, it can be moved from one place to another without trouble or expences and is not subject to the loss to which metallic money is exposed from wear and friction. Let us only imagine that we had nothing but metallic money in the United Kingdom and were all obliged to receive our rents and our dividends and to carry on all our commercial transactions in such money and we shall have some idea of the immense benefits from the use of paper money. These then are the advantages which we derive from the establishment of Banks which issue paper money, but the public are apt to suppose that they confer other advantages and that our commerce is greatly benefited by the discounting of merchants bills which is a separate trade and would be equally carried on if the two

is in fact the precise way in which the circulation of London and the country is now regulated—' is del. here.] The only difference in the way proposed, and that by which the circulation is now regulated is this that if there be need of an increased quantity of circulation in the country now the country banker can increase the quantity of his notes and lend them at interest, or he can increase his gold deposits and increase his issues at the same time; in fact by buying gold coin with his notes. By the plan proposed he can do neither of these but the commissioners can; when they buy gold and procure the gold to be coined they in fact increase their issues and their deposits of gold coin at the same time, when they purchase govᵗ securities in the market they create an additional number of notes, and lend them at interest.'

businesses of issuing paper money and discounting bills were entirely separated.

Let me suppose that Government should take into its own hands one part of this joint business and should be the sole issuer of paper money in the kingdom, liable to the same obligation of paying their notes on demand in specie. It is known that the permanent Capital of the Bank is nearly 15 millions, which is all lent to Government at an interest of 3 pc^t p^r Ann^m.—It is known also that the Bank have made advances to Government on Excheq^r-bills, and on[1] an annuity which is to terminate at the end of 45 years. Let us suppose these advances to amount to 10 millions, and the whole debt of Government to the Bank to be 25 millions. Now then let us further suppose that at the expiration of the Charter Gov^t pays in notes of its own these 25 millions to the Bank and at the same [time][2] compels the Bank of Eng^d and all other Banks to call in their paper. It is evident that there would only be a substitution of one kind of paper for another there would neither be an increase or a diminution of quantity, and consequently there would be no diminution in the quantity devoted to mercantile discounts. On the contrary the Bank might greatly increase the amount of the particular fund which they now devote to such purposes. They would be in[3] possession of 15[4] millions of capital after paying all their debts and might employ the whole of this amount in discounting commercial bills. The probability is that no such amount would be lent for that particular purpose, and that the Bank would actually be obliged to invest a large portion of this capital in the public funds of the country. That however which I am desirous of proving is that there would be no want of power in the Bank to afford precisely the same accomodation to trade as they now do and therefore that it is no argument against the Gov^t issuing the paper money to urge that the trade of the country would be in want of its usual facilities. To make this more manifest let me suppose the following to be a statement of the affairs of the Bank

Loan to Gov^t —	15,000,000	Bank notes —	15,000,000
D^o ————	5,000,000[5]	Deposits	5,000,000
Bills discounted	3,000,000	Balance	
Bank Treasure	15,000,000[6]	constituting the capital of the Bank	18,000,000

---

1 'the half pay of the' is del. here.   4 Replaces '25'.
2 Omitted in MS.   5 Replaces '15,000,000'.
3 'immediate' is del. here.   6 Replaces '25,000,000'.

After the paym.ᵗ from Government of 15 millions and the withdrawing of 15 millions of Bank notes the acc.ᵗ would stand as follows

Loan to Gov.ᵗ —	5,000,000	Deposits —	5,000,000
Bills dis.ᵗ —	3,000,000	Bal.ᶜᵉ —	18,000,000
Treasure	15,000,000		

[Sketch of the Regulations for *A Plan for the Establishment of a National Bank*.]

Let there be a National Bank established in London and oblige all other Banks, the Bank of England included to call in all their notes in certain proportions at fixed periods during 3 years after which there shall be no paper money in circulation excepting that which is to be issued by Government.—

Let the Government paper be a legal tender.

Let the Govern.ᵗ Bank pay the Bank of England the debt due to them of £14,686,000 in Gov.ᵗ notes.

Let them further buy with their notes the whole stock of gold bullion of which the Bank is possessed at £3. 17. 6 p.ʳ oz—if the Bank is willing to sell it.—

Let any other debt due by Gov.ᵗ to the Bank be paid in Gov.ᵗ Bank notes.—

Let a calculation be made by a return of the Stamp duties on Promissory notes of the amount of Country Bankers notes in circulation.

Let this amount be added to the amount of Bank of England notes in circulation.—

If the aggregate amount of the Gov.ᵗ notes to be issued in payment to the Bank for debt and bullion, be less than the aggregate amount of Bank of England and Country Bank notes let the Gov.ᵗ issue a further amount of notes either in the purchase of bullion or of funded or unfunded debt as may be thought most expedient by those to whom the management of this important concern be confided.—

Let the Government Bank ever after regulate its issues by the price of gold bullion and the foreign exchanges.

The Gov.ᵗ Bank shall be obliged to pay its notes in coin or bullion.—

It shall be obliged to give its notes at all times in exchange for gold coin of lawful weight, and shall also be obliged to buy whatever gold standard bullion may be offered to them at £3. 17. 6 per oz.—

NOTES FROM RICARDO'S
MANUSCRIPTS
1818–1823

FRAGMENTS ON TORRENS
CONCERNING VALUE
1818

NOTE ON FRAGMENTS ON TORRENS

EARLY in September 1817 Robert Torrens wrote a review of Ricardo's *Principles*: it was offered to the *Edinburgh Review*, which did not accept it.[1] Following this there were discussions concerning the theory of value between Ricardo and Torrens. Ricardo refers in particular to 'a long conversation' with Torrens on the question of value, 'without convincing each other', which probably took place in February 1818;[2] and Malthus in a letter of that month expresses surprise 'that Major Torrens should puzzle himself so long with his peculiar objections to your measure of value'.[3]

One of Torrens' objections can be inferred from the paragraph added in edition 2 of Ricardo's *Principles*[4] which begins: 'The same result will take place if the circulating capitals be of unequal durability'; and which, as Ricardo wrote to McCulloch, 'more fully answers Major Torrens' objection'.[5] This is the same problem as is discussed in the two Notes printed below as (A 1) and (A 2); and we can therefore conjecture that these are contemporary with the discussions of February 1818.[6]

In edition 1 of his *Principles* Ricardo had said that, after capital had accumulated in the hands of persons who set labourers to work, relative values of commodities 'occasioned by more or less labour being required to produce them', were also affected by a rise of wages (*a*) when 'fixed and circulating capitals were in different proportions', and (*b*) when fixed capital was 'of different durability'.[7] Now Torrens (in a Note which has not

---

[1] Below, VII, 179.
[2] *ib.* 338, n. 2.
[3] *ib.* 253.
[4] Above, I, 61 n.
[5] Below, VII, 338.
[6] One sheet of (A 1) bears the watermark of 1817 and has on the back of it in Ricardo's handwriting some particulars of the 4th Report of the Committee on Finance of 5 June 1817.
[7] Above, I, 56. An alternative version of the same conditions was: 'if the fixed capital employed be either of unequal value or of unequal duration' (*ib.* 53).

been found) appears to have confronted him with a source of variation which did not fit into either of these categories.

In the paragraph added in edition 2 of the *Principles*, Ricardo dealt with the problem by introducing a third category, *i.e.*, one in which 'the circulating capitals be of unequal durability'.[1] But in the Note (A 1) he had adopted a different solution. He included the case under discussion within the first of the two existing categories: 'in this case the raw material in both manufactures is really fixed capital of equal duration, but of unequal value'.[2]

He evidently noticed immediately that the inclusion of raw material in the category of fixed capital could not be limited to 'this case'; and there follows the interesting passage crossed out in the manuscript, in which he extends the definition of fixed capital to include all that is used in production 'except that which resolves itself into wages' (thus leaving wages as the sole constituent of circulating capital). This was a radical departure from his distinction between the two sorts of capital as being one of degree, which he declared it to be in the *Principles* (above, I, 150). The distinction which he here arrived at under the name of fixed and circulating capital coincided with that between constant and variable capital later established by Marx. This interpretation of fixed and circulating capital was first advanced in a published work by George Ramsay in his *Essay on the Distribution of Wealth*, 1836, whom Marx regarded as the originator of this notion.[3] However, Ricardo reverted to his original definition, and emphasised it in edition 2 of the *Principles* (above, I, 31).

In the autumn of 1818 Torrens met McCulloch in Edinburgh and discussed with him Ricardo's theory of value. They agreed to continue their argument in the *Edinburgh Magazine* in amicable battle.[4] An article by Torrens appeared in the October number of the *Edinburgh Magazine* in the form of a letter to the Editor, signed 'R', under the title 'Strictures on Mr Ricardo's Doctrine respecting Exchangeable Value'. In this Torrens declared that

---

[1] Below, VII, 338 and above, I, 61: see also the paragraph added in I, 31.
[2] Below, p. 311.
[3] *Theorien über den Mehrwert*, ed. 1923, vol. III, p. 381–2.
[4] Below, VII, 316.

Adam Smith was correct in maintaining that 'after stock has accumulated in the hands of particular persons who set industrious people to work by advancing them wages and material, the quantity of labour employed in production is not the circumstance which determines the exchangeable value of commodities'. Since the market price of commodities exceeds the wages of the labour by which they are produced and the rate of profit on capital tends to equality in different industries, and since 'equal capitals generally put unequal quantities of labour in motion', it follows inevitably: 'first that the products obtained by the employment of equal capitals will be equal in value; and, secondly, that things on the production of which equal quantities of labour were bestowed will not be equivalent to each other in the market'. This doctrine that the products of equal capitals will be equal in value he qualified by the statement that 'when capitals equal in amount, but of different degrees of durability, are employed, the articles produced, together with the residue of capital, in one occupation, will be equal to the things produced, and the residue of capital in another occupation'.[1]

It was probably soon after he had seen Torrens' article on 25 November[2] that Ricardo entered in one of his commonplace books[3] the parallel quotations of Torrens' objections side by side with the passages in his own *Principles* which proved them groundless.

McCulloch wrote a reply to Torrens, dated 2 Nov. 1818, which was published in the November number of the same magazine over the signature 'M'. Ricardo shared Mill's dissatisfaction with McCulloch's vindication[4] and himself wrote an answer to Torrens' attack, and sent a copy of this to Mill.[5] This answer was not written with the intention of publication ('I have not entered into a long dissertation in my answer to Torrens. I wrote

---

[1] *Edinburgh Magazine*, Oct. 1818, p. 337.
[2] Below, VII, 332, n. 3.
[3] This entry follows one from the *Edinburgh Review* of September 1818 and precedes one from Montesquieu's *Spirit of Laws*,

which he says in a letter to Mill on 28 Dec. 1818 that he had been reading (below, VII, 382).
[4] Below, VII, 364.
[5] Below, VII, 376. Ricardo had completed this reply by 12 Dec. 1818 (*ib.* 360).

it for my own satisfaction and with no idea of publishing it')[1]. Unfortunately this reply has not been found. In sending the copy of it to Mill, however, Ricardo made an important comment upon what he considered to be his true difference of opinion with Adam Smith, which affords some indication of the tenor of the missing reply to Torrens.[2] Torrens' theory was reproduced in closely similar terms in 1821 in his *Essay on the Production of Wealth*, which is discussed by Ricardo in his paper on Absolute Value and Exchangeable Value (below, pp. 393–6).

Notes (A 1) and (A 2) are written, in the handwriting of Ricardo and Torrens respectively, on separate sheets of notepaper, and were found among the Mill-Ricardo papers.

The commonplace book containing the parallel passages (B) is in Ricardo's Papers. This item was published in *Minor Papers on the Currency Question, 1809–1823*, Baltimore, The Johns Hopkins Press, 1932. The page references, which in the original are to ed. 1 of Ricardo's *Principles*, have been adjusted to the pagination of Vol. I of the present edition; words underlined in the MS have been printed in italics.

[1] Below, VII, 372.   [2] *ib.* 377.

[RICARDO ON TORRENS]

According to Major Torrens supposition 5 days labour are necessary to produce a certain quantity of flax and 90 days labour are further required to make that flax into Cambric.

To make the coarse linen he supposes that 40 days labour are necessary to procure the flax and 20 additional days to work it into linen.

Under these circumstances I say that the cambric will have a value superior to the linen in the proportion of 95 to 60.

Major Torrens says that before society is divided into the two classes of capitalists and labourers the cambric will be twice the value of the linen, but after such division it will be of equal value,[1] and therefore he contends that the principle

---

[1] To understand how Torrens may have reached these results in the missing note to which Ricardo is replying, it must be kept in mind that (as appears from the sequel in Ricardo's Note and from Torrens's reply to it) he was assuming: (*a*) that one day's labour produces two days' subsistence, (*b*) that 'a capital' consisting entirely of subsistence is used in the first year to produce both the raw material and the subsistence which are required to manufacture the finished product in the second year. The quantity of labour necessary to produce a commodity is treated by him as including the labour employed during the first year in producing the subsistence consumed by workers in the second year. On this calculation the cambric requires *twice* as much labour to produce as does the coarse linen (cambric: 5 days' labour for producing flax + 45 days' labour for producing subsistence for the second year + 90 days' labour for manufacture = 140 days' labour; coarse linen: 40 for flax + 10 for subsistence + 20 for manufacture = 70 days' labour). But both the cambric and the coarse linen are produced by *equal initial capitals*: namely, 50 days' subsistence in each case (5 + 45 and 40 + 10).

Ricardo, however, does *not* count the labour employed in producing the subsistence for the second year as part of the labour required to produce cambric and coarse linen; and accordingly arrives at a value-ratio of 95:60 (*i.e.* 5 + 90 for the former and 40 + 20 for the latter).

which I endeavor to establish of commodities being valuable only in proportion to the labour necessary to produce them, when the fixed capital of the manufacturer is of the same value and of equal duration is not true.

To support his opinion Major T supposes that men having all the requisites to work should employ their labour not on the commodity which is ultimately to be produced but on some other nowise necessary to its production.

Thus he supposes that the manufacturers of cambric employ their labour in producing food, and while consuming the food they manufacture their flax into cambric; but as this is not the most economical course for the manufacturers to pursue Major Torrens should shew why they should follow it; why when they had 50 days subsistence they should rather employ men in producing subsistence than in producing cambric, the commodity they intend to sell in the market.

Suppose the Capitalist to have at his command 95 days labour, and that the materials mentioned would produce 100 yards of cambric; he can at once produce them, for it is acknowledged that 5 days labour will produce the flax, and 90 will manufacture the flax into cambric.

The manufacturer of coarse linen requiring also by the supposition 60 days labour to produce 100 yards, viz. 40 for the flax, and 20 for the manufacture of the flax into linen; 95 days labour will give him $158\frac{2}{8}$ yards, consequently the value of cambric will be to that of linen as $158\frac{2}{8}$ to 100—or as 95 to 60.

But the same quantity will be given when society is divided into two classes if the circumstances are as here supposed, for either the two capitals will be of equal or of unequal value. If equal the returns must be equal which can only be while 95 yards of linen will exchange for 60 yards of cambric,—if unequal the returns must be unequal and must be in the proportion of 95 to 60 to yield the same number of yards and give to each capitalist the same rate of profit.

But the circumstances here supposed never take place, a man having 50 days labour at his disposal cannot produce flax, and then cambric; for though 5 days labour only may be necessary to produce the flax, of which the cambric is made, he must probably wait 6, 9 or 12 months before he can add the labour to it necessary to make cambric.

It is therefore requisite to consider the case as stated by Major Torrens where he supposes that two men have equal capitals each of the value of 100 days subsistence—the capital of one consisting of flax of the value of 10 days subsistence and food of the value of 90 days subsistence; the capital of the other consisting of flax of the value of 80 days subsistence, and of food of the value of 20 days subsistence. Will not these commodities says Major T be of equal value being the products of equal capitals? I answer yes.[1] But continues Major T if you agree that they will be of equal value is it not evident that they are not the result of the same quantity of labour, you yourself having shewn that one required only 60 days labour the other 95? To which I answer that the proposition in my book requires that they should be of equal value although there be different quantities of labour employed in their production, because in this case the raw material in both manufactures[2] is really fixed capital of equal duration, but of unequal value. That employed in the production of linen being 8 times more valuable, than that employed in the production of the cambric.

[1] There is attached here a footnote: 'See Note 1', but the note referred to is not extant.

[2] 'in both manufactures' is ins.

[It appears then that every thing is fixed capital which is employed on production except that which resolves itself into wages. If with a capital of £1000 I manufacture commodities made of Iron that part of my capital only can be considered as circulating which is exclusively devoted to the payment of wages.][1]

To shew this, let us take a strong case. Suppose 5 mens labour to be employed for a year in making iron; it will sell not only for the labour which produced it, but for as much more as the profits on the capital which employed the 5 days labour; suppose this profit to be added to the capital, and to employ 6 men for the next year in producing the same commodity; and that this be sold and the profit added to the capital, and so on for twenty years; and that at the end of that period, the iron produced will sell for £100. Suppose now another man possessing a capital equal to the employment of 5 men for a year, should make them work in planting a piece of ground, which affords no rent, with acorns. It is evident that at the end of twenty years, the wood growing on his land should be of the value of £100; for as he started with a capital equal to that of the man who employed the labour he could command on iron, and as the capitals had in both cases accumulated for 20 years without affording any advantage in the interim to their owners, their results must be equal to afford the same profits. Now the whole quantity of labour realized in the wood is only that of 5 men for a year, that employed on the iron very considerably exceeds the labour of 100 men employed for a year. Here then are two commodities of equal value one of which is the production of more than 5 times the quantity of labour employed on the production of the other.

[1] This paragraph is deleted.

Now supposing Iron to be necessary in one manufacture and wood in another, altho' their cost should be equal, and all other parts of the circulating capital of the manufacturers, who work on these commodities as raw material be also equal, and the prices of their finished commodities be equal, yet those finished commodities would be the result of unequal quantities of labour, because unequal quantities were necessary to the production of the raw materials of each. Thus suppose a cutler to employ a capital of £1000—£100 of which consisted of steel[1], and an upholsterer to employ an equal capital of £1000—£100 of which consisted of wood, the steel made by the cutler in one year, and the furniture made by the upholsterer in the same time would[2] sell for the same money, but as the iron employed would contain much more labour than the wood, the finished commodity in iron would continue in its finished state to represent more labour than the finished commodity in wood, altho the same quantity of circulating capital had been subsequently employed on them. In the same way it might be proved that a carpenter and upholsterer employing the same amount of capitals but an unequal value of wood as their raw material, though they would sell their finished goods for the same money, yet those goods would represent different quantities of labour. This last is Major Torrens case and is in my opinion completely answered by shewing that in the production of the raw material different quantities of fixed capital were used.

[1] 'in its rude state' is del. here.   [2] 'would' replaces 'ought to'.

(A 2)

[TORRENS ON RICARDO]

If there is any surplus in the form either of profit or of rent the labour of a man must produce more than the subsistence of a man. I will therefore say for the sake of illustration that a days labour produces two days subsistence.

A has a capital produced by 50 days labour and consisting of subsistence for 90 and flax equivalent to subsistence for 10 and employs 90 labourers in converting the flax into lace; *B* has a capital produced by 50 days labour and consisting of subsistence for 10 and flax equivalent to subsistence for 90 and employs 10 labourers in converting the flax into coarse cloth.

Now in this case the lace and the cloth will be of equal value because they are the results of the employment of equivalent capitals and the results of equivalent capitals must be equivalent otherwise the profits of stock will not be equal.

But though the lace and the cloth are of equal value they are not the products of equal quantities of labour. The subsistence and material advanced for [the][1] production of the lace was raised by 50 days labour [and 90] days were employed in working it up; while [the] subsistence and material advanced for the production of the cloth was raised by 50 days labour and only 10 days were employed in working it up. In the one case 140 days labour are employed; in the other case only 60 days labour are employed.

Ricardo objects to this case and says that I should not take into the calculation the labour employed on producing the subsistence. I do not admit the validity of this objection but for argument I concede the point and throw out the

[1] MS torn here and below.

labour which produces the subsistence. The case then stands thus. To prepare the lace 90 days labour are employed on material produced by 5, to prepare the cloth 10 days labour are employed upon material produced by 45 day labour. Yet still the value of the lace and the cloth must be equal because the two articles cannot be produced but by the expenditure of equivalent capitals.

(B)

[AN ENTRY IN RICARDO'S COMMONPLACE BOOK]

Major Torrens under the signature of R in the Edinburgh Magazine for Oct.ʳ 1818 has observed as follows on Mr. Ricardo's doctrine respecting exchangeable value

In Mr. Ricardo's book on the Principles of Political Economy in which his doctrine of value is given he says as follows

Dr. Smith says that "in that rude state of society which precedes both the accumulation of stock, and the appropriation of land, the proportion of labour necessary for acquiring different objects, seems to be the only circumstance, which can afford any rule for exchanging them for one another. If, among a nation of hunters, for example, it usually costs

In the early stages of society, the exchangeable value of these commodities or the rule which determines how much of one shall be given in exchange for another, depends *solely* on the comparative quantity of labour expended on each.

Page [12]

Though Adam Smith fully

twice the labour to kill a beaver which it does to kill a deer, one beaver should naturally exchange for, or be worth two deer. It is natural that what is usually the produce of two days or two hours labour, should be worth double of what is usually the produce of one day's or one hour's labour."

Smith however limits this principle to the first and rudest period of society, and contends, that as soon as stock accumulates in the hands of particular persons who set industrious people to work by supplying them with subsistence and materials, the quantity of labour commonly employed in acquiring or producing any commodity is not the only circumstance which can regulate its exchangeable value in the market. *This limitation of the principle is represented as a great and fundamental error by Mr. Ricardo*, who contends that in the most advanced periods of society, as well as in that rude and simple state which

recognized the principle that the proportion between the quantities of labour necessary for acquiring different objects is the only circumstance which can afford any rule for our exchanging them for one another, yet he limits its application to "that early and rude state of society which precedes both the accumulation of stock *and the appropriation of land*"; as if, when profits *and rent* were to be paid, they would have some influence on the relative value of commodities, independent of the mere quantity of labour that was necessary to their production.

Adam Smith however has no where analyzed the effects of the accumulation of capital, *and the appropriation of land*, on relative value. It is of importance therefore to determine how far the effects which are avowedly produced on the exchangeable value of commodities, by the comparative quantity of labour bestowed on their production, *are modified or altered by* precedes the accumulation of stock, and the separation of the community into capitalists and labourers, the labour bestowed upon production is the *only* foundation of exchangeable value.

This is the radical difference between Dr. Smith and Mr. Ricardo.

Mr. Ricardo admits, that when equal capitals are of different degrees of durability, the products of equal quantities of labour will not be of equal value; *and this he states as an exception to his general principle*, that the labour expended on production determines exchangeable value: But as equal capitals seldom possess precisely equal degrees of durability, this, instead of limiting *what he calls the general principle*, subverts it altogether, and proves, that the relative worth of all things is determined, not by the quantities of labour required to procure them, but by the universally operating law of competition,

the accumulation of capital, and the payment of rent.

Page [22–3, n.]

Besides the alteration in the relative value of commodities, occasioned by more or less labour being required to produce them, they are also subject to fluctuations from a rise of wages, and consequent fall of profits, if the fixed capital employed be either of unequal value, or of unequal duration.

Page [53]

Thus we see, that with every rise of wages, in proportion as the capital employed in any occupation, consists of circulating capital, its produce will be of greater relative value than the goods produced in another occupation where a less proportion of circulating, and a greater proportion of fixed capital are employed.

Page [58]

It appears, then, that in proportion to the quantity and

which equalises the profits of stock, and, consequently, renders the results obtained from the employment of equal capitals of equal value in exchange.

No proposition, physical or moral, can admit of a more rigid demonstration than the principles laid down by Dr. Smith, that, after stock has accumulated in the hands of particular persons who set industrious people to work by advancing them wages and material the quantity of labour employed in production is not the circumstance which determines the exchangeable value of commodities.

durability of the fixed capital employed in any kind of production, the relative prices of those commodities on which such capital is employed, will vary inversely as wages; they will fall as wages rise.

Page [62–3]

It appears then that the accumulation of capital by occasioning different proportions of fixed and circulating capital to be employed in different trades, and by giving different degrees of durability to such fixed capital, introduces a considerable modification to the rule, which is of universal application in the early states of society.

Page [66]

A NOTE ON PRICES AND TAXATION

1821

THIS Note is concerned with the question whether a tax on commodities could raise prices without an increase in the quantity of money. This was a matter on which Ricardo twice changed his mind. In 1811 in his *Reply to Bosanquet*[1] he held that this was possible. In 1817 in edition 1 of the *Principles* he denied the possibility; but in edition 3 he reverted to his earlier view, adding two footnotes in which he accepted the possibility 'on further consideration'[2]. The argument of the Note printed below is so closely similar to that of the footnotes added to edition 3 in 1821 as to indicate that it belongs to this period.

Soon after the publication of edition 3 the same problem was discussed by the Political Economy Club, in the form of the following question proposed by Torrens on 30 April 1821: 'The quantity of Money being constant, would a general tax upon all commodities in a country raise their prices?'[3] This and a similar question proposed by Tooke at a later meeting were discussed at a series of meetings up to June 1823. Ricardo describes one of these discussions in a letter to McCulloch of 8 Feb. 1822.[4]

The MS consists of a single half-sheet, one side of which is in Ricardo's handwriting. At the bottom of it Trower writes 'turn over', and on the back of it he adds his own comments. The MS was found among Trower's papers and later passed into Dr. Bonar's possession. It was printed in Appendix B to *Letters of Ricardo to Trower*, edited by Bonar and Hollander, 1899.

[1] Above, III, 242–3.
[2] Above, I, 213, and cp. 169.
[3] *Political Economy Club, Minutes 1821–1882*, p. 40 ff.
[4] Below, IX, 158–9.

[A NOTE ON PRICES AND TAXATION]

[RICARDO]

A B and *C* each lay out £100 p^r Ann^m in Corn, when its price is 40/ p^r quarter, they each buy 50 quarters. But Government imposes a tax of 10/- p^r quarter on corn, and consequently the price of corn rises from 40 to 50 shillings, and the whole 150 quarters consumed will cost £375, instead of £300. In consequence however of the additional price, *A*, *B*, and *C*, can each, only purchase 40 quarters, instead of 50;—and therefore they will together purchase 120 quarters instead of 150. There will remain 30 quarters to be disposed of[,] which will be purchased by Government at the market price of 50/- and therefore for £75. This sum of £75 is precisely the sum which Government has raised by the tax of 10/- on 150 quarters, I think therefore I have shewn that although it is true that 150 quarters of corn will be disposed of for £375 instead of for £300 no additional quantity of money will be required for the purpose of purchasing it.—

[TROWER]

No additional money is required to purchase it, because although more money is *paid* for the corn in consequence of the Tax, yet the cost of production of the corn, its natural price, is not increased. And the seller of the corn pays over to Government the extra price he receives in consequence of the Tax. This money, so paid to Government, is given to other persons, by whom that portion of the Corn is purchased, which used to be bought by the tax payers before the Tax was imposed.

So that the same £300 purchases the Corn whose price is raised by the Tax to £375. And it is enabled to do this in consequence of the *increased ratio* of its circulation, which the imposition of the tax occasions. Before the tax was imposed the 300 purchased 150 quarters of Corn for 300, now it first purchases 120 quarters @ 50/- amounting to 300; and then afterwards, that portion of it which was paid for the tax, vz.ᵗ 75, purchases the remaining 30 quarters @ 50/- amounting to 75. So that that portion circulates twice where before the Tax was imposed it only circulated once.

Thus the only effect of the Tax is to take from the payers of it the power of purchasing 30 quarters of Corn, and to transfer that power to other persons; and this is effected by causing the money to pass through the hands of the seller of the Corn to Government and from Government to these other persons. The increase in the ratio of circulation is equal to the amount of the Tax—vz.ᵗ 25 pC.ᵗ

ON BLAKE'S 'OBSERVATIONS ON THE EFFECTS PRODUCED BY THE EXPENDITURE OF GOVERNMENT'

1823

Observations on the Effects Produced by the Expenditure of Government during the Restriction of Cash Payments, by William Blake, F.R.S., was published on 8 March 1823.[1] The author states in the preface that he had written it in February 1822. Sometime between these two dates ('before he printed it') he showed it to Ricardo, who afterwards wrote: 'I used the privilege of a friend in freely giving him my sentiments upon it: he was kind enough to give to my remarks the most attentive consideration, but he at last came to the conclusion that he had taken a correct view of the subject.'[2]

This exchange of 'sentiments' before publication however is distinct from the controversy contained in the papers printed below, which took place *after*, probably immediately after, publication. Ricardo wrote a series of remarks on the margins of his own copy of the published *Observations*; he wrote them first in pencil, and then went over them carefully in ink, no doubt to enable his friends to read them.[3] Blake dealt with Ricardo's criticisms one by one, in a reply which extends to 19 quarto pages of MS.

McCulloch, in a letter to Ricardo on 21 March 1823, sharply criticised Blake's pamphlet, but he wished to have Ricardo's opinion before attacking it in print, for he did not trust his own judgement in matters of exchange: 'I should esteem it as a most particular favour if you could find time to give me a few remarks on Mr. Blake's pamphlet'.

It was probably this hint that set Ricardo working on the review which is printed below from the MS. However, he did not finish it, nor did he send it to McCulloch. He wrote him instead a letter on 25 March 1823, which follows closely the argument of the first part of the review, but sets it out more clearly and briefly. There can be little doubt that the review was written just before that letter.

---

[1] Advt. of the Publishers (John Murray and E. Lloyd & Son) headlined 'To-morrow, 8vo, 4*s*.' in *Morning Chronicle*, 7 March 1823.

[2] Letter to McCulloch of 25 March 1823, below, IX, 275.

[3] Occasionally the ink version differs from the pencil one, but in such cases the pencil script is mostly illegible. From the quotations given in Blake's replies it is clear that he had before him the ink version as printed here.

McCulloch published a long review of Blake in the form of a leading article in the *Scotsman* of 12 April 1823. But notwithstanding the guidance he had received it did not meet with Ricardo's approval, as is made clear in a letter to McCulloch of 3 May 1823.[1]

In the present edition each remark has been given a roman number. In each case, a short quotation from Blake's pamphlet is printed first, in small type; then Ricardo's comment upon it, in larger type; finally Blake's reply, in small type. To the first there is prefixed the page reference to the pamphlet, to the second the letter [R.], to the third the letter [B.]. The quotations are only intended to identify the sentence to which the comment is directly attached; they do not attempt to enable the reader to follow the line of Blake's argument.

Ricardo's notes and his review are here published for the first time. Blake's replies have been printed in Ricardo's *Minor Papers on the Currency Question*, ed. J. H. Hollander, Baltimore, The Johns Hopkins Press, 1932.

The original copy of Blake's pamphlet annotated by Ricardo is in the Library of Somerville College, Oxford. I am indebted to Professor F. A. Hayek for finding it and to the Librarian for making it available. This copy is inscribed 'From the Author', not in Blake's hand. The volume of pamphlets at the end of which it is bound up[2] bears the printed label: 'This book formed part of the Library of the late JOHN STUART MILL, presented to the College by Miss Helen Taylor, in 1905.'

The MS of Blake's reply is in Ricardo's Papers.

The MS of Ricardo's review is in the Mill-Ricardo Papers.

---

[1] Below, IX, 284 ff.

[2] The other pamphlets in the volume are Ricardo's *Protection to Agriculture*, 3rd ed., 1822 and Whitmore's *Letter on the Present State and Future Prospects of Agriculture*, 2nd ed., 1823, inscribed 'From the Author': there are no MS notes on them. The volume is uncut, bound in boards with vellum back and on the back the titles are written in ink in Ricardo's handwriting.

[NOTES ON BLAKE'S 'OBSERVATIONS ON THE EFFECTS PRODUCED BY THE EXPENDITURE OF GOVERNMENT' 1823 WITH BLAKE'S REPLIES]

I

[Blake's *Observations*, p. 7.] As the law now stands upon this point, the coin is permitted to be exported, and therefore no alteration whatever would take place in the price of gold so long as the merchant exporter could apply at the Bank and convert the paper currency into exportable coin.

[Ricardo's note.] How long could he do so? Would the few millions of gold in the Bank, the greatest part of which is absolutely required to keep up a money circulation, have the effect ascribed by the author?

[Blake's reply.] The author merely says that no alteration would take place in the price of Gold *so long as* the merchant could convert paper into Gold at the Bank. If the critic is *determined* to ask *how long* the author answers it would depend upon the amount of foreign expenditure; if that was very large the Bank would *soon* be drained.

II

[p. 9.] It is manifest to common sense, that with such an alteration in the exchange, there must be a corresponding and proportional alteration in the price of bullion.

Now, if the paper currency of the kingdom is not convertible into coin, what is there in this demand for bullion that can have any influence on the amount of the currency?

[R.] The exportation of commodities would prevent the rise of bullion. We have a debt to pay, why should it be assumed that the payment must be made in bullion to the exclusion of commodities. Every fall in the exchange is a bounty on the exportation of commodities.

[B.] The exportation of commodities would prevent the rise of Bullion if a *sufficient* quantity could be got out at a small variation in the Exchange but when the Expenditure is very large foreigners will not take our goods unless we can sell them cheap and we cannot sell them cheap enough to make the foreigner buy large quantities except the Exchange becomes adverse to a sufficient degree.

III

[p. 9.] It is curious to observe, in the examinations of the merchants on this point before the committees of 1810 and 1819, the extreme perplexity they evinced, when pressed to explain how the value of gold could rise partially here, without a corresponding rise on the Continent;

[R.] I should not call this a rise in the value of gold in England but a fall in the value of money peculiar to England.

[B.] When the Exchange became adverse so as to exceed the expenses of the transit of Bullion considerably the author maintains that the value of Bullion would rise although the currency remained at an invariable value.

IV

[pp. 9–10, consecutive to preceding quotation.] and with what complacency the examiners seem to have regarded the steadiness of its price on the Continent, as a proof that its high price here must have arisen from depreciation dependent upon over issue.

Now there is nothing whatever in the effect just described, that in the slightest degree indicates the currency to have changed its value in relation to commodities in general. It marks neither more nor less than that gold acquired an artificial increase of value in this country, in consequence solely of the premium on foreign bills.

[R.] The complacency was well founded. I do not know what sense the author gives to the word value when he talks of an artificial increase in the value of gold in this country. Can this artificial increase of value exist for years. The subject in dispute is, was gold increased in value when it differed from the value of paper or was paper low? The author answers gold had increased in value. I ask for his proofs and he answers that though gold rose other commodities did not rise. The fact however is directly the reverse—the author himself acknowledges it and endeavours to account for it by a theory of his own built upon a great government expenditure. He acknowledges that in our paper currency gold and all commodities rose in value whilst no such rise took place abroad, and yet he denies that it was our peculiar currency which fell in value.

[B.] This artificial increase of value might exist for years if the expenditure created an adverse Exchange for years—the author purposely avoids at present the discussion respecting the price of commodities generally—all that he contends for is that with an adverse exchange exceeding the expenses of the transit of Bullion—the price of Bullion must rise *although* currency remained unaltered and the prices of commodities generally remained the same—the demonstration is given first independently of all application to existing circumstances—then application is made afterwards.

V

[p. 10, consecutive to preceding.] The restriction on the specie payments of the Bank virtually precluding the accustomed contraction of the currency, it no longer rose to a level with the gold; and the excess of the market price above the mint price, marked the height to which the gold had risen.

[R.] Here the question in dispute is taken for granted. Did gold rise or paper fall? In either case the price of bullion would appear high and the exchanges unfavorable.

Goods rose as well as gold, and therefore the probability is in our favor.

[B.] The question is not taken for granted—the inference is drawn from the preceding demonstration. If there was no other cause for the rise of goods the probability would be in favor of the critic's opinion that the paper altered—but why will not the critic be content to examine the demonstration whether Gold would or would not rise even though the paper did not alter.

VI

[p. 10, consecutive to preceding.] Admitting then, that if the Bank had been paying in specie, the difference in the value of gold would not have shown itself, would it not be a strange confusion to say that the restriction was the cause of the increased value?

[R.] We say the restriction was the cause of the increased price. We have doubts about the increased value of gold.

[B.] If the critic doubts whether the Gold increased in value let him remain sceptical till the author removes those doubts let him attend first to the demonstration that the price of Gold *might* alter and afterwards to the facts which prove that it *did* alter.

VII

[p. 11.] The moment the term depreciation is applied to the currency, it is assumed as the cause of the increase of prices generally. If an adverse exchange raises the price of bullion 20 per cent. above the Mint price, it is supposed to account for an increase in the price of commodities to the extent of 20 per cent. also; than which nothing can be more fallacious.

[R.] This is not precisely what we say, for bullion itself may have varied all over the world.

[B.] The critic and his friends may not mean what is here stated but the public certainly misapply the term depreciation and do not use it in the sense ascribed to it by the critic. The author is writing for the public.

VIII

[p. 13.] And in another part of his evidence he [Mr. Ricardo] says, 'I think it quite possible that a bank note may be depreciated, although it should rise in value, if it did not rise in value in a degree equal to the standard.'

[R.] I believe all the other witnesses agreed with Mr. Ricardo in this explanation of the meaning of the word depreciation.

[B.] The author agrees with the critic that Mr. Ricardo is consistent in his use of the term depreciation—although some passages in the pamphlet on the protection of Agriculture might lead to an opposite inference—but the author very much doubts whether the other witnesses are equally consistent—he believes that they frequently confound the two senses when their attention is not immediately drawn to the distinction.

IX

[pp. 13–14.] This question—whether the currency or the gold had altered?—was continually put to the witnesses by the committee in 1810 and 1819, and never received a precise and definite reply. To read the evidence, one would imagine both the examiners and the examined were alike perplexed. If the witness affirms, that gold has risen in value because it is wanted for exportation (which is quite correct), he is immediately asked, whether it has risen in the general market of the commercial world, whether there was any greater demand for gold on the Continent, or whether there was any scarcity in the supply there?

[R.] What should make gold go from England to the Continent where it did not go before unless it had fallen in England or had risen abroad? To say that it rose in value in England and remained steady abroad, and yet that it was profitable to export it is a manifest contradiction.

[B.] How can the critic ask such a question? The reason is obvious. If the premium on the foreign Bill was greater than the loss from the difference of prices the Gold would go. It might go too at a loss, if the loss was less upon the Gold, than upon the export of goods. The critic seems to forget that there was an expenditure that must be provided for coute qui coute.

X

[p. 14.] Whereas, the true and proper answer would have been, It has not risen in the general market of the world; it is not in greater demand abroad; there is no scarcity in the supply there. If goods could be exported without loss, they would answer the purpose as well as gold. The demand is for foreign payment, not for gold; and it rises in value in this country, and this country alone, because the exchange has become so adverse as to create a large premium on a foreign bill, and a profit is to be obtained by the export of gold.

[R.] A large premium on a foreign bill undoubtedly makes it profitable to export gold if its price does not rise in the same degree as the bill, but is not this true also of every other commodity? does it not become profitable to export them as well as gold? Why does the author always speak of gold as a commodity differing from all others and as alone calculated to discharge the expense of a foreign expenditure. Bills of exchange never really discharge a balance of debt, debts must be paid by things having value, a bill of exchange has none. If we observe that gold is regularly for years exported from one country into another shall we be wrong in saying that it is dearer or of greater value in the importing than in the exporting country?

[B.] Here the critic answers his own preceding question, and explains the supposed contradiction—but he asks—'Why does the author always speak of Gold as alone calculated to discharge the foreign expenditure?' This is a strange question in a note upon a passage where the author expressly says—'If goods could be exported without loss they would answer the purpose as well as gold, the demand is for foreign payment, not for gold'. The author is perfectly aware that the foreign expenditure must be discharged by goods (except where it is very trifling) but he is also aware that goods have to come in competition with the goods of the foreigner in the foreign market, and that consequently he must sell them cheap in order to make the foreigner buy; but he cannot sell them cheap unless the Exchange is adverse in proportion to the quantity of goods that must be sent—whereas gold is nearly sure of a market. Goods go first. When the premium on the Bill exceeds the expenses of the transit of Bullion —Bullion goes. And as I have said in a note p. 8. a half p cent profit would drain the country of all disposable Bullion. After that drain, goods must liquidate the balance—but in proportion as that balance is large, must the Exchange be depressed, before the goods can be sold cheap enough abroad. When the Exchange is thus depressed, what Gold remains in the country for the purpose of manufacture must be sold at a proportionally high price, for without that high price all would go.

XI

[pp. 15–16.] The price of corn, of cloth, of every other commodity, might remain precisely the same, and nothing alter but the price of gold. Not only might it vary to any extent without altering the price of these articles, but for any length of time too, provided the foreign expenditure continued upon the same scale that first induced the adverse exchange, and was constantly creating a fresh adverse balance, as the export of bullion or of other commodities was tending to liquidate it.

[R.] This idea of commodities remaining at the same price while gold rises considerably, and no impediment is offered to foreign commerce, appears to me to have no foundation.

[B.] I do not believe that Gold would have remained at so high a price as it reached during the war, unless impediments had been thrown in the way of foreign commerce. It was during the Milan decrees and American Embargo that Gold *continued* at a very high price; from 1800 to 1802 and to 1808 it was scarcely more than 4£. ℘ oz. It is not denied either that the price of such goods as suited the foreign market might rise—but this would be a rise from demand not from an alteration in the value of currency neither would it affect *all* commodities. It could not in this country for instance affect the value of our Corn.

XII

[p. 17.] It will be asked, however, does not this excess [of the market price above the mint price of gold] imply a derangement in the currency? Does it not imply a greater amount of circulating medium than could have existed under similar circumstances, if the Bank had been paying in specie? Undoubtedly it does.

[R.] This is the sole admission that my theory requires.

[B.] This is the sole admission too that I require. I think it ought to conform to Gold—but I am examining whether Gold rises, not whether the currency ought not to rise also.

XIII

[p. 18.] But how is the currency to be so regulated? And to whom is the regulation to be committed? To the bank directors? By no means. Much of unmerited odium, as I believe these gentlemen to have incurred,...

[R.] What odium have they acquired except that of ignorance? is that unmerited?

[B.] The public certainly charged the Bank Directors with taking advantage of their privileges to enrich themselves and proprietors at the expense of other classes—they were charged too with the murder of all the poor wretches hanged for forgery &c. &c.

XIV

[pp. 19–20.] After this examination it may be assumed, that provided the paper be not convertible at option into coin or bullion, the price of gold will be advanced by an adverse exchange; and yet, that the currency may remain at its natural level, that is, unaltered in value, and be maintained in its exact and perfect relative proportion to the commodities to be circulated by it.

[R.] This is undoubtedly a possible case, and would happen if gold generally rose in value all over the world, but the proof to be given of that rise should be very satisfactory before it ought to be admitted.

[B.] It is more than a possible case it is a demonstrable case. Gold *must* advance under an adverse exchange, with a currency not convertible *although invariable in value*. It would happen too although Gold remained perfectly steady all over the world.

XV

[pp. 20–21.] Not only is there a general accordance between the exchanges and price of bullion whether rising or falling, but if taken for any long periods of time the connexion may be stated to be absolutely invariable.

[R.] The connexion cannot be otherwise than invariable after a certain limit of unfavourable exchange is passed. —

[B.] What does the critic mean? If the connexion is invariable how can the inference be denied that an adverse Exchange must raise the price of Gold here?

XVI

[p. 21, consecutive to preceding] Whilst, on the contrary, no such connexion has subsisted between the amount of Bank issues and the high price of gold: nay, so far from it, that for months together they are found to run in opposite directions.

It was this want of connexion, between the amount of Bank notes and the price of bullion, that first led me to suspect the accuracy of the theory, that attributed the high price of gold to the over-issues of the Bank;...

[R.] "Over issues of the Bank" Is not every thing an overissue after the market price of gold rises above the mint price, whether caused by a real rise in the value of gold or a real fall in the value of paper?

[B.] Yes overissue in the sense in which it is used by *consistent* political Œconomists but not in the sense in which the public use it—viz. that notes have been issued in such excess as to alter the value of currency in respect *to all* commodities; there is a material difference between "overissue" and "non-contraction".

XVII

[p. 29, n.] England might send hardware to Spain, Spain might send wool to France, and France send wine to England; in which case the respective debts and credits would be liquidated through a circuitous remittance, known technically by the term arbitration of exchange. The direct exchanges, however, between England and Spain would be in favour of England; between Spain and France, in favour of Spain; and between France and England, in favour of France.

[R.] The author appears to me to have fallen into a great error in this passage and I should be willing to rest the truth of our different theories on this proposition. In the case supposed the exchanges of all the three countries would be at par. If not an exchange broker might get 3 pc^t by merely sending a bill to Spain with instructions to forward it to France and from France again to England—This bill would effect all the payments.

[B.] If the author has fallen into an Error here, he has done it upon the authority of one of the most intelligent practical and extensive Exchange Merchants with whom he is acquainted and one who in his Evidence before the Committee on Resumption of Cash payments was disposed to view the author's opinions with great distrust. The author apprehends [1] the critic to mistake the theory of Exchange—he speaks this with great deference. There is no doubt that the tendency of the Exchange under the supposed circumstances would be to a state of par—but during an intercourse such as the author has supposed deviations would occur that would give rise to exchange operations by which the deviations would be corrected—previously to such correction the language used by the critic would subject him to the contradiction stated in the note. If *there were only two countries trading together* their exports and imports would balance upon the whole and the tendency of the Exchange would be to a par—but temporary deviations would occur and during those deviations Exchange operations w^d take place.

XVIII

[pp. 30–31.] There is another powerful auxiliary to rectify the fluctuations of the exchange. For as soon as the premium on a foreign bill has exceeded the limits which will repay the exporter the expenses of transmitting bullion, the coin itself will be exported in payment of the adverse balance. This will lead to a contraction of the currency, and an artificial elevation of its value; and this elevation of the value of the currency, lowering the prices of produce, will still further increase the profits upon export, and diminish the profits upon import....Now it is this fall of price, arising from the forced contraction, that enables the exporting merchant to gain augmented profits upon all his exports; he would buy cheaper here, and sell at the same price abroad.

[R.] So he would without a contraction of currency. The author appears to forget here that it is only the fall in the

[1] Replaces 'I apprehend'; and, below, 'he speaks' replaces 'I speak'.

real, and not in the nominal exchange, which operates as a bounty on exportation.

[B.] The author admits himself to have been asleep when he wrote this passage or that he had forgotten the distinction which his own pamphlet on the Exchange was (as far as he knows) the first to point out—but he cannot understand how the critic should admit of any distinction between real and nominal Exchange since as far as the author is enabled to understand the critic's theory he supposes all variations in the exchange to depend upon a previous alteration in the value of currency and this is precisely what the author means by a nominal Exchange. No export or import of goods can rectify a nominal Exchange. Export or import of currency would be the only remedy. How does the critic shew upon his theory of Exchange that it could ever afford a bounty on the exportation of goods?

XIX

[p. 42.] Every manufacturer is aware, that during the pressure of unusual demand, he can well afford to pay higher wages to his workmen; because he not only reimburses himself for the extra advances, but is enabled to increase the price of his articles so as to augment his profits also. In a particular case then, his power of adding wages to the price will depend upon the demand compared with the means of supplying that demand. But the same reasoning will apply to the whole mass of manufacturers, provided a general demand arises for their commodities beyond the customary powers of supply.

[R.] The author appears to me to fall into an error when he supposes that because an individual manufacturer may raise the price of his commodities when he has increased wages to pay that therefore the whole mass of manufacturers may do the same. The two cases are widely different.

[B.] The author does not suppose the same reasoning will apply to *the whole mass* of manufacturers *unless a general demand* arises beyond the customary powers of supply. And this question leads to his following discussion—whether such a general demand can occur or not.

XX

[pp. 50–51.] Assuming then twenty millions to be wanted for the service of the year, let us suppose that this amount of capital is taken from an employment where it is reproduced with a profit, and that it is transferred to be expended unproductively, so that at the end of the twelve-month, no traces of it shall appear. This is precisely what is meant by converting capital into revenue.

Now twenty millions of circulating capital thus borrowed will, of course, throw out of work all the hands employed by the capitalists who lend it. The persons thus deprived of employment would be chiefly artisans, and might, one with another, earn £40 per annum each. At this rate, the twenty millions of capital would give employment to five hundred thousand workmen, and as many of these might be heads of families, there could hardly be (taking workmen and their families together) less than one million of souls depending for subsistence upon their employment.

[R.] Why suppose all capital to be circulating capital?

[B.] The author does not suppose all capital to be circulating capital but he supposes that Government obtains circulating capital alone and therefore his reasoning is confined to a change in the employment of circulating capital.

XXI

[p. 51, consecutive to preceding.] To prevent the convulsion incident to such a diversion of capital, let us suppose that government employs a certain number as soldiers, and that the remainder could find work in manufacturing the warlike stores and accoutrements,* all of which are to be consumed, according to the conditions, unproductively. In this way, no inconvenience would be felt; the whole million of souls would be provided for, and it would be a fair representation of the change of productive capital into unproductive revenue.

[R.] *They could not find work in these manufactories if the former supposition be realised namely that there should be a destruction of capital equal to 20 millions.

[B.] The author in order to give every advantage to the opposite arguments supposes that the men thrown out of work by the diversion of circulating capital find employment from the *same capital* distributed by Government amongst troops and manufactories of warlike stores.

XXII

[pp. 51–52, consecutive to preceding.] Thus far the process goes on very smoothly; and were we to stop here, no other difficulty would ensue, except that which attends all violent transitions. But what is to be done the second year? Government requires a further supply of twenty millions, which is to be borrowed in the same manner, and with the same consequences. Five hundred thousand more artisans are thrown out of work, who with their families constitute a second million of persons wanting the means of subsistence, in addition to the million of the former year.

[R.] Again all capital is supposed to be circulating capital.

XXIII

[p. 52, consecutive to preceding.] Continuing, then, the same supposition, that government could apply, as before, the twenty millions of money in providing work for the discharged artisans, we should still have two millions of persons to support with a fund equal only to the supply of one million: the third year would give three millions of people to be employed by a fund of the same limited power, and thus in succession as long as the war lasted. So that at the end of the late struggle, after twenty-two years of war, there would be a destruction of four hundred and forty millions of capital, and twenty-one millions of souls would have been left without subsistence, or any possibility of finding employment.

A more striking example of a moral *reductio ad absurdum* could hardly be imagined; and yet, extravagant and preposterous as this conclusion may appear, I am not aware of any exaggeration.

[R.] Who has ever supposed this? The author raises a phantom of the imagination and then demolishes it. There can be no doubt that a nation may make great inroads on its capital. In point of fact it never does, because public extravagance is made up by private frugality and savings.

[B.] Many persons have supposed this. I have imagined that nothing more was required than to convert capital into revenue in order to account for the high prices of the last 20 years. It was absolutely necessary to shew that such a conversion upon the scale that occurred during the war must have entailed irretrievable ruin unless some counteracting cause corrected the mischief. The author may have mistaken the best mode of conducting his argument but the mode adopted appeared to him to make a deeper impression.

XXIV

[pp. 54–55.] It appears to me that the error lies in supposing, first, that the whole capital of the country is fully occupied; and, secondly, that there is immediate employment for successive accumulations of capital as it accrues from saving. I believe there are at all times some portions of capital devoted to undertakings that yield very slow returns and slender profits, and some portions lying wholly dormant in the form of goods, for which there is not sufficient demand. I believe, too, that when capital accumulates rapidly from savings, it is not always practicable to find new modes of employing it. Now, if these dormant portions and savings could be transferred into the hands of government in exchange for its annuities, they would become sources of new demand, without encroaching upon the existing capital.

[R.] Suppose these dormant portions to consist of goods for which there is no market, how will the government expenditure procure a market for them? How should they do it if the proprietors cannot? In point of fact these dormant portions never find their way into the hands of Government.

[B.] Some dormant portions may not find their way to the hands of Government, and may be irretrievably lost by miscalculation, such as machinery that is rendered useless by the invention of that which is more perfect. But suppose a quantity of cotton or woollen goods without a market, such goods may be bought by the working classes receiving more wages from full employment in consequence of the capital which Government distributes. It would be effected through the circulation of money which alone passes through the hands of Government. But substantially it would be as if Government granted an annuity for the woollens and cottons and then distributed those woollens and cottons as wages for which it would receive as an equivalent the warlike stores fabricated by the workmen.

XXV

[p. 55, consecutive to preceding.] Unless savings were actually accumulating simultaneously with the expenditure of government, it appears to me that all the mischief described in the foregoing pages would have followed, and that long before the expiration of the contest our efforts must have been completely paralysed.

[R.] Who denies that savings actually accumulate simultaneously with the expenditure of Government? It is the only theory by which the actual phenomena of the last 25 years can be explained.

[B.] No one denies it, whose attention is strictly drawn to the subject but an author is obliged in the conduct of his argument frequently to introduce propositions which no one denies. No one denies the propositions of Euclid, are they not therefore to be published.

I am disposed to think however that the same capital may be made to produce more work or if I may use the expression—may be put to harder work under the influence of great demand by quicker rapidity of return—but I did not venture to hazard the opinion without more maturely weighing it and chiefly out of deference to the authority of the Critic himself. If this opinion should be well founded—then the extravagance of Government might be supplied to a certain extent at least without having recourse to the supposition of simultaneous saving.

XXVI

[pp. 55–56.] It will be contended, no doubt, that if the savings had remained in the hands of the capitalist, they would have equally been a source of demand as when transferred to the government; but this is the very point at issue.

[R.] This will not be contended, because profits have a tendency to fall as capital increases, and vice versa. A Government expenditure reduces capital and increases profits and therefore render every given proportion of profits more efficacious as a fund for replacing expended capital.

[B.] I do not see the bearing of the Critic's remark in this case. The author is speaking of demand and the Critic seems to be speaking of Profits.

XXVII

[p. 56.] Now, whenever savings are made from revenue, it is clear that the person entitled to enjoy the portion saved is satisfied without consuming it. It proves that the industry of the country is capable of raising more produce than the wants of the community require.

[R.] There would be more in this argument if a man had a right to consume all which his capital contributed to produce. As it is every thing produced is actually consumed.

[B.] It proves that the person whose capital has been raising him a revenue was supplied with a revenue that he did not want for the purpose of consumption. If that revenue is made to produce again, there will be two portions of revenue the 2$^\text{d}$ year not wanted for consumption. It appears to me that there must be some limit *to the degree* in which this process can go forward.

XXVIII

[p. 56, consecutive to preceding.] If the quantity saved is employed as capital in reproducing a value equivalent to itself, together with a profit, this new creation, when added to the general fund, can be drawn out by that person alone who made the savings; that is, by the very person who has already shown his disinclination to consume.

[R.] It is not all drawn out by him: the greatest part is drawn out by the workmen he employs and is actually consumed by them.

XXIX

[p. 57, consecutive to preceding.] When once the division of labour has taken place, the efforts of each individual are directed to the fabrication of some specific commodity. He fabricates it in the hopes that there will be a demand for all that he can produce. If every one consumes what he has a right to consume, there must of necessity be a market. Whoever saves from his revenue, foregoes this right, and his share remains undisposed of.

[R.] I deny this, it is disposed of when it becomes a fund for future production.

[B.] His share remains undisposed of in the consumption of that year. Whether it will be disposed of in the following year as a fund for reproduction depends upon the opportunity of finding what M. Say calls un emplacement.

XXX

[p. 57, consecutive to preceding.] Should this spirit of economy be general, the market is necessarily overstocked, and it must depend upon the degree in which this surplus accumulates, whether it can find new employment as capital. For it is quite evident, that to continue to fabricate the same sort of goods that have been already rejected would only tend to increase the evil.

[R.] This is to suppose demand to be limited which is not true either in theory or practice.

[B.] There can be no doubt that there will be no progressive improvement without accumulation but it is a question of degree and whether capital may not increase faster than the employment for it. I am not aware that I can state my opinion more clearly than in the text. It seems that the Author and the Critic differ here materially and the Author is sorry to find such a difference with a person to whose opinion he looks up with so much respect. There seems to be no alternative but to agree to differ.

XXXI

[p. 58.] This doctrine, I think, has been pushed a little too far. It proceeds upon the assumption that every addition to capital necessarily creates its own demand; but in applying the theory to the actual circumstances of mankind, some inseparable conditions appear to me to have been overlooked. It takes for granted, that new tastes, new wants, and a new population, increase simultaneously with the new capital; a supposition which is not consonant with the fact.

[R.] It is not necessary that in such a country as England new tastes and new wants should be generated—the old tastes are sufficient for the purpose. Tastes and wants exist already in a sufficient degree, give but the means of satisfying them and demand follows.

[B.] Conceive the immense revenue that is at present spent for the luxury of having Physicians, Lawyers, Clergymen, Musicians, Players Buffoons, &c. &c. suppose those tastes to be annihilated what would become of the revenue or how would it be disposed of—Have those tastes grown up suddenly? have they not been the growth of centuries—May not the means of indulgence in them increase faster than the desire of indulgence— Does not saving imply a want of desire to indulge? There was a time when these tastes did not exist—would production have gone on without them. I cannot conceive production for the sake of production—without an ultimate desire to gratification by consumption.

XXXII

[pp. 59–60.] But this proposition implies that there is not more corn and cloth in the whole than the two classes of capitalists [producing corn and cloth] want to consume. If more than that is produced, the surplus is absolute waste on both sides; and all the labour thrown away.

[R.] True. This is what the Political Economists of the present day call glut arising from miscalculation. They do not say there may not be a glut of 2 or of 10 commodities but they say there cannot be a glut of all.

[B.] The author has supposed a case of a country divided into two sets of capitalists, one producing food and the other clothing —but where the division of labour was complete. If these persons produce more food and clothing on the whole than is wanted, there will be general glut. It is not a case of two or ten com- modities—but of all commodities—the author having supposed no other production than cloth and corn.

XXXIII

[p. 60.] How is it possible for this process to continue without a fall in prices, and a lower rate of profit to the capitalist?

[R.] Certainly not possible without a lower rate of profit in the particular trade.

XXXIV

[pp. 60–61, consecutive to preceding.] The difficulty of finding employment for new capital is acknowledged by all practical men. They continually feel and complain that every channel is full. The evidence is brought home to them, by the general accumulation of commodities undisposed of, and stored in the warehouse. These are the records of so much capital in a state of actual stagnation, neither affording profit to the owner, nor employment to the workman, and discouraging all future exertion.

[R.] When markets are dispersed and competition active great mistakes are made in the application of capital to the production of particular commodities, but this only proves the great risk of miscalculation, it does not impugn the general principle that if there were no mistakes there would be no glut.

[B.] This case therefore if founded does impugn the general principle. It shews that there may be more of every thing than is wanted—unless new tastes are introduced.

XXXV

[p. 62.] The immediate means of purchasing which government possesses is derived from the sale of annuities.

[R.] Will the sale of annuities create a demand for cloth and corn which were before and are still in excess?

[B.] The sale of annuities gives Government money with that money a demand is made for commodities the cost of those commodities is chiefly made up of wages—the money therefore distributed as wages enables the workmen to buy the cloth and corn which were in excess. Without the demand of Government those extra wages would not have been distributed.

XXXVI

[p. 62, consecutive to preceding.] The power of levying taxes in perpetuity, and of transferring the income arising therefrom to individuals, enables the government to collect all those savings that find no immediate employment as capital,* and to devote them to expenditure.

[R.] *In what shape does this capital exist which is to be devoted to expenditure?

[B.] It exists in the shape of goods unemployed for want of demand—as soon as the extra employment is given to workmen their wages purchase the goods.

XXXVII

[p. 63.] No proposition is more generally admitted, than that the market rate of interest paid for the loan of capital is proportionate to the profits that can be made from the employment of it.

[R.] This proposition cannot be admitted without great qualification.

[B.] There can be no doubt that the *market* rate of interest must be a tolerably correct index of the rate of profits.

XXXVIII

[p. 64, consecutive to preceding.] If profits, then, were regulated solely by those made upon the last quality of land taken into cultivation, we should observe in all countries a regular fall in the market rate of interest as the population increased, and was compelled to have recourse to inferior land. Now it is not denied that such has been the usual course of the rate of interest;...

[R.] Not if great improvements were at the same time made in agriculture, nor if wages fell from a too abundant supply of labourers.

XXXIX

[p. 65.] These facts are in direct opposition to the theory of profits being regulated *always* by the quality of the last land taken into cultivation; . . .

[R.] This is not a correct representation. I say that profits depend *always* upon wages—that wages depend upon demand and supply, and are also mainly regulated by the price of food, and that the price of food depends on the productiveness of the last capital employed on the land. I see the greatest difference between this proposition and that in the text.

[B.] The critic will see that the text is a repetition of what was expressed before nearly in his own words—at p. 58.

XL

[p. 67.] The trade with India is thrown open, and instantly the different presidencies are glutted with English goods, without any diminution in the supply of the home market.

[R.] Who says without any diminution in the supply of the home market?

XLI

[pp. 69–70.] The demand, however, of a large manufacturing population, receiving high instead of low wages, and *in full employment*, is an efficient and powerful cause, that must produce an immediate effect upon consumption, more especially of food and the raw materials of coarse clothing.

The numbers in the higher classes of society bear no sort of proportion to that of the working class. We are apt to dwell upon the expenditure of the former, as if their revenues were the great source of national demand; forgetting that the bulk of the gross annual produce is consumed by workmen whilst preparing commodities to gratify the tastes of capitalists. A return of 10 per cent. has been thought a fair profit to the possessor of capital. For every £100, then, of circulating capital that is distributed

amongst workmen as wages, which is the measure of their consumption, the possessor himself can consume but to the extent
of £10.

[R.] Compare this passage with that in page 56. marked[1].

[B.] p. 70. and p. 56. do not disagree. In the latter case the
capitalist and the workmen both consume their respective portions—in the former it is supposed that the capitalist does not
consume his portion and therefore there would be no motive for
distributing the capital amongst the workmen.

XLII

[p. 70, consecutive to preceding.] If, in consequence of brisk
markets, the artisans are employed fourteen hours a day instead
of twelve, and they receive wages in proportion, the demand for
goods suited to their consumption will be increased in the same
ratio as the wages. An increased exertion amounting to one-sixth
would be tantamount to an increase of population to the same
extent; and a population, too, possessing the means of effective
demand.

[R.] What is the complaint? a redundant production
which cannot find a market. What is the remedy? a demand
by Government which immediately leads to an increased
production leaving the former surplus just what it was.

[B.] The demand of Government leads to an increased production, but the workmen having more wages consume the
excess that was previously existing and the government consumes
the stores that are produced. There are two extra consumptions
and only one extra production.

XLIII

[p. 71.] When the capitalist furnishes an extra quantity of
goods, he acquires a greater amount of profits, but not a greater
rate of profits.

[R.] Surely to[o] a greater rate of profits if the machinery
and buildings are adequate to the performance of the increased
work. They do not rise in price or in value.

[1] Quotation XXVIII.

[B.] There may be some inaccuracy in the Author's expression here but he did not mean in this passage that the increased work was produced from the same capital. The latter part of the paragraph evidently shews that more wages were given to the workmen which implies that more capital was employed.

XLIV

[p. 72.] But it does appear to me, that not only was there an increased amount of wages and profits from the extra work done [during the war], but also an increased rate of both, and that this was effected through the medium of prices.... I am, therefore, disposed to concur with Mr. Malthus, that the rise of wages which took place during the war did actually afford a greater remuneration to the labourers.

[R.] Profits and wages were both higher it seems. Was this general? If you say yes I ask how they can both be higher if the value of commodities is at all times equal to the value of wages and profits together?

[B.] Wages and profits together cannot (perhaps) be higher unless there is a large class of consumers who do not produce—but with such a class a new distribution may take place affording higher wages and profits at the expense of that class.

XLV

[pp. 73–74.] If A, having a certain capital, and employing a certain number of labourers in raising corn, has to exchange his produce with B, who, with a similar capital and number of workmen, is fabricating cloth, it is evident that no advantage could accrue to either of them by increasing the price at which they interchanged the corn and the cloth. But if both A and B have to contribute a fixed sum for the expenses of government, for the payment of public creditors, for the interest on capital borrowed, for the support of the clergy, it is their interest to interchange commodities at the highest prices that can be obtained.

[R.] This is only proving that it is the interest of all producers at all times to depreciate the value of money, because by so doing they defraud the public creditor. No proposition can be more true. I do not see how the payment of the clergy or the expences of the government can affect this question, they must vary with the alteration of prices because they are not fixed payments.

[B.] Great part of the Clergy receive nominal sums for their livings and curacies—by the expenses of Government was here meant the consolidated fund and the nominal sum paid to the Stockholders.

XLVI

[pp. 74–75.] In times of peace, when more is produced than finds a ready consumption, there is a difficulty in raising prices as wages rise. But in time of war, when there is an unusual demand, when the markets are more scantily supplied in proportion to the extent of consumption, when the supply can only be obtained by increased exertion on the part of the capitalists and the labourers, then it is that the working classes reap their harvest, and acquire not only the increased wages and profits to which they are entitled from the addition to the annual produce, which their extra exertion has created, but an increased rate both of wages and profits.

[R.] Is war then the interest of the country?

XLVII

[p. 75.] A given number of workmen, and a given number of capitalists employing them, are called upon to furnish an extra quantity of work. Is it possible to conceive that they will not take advantage of the urgent necessities of the buyer, even if they could produce the articles wanted without additional sacrifices? But if the men are to work thirteen hours a day instead of twelve, and the machinery is to be watched night and day, and the employers to devote more time to superintendence, are they not entitled to a greater remuneration?

[R.] I do not call it an increase of wages if the men are paid more only because they do more.

[B.] When men are paid more because they do more, they receive increased wages but certainly not a higher rate of wages. It is not necessary for the author's argument to suppose that workmen received higher wages—if they received more wages their effectual demand would be proportionally increased. The author cannot help thinking that workmen must have received higher wages during the war than previously to the war—but it is an incidental remark that might have been omitted without prejudicing his argument.

XLVIII

[p. 76.] During the progress of the war, five hundred and nine millions sterling were in this way devoted to the purchase of commodities intended for consumption, instead of being devoted to reproduction.

[R.] Much more than 509 millions must have been expended by Government.

[B.] Much more was spent by Government but not in the form of loans—the sum is taken from Dr. Hamilton and includes all sums funded either in loans or Exchequer Bills. The sums derived from war taxes was only a transfer of Income and has therefore been omitted by the author.

XLIX

[pp. 78–79.] When commodities become high priced, and continue so for a length of time, it is sometimes argued that this circumstance of itself is proof of a depreciation of the currency.... Be it so: but let us understand each other.... Let us not invalidate the fixed contracts between man and man....

[R.] Very good and so is almost all that follows.

[B.] The only few words of comfort that the author receives for all his labours.

L

[p. 93.] This [glut] might arise partly from the cessation of our own demand, and partly from the cessation of demand which the war expenditure of other governments had created.

[R.] Have you not in a former part ridiculed the idea of the war having made much difference in the quantity consumed?

[B.] Allusion is here made perhaps to the remark at p. 69, where the author does not mean to *ridicule* the idea of greater consumption but to *inforce* it. He does not think the mere waste of war adds much to consumption. But a population fully employed and receiving more[1] wages (not higher wages) he conceives to be tantamount to an extra population for the time being.

LI

[p. 94.] To those who imagine consumption not to be a necessary ingredient of demand, and that in order to make a market for commodities, it is only necessary to produce more, these phenomena [of the universal distress] offer problems not very easy of solution; nor is the difficulty less for those who conceive the previously existing capital to have been diminished by being converted into revenue. Accordingly, every drowning theorist has caught at the various straws that crossed him.

[R.] Drowning theorist! I am not one for I as well as you say the supply was too great for the demand.

[B.] The author certainly did not apply the term drowning Theorist to the Critic but perhaps the Critic may be included in the class of those who just keep their heads above water by supposing a cycle of abundant harvests since the termination of the War.

[1] Replaces 'extra'.

[AN UNFINISHED REVIEW OF BLAKE'S 'OBSERVATIONS ON...THE EXPENDITURE OF GOVERNMENT' 1823]

Mr. Blake is a gentleman whose reputation must be well known to our readers, he was[1] the author of one of the few good pamphlets which were published on the bullion question in the year [1810][2]. In that pamphlet Mr. Blake explained in a perspicuous manner the theory of Exchanges and the laws which governed the variations in the nominal and real course of exchange. We opened his present publication with considerable interest, but although we saw the same marks of ability in the clearness of his statements we must confess we finished the perusal of his tract with regret and disappointment. Mr. Blake appears to us to agree with those whose theory he attacks without being himself aware of it, and to confirm by his authority every principle which he has with so much pains attempted to overturn. This remark is perhaps only strictly and fairly applicable to the first part of his Essay, but if this be established there will not remain much matter of dispute between him and those whose opinions he attempts to controvert. Those who have written on the subject of the currency it will be recollected maintain that during the war and the Bank restriction act the prices of gold and of all commodities have been raised by the overissues of paper money; that during such depreciation many loans have been made, the interest on which, now that the standard is restored, and money has regained its former value is paid in a medium more valuable than that in which the debt was contracted, and that as the prices of gold and of all commodities have fallen since the cessation of the restriction

---

[1] 'he was' replaces 'for being'.   [2] Blank in MS.

on Bank payments, it may be justly attributed to the rise in
the value of money. It is Mr. Blake's object to prove that
money has not varied in value—that when commodities and
gold were high in price it was they which had risen and not
money that had fallen, and that now that gold and commodities have fallen in price, the fall is really in them and
that it would be a great mistake to say that money had fallen [1]
in value.

Now all this we confess appears to us to be a dispute about
words for Mr. Blake agrees with his opponents [2] in thinking
that the rise in the price of gold and of commodities during
the war, and the subsequent fall since the peace, would not
have taken place if there had not been a restriction on specie
payments. In that case Mr. Blake says gold and bank notes
must have agreed in value and therefore goods would not
have been high in this more valuable medium. He agrees
with his opponents too that the present prices of goods and
gold would have been just as they now are. Every one is
agreed as to the actual phenomena; a high price of gold and
commodities, during the war; an unfavorable exchange to a
degree without example; a great injustice to the public
creditor in his being prevented from receiving his dividends
in a medium as valuable as gold; a fraud on all other creditors
but one party says all these effects followed from a depreciation in the value of money, no says Mr. Blake that is not the
right way of stating the case, it proceeded from the increased
value of gold, to which increased value money ought to have
conformed, but as it was prevented from doing so by the
interference of the legislature a great mass of injustice was
the consequence. Here then is a perfect agreement as to the
effects but one party calls the cause a fall in the value of
money, the other a rise in the value of gold. A dispute about

[1] Should be 'risen'.   Mr. Blake as well as himself
[2] Replaces 'for the opponents of   agree'.

a point so trifling appears to us totally unworthy of Mr. Blake's talents, but if it were worthy we think he has utterly failed in proving his view correct. A rise in the value of gold necessarily implies a relative[1] fall in the value of commodities, we should expect then to find that after this great rise in gold an ounce of that metal would exchange for a larger quantity than before of commodities. Did it do so? quite the contrary; if any thing gold was of a less exchangeable value than before. Mr. Blake acknowledges this and endeavors to get over the difficulty by a supposed rise in the value of all commodities in consequence of the great expenditure of Government. This cause appears to us to be utterly inadequate to produce the alleged effect. If it could be conceded, which I think it could not, that the prices of all the commodities demanded by Government could be affected for 15 years together by their increased expenditure even then the rise would be only in those commodities, and not in others for which there would necessarily be rather a diminished than an increased demand. Mr. Blake invariably contends that a large government expenditure is a great stimulus to an increase of industry and of production. Suppose this true it in no way accounts for the increased prices of things which are not demanded by Government. Mr. Blake says this increased demand will induce labourers to work extra hours —these labourers will receive increased wages, these wages will be expended on all sorts of commodities and consequently they will all rise. But from whence do these increased wages come? from the contributions of all other classes. If labourers can demand more these other classes must demand less and consequently the aggregate of demand must be precisely the same, if we except only the government demand which Mr. Blake supposes will be met by an increased supply added to the former supply all[2] raised by the same

[1] 'relative' is inserted. [2] The last six words are ins.

amount of capital and by the same number of labourers, only working[1] for a greater number of hours. It is evident then that Mr. Blake has by no means proved that independent of the increased demand of government there would be any other increased demand in the country.

But can Mr. Blake's proposition, that with the same capital by means of increased exertion and industry, the increased quantity of commodities, required by Gov.^{t}, can be produced, without occasioning any diminished supply of commodities in any other quarter?[2] If industry be encouraged in one department it is discouraged in another. Wages are always advanced to the workmen before the commodity is produced—the means of employing workmen are not increased at any rate in the first instance. If more warlike stores be produced more capital must be employed in that line whether the same labourers do more work or new labourers are employed, for the very wages which pay them for their work constitute a part of the capital of the master. How is his capital to be augmented but at the expense of some other persons?—how can the same identical commodities be paid to two persons at the same time for wages?

There appears to us this sort of contradiction in Mr. Blake's statement, The gunsmith, the army clothier, the gunpowder manufacturer are all to produce an increased quantity of commodities—they are to have an increased quantity of capital to enable them to do so and yet this additional quantity is to be found without influencing the production of any other commodity.

---

[1] 'working' is ins.

[2] The following is deleted here: 'Government like all other purchasers must go to market with equivalents to offer in exchange for the goods it wants, but it has none of its own and can only obtain them by appropriating to itself the equivalents of some other persons. If then Gov.^{t} can give more to the individual workmen whom they employ other people have less to give.'

ABSOLUTE VALUE
AND EXCHANGEABLE VALUE
1823

NOTE ON 'ABSOLUTE VALUE AND
EXCHANGEABLE VALUE'

THIS paper on Absolute Value and Exchangeable Value, of which we have a complete rough draft and an unfinished later version, was written by Ricardo in the last few weeks of his life. Besides presenting his own views on the subject of a measure of value, the draft contains criticism of the measures advocated by Malthus, McCulloch, Mill and Torrens; while what there is of the later version discusses only those of Malthus and McCulloch.

The existence of these writings was hitherto unknown. They were found among the Mill-Ricardo papers, and are now published for the first time. A hint of their existence which had been given by McCulloch in the early anonymous versions of his *Life and Writings of Mr. Ricardo*[1] has been completely overlooked. He stated that Ricardo, on retiring to Gatcomb in the summer of 1823, 'engaged, with his usual ardour, in a profound and elaborate investigation concerning the absolute and exchangeable value of commodities. But he was not destined to bring this investigation to a close!' In the later and better known versions of the *Life*, however, this allusion was dropped.[2]

Prompted by his disagreement with Malthus's *Measure of Value*, which was published in April 1823, there was a prolonged correspondence on the subject between Ricardo and Malthus, which later extended to his other friends. During McCulloch's visit to London between the middle of May and the end of June 1823 he joined in a number of discussions on this question which took place among Ricardo's circle: discussions once referred to by Mrs. Grote as 'the interminable controversy about the

---

[1] See *Edinburgh Annual Register for 1823* and the pamphlet *Memoir of the Life and Writings of David Ricardo*, London, 1825.
[2] In these later versions, such as the one prefixed to his own edition of Ricardo's *Works*, 1846, p. xxix, McCulloch merely speaks of Ricardo's engaging 'in elaborate inquiries regarding some of the more abstruse economical doctrines.'

"measure of value"'.[1] After these conversations Ricardo wrote to Malthus: 'McCulloch and I did not settle the question of value before we parted—it is too difficult a one to settle in a conversation'; adding that he himself had promised 'to bestow a good deal of consideration on it' during his holiday.[2] And on 8 August Mill, in a letter to Ricardo, remarked: 'He [McCulloch] also told me that you were to reconsider the subject with your pen in your hand'.[3]

The paper which was the product of Ricardo's reconsideration must have been sent to Mill after Ricardo's death, together with the *Plan for a National Bank*; but unlike the latter it was apparently regarded by Mill as not suitable for publication. Ricardo himself evidently felt dissatisfied with his results: in his last letter to Mill on 5 Sept. 1823 he confessed that he had 'been thinking a good deal on the subject lately, but without much improvement.'[4]

Yet this paper has importance since it develops an idea which existed previously in Ricardo's writings only in occasional hints and allusions: namely, the notion of a real or absolute value underlying and contrasted with exchangeable or relative value.

The draft was written on odd pieces of paper paginated 1 to 18. Some of them are covers of letters addressed to Ricardo; those which bear postmarks being dated in all but two cases between 6 and 9 Aug. 1823, and some insertions (below p. 364, n. 2 and n. 4, and p. 365, n. 2) being written on a letter-cover postmarked 23 Aug. 1823. We may, therefore, conclude that this draft was mainly written not earlier than the second week of August[5], and was revised not earlier than the last week of that month.

The later version is neatly written on seven uniform sheets of paper with scarcely any corrections. It breaks off at the end of a page. This version must have been written between the last

---

[1] Quoted below, IX, 301.
[2] *ib.* 303.
[3] *ib.* 334.
[4] *ib.* 387.
[5] The fact that two pages are postmarked respectively 28 and 29 July 1823, does not affect the above conclusion, since these consist of the final page and a page added later.

few days of August and 5 September when Ricardo fell ill, since it contains passages from McCulloch's letter of 24 August, from Malthus's letter of 25 August, and from Ricardo's reply to Malthus of 31 August.[1]

The papers here printed thus belong to the period between the beginning of August 1823 (after he had completed his *Plan for a National Bank*) and the onset of his fatal illness in the first few days of September.

Besides the draft and the later version there are two sheets which mark stages of transition between them. The first of these (*a*) is printed below in full at the end of the draft (below, pp. 396–7). It is written on a letter-cover postmarked 18 August 1823.

The other sheet (*b*) is closely similar to the opening pages of the later version, including the two headings 'Exchangeable Value' and 'Absolute Value'. But it contains a paragraph which is a revision of a passage of sheet (*a*) and which does not re-appear in the later version. This is given below, p. 399, n.

[1] See below, pp. 409–10.

[ABSOLUTE VALUE AND EXCHANGE-ABLE VALUE]

[*A Rough Draft*]

The only qualities necessary to make a measure of value a perfect one are, that it should itself have value, and that that value should be itself invariable,[1] in the same manner as in a perfect[2] measure of length the measure should have length and that length should be neither liable to be increased or diminished; or in a measure of weight that it should have weight and that such weight should be constant.

Altho' it is thus easy to say what a perfect[3] measure of value should be it is not equally easy to find any one commodity[4] that has the qualities required. When we want a measure of length we select a yard or a foot—which is some determined definite length neither liable to increase or diminish, but when we want a measure of value what commodity that has value are we to select which shall itself not vary in value[5]? Mr. Malthus has recommended the pay of a day's labour whatever it may happen to be as a perfect measure[6] of value*—labour has value, and so far no objection

* If for example the pay for a day's labour were 2 shillings this month or year and 1 shilling or four shillings next month or year he would say the two shillings, one shilling or four shillings were all of equivalent value, because they could each in their time command the same quantity of labour.[7]

---

[1] First written 'The only quality necessary in a measure of value is invariability'.
[2] 'a perfect' is written above 'the' as an alternative.
[3] 'perfect' is inserted.
[4] 'commodity' is ins.
[5] Replaces 'not be subject to a variation of value'.
[6] Replaces 'the hire of labour as a measure'.
[7] This note is ins.

can be made to it, but is its value invariable? No one will assert that it is, and least of all should Mr. Malthus who has written ably on the subject of population, and endeavored to shew the great effects which are produced on the value of labour by the increase of numbers[1] when it is not proportioned to the increase of the capital which is to employ them.

Suppose the capital of a country to continue unaltered, and the population to be greatly increased in consequence of the influx of a great number of people from foreign countries or that by unwise laws at home injudicious encouragements are given to marriage, and to the birth of children, can it be denied that labour would fall in value, and that every commodity in the country excepting indeed those which are produced by a day's labour only[2] would exchange for a greater quantity of it? Would it be just in this case, to do what Mr. Malthus requires of us, to say that all commodities had fallen in value, and that labour alone had remained invariable, when we should all know that nothing had occurred to alter the value or price[3] of these commodities, but that the alteration had been specifically in labour, which had greatly increased in quantity, and had consequently made the supply excessive as compared with the demand. Now let us suppose an opposite case, let us suppose that while the capital of the country remained the same an epidemic disorder carried off a vast number of the people[,] would not the supply of labour have diminished as compared with the demand, would not every commodity in the country (excepting again those commodities which are produced by a day's labour and which therefore are always equivalent to a day's labour)[4] exchange for a smaller

[1] 'numbers' replaces 'mankind'.   [3] 'or price' is ins.
[2] The last eleven words are ins.   [4] The words in brackets are ins.

quantity of it, and would it not be correct to say that labour had risen in value, and not as Mr. Malthus requires us to say that all commodities had fallen in value.—

It is I believe contended by Mr. Malthus and[1] acknowledged on all hands that if all commodities were produced with labour alone and brought to market immediately[2] after having had one day's labour bestowed on them,[3] commodities would then be valuable in proportion to the number of mens labour bestowed on them. If 5 men were employed for one day in cutting down trees which were found in a Forest that was no man's property, the trees would be of 5 times the value of the game which one man could kill in a day. This is true, but it would not be true that if one man was 365 days in cutting down trees and at the end of that time brought his trees to market they would then be of the same value. In this case the game killed in one day, or the fifth part of the trees cut down in a day would be equally a good measure of value and all the commodities brought to market might be estimated by this measure. The measure would be invariable while the same quantity of labour was required to kill game or fell trees, and commodities could not vary in such a measure for any other reason than because the labour of fewer or more men[4] for a day was required to produce them. Thus if the same number of trees could by some improvement of skill[5] be felled by 4 men they would be worth only 4 times the produce of a days labour by one man in the killing of game.

[1] 'contended by Mr. Malthus and' is ins.
[2] 'immediately' is ins.
[3] The following was ins. here and then del.: 'and no longer time was to elapse before they were so brought to market'.
[4] 'the labour of fewer or more men' is written above 'more or less labour' as an alternative.
[5] 'by some improvement of skill' is ins.

If then all commodities were produced by labour employed only for one day Mr. Malthus's proposed measure would be a perfect one, for however abundant or however scarce might be the number of hands yet the exchangeable value of a day's labour would be always precisely the same as[1] the commodities that a day's labour could produce.[2]

If *all* commodities required a year's time before they were in a state to be brought to market, and required the continued labour of men to produce them during that time, then again they would be valuable according to the number of men employed on their production. If a piece of furniture were twice the value of a piece of cloth, it would be so because double the number of men had been occupied in producing one that[3] had been employed in producing the other. In this case too any commodity which continued uniformly to require the same quantity of labour would be an accurate measure of value. It would in fact be invariable, and the variations in the relative value of this commodity to others, when they occurred, would be owing to some alteration in the facility or difficulty of producing those other commodities, by which a less quantity of labour was employed on them. This is in fact the measure which I have proposed as the nearest approximation to a perfect measure.[4]

If all commodities required 2 years time before they could be brought to market the same argument would apply: either would be a good measure of value while it required the same quantity of labour to produce it and if any varied

---

[1] In MS, by mistake, 'as' is replaced by 'in'.
[2] This sentence, evidently intended for insertion at this place, was written later on a separate sheet.

[3] Replaces 'than'.
[4] This sentence was written later on a separate sheet and marked for insertion here.

in this measure it would only be because more or less labour was required for its production.[1]

If all commodities were produced by labour employed only for one day there could be no such thing as profits for there would be no capital employed, beyond that of which every labourer is in possession before he commences to work—there could as we have seen be no variation in the value of labour, but commodities would vary as labour was more or less productive. If a labourer by a day's labour could get a thousand shrimps 1000 shrimps would be of the value of a day's labour and if he could get only 500, 500 would be of the same value. If a labourer could pick up on the sea shore as many grains of gold as are coined into 2 shillings, 2 shillings would be of the value of a day's labour and if he could pick up half the quantity one shilling would be of the same value.[2]

But of the commodities which are brought to market after the lapse of one year or of two years there are in fact two classes of persons who are joint proprietors. One class gives its labour only to assist towards the production of the commodity[3] and must be paid out of its value the compensation to which it is entitled, the other class makes the advances required in the shape of capital and must receive remuneration from the same source.[4] Before a man can work for a year a stock of food and clothing and other necessaries must be provided for him. This stock is not his property but is the property of the man who sets him to work. Out of the finished commodity they are in fact both paid—for

[1] The words following the colon are ins.
[2] This paragraph was written later on a separate sheet evidently for insertion here.
[3] Replaces 'to assist its pro-duction'. (The reading of both versions is uncertain.)
[4] First written simply: 'One class gives its labour only, the other class makes the advances required.'

the master who sets him to work and who has advanced him his wages must have those wages returned with a profit or he would have no motive to employ him, and the labourer is compensated by the food clothing and necessaries with which he is furnished, or which is the same thing which his wages enable him to purchase. It greatly depends then on the proportion of the finished work which the master is obliged to give in exchange to replace the food[1] and clothing expended on his workman what shall be his profits. It not only depends on the relative value of the finished commodity to the necessaries of the labourer, which must always be replaced, to put the master in the same condition as when he commenced his yearly business but it depends also on the state of the market for labour (or on the quantity of necessaries which competition obliges the master to give for these necessaries)[2], for if labour be scarce the workman will be able to demand and obtain a great quantity of necessaries (or which is the same thing to the master luxuries)[3] and consequently a greater quantity of the finished commodity must be devoted to the payment of wages and of course a less quantity remains as profit for the master. The profits of the master depend then on two circumstances first on the comparative value which necessaries bear to the finished commodity, secondly on the quantity of necessaries and enjoyments which the labourer by his position can command. If however commodities were all the result of labour, employed for[4] and brought to market precisely in the same length [of][5] time, the rise or fall of wages,[6] either in con-

---

[1] 'food' replaces 'stock'.
[2] The words in brackets are ins.
[3] The words in brackets are ins. In MS 'luxuries' is replaced by 'other enjoyments equally valuable with luxuries'; 'luxuries' apparently being a mistake for 'necessaries' in this amended wording.
[4] 'employed for' is ins.
[5] Omitted in MS.
[6] 'wages' is written above 'labour' as an alternative.

sequence of the rise or fall of necessaries advanced to the labourer or in consequence of the favorable or unfavorable position in which he stands in relation to his employer, will not produce any effect whatever on the relative value of one commodity to another and consequently any commodity which continues always to require the same quantity of labour to produce it will be a perfect measure of value. For if the manufacturer of cloth should demand in exchange for his cloth more furniture, in consequence of the greater quantity of his commodity which he was obliged to part with in order to replace the advances which he made[1] to his workmen, the upholsterer would answer that the very same circumstance operated with equal force upon him as he also was obliged to part with more of his furniture to satisfy the demands of his workmen.

Either of these commodities would be a correct measure of value and would therefore shew correctly all the variations which took place in the value of commodities provided there was no other cause of the variation of commodities but the[2] increased or diminished difficulty of producing them. Though this is by far the greatest cause[3] it is not strictly the only one.[4] If by a day's labour fewer shrimps were obtained and nothing altered in regard to cloth and wine[5] shrimps would sell for more wine and for more cloth and exactly in proportion to the increased quantity of labour required to procure them. The same may be said of wine (supposing that to be the commodity requiring more labour),[6] if measured either by cloth or shrimps, and of cloth if measured

---

[1] 'made' replaces 'was obliged to make'.
[2] The last twelve words are written above 'they were caused by any' as an alternative.
[3] 'of all' is del. here.

[4] This sentence is ins.
[5] The last seventeen words are written above 'to get shrimps it required more labour', which however is not del.
[6] The words in brackets are ins.

by wine or shrimps, but they would be still liable to variations in value from variations in the value of labour which though comparatively of rare occurrence cannot be omitted in this important enquiry.

Either[1] of these commodities would in the case supposed correctly indicate all variations in value because they would themselves be invariable, but difficulty or facility of production is not absolutely the only cause of variation in value there is one other, the rise or fall of wages, which though comparatively of little effect and of rarer occurrence yet does affect the value of commodities and must not be omitted in this important enquiry.

As this increase of wages then would operate equally on all, it could not be admitted as a plea either to raise the value of their commodities in relation to others, or in relation to that which[2] for the general accommodation was recognised as the common measure.

It appears then that we should have no difficulty in fixing on a measure of value, or at least in determining on what constituted a good measure of value, if all commodities were produced exactly under the same circumstances—that is to say if all required labour only without advances, to produce them, or all requiring labour and advances[3] could be produced and brought to market in[4] precisely the same time.

The difficulty then under which we labour in finding a measure of value applicable to all commodities proceeds from the variety of circumstances under which commodities are actually produced. Some, such as shrimps and a few

---

[1] This paragraph was evidently intended as an alternative to the preceding one.
[2] 'by universal' is del. here.

[3] 'and advances' is ins.
[4] 'and brought to market in' replaces 'with precisely the same amount of advances and for'.

others, are the result of a few hours labour without any advances which are actually acknowledged to be such; others such as cloth is the result not of labour only, but of advances made probably for a year before the finished commodity is brought to market. Others again such as wine mellowed by age after being kept long in the merchant's cellar, is the result also of labour and advances but advances made for a much greater length of time than in the case of the cloth, and therefore requiring an increased price to afford the regular profit on such advances.

Now while these commodities continued to be produced precisely in the same way—shrimps would be an excellent measure of value for all things produced under the same circumstances as shrimps are produced, cloth for all commodities produced under the same circumstances as cloth, and wine for all commodities produced under the same circumstances as wine, but shrimps would be very far from an accurate measure of value for cloth or wine, cloth not a good one for shrimps or wine and wine a very inaccurate measure for shrimps and cloth. If for example labour rose from one of the two causes mentioned before, namely the higher relative value of food and other necessaries, or the advantageous position in which the labourer found himself placed, it would affect all commodities produced under the same circumstances as shrimps alike, and therefore their relative value would continue unaltered—it would affect all commodities produced under the same circumstances as cloth alike, and therefore their relative[1] value would also remain unaltered—it would affect all commodities produced under the same circumstances as wine alike and therefore their relative value would also continue unaltered. Altho' each would bear the same relative value to things produced

[1] 'relative' is ins.

under circumstances precisely similar, yet each would not bear the same relative value to the other which was not produced under similar circumstances. In proportion as labour rose a given quantity of shrimps would exchange for more cloth, for the whole value of cloth is not the reward of labour, a part constitutes the profits of the master who makes the advances, (while the whole value of the shrimps is the reward of the labourer and he has nothing to allow out of it for profits on capital or advances)[1] and for the same reason they would exchange for more wine, for a still greater portion of the value of the wine is made up of the profits on advances and a less portion of the wages[2] of labour. If then we constituted the shrimps the measure of value of all things, cloth and wine would fall in such measure altho' nothing had altered in respect to the circumstances of[3] actual labour and advances under which all these commodities were produced. If we constituted cloth the measure of value wine would fall in such measure and shrimps would rise, and if we chose wine as the measure both cloth and shrimps would rise but in unequal degrees the shrimps in which nothing but labour entered would rise a great deal, cloth in which there were profits as well as labour would rise in a more moderate degree.

In this then consists the difficulty of the subject that the circumstances of time for which advances are made are so various that it is impossible to find any one commodity which will be an unexceptionable measure, in those cases in which wages rise and in which consequently profits fall, or in those in which wages fall and profits consequently rise.

What are we to do in this difficulty, are we to leave every one to chuse his own measure of value or should we agree

---

[1] The words in brackets are ins.　　[3] 'of' replaces 'as far as regards'.
[2] Replaces 'and not of wages'.

to take some one commodity and provided it were always produced under the same circumstances constitute that as a general measure to which we should all refer that we may at least understand each other when we are talking of the rise or fall in the value of things. When Mr. Malthus speaks of the rise or fall in the value of commodities he estimates value by shrimps, or by commodities produced under similar circumstances in which shrimps are produced, and which are[1] wholly made up of labour. When Mr. Ricardo speaks of the rise or fall in commodities he estimates value by commodities produced under the same circumstances as cloth or gold, always supposing that cloth or gold require capital as well as labour to produce them, and always require them in the same proportions, for on no other conditions does he hold them to have any of the characters of invariability without which character there can be no measure. Now against Mr. Malthus's measure I object that it assumes labour itself to be invariable; that under all the circumstances of a redundant or a deficient population, under all the circumstances of an abundant supply or of a great demand for labour, it supposes labour to be of the same value. Labour might and probably would be of the same value, whatever might be its redundancy or deficiency, as compared with shrimps and other things produced by labour only, but it would vary prodigiously in value as compared with corn, with clothes, with furniture, with wine and millions of other things. We should as I have already observed be always required to say that it was these millions of commodities that had varied in value whether the cause of the variation was a deficiency of labour in the market, or an abundance of commodities from new facilities of producing them,—now I confess I prefer a measure, though

[1] In MS 'are' is replaced by 'is'.

confessedly an imperfect one, which will give some idea whether when labour varies as compared with commodities it is the value of labour which has undergone a change, or whether it is the commodity which rises or falls. Now this is what Mr. Ricardo's measure does.

It is not like Mr. Malthus's measure one of the extremes it is not a commodity produced by labour alone which he proposes, nor a commodity[1] whose value consists of profits alone, but one which may fairly be considered as the medium between these two extremes, and as agreeing more nearly with the circumstances under which the greater number of[2] commodities are produced than any other which can be proposed. He does not propose it as a perfectly correct measure for none such can be obtained but as one more nearly approaching to that character than any that has been suggested. In this measure, if labour became abundant or scarce, it would, like all other things, rise or fall. If it became difficult, from the appropriation of land to agriculture, to obtain an additional supply of corn without the expenditure of more capital for each quarter obtained, corn would rise, and nearly in proportion to the increased difficulty. In Mr. Malthus's measure provided the labourer were always paid the same quantity of corn for his labour the value would always be the same although to obtain this same quantity double the expenditure of labour and capital might be necessary at one time to what was necessary at another. If by improvements in husbandry corn could be produced with half the expenditure of labour and capital it would by Mr. M be said to be unaltered in value provided the same quantity and no more was given to the labourer as wages. It is indeed acknowledged by Mr. Malthus, (and how

[1] 'produced by' is del. here.
[2] 'the greater number of' replaces 'most'.

could it be denied?)¹ that under such circumstances corn
would fall very considerably in money price—it would fall
also in the same degree in exchangeable value with all other
things, but still Mr. M says it would not fall in absolute value,
because it did not vary in his measure of value. On the
contrary all these things as well as money would under the
circumstances supposed vary in this measure and therefore
he would say they had all risen considerably in value. He
would say so altho' with respect to any one or more of them
great improvements may have been made in the means of
producing them by the application of machinery, or from
any other cause which should render it cheap in price and
lower in exchangeable value with regard to all things corn
and labour excepted. In Mr. Ricardo's measure every thing
to which such improvements were applied would fall in
value[,] and price and value would be synonymous while
gold the standard of money cost the same expenditure of
capital and labour to produce it. If the commodity chosen
for Mr. Ricardo's measure, whose value confessedly consists
of profit and labour, were divided in the proportion of 90
for labour and 10 for profit—it is manifest that with every
rise of 1 pc^t in² labour a commodity produced by labour
alone would rise one per cent.³ If the measure was perfect
it ought not to vary at all. Now suppose any other commodity whose value is made up of 40 pc. for profit and
60 pc. for labour, how much would that fall with 1 pc. rise
in wages? Probably about 3 pc^t These are the two extremes,
and it is evident that by chusing a mean the variations in
commodities on account of a rise or fall in wages would be
much less than if we took either of the extremes.⁴

¹ The words in brackets are ins.
² '1 pc^t in' is ins.
³ 'one per cent.' replaces 'one

tenth in such a measure.'
⁴ The last four sentences, beginning 'If the measure', replace:

By many it is contended that the sole way of ascertaining value is by estimating the commodity whose value we wish to ascertain in the mass of commodities—that if at one time it will exchange for more of these than it did at another we may justly say that it has risen in value and vice versa. Now the objection to this is that it assumes invariability in the value of the mass of commodities, for as has been already observed nothing can be a proper measure of value which is not itself exempted from all variations. In our own times great improvements have been made in the mode of manufacturing cloth, linen and cotton goods, iron, steel, copper, stockings—great improvements have been made in husbandry all which tend to lower the value of these goods and of the produce of the soil and yet these are made a part of the measure by which you would measure the value of other things. Col. Torrens does not scruple to confound two things which ought to be kept quite distinct—if a piece of cloth will exchange for less money than formerly he would say that cloth had fallen in value but he would also say that money had risen in value because it would exchange for more cloth. This language may be correct as he uses it to

'Suppose wages to rise 5 pc^t, how much would a commodity of the value of £100 produced wholly by labour rise in Mr. Ricardo's measure? The answer is 10/- consequently it would become of the value of £100.10.—If the measure was perfect it ought not to vary at all. Now suppose wine or any other commodity to be made of the values of profit and labour—of the former 40 pc^t and the latter [actually written 'former'] 60 pc^t and that wages as before rise 5 pc^t the commodity would in the measure proposed by Mr. Ricardo fall'.

The difference between the two versions seems to be this. In the earlier calculation (referred to in this and the two preceding footnotes) of the change in value Ricardo was neglecting the fall of profit which is caused by the rise of wages. In the revised calculation (as given in the text) he takes into account the effect upon value of the fall in profit, and assumes that in the commodity chosen as a measure the fall of profit is equal to the rise of wages.

express only exchangeable value but in Political Economy we want something more we desire to know whether it be owing to some new facility in manufacturing cloth that its diminished power in commanding money is owing, or whether it be owing to some new difficulty in producing money. To me it appears a contradiction to say a thing has increased in natural[1] value while it continues to be produced under precisely the same circumstances as before. It is a contradiction too according to the theory of Col. Torrens himself for he says that commodities are valuable in proportion to the quantity of capital employed on their production. If less capital then be required to produce cloth, cloth will fall in value—in this we all agree but would it not be wrong while the same quantity of capital was required to produce money to say that money had risen in value. It has risen in value as compared with cloth he will say. It is undoubtedly of a higher relative value than cloth but how it can be said to have risen in value because another commodity had fallen in value does not appear clear to me nor can it be warranted but by an abuse of language.

Mr Mill says[2] that commodities are valuable according to the quantity of labour worked up in them and when the objection is made to him[3] that cloth and wine which has been kept several years are not valuable in proportion to the quantity of labour worked up in them as the wine must in its price pay a compensation for the time that the merchants capital has been invested in it he answers[4] that such an objection shews that the principle contended for is too strictly applied. The wine is not valuable exactly in pro-

[1] 'natural' is ins.
[2] First written 'Mr. MCulloch to whom the public is indebted for'; then replaced by 'Mr. MCulloch and Mr Mill say'; finally as above.
[3] 'him' replaces 'them'.
[4] 'he answers' replaces 'they answer'.

portion to the quantity of labour worked up in it, but that its value is regulated by the value of the commodity in which labour is worked up, and which for a sufficient reason has been chosen as the measure of value. But this is not exactly true. Wine now bears some relative value to cloth and let us suppose cloth the measure of value. Next year[1] a greater proportion of the finished commodity is paid for labour in consequence of a scanty supply of or a greater demand for labour. It becomes necessary then that wine should alter in relative value to cloth, although there is the same quantity of labour, neither more nor less, worked up in the cloth. If it did not so alter, if wine did not fall in this measure, the wine manufacturer's profits would be greater than those of the clothier, and consequently competition would immediately operate on that trade. How can Mr. Mill then be right in saying that the value of wine is regulated by the quantity of labour worked up in cloth the measure, when it may exchange for a greater or smaller quantity altho' no alteration has taken place in the mode of producing it.[2]

Mr. MCulloch defends the principle on a somewhat different ground—he estimates the quantity of labour employed by the quantity of capital employed. If I employ £1000 this year in erecting the walls of my house, £1000 the next in laying the timbers, £1000 the next in finishing and completing it my house ought not to be of the value only of a commodity on which so much labour was employed as £3000 could pay for one year, which is really all the labour which is put in the house but something more. If profits were 10 pc[t] a commodity on which £3000 worth of labour was bestowed in one year, cloth for example,[3]

---

[1] 'labour rises in price [replaced by 'value']' was first written here, then del.

[2] This sentence is ins.

[3] 'cloth for example,' is ins.

should be of the value of £3300 but the house would be of
the value of £3641.—for £1000 expended the first year
ought at the end of it to be worth £1100 and this £1100 the
second year would be of the value of £1210 and the third
year this again would be of the value of £1331 con-

sequently the house ought to sell for $\left.\begin{array}{r} £1331 \\ 1210 \\ 1100 \\ \hline 3641 \end{array}\right\}$ which is £341

more than the other commodity would sell for. Now in the
house more labour is realised than in the other commodity
according to Mr. McCulloch because the capitals employed
for three years were not equal to £3000 employed for one
year but to £3410[1]; for 1000 £ was employed the first year,

£1100 the next and 1210 the next $\left(\begin{array}{r} 1000 \\ 1100 \\ 1210 \\ \hline 3410 \end{array}\right)$ and 10 pc. profit

on 3410 is equal to £341 the difference between the value of
the cloth and the house. I have a right says Mr. MCulloch
to estimate the value of my house by the quantity of[2] labour
which I might have realised in a commodity if I could have
realised the profit from year to year. On an oak tree at the
end of 73 years I have only perhaps expended as much
labour as 2 shillings could command, but if my profits had
been received at the end of each year, at the end of the first
year I should have had 2.2 shillings at the end of the second
2.42 shillings and at the end of 73 years my 2/- would have
amounted to £100, I contend then that in saying my tree is
of a value equal to the labour which is expended upon it,

---

[1] First written 'the capitals employed for one year were not
£3000 but £3410'. This last
figure is a mistake for £3310.

[2] 'quantity of' is ins.

I am not to be supposed to maintain that as much labour has been actually expended on the tree as on a commodity such as cloth which sells for £100 for that would be absurd[1], but that if from year to year I had realised my original 2/- with the profits on it I should this last year have been able to employ as much labour for this particular year as the clothier and therefore the commodity which I should have had to sell would have been of the same value as the cloth, or of[2] the tree. Mr. MCulloch may be quite right in saying what he does but in that case he is only contending for the propriety and correctness of the measure of value which he adopts in which he in fact estimates the value of all things and gives his reasons for so doing, but that language is not strictly correct which affirms that commodities bear a relative value to each other according to the quantity of labour worked up in each.—To enable the capitalist of 2/- who received no fruits of it for 73 years to be on a par with those who employed labour all the time with annual profits of 10 pc[t] he should sell his tree for £100—that is undoubtedly true and no one contests it[3]—but supposing labour so rises as to sink profits to 5 pc[t] 2/- expended for the next 73 years without any revenue derived from it for the whole of that time should produce only £35.—. The subject is a very difficult one for with the same quantity of labour employed a commodity may be worth £100 or £35 of a money always produced under the same circumstances, and always requiring the same quantity of labour. Mr. MCulloch in fact shews as Mr. Malthus might do that if you grant his measure to be a correct one it is adequate to the object of measuring commodities, but the dispute really is about the invariability of the measure chosen. If that chosen by Mr MCulloch be

[1] 'for that would be absurd' is ins.
[2] 'or of' replaces 'and as .
[3] The last nine words are ins.

invariable Mr. Malthus's is not invariable, and if Mr. Malthus's be invariable Mr. MCulloch's is not.

1. All[1] commodities having value are the result either of immediate labour, or of immediate and accumulated labour united.

2. The proportions in which immediate labour and accumulated labour enter into different commodities are exceedingly various and will not admit of definite enumeration.

3. That part of the value of a commodity which is required to compensate the labourer for the labour he has

---

[1] An earlier draft of the series of propositions which begins here reads as follows:

'All commodities having value are the result of labour alone, or of labour and capital united.

'A commodity which is the result of labour and capital, and whose value therefore resolves itself into wages and profit is the only one which under any circumstances can be an accurate measure [first written 'A commodity made up of labour and profit is the only one calculated for a measure] of the value of other commodities made up also of labour and profits.

'To be an accurate measure of value even of such commodities other conditions are necessary—first it must require the same length of time to bring the commodities which are measured and the commodity by which they are to be measured, to market. And the commodity which is to be the measure should always require the same quantity of labour to produce it.

'A commodity made up of labour only without any advance of a capital for a day [the last nine words are ins.] is a good measure of value of all commodities which are produced under the same conditions, provided the commodity which is the measure be always produced by the same quantity of labour.

'A commodity produced by labour only without advances is not a good measure of value for commodities in the production of which advances are required.

'A commodity which requires one year to produce it and bring it to market is not an accurate measure of the value of commodities which require 2 or more years to effect the same object.

'When commodities are produced in the same time their values are in proportion to the quantity of labour bestowed on their production.

'When they are produced in unequal times their values are directly in proportion to the quantity of labour employed together'—here the draft breaks off.

bestowed on it is called wages, the remaining part of its value is retained by the master and is called profit. It is a remuneration for the accumulated labour which it was necessary for him to advance, in order that the commodity might be produced.

4. If I have a foot measure I can ascertain the length of a piece of cloth, of a piece of muslin, or of a piece of linen and I can not only say which is the longest and which the shortest, but also what their proportional lengths are.

5. In the same way if I take any commodity having value and which is freely exchanged for other commodities in the market, I can ascertain the proportional value of those other commodities. I can discover for example that one is twice, another one half and another three fourths of the value of the measure of which I make use for ascertaining their value.

6. There is this difference however between a measure of length and a measure of value, with respect to the measure of length we[1] have a criterion by which we can always be sure of regulating it to[2] the same uniform length or of making a due allowance for any deviation.[3] (In the measure of value we have no such criterion.)[4] If I have any doubt whether my foot measure is of the same length now that it was of 20 years ago I have only to compare it with some standard afforded by nature, with a portion of the arc of the meridian—or with the space thro' which a pendulum swings in a given portion of time. But if I have similar doubts with respect to the uniformity of the value of my measure of value at two distant periods what are the means by which I should arrive at the same degree of certainty as in the case of the measure of length.

---

[1] 'we' replaces 'I', here and six words below.
[2] Replaces 'of its remaining of'.
[3] The last nine words are ins.
[4] The words in brackets are ins.

6[*]. We are possessed then of plenty of measures of value and either might be arbitrarily selected for the purpose of ascertaining the relative value of commodities at the time they are measured, but we are without any by which to ascertain the variations in the values of commodities for one year, for two years or for any distant portions of time. I cannot for example say that linen is 20 pc^t cheaper now than it was a year ago unless I can with certainty say that the commodity in which I ascertain its value at the two periods had been itself invariable, but by what test shall I ascertain whether its value has remained fixed or has also altered. I can have no difficulty in asserting that a piece of cloth which measures 20 feet now is twice the length of a piece of cloth which was measured a year ago—I have no means whatever of ascertaining whether it be of double the value.

7. The difficulty being stated, the question is how it shall be best overcome, and if we cannot have an absolutely uniform measure of value what would be the best approximation to it?

8. Have we no standard in nature by which we can ascertain the uniformity in the value of a measure? It is asserted that we have, and that labour is that standard. The average strength of 1000 or 10,000 men it is said[1] is nearly the same at all times. A commodity produced in a given time by the labour of 100 men is double the value of a commodity produced by the labour of 50 men in the same time. All then we have to do it is said to ascertain whether the value of a commodity be now of the same value as a commodity produced 20 years ago is to find out what quantity of labour for the same length of time was necessary to produce the commodity 20 years ago and what quantity is necessary to produce it now. If the labour of 80 men was

---

[1] Replaces 'A man's strength'.

required for a year then and the labour of 100 is required now we may confidently pronounce that the commodity has risen 25 pc.ᵗ—

9. Having discovered this standard we are in possession of an uniform measure of value as well as an uniform measure of length[;] for suppose 1000 yards of cloth or 100 ounces of gold to be the produce of the labour of 80 men we have only to estimate the value of the commodity we wish to measure at distant periods by cloth or gold, and we shall ascertain what variations have taken place in its value, and if we have any doubt whether our measure itself has varied in value there is an easy method of correcting it by ascertaining whether the same quantity of labour neither more nor less is necessary to produce the measure, and making a correction or allowance accordingly.

10. This measure would have all the merit contended for if precisely the same length of time and neither more nor less were necessary to the production of all commodities. Commodities would then have an absolute value ˌdirectly in proportion to the quantity of labour bestowed upon them. But the fact is otherwise, some commodities require only a day for their production, others require 6 months, many a year and some 2 or 3 years. A commodity that requires the labour of 100 men for one year is not precisely[1] double the value of a commodity that requires the labour of 100 men for 6 months; a commodity that requires the labour of 100 men for two years is not precisely of twice the value of a commodity which requires the same quantity of labour for one year, nor of 24 times the value of a commodity produced with the same quantity of labour in one month. Nor is the value of a commodity produced with the labour

[1] 'precisely' is ins. here and three lines below.

of 100 men in one month 30 times the value of one produced with the same quantity of labour in one day.

It might nevertheless be said that if we even allow that no measure of value can be an universally accurate one for ascertaining the relative variations of commodities produced under different circumstances of time, yet that one might be found which would inform us of the relative value of the same commodity at different periods—that if for example the same quantity of cloth required now 100 men to make it and 20 years ago required 80 men we might say its value had increased 25 pc^t, and the same might be said of every other commodity which required a fourth more labour whether produced in 1 day 1 month 1 year or 5 years. But if wine produced in 5 years and cloth produced in one, each required one fourth more labour to produce them they would not exchange for the same proportional increased quantity of any commodity whatever. If for example I valued them in a commodity produced during the whole time with one uniform quantity of labour[1]

11. A commodity produced in two years is worth more than twice[2] a commodity produced with an equal quantity of labour in one year for if profits be 10 pc^t £100 employed for one year will produce a value equal to £110 and £110 employed the second year will produce a value equal to £121, therefore 100 in two years will produce £121

$$\begin{array}{r} \text{and 100 in one year} \quad 110 \\ \hline £231 \end{array}$$

If then a commodity be produced in one year by such a quantity of labour as £100 will employ it ought to be worth at the end of the year £110 but if an equal quantity

---

[1] This unfinished paragraph is written on a separate sheet.   [2] 'the quantity of' is ins. here apparently by mistake.

of labour be further employed upon it, if the labour which a sum of £100 can command be employed the second year the whole value of the commodity would be £231.— This value would be necessary in order to afford the fair remuneration of profits but[1] if it were valued according to the quantity of labour employed on it, its value would be only £220. Its value therefore is not regulated by the actual quantity of labour bestowed upon it.[2]

Suppose however the labour that £200 can employ upon it be worked up in it the first year it will at the end of the year be worth £220—but if it be a commodity that improves by age such as wine and it be kept in a cellar for one year more at the end of the second year its value should be £242. Here then are 3 commodities all with the same quantity of labour employed upon them for the same time, one of which is of the value of £220—one of the value of £231 and one of the value of £242.

12.[3] Suppose now labour to rise in value, and profits to fall—that from 10 pc^t they fall to 5 pc^t, the value of one commodity will be £210, of the other £215.25—and of the third £220.5. But if the first of these be the measure of value, it cannot itself vary, and therefore will be still of the value of £220. In this case the second will be £225.5 and the third £231. Measured then by the first, the second will have fallen 2.38 pc^t, the last 4.54 pc^t. While as far as labour is concerned in their production nothing has occurred to alter the value of these different commodities, because the same quantity of labour neither more nor less is worked up in them they vary however and vary very unequally.[4] It is true that the labour actually worked up in these com-

---

[1] The first part of this sentence up to this point is ins.
[2] This sentence is ins.
[3] Misnumbered '13' in MS.
[4] 'But may it not be said in answer to this' is del. here.

modities is the same under every supposition you[1] have
made, and therefore it is not strictly correct to say that
commodities only vary[2] on account of the quantity of labour
worked up in them being either increased or diminished, for
we see they may vary also[3] merely on account of an alteration
in the rate of profits, and wages—that is to say on account
of the different proportions in which the whole result of
labour is[4] distributed, between master and workers.[5] But
does this prove the measure proposed an imperfect one?
May I not say that I estimate the value of commodities once
a year—that at the end of the first year the wine on which
£200 has been employed is worth £220 and both the other
commodities on which only half the labour has been employed for the same time £110. So far their values agree
with the quantities of labour employed, and if you were to
alter profits to 20 pc^t or to 5 pc their relative value would be
precisely the same.[6] If you employ the first of these capitals
without employing any labour its value must be the same
precisely as if you employed an equal value in the support
of labour and therefore if profits be 10 pc^t they will both be
of the value of £242 the second year. In the second case
you actually employ only as much labour as £210 can
employ (only such a capital as is equal to £210 employed in
labour)[7] and therefore you obtain only a value of £231. If
the measure of value be[8] produced in a year, the commodity to be measured must be valued annually, and must
not be valued by the quantity of labour actually employed

---

[1] 'you' replaces 'I'.
[2] 'in proportion to' is del. here.
[3] 'also' is ins.
[4] 'the whole result of labour is'
replaces 'they are'.
[5] This phrase, beginning 'that is
to say', is ins.

[6] At this point there is an incom-
plete insertion which reads: 'The
wine would be always of'.
[7] The words in brackets are ins.
[8] Replaces 'If the employment be
yearly—the measure of value
must be'.

on the commodity, but by the quantity which its value could employ[1] if devoted to the production of the commodity which is the measure.

We have already had occasion to remark that a measure of value which is the result of immediate[2] labour only without any advances whatever, as in the case of shrimps or any other commodity which requires a day's or a few hours labour to produce it; or a measure of value[3] which is the result of immediate labour and of accumulated labour, that is of labour and capital expended for a given time[,] a year for example[,] are equally accurate measures of value if confined respectively to the class of commodities which are produced precisely under the same circumstances as themselves. If gold and cloth be produced under the same circumstances of labour and capital united, for the same time, then will either of them be an accurate measure by which to estimate the variations in other things also produced under the same circumstances[4] provided the gold or cloth be always produced with the same quantity of labour—and if shrimps and broken stones prepared for the roads be produced also under similar circumstances either of them will also be an accurate measure of the value of commodities produced by a days labour without advances in the same manner as shrimps and stones, but the stones or shrimps will not accurately measure the value and variations of the commodities produced under the same circumstances as cloth and gold, nor will cloth and gold measure accurately the variations in the commodities produced under the same circumstances as shrimps and stones. This then seems to hold universally true that the commodity valued must be

---

[1] 'employ' replaces 'produce'.
[2] 'immediate' is ins.

[3] The last two lines, beginning 'as in the case', replace 'or'.
[4] The last six words are ins.

reduced to circumstances precisely similar (with respect to time of production)[1] to those of the commodity in which the valuation is made. Tho' wine be not fit to drink for 3 years after it is made, in the first year some if not all the labour has been bestowed, cloth and gold is a good measure of its value at that period. Whatever its value may be at that period we may enquire what quantity of labour that capital would employ if bestowed on the production of cloth or gold, and then again after another year has elapsed the wine would be worth more cloth and gold by all the profits which such a capital is calculated to produce. The third year it would be still more valuable and so on as long as it was advantageous to keep it. If I am possessed of equal values in cloth and in wine I have equal powers with either to employ labour. If I dispose of the cloth and employ labour, in the production of cloth, and for the satisfaction of the wine drinker lock up the wine in my cellar and forbear selling it for one year ought I not to obtain an additional value for it equal to that which the cloth which I have produced will enable me to get. If I had 100 pieces of cloth and by the exchange for food raw material &c.ª and the employment of 50 men for a year I obtain 120 pieces of cloth, as my cloth has increased one fifth in quantity and value, ought not my wine to increase also one fifth in value. Tho' it is not strictly right to say that these two commodities are valuable in proportion to the quantity of labour actually bestowed on them, would it be not correct to say that the value of the wine after two years was in proportion to the labour actually employed on it the first year, and to the labour which might have been employed on wine or on some other commodity if it had been brought to market after the first year of its production.

[1] The words in brackets are ins.

An oak which is the growth of 100 years in like manner has perhaps from first to last only one day's labour bestowed upon it, but its value depends on the accumulations of capital by the compound profits on the one day's labour and the quantity of labour which such accumulated capital would from year to year have employed.

Iron is the production of many days perhaps a year's labour before it is finally brought to market, and accordingly is accurately measurable by a commodity produced under the same circumstances as itself such as cloth and gold—but we may make use of the[1] measure for commodities of the produce of one day's labour such as shrimps and broken stones if we reduce the iron in its rude state to the same condition as the shrimps and stones.

When the ore is first dug from the earth the quantity obtained by one man's labour in one day will probably be of the same value as the shrimps or broken stones obtained by the labour of one man for one day. After the second day it will be of more than double the value, because it will not only be increased in value by the second day's labour but by the profit on a capital advanced for one day and which is equal to a man's wages for one day. This case in days is precisely similar to that for years in our former supposition respecting the cloth and wine, one the produce of one year's labour the other the produce of two years labour. If the Iron should have 365 days labour bestowed upon it, it will be more than 365 times the value of the ore when it was first dug by one day's labour from the mine, because it will have all the successive profits on the advances which were made and which if realised at any of the intermediate periods would have commanded a greater quantity of labour than had been actually expended.

[1] 'other' is del. here.

If we succeeded in our object we have shewn that one of these measures is best calculated to measure one class of objects and that another of them is more applicable to a different class. But as it is desirable that we should have one measure of value only which it is acknowledged cannot be accurate for all objects, to which shall we give the preference[:] to that commodity which is the result of continued labour for one year, and whose value must consequently include profits as well as wages, or that commodity which is the result of the labour of one day only and which consequently does not require advances and does not include profits. The choice is in some degree arbitrary and should be governed only by expediency. If the generality of commodities which are the objects of the traffic of mankind were produced under the circumstances of the shrimps and stones, shrimps or stones should be the measure of value and whenever we said a thing had risen or fallen in value it should always be in reference to that measure; if the generality of commodities were produced under circumstances similar to those under which wine is produced and required 2 or 3 years before it could be brought to market then a commodity similar to wine should be the general measure of value. But if as is most certain a much greater proportion[1] of the commodities which are the objects of exchange amongst men are produced under circumstances similar to those under which gold and cloth are produced and are the result of labour and capital applied for a year, then gold or cloth is[2] the most proper measure of value (while they require precisely the same quantity of labour and capital[3] to produce them)[4] and to that measure should we always refer when we

---

[1] 'a much greater proportion' replaces 'the generality'.
[2] Replaces 'gold and cloth are'.
[3] 'and capital' is ins.
[4] The whole sentence within brackets is ins.

are speaking of the rise or fall in the[1] absolute value of all other things.

It cannot have escaped the attention of the reader that for the measure which I have proposed I have not claimed the character of perfection—I have now and at all other times acknowledged that it was not under every circumstance a measure against which no objections could be urged; on the contrary when I first proposed it I shewed that there were many cases of exception where it could not be correctly denominated an accurate measure of value—I claimed for it only the preference over all measures which had up to that time[2] been proposed. Mr. Malthus was the first who questioned the correctness of the principle on which this measure was founded. He made use of the very exceptions which I had mentioned to shew its inaccuracy as a general measure of value, and insisted that though it was a correct measure of value for all commodities produced under like circumstances with itself, for all others it was an incorrect one, and could not on the one hand measure the variations in those things which were the produce of labour alone as shrimps and broken stones[3], nor of commodities produced with advances employed for a much longer time than those employed on the production of the measure itself. Mr. Malthus was perfectly right in these observations and in fact I had made them myself before he made them[4], but what has Mr. Malthus subsequently done he has himself written a pamphlet to recommend a general measure of value against which every objection which he has made against mine exists in full force. He in fact constitutes as his measure a commodity which is produced by labour alone, and has not

---

[1] 'value' is del. here.
[2] Replaces 'thitherto'.
[3] 'and broken stones' is ins.
[4] 'him' is written above 'he made them' as an alternative.

appeared to see that if a commodity produced by labour and capital united is a bad measure of value for a commodity produced by labour alone, a commodity produced by labour alone must be a bad measure of value for a commodity produced by labour and capital united. What should we think of a man who should object to a yard measure for measuring [the][1] dimensions of a foot and yet propose the foot measure for measuring the dimensions of a yard? He might say that the foot was a more convenient measure than the yard, but he could not say that the one was an accurate measure founded on a principle, and the other an inaccurate measure founded on no principle, for it would be certain that if 1 yard were equal to 3 feet, 1 foot would be the third part of 1 yard and therefore the expressions of one foot and the third part of 1 yard, or 1 yard and 3 feet would be equivalent. Mr. Malthus has in fact made an objection against my measure to which his own is more peculiarly liable. It is in fact founded as he tells us himself on the quantity of labour necessary to production, but necessary to the production of a few particular commodities, and in these he estimates the value of all other things. A pipe of wine for example he says is equivalent to so much of his measure as would require the labour of 1000 men to produce it, in one day—that does not mean that 1000 men's labour for one day or the labour of 500 men for 2 days have been bestowed on the wine, but it means that the wine will exchange for more labour than it cost, and therefore if it cost the labour of 200 men for one day the value of the labour of 800 men will constitute the profit and the whole value of the wine is divided into fifths one fifth of which is the value of the wages and four fifths the value of the profits. If it had sold for 900 then it would have been

[1] Omitted in MS.

divided into ninths of which 2 would have constituted wages
and 7 profits.[1] But if it cost 20£ and will sell for £100—or
20 yards of cloth and will sell for 100, these facts would be
equally indicated. In saying this then Mr. Malthus appears
to me only to repeat that the value of all commodities
resolves itself into wages and profits, and therefore all above
the value of wages which is produced when sold constitute
profits. This is a proposition which no man will dispute
but which may be equally known whether we use gold,
silver, cloth, hats, wine or labour for our measure of value.
It in fact indicates nothing but the proportions in which the
finished commodity is divided amongst the master and his
workmen. Labour says Mr. Malthus never varies in itself,
a day's labour is always worth a day's labour, therefore
labour is invariable and a good measure of value. In this
way I might prove that no commodity ever varied and
therefore that any one was equally applicable as a measure
of value, as for example gold never varies in itself and
therefore is an invariable measure of value—cloth never
varies in itself and therefore is an invariable measure of
value, but labour, gold, and cloth vary in each other—they
vary in all other commodities, and therefore they are not all
invariable and we are as far as ever from the object of our
search which is not a measure invariable in itself but invariable in some standard which is itself fixed and unalterable. If no commodities but those which are the result of
one day's labour existed in the world Mr. Malthus would
have obtained this desirable standard, for as[2] the average
strength of a man is at all times nearly the same, the labour

---

[1] The last five lines, beginning
'the value of the labour of 800
men', are written as an alternative
above 'then is the value of the

wine made up of 200 of labour
and 800 for profits'.
[2] 'one man's strength' is del.
here.

of 1000 men in one commodity for one day would be equal in intensity and therefore equal in value to the labour of 1000 men in another commodity and for this reason the commodities themselves would be of equal value but as the result of the labour of 1000 men for 365 days is and always will be of considerably [1] more value than 365 times the result of the labour of 1000 men for one day Mr. Malthus cannot claim the character of invariability for his measure which he refuses to accord and justly refuses to accord to the measure proposed by others.

"After capitalists become a distinct class from labourers, competition turns, not upon the quantity of labour, but on the amount of capital expended in production; and the results obtained after the employment of equal capitals, will always tend to an equality of value in the market".[2] Col! Torrens means that if two equal capitals be employed for the same time the commodities produced will be of equal value. No one can doubt the truth of this proposition, but I may ask Col! Torrens what he means by equal capitals? If he answer I mean what I have often mentioned equal quantities of loaves and suits of cloathing for the support of labourers I understand him, but I again ask him to compare the capital of the clothier consisting of buildings steam engines, raw material &c.ª, with the capital of the sugar baker consisting of a very different set of commodities, and then to tell me what he means by equal capitals—he must answer that by equal capitals he means capitals of equal value. Now how does he discover that they are of equal value? he will tell me by comparing them with a third commodity which will accurately determine their relative value—he is quite correct

[1] 'considerably' is ins.
[2] *An Essay on the Production of*   *Wealth*, by Robert Torrens, London, 1821, p. 38.

but suppose now something occurs to alter the value of the clothiers capital as compared with the sugar bakers the means are undoubtedly easy of ascertaining what the alteration is in the relative value of these two capitals but what I want to know [is]¹ in which the alteration has taken place and here Col! Torrens' rule fails me. I can only know that their relative value has altered but I have no measure by which I can tell whether the capital of the one has fallen or the capital of the other has risen. A yard of cloth may be worth 5 loaves of sugar. The difficulty of producing cloth and sugar may be increased two fold, or it may be doubly easy to produce them both, in neither of these cases will the relative value of these two commodities alter, a yard of cloth will be still worth 5 loaves of sugar, and because their relative value has not altered Col. Torrens would lead you to infer that their real value has not altered—I say their real value has certainly altered, in one case they have both, the yard of cloth and the 5 loaves of sugar, become less valuable, in the other they have both become more valuable. If Col. Torrens says that he also says they are altered in real value I ask by what rule he estimates the alteration—if he says by comparing them with a third or fourth commodity I ask him for his proof that they have not altered [in]² value for it can not be too often repeated that nothing can be a measure of value which is not itself invariable. If he says that this third or fourth commodity are invariable then he has found out an invariable measure of value and then I ask him for his proof of its invariability. But instead of making any such claim he says expressly there is no measure of absolute³ value and all we can know any thing about is relative value. When Col! Torrens says⁴ that equal capitals

---

¹ Omitted in MS.
² Omitted in MS.
³ 'absolute' is ins.
⁴ Replaces 'But is it true'.

will produce equal values he must then clearly define what he means by equal capitals, and he ought to add "when employed for equal times" for equal capitals do not produce equal results unless they are employed for equal times.

"Exchangeable value &cᵃ &cᵃ Page 56.[1]

"Nothing can be an accurate measure of value &cᵃ &cᵃ— 59[2] In page 49 Col. Torrens says the exchangeable value of cottons would fall one half if they could only purchase half the former quantity of commodities altho' they might at the same time exchange for double the former quantity of wine, corn, labour, or money.[3] But suppose that their exchangeable value rose relatively to as many commodities as it fell relatively to others we should not then say its exchangeable value had fallen. I suppose Col. Torrens would say their exchangeable value had both risen and fallen, according to the goods [with][4] which he compared them. But if I asked him whether their value, leaving out the word exchangeable, had altered, he would be puzzled for an answer. Now with respect to the correctness of Col. Torrens' definition of exchangeable value no one questions it, no one who has preceded him in these enquiries who has not nearly said the same thing on the subject as he has himself, but there are writers deeply impressed with the importance of possessing an absolute measure of value to which all things may be referred, and the question is not whether an accurate measure

[1] 'Exchangeable value is determined, not by the absolute, but by the relative cost of production.' *Production of Wealth*, p. 56.
[2] 'Nothing can be an accurate measure of value, except that which itself possesses an invariable value.' *ib*. p. 59.
[3] 'If cotton would purchase only half the former quantity of commodities in general, while it purchased twice the quantity of some particular commodity, such as corn, or wine, or labour, or money,—then its exchangeable value would have sunk one half, while its price, as expressed in corn, or wine, or labour, or money, became double.' *ib*. p. 48.
[4] Omitted in MS.

of this description can be obtained, but whether any thing approximating to it can be suggested?

[The following is the draft described as sheet (*a*) in the introductory Note, above, p. 360]

It is a great desideratum in Polit. Econ. to have a perfect measure of absolute[1] value[2] in order to be able to ascertain what relation commodities bear to each other[3] at distant periods. Any thing having value is a good measure of the comparative value of all other commodities at the same time and place, but will be of no use in indicating the variations in their absolute value[4] at distant times and in distant places. If I want to know what the relative values of cloth, leather, copper and lead bear to each other I may successively compare them to gold, iron, corn or any other commodity—if a given quantity of cloth be worth twice a like quantity of leather, it will also be worth twice the value of the gold, or iron or corn which a like quantity of leather will exchange for. But if I want to know whether cloth be of a greater absolute value[5] now than at a former period I can know nothing of this fact, unless I can compare it to a commodity which I am sure has itself not varied during the time for which the comparison is to be made. If for example a piece of cloth is now of the value of 2 ounces of gold and was formerly of the value of four I cannot positively say that the cloth is only half as valuable as before, because it is possible that the gold may be twice as valuable as before. That the cloth is only half as valuable as before must depend therefore

[1] 'absolute' is ins.
[2] This phrase echoes Blake's 'that great desideratum in political economy, an uniform measure of value' (*Observations on...Expenditure*, 1823, p. 19).
[3] 'now bear to the same commodities' is written as an alternative above 'bear to each other'.
[4] 'their absolute value' replaces 'the value of commodities'.
[5] 'of greater absolute value' replaces 'more valuable'.

on the invariability of the measure by which I endeavor to ascertain the fact. If to determine the value of gold I compare it with some other one commodity or many other commodities how can I be sure that that one commodity or all the other commodities have not themselves varied in value. I may be asked what I mean by the word value, and by what criterion I would judge whether a commodity had or had not changed its value. I answer, I know no other criterion of a thing being dear or cheap but by the sacrifices of labour made to obtain it. Every thing is originally purchased by labour—nothing that has value can be produced without it, and therefore if a commodity such as cloth required the labour of ten men for a year to produce it at one time, and only requires the labour of five for the same time to produce it at another it will be twice as cheap. Or if the labour of ten men should be still required to produce the same quantity of cloth but for 6 months instead of twelve cloth would fall in value.

That the greater or less quantity of labour worked up in commodities can be the only cause of their alteration in value is completely made out as soon as we are agreed that all commodities are the produce of labour and would have no value but for the labour expended upon them. Though this is true it is still exceedingly difficult to discover or even to imagine any commodity which shall be[1] perfect general measure of value, as we shall see by the observations which follow.

[1] 'or even to imagine any commodity which shall be' replaces 'any'.

[ABSOLUTE VALUE AND EXCHANGE-ABLE VALUE]

[*Later Version—Unfinished*]

EXCHANGEABLE VALUE

By exchangeable value is meant the power which a commodity has of commanding any given quantity of another commodity, without any reference whatever to its absolute value. We should say that an ounce of gold had increased in exchangeable value in relation to cloth if from usually commanding two yards of cloth in the market, it could freely command or exchange for three: and for the same reason we should under the same circumstances say that the exchangeable value of cloth had fallen with respect to gold, as three yards had become necessary to command the same quantity of gold that two yards would command before. Any commodity having value will measure exchangeable value, for exchangeable value and proportional value mean the same thing. By knowing that an ounce of gold will at any particular time exchange for two yards of cloth, ten yards of linen, a hundred weight of sugar, a quarter of wheat, 3 quarters of oats &cᵃ &cᵃ we know the proportional value of all these commodities, and are enabled to say that a yard of cloth is worth 5 yards of linen, and a quarter of wheat 3 times the value of a quarter of oats.

ABSOLUTE VALUE[1]

All measures of length are measures of absolute as well as relative length. Suppose linen and cloth to be liable to contract and expand, by measuring them at different times with a foot rule, which was itself neither liable to contract or expand, we should be able to determine what alteration had taken place in their length. If at one time the cloth measured 200 feet and at another 202, we should say it had increased 1 per cent. If the linen from 100 feet in length increased to 103 we should say it had increased 3 per cent, but we should not say the foot measure had diminished in length because it bore a less proportion to the length of the cloth and linen. The alteration would really be in the cloth and linen and not in the foot measure. In the same manner if we had a perfect

[1] In an earlier draft, described above (p. 360) as sheet (*b*), this section opened as follows:

'But although in the case just supposed we should know the relative value of these commodities we should have no means of knowing their absolute value. If an ounce of gold from commanding two yards of cloth came to command 3 yards of cloth it would alter in relative or exchangeable value to cloth but we should be ignorant whether gold had risen in absolute value or cloth had fallen in absolute value. Suppose lead to be a measure of absolute value, and that when an ounce of gold exchanged for two yards of cloth it was of the same value as 2 cwt of lead and that when it was worth 3 yards of cloth it was worth also 3 cwt of lead then cloth would not have varied in absolute value, but gold would have risen 50 pc^t. If on the contrary the ounce of gold continued of the same value as 2 cwt. of lead then when it exchanged for 3 yards of cloth cloth would have risen 50 pc^t in absolute value and gold would not have varied. The question is can we obtain such a measure of absolute value and what are the criteria by which we are to satisfy ourselves that we have obtained. Into that question we now propose to enter.

'No one can doubt that it would be a great desideratum in political Ec. to have such a measure of absolute value in order to enable us to know[,] when commodities altered in exchangeable value[,] in which the alteration in value had taken place'. Here the draft broke off and started again with the paragraph 'All measures of length'.

measure of value, itself being neither liable to increase or diminish in value, we should by its means be able to ascertain the real as well as the proportional variations in other things and should never refer the variation in the commodity measured to the commodity itself by which it was measured. Thus in the case before stated when an ounce of gold exchanged for two yards of cloth and afterwards exchanged for three, if gold was a perfect measure of value we should not say that gold had increased in value because it would exchange for more cloth but that cloth had fallen in value because it would exchange for less gold. And if gold was liable to all the variations of other commodities, we might, if we knew the laws which constituted a measure of value a perfect one, either fix on some other commodity in which all the conditions of a good measure existed, by which to correct the apparent variations of other things, and thus ascertain whether gold or cloth, or both had varied in real value, or in default of such a commodity we might correct the measure chosen by allowing for the effect of those causes which we had previously ascertained to operate on value.

By many Political Economists it is said that we have an absolute measure of value, not indeed in any one single commodity but in the mass of commodities. If we wanted to ascertain whether in the case just supposed of the cloth and gold[1] the variation had been in the one or in the other we could immediately ascertain it by comparing them alternately to many other commodities and if the gold preserved the same relation as before with these commodities then the cloth had varied, but if the cloth remained as before we might safely conclude that gold had varied.

This measure might be an accurate one on many occasions, but suppose that on such a comparison I found that with

[1] In MS 'whether' is repeated here.

respect to a great number gold had altered in value, and with respect to another large number it had not altered in value, but cloth had; how should I determine whether the cloth or gold had varied? Suppose further that with respect to any twenty or thirty with which I compared them the results were the same, how should I know that the commodities to which I thus compared them had not themselves altered in value? If it be admitted that one commodity may alter in absolute value, it must be admitted that 2, 3, 100, a million may do so, and how shall I be able with certainty to say whether the one or the million had varied.

There can be no unerring measure either of length, of weight, of time or of value unless there be some object in nature to which the standard itself can be referred and by which we are enabled to ascertain whether it preserves its character of invariability, for it is evident on the slightest consideration that nothing can be a measure which is not itself invariable. If we have any doubts respecting the uniformity of our measure of length, the foot, for example, we can refer it to a portion of the arc of the meridian, or to the vibrations of the Pendulum under given circumstances and by such means can correct any accidental variations. If we have any doubts respecting our clocks and watches we regulate them by the daily revolution of the earth on its axis, and by similar tests we are enabled to correct our measures of weight and our measures of capacity, but to what standard are we to refer for the correction of our measure of value? It has been said that we are not without a standard in nature to which we may refer for the correction of errors and deviations in our measure of value, in the same way as in the other measures which I have noticed, and that such standard is to be found in the labour of men. The average strength of a thousand or of ten thousand men it is asserted is always nearly the same, why then not make the labour of man the unit or standard measure of value? If we are in possession of any commodity which requires always the same quantity of labour to produce it that commodity must be of uniform value, and is eminently well qualified to measure the value of all other things. And if we are not in possession of any such commodity, we are still not destitute of the means of accurately measuring the absolute value of other things, because by correcting our measure, and making allowance for the greater or less quantity of labour necessary to produce it we have always the means of referring every commodity whose value we wish to measure to an unerring and invariable standard. If this test were adopted it has been said every commodity would be valuable according to the quantity of labour required to produce them,—that if a quantity of shrimps required the labour of ten men for one day, a quantity of cloth the labour of ten men for one year, and a quantity of wine required the application of the labour of ten men for two years, the value of the cloth would be 365 times that of the shrimps, and that of the wine twice the value of the cloth. It is further said that if a commodity produced 20 years ago, such as cloth, required the labour of 10 men for a year, and now requires the labour of 12 men for the same time it would have increased one fifth or twenty per cent in value and that in fact it would in the market exchange for one fifth more of a commodity on the production of which the same quantity of labour had been uniformly employed.

Of all the standards hitherto proposed this appears to be the best but it is far from being a perfect one. In the first place it is not true that the cloth produced under the circumstances supposed would be precisely 365 times the value of the shrimps for in addition to such value, if profits were 10 pc^t, 10 pc^t must be added on all the advances made for the time they were made before the commodity was brought to market. It would not be true either that the wine would be of only twice the value of the cloth, it would be more for the clothier would be entitled to one years profits only, the wine merchant would be entitled to two. In the second place if profits fell from 10 pc^t to 5 pc^t, the proportions between the value of wine, of cloth, and of shrimps would alter accordingly, although no alteration whatever took place in the quantity of labour necessary to produce these commodities respectively. Now which of these commodities should we chuse for our standard? they would be all unerring, if the quantity of labour employed on production were the sole test of value, and yet we see that without any alteration in the quantity of that labour they all vary with respect to each other. If we selected cloth, when profits fell to 5 pc^t shrimps would rise in value, and wine would fall. If we selected wine shrimps would rise very considerably, and cloth would rise in a slight degree; and if we selected shrimps both wine and cloth would fall considerably, but the wine more than the cloth.

If all commodities were produced by labour alone, without any advances, and were brought to market in one day, then indeed we should possess an uniform measure of value, and any commodity which always required the same quantity of labour to produce it would be as perfect a measure of value, as a foot is a perfect measure of length, or a pound a perfect measure of weight.

Or if all commodities were produced by labour employed upon them for one year, then also would any commodity always requiring the same quantity of labour be a perfect measure.

Or if they were all produced in two years the same would be equally true, but while commodities are produced under the greatest variety of circumstances, as far as regards the time at which they are brought to market, they will not vary only on account of the greater or less quantity of labour necessary to produce them but also on account of the greater or less[1] proportion of the finished commodity which may[2] be paid to the workman, accordingly as labour is abundant or scarce, or as the necessaries of the workman become more difficult to produce, and which is the only cause of the variation of profits. A commodity produced by labour alone in one day is totally unaffected by a variation in profits, and a commodity produced in one year is less affected by a variation in profits than a commodity produced in two.

It appears then that any commodity always produced by the same quantity of labour, whether employed for a day a month a year or any number of years is a perfect measure of value, if the proportions into which commodities are divided for wages and profits are always alike, but that there can be no perfect measure of the variations in the value of commodities arising from an alteration in these proportions, as the proportions will themselves differ according as the commodity employed for the measure may be produced in a shorter or longer time.

It must then be confessed that there is no such thing in nature as a perfect measure of value, and that all that is left to the Political Economist is to admit that the great cause of the variation of commodities is the greater or less quantity of labour that may be necessary to produce them, but that there is also another though much less powerful cause of their variation which arises from the different proportions in which finished commodities may be distributed between

[1] 'or less' is ins.   [2] Replaces 'must'.

master and workman in consequence of either the amended or deteriorated condition of the labourer, or of the greater difficulty or facility of producing the necessaries essential to his subsistence.

But though we cannot have a perfect measure of value[,] is not one of the measures produced by labour better than another, and in chusing amongst measures which are all acknowledged to be imperfect which shall we select[,] one which is produced by labour alone, or one produced by labour employed[1] for a certain period, say a year?

To me it appears most clear that we should chuse a measure produced by labour employed for a certain period, and which always supposes an advance of capital, because 1st it is a perfect measure for all commodities produced under the same circumstances of time as the measure itself—2dly By far the greatest number of commodities which are the objects of exchange are produced by the union of capital and labour, that is to say of labour employed for a certain time 3dly That a commodity produced by labour employed for a year is a mean between the extremes of commodities produced on one side by labour and advances for much more than a year, and on the other by labour employed for a day only without any advances, and the mean will in most cases give a much less deviation from truth than if either of the extremes were used as a measure. Let us suppose money to be produced in precisely the same time as corn is produced, that would be the measure proposed by me, provided it always required the same uniform quantity of labour to produce it, and if it did not provided an allowance were made for the alteration in the value of the measure itself in consequence of its requiring more or less labour to obtain it. The circumstance of this measure[2] being produced in the

[1] Replaces 'advanced'.   [2] 'agreeing exactly with' is del. here.

same length of time as corn and most other vegetable food which forms by far the most valuable article of daily consumption would decide me in giving it a preference.

Mr. Malthus proposes another measure and he supposes a money to be picked up by the labour of a day on the sea shore and whatever quantity can be so uniformly picked up is according to him not only the best but a perfect measure [of][1] value. Thus suppose a man by a day's labour could always pick up as much silver as we call 2/- a day's labour and 2/- would be of equal value and either in Mr. Malthus's judgment would be a perfect measure of value.

Now that it cannot be a perfect measure of value must be evident from the foregoing observations, but it is singular that Mr. Malthus himself after the admissions which he has made for it should claim for it that character. Mr. Malthus acknowledges that if all commodities were produced by the union of capital and labour in the same time that corn is produced[,] that corn always requiring the same quantity of labour or gold produced under the same circumstances as corn would be a perfect measure of value. Mr. Malthus admits then that for a large class of commodities the measure proposed by me is a perfect one, and that it would be a perfect one for all if the case were as I have just supposed it. Now let me suppose that corn, cloth, gold and[2] various other commodities to be produced in the same time, and that gold is the measure and always produced with the same quantity of labour. Let me also suppose that labour becomes scarce and is universally paid by a larger proportion of the finished commodity, will corn, or cloth rise in price? Will it exchange for more gold the general measure? Mr Malthus has admitted and will admit that it would not, because this rise of wages will affect all equally, and will

[1] Omitted in MS.   [2] 'poultry' is del. here.

therefore leave them in the same relative situation to each other. If the labourers in agriculture receive ¾ of the produce, in lieu of one half, as wages, the labourers in the gold mines, and in the clothiers manufactory will do the same and consequently the prices of these commodities, their value in this (under these circumstances acknowledged) perfect measure will remain unaltered. Now suppose Mr. Malthus' money obtained by the labour of a day to be the measure of value, will corn and cloth under the former supposition of a larger proportion of the whole produce being paid to the workman remain of the same value? certainly not, every quarter of corn will command less labour, less of Mr. Malthus' money and therefore will be of less value. Here then are two measures both perfect according to Mr. Malthus in one of which the same commodities will remain stationary that vary in the other.

If I had no[1] argument to advance against the expediency of adopting[2] Mr Malthus's proposed measure, this is I think conclusive against the claim which he sets up for its universal accuracy and perfection, but I have many reasons to urge against its adoption on account of its inexpediency.

Let me suppose that some great improvement was discovered in agriculture by means of which we might without any additional labour on the land produce 50 pc.t more of corn. According to my mode of estimating value, without any regard to what was paid to the workman corn would fall in the proportion of 150 to 100. According to Mr. Malthus mode of estimating the value of corn, it would not depend at all upon the difficulty or facility of producing it, but solely on the quantity paid to the labourer. Altho' you could produce 50 pc.t or 100 pc.t more with the same labour he would say it was of the same value if the labourer

---

[1] 'other' is del. here.   [2] 'the expediency of adopting' is ins.

received no more than before—according to him commodities are not valuable in proportion to the difficulty or facility of producing them, but their value depends wholly not on the proportion but on the actual quantity paid to the labourer. A man can buy in our present money a loaf and a half of bread for the same money that he could before buy only a loaf: he can do so because the facility of producing it is increased 50 pc.^{t} and yet Mr. Malthus would constrain us to say that corn had not fallen in value, but that money had risen in value if the labourer received the same quantity of corn.

An epidemic disorder prevails in a country to so great a degree as to sweep off a very large portion of the people and in consequence all the employers of labour are obliged to give a much larger proportion of their finished commodities to their labourers, this in my estimate of value would have no effect whatever on the price of goods, but it would have a great effect on the price of labour. Wages I should say were high and specifically because labour was scarce as compared with capital, not so Mr. Malthus he would say that labour remained precisely of the same value, and that all commodities without exception[1] which were the produce of labour and capital had undergone a considerable reduction of value.—

A vast number of people come into this country from Ireland and by their competition sink the price of labour. Mr. Malthus assures us that labour has not altered in value, but that all commodities, in the production of which no new difficulty has occurred, have very considerably increased in value.

I know and am ready to confess that however these expressions might be contrary to general usage, if Mr.

[1] 'without exception' is ins.

Malthus had shewn that the alteration he proposed rested on a sound principle, we ought, at least amongst Political Economists, to have adopted them, but I contend that his selection rests on no sound principle whatever,—that it is an arbitrary choice, and that it has no foundation in reason and truth. My measure says Mr. Malthus is an invariable one because it will measure both wages and profits. "I can see no impropriety he says in saying with Adam Smith and myself that labour will measure not only that part of the whole value of the commodity which resolves itself into labour but also that which resolves itself into profits"[1] Nor no body else if the object be to determine the proportions into which the whole value is divided between the capitalist and the labourer, but what proof does this afford of its being an invariable measure of value? Would not gold, silver, iron, lead, cloth, corn all confessedly variable measures equally effect the proposed object? The question is about an invariable measure of value, and the proof of the invariability of the proposed measure is that it will measure profits as well as labour, that is to say that it will do what every other measure without exception variable or invariable will equally accomplish.[2]

But the conditions of the supply of every commodity says Mr. Malthus are that it should command more labour than it cost, and therefore labour is a particularly appropriate measure. That is saying in other words that wherever advances are made, if those advances only are returned, and nothing remains for profit, the commodity will not be produced. This is a proposition which no one denies but it does not afford the least proof of the invariability of the value of labour, for if a man value his advances, in labour, and his

---

[1] Malthus' letter of 25 Aug. 1823, below, **IX**, 363.　　[2] See Ricardo's letter to Malthus, 31 Aug. 1823, *ib.* 380–1.

returns in the same medium, his profits will be increased if labour during the interval that he is obtaining the returns become very abundant, they will be reduced to little or nothing if labour become scarce. But so also they would be if he made these estimates in money. If labour rose in money he would realise less money for profits when he was obliged to give a great deal of money to his labourers, he would realise more money for profits if in consequence of the fall of the price of labour he had to pay his labourers a small quantity of money. Mr. Malthus appears to me wholly to fail in his proof of labour being invariable in value.

Mr. MCulloch has a different theory—he does not he says[1] pretend to establish any general invariable measure of value, but all he aims at is to lay down the rule by which the relative value of commodities may be determined and this he says depends on the quantity of labour worked up in them. If one commodity is twice the value of another, it is because it has twice the quantity of labour employed on it. It is objected to Mr. MCulloch that this does not appear to be the fact, that an oak tree worth £100 has not had perhaps from the first moment it was planted[2] as much labour employed on it as would cost 5 shillings while another commodity of the value of £100 had really had 100 pounds worth of labour bestowed on it. Mr. MCulloch answers that he estimates the labour in a commodity by the capital which has actually been devoted to its production, and if you again object that only 5/- worth of capital has been bestowed on the tree he denies this and says 5/- employed for a day will when profits are 10 pc.^{t} be equivalent to 5/6 in a year, that after the 1.st year, and for the second year 5/6 is employed as capital which at the end of the 2.^{d} year becomes a capital

[1] Cp. McCulloch's letter of 24   [2] 'had' is repeated here in MS
Aug. 1823, ib. 369.

of 6/0½ and so from year to year because you forbear using
any part of the capital it becomes in the course of time worth
£100, in the same manner as if you employed 5/- for one day
on the land, in a year it would be worth 5/6. This 5/6 will
employ more labour and will at the end of another year
produce 6/0½ and so on from year to year till it amount to
£100. That in fact there is not so much actual labour
bestowed on the tree as on the corn which may sell for £100
but that equal capitals have been actually expended on them
if you make due allowance for the forbearance of the owner
of the 5/- expended on the tree in not appropriating to
himself any part of the accumulations which the tree made
from year to year. If you suppose the growing tree brought
to market every year the first year it will be worth 5/6 the
second 6/0½ and so on; that in fact these successive purchasers
actually advance such a sum of capital to become possessed
of the tree, till at last £100 is advanced. Mr. MCulloch asks
what are these advances but capital, what is capital but labour
how then can it be denied that equal quantities of labour
yield equal values. If you ask Mr. MCulloch whether the
labour of 52 men for one week be not the same quantity
of labour as the labour of one man for 52 weeks, he will
answer, no, it is not the same, for after each week a man
who receives the profit on his work has an increased capital
with which to work the second week and so on from week
to week; the second man who employs his capital for
52 weeks without receiving any profit during the interval is
equally entitled to these successive accumulations, and therefore his capital is to be estimated by the same rule as the
man's capital who realises an increased capital every week,
by adding to the original capital the further capital which
his profits enable him to cultivate. The only doubt one can
feel on this subject is the accuracy of the language used by

Mr. MCulloch—it might be right to say that commodities were valuable in relation to each other according to their cost of production, or according to the quantity of capital employed on them for equal times, but it does not appear correct to say that their relative value depended on the quantity of capital worked up in them

[The MS breaks off here]

APPENDIX

APPENDIX

The 'Ingenious Calculator'

IN 1797 the Bank of England, although unwilling to disclose the absolute figures for their cash and for their discounts, had delivered to the Secret Committee of the Lords on the Suspension of Cash Payments two separate 'scales' (or, as they would now be called, index numbers) for cash and for discounts over the years 1782 to 1797. These scales were printed in the Appendix to the Report.

Ricardo, in *Economical and Secure Currency*, says that 'by comparing these tables with each other and with some parts of the evidence delivered before the Parliamentary Committees, an ingenious calculator discovered the whole secret which the Bank wished to conceal.'[1] He refers again to the same 'ingenious individual' in his *Plan for a National Bank*.[2] But in neither of these cases does Ricardo quote his source or give any clue to the identity of the calculator.

Dr Bonar has suggested that it might be Thomas Tooke.[3] Tooke's first contribution to the question, however, was in 1829 when he applied the key furnished by the calculator of 1797 to the further scales disclosed to the Committees of 1819.[4]

If we look into the matter further the following facts emerge.

The 'ingenious calculator' published his results in an article 'On the Finances of the Bank', dated 'London, Oct. 16, 1797', which appeared in the *Monthly Magazine* for October 1797; he signed himself 'M. N.'

The article was reprinted by Alexander Allardyce in his *Address to the Proprietors of the Bank of England*, 3rd ed., 1798,[5] where he refers to the author as 'a writer, eminent for financial knowledge and acuteness'.[6] In a MS note in a copy of Allardyce's

---

[1] Above, p. 99 and cp. p. 112 n.
[2] Above, p. 279.
[3] 'Who was the "ingenious calculator" who found out the Bank's cash and bullion in 1797; was it Tooke?' (*Economic Journal*, 1923 p. 414.)
[4] See below, p. 418.
[5] Appendix, pp. 82–90.
[6] *Address*, p. 32.

book which belonged to Lord Henry Petty (afterwards Lord Lansdowne) 'M. N.' is identified as 'Mr. Morgan'.

No doubt Ricardo read the article in Allardyce's book, which had been sent to him by Grenfell when he was writing *Economical and Secure Currency*;[1] having guessed his identity, he must have written about it to Grenfell, for the latter, writing on 20 September 1815, asked him: 'Where is the calculation of Mr. Morgan, as to the Cash and Bullion of the Bank in 1793 &c.?'[2]

This Mr. Morgan was no doubt William Morgan (1750–1833), F.R.S., actuary to the Equitable Assurance Society and author of many financial pamphlets.

Morgan discovered the key for deciphering what he calls the 'cabalistical numbers' of the Bank in an unpublished part of the evidence: he had 'very good reason for believing (although the circumstance is not inserted in either of the reports) that one of the Directors acknowledged that the Bank, in the course of six days before it stopped payment, had been drained of its cash after the rate of £100,000 each day.' Since the scale had been given both for 18 and 25 February 1797 (the beginning and the end of the period in question) he was enabled to calculate the absolute figure of the cash for all the dates included in the scale. The differences between the figures thus obtained and the aggregate figures for cash and bills discounted, which were published, gave the amount of bills discounted.

In 1810, at the request of the Bullion Committee, the Governor and Deputy Governor of the Bank again 'furnished a comparative Scale, in progressive numbers, shewing the increase in the amount of their discounts from the year 1790 to 1809, both inclusive.' But, no doubt as a result of their previous experience, they requested that the document should not be made public; the Committee therefore returned it to the Bank.[3] Another leakage occurred, however, when the following letter appeared in the *Morning Chronicle* of 15 October 1810. As it also gives the voting in the Committee, which is not available in full elsewhere, it is here reprinted.

[1] See below, VI, 260.   [3] *Bullion Report*, 8vo ed., p. 62.
[2] Below, VI, 275.

Bullion Report.

To the Editor of the Morning Chronicle.

Sir,
　　Happening to call upon a friend of mine the other day, who was a Member of the Bullion Committee, I found on his table the printed Report of that Committee, and on looking at the beginning of it I noticed in my friend's handwriting, opposite to the title-page, what follows:—

Scale of Discounts.

Anno	1797	...	...	241
	1798	...	...	200
	1799	...	...	251
	1810	...	...	688

I presume this must be the account delivered by the Bank of England to the Committee, for the purpose of shewing the rate of increase on their discounts since they have ceased paying in cash; and from this statement it appears that their discounts have increased since 1797, in the enormous proportion of 688 to 241, that is, that it has nearly trebled its amount. Why this statement was not printed with the other documents I am at a loss to conjecture. If the Bank Directors were anxious for its being withheld from the public, it proves that they are conscious that under this head of issue at least, they have made profits which they are desirous should not be publicly disclosed.
　　In another part of the same page I read what follows in my friend's handwriting.

For	Against
Horner	Chancellor of the Exchequer
Henry Thornton	Long
Sharp	Thompson
Huskisson	Manning, Deputy Governor of the Bank
Tierney	Irving
Grenfell	
Parnell	
Brand	
George Johnstone	
Dickenson	Baring spoke *"for"*,—voted *"against."*
Magens	Foster—Absent on day of voting.
Davies Giddy	Sheridan—ditto, only attended once.
Abercrombie	Lord Temple—ditto, never attended.

I make no comment upon this interesting manuscript; I only desire that these several names may be adverted to when the Bank Directors and learned Counsel insinuate that the great question was carried as a *Party* Question.

A. B.

It is probably to this publication that Ricardo refers in his *Notes on the Bullion Report*, when he writes that he is 'credibly informed' as to the proportion in the increase in discounts since the suspension of cash payments.[1]

Its authenticity was confirmed in the House of Commons on 5 April 1811, when Huskisson, in anticipation of the Bullion debate, moved unsuccessfully for the production of the scale in question, saying that it 'had been communicated to the Committee by the Governor of the Bank, under an injunction not to insert it in the Report, and it had since been published in one of the daily vehicles of intelligence.'[2] Alexander Baring, opposing the motion, observed that 'a loose paragraph in the papers possessed no authenticity but what was conferred on it by the hon. gentleman himself'.[3]

Similar scales, brought up to date and on the same basis as those of 1797, were again supplied by the Bank to the Lords' and Commons' Committees on the Resumption of Cash Payments in 1819, and again they were withheld from the public.[4] Tooke published them for the first time in 1829, by permission, together with the absolute figures which he worked out with the aid of the key supplied by the 'ingenious calculator' of 1797.[5]

The absolute figures for cash and for discounts, including the periods (though not the actual dates) of the scales of 1797, 1810 and 1819 were finally disclosed to the Bank Charter Committee of 1832 and published in Appendix 5 to their Report.

---

[1] Above, III, 358.
[2] *Hansard*, XIX, 731.
[3] *ib.* 734.
[4] See Lords' Second Report, p. 31 and Commons' Second Report, p. 152. Two of the numbers were mentioned in the evidence before the Commons' Committee, *ib.* p. 45.
[5] *A Letter to Lord Grenville, on the Effects Ascribed to the Resumption of Cash Payments on the Value of the Currency*, by Thomas Tooke, London, Murray, 1829, pp. 42–6.

Tables of corresponding pages

for Ricardo's Pamphlets in the original editions, 1815–24,
McCulloch's edition (Works, 1846 etc.),
Gonner's edition (Economic Essays, 1923 etc.),
and the present edition.

ESSAY ON THE INFLUENCE OF A LOW PRICE OF CORN ON THE PROFITS OF STOCK

Editions 1–2 1815	McCulloch's edition	Gonner's edition	Present edition	Editions 1–2 1815	McCulloch's edition	Gonner's edition	Present edition
1–2	369	223	9	26–8	381	239–40	26
3–4	371	225–6	10	28–9	381–2	240–1	27
4–6	371–2	226–7	11	29–31	382–3	241–2	28
6–7	372–3	227	12	31–2	383	242	29
7–9	373	227–8	13	32–4	383–4	242–3	30
9–10	373–4	228–9	14	34–5	384	243–4	31
10–12	374	229–30	15	35–7	384–5	244–5	32
12–13	374–5	230–1	16	37–8	385–6	245–6	33
14	376	232	17	38–40	386	246–7	34
13–16	375	231–3	18	40–1	386–7	247–8	35
16–17	375–7	233–4	19	41–2	387	248–9	36
17–19	377–8	234	20	42–4	387–8	249	37
19–20	378	234–5	21	44–5	388–9	249–50	38
20–2	378–9	235–6	22	45–7	389	250–1	39
22–3	379	236–7	23	47–8	389–90	251–2	40
23–5	379–80	237–8	24	48–50	390	252–3	41
25–6	380–1	238–9	25				

PROPOSALS FOR AN ECONOMICAL AND SECURE CURRENCY

Editions 1–2 1816	McCulloch's edition	Gonner's edition	Present edition	Editions 1–2 1816	McCulloch's edition	Gonner's edition	Present edition
1–2	393	153	51	72–3	424	194–5	97
2–4	393–4	153–4	52	73–5	424–5	195–6	98
4–5	394	154–5	53	75–6	425	196–7	99
5–7	394–7	155–7	54	76–8	425–6	197	100
7–9	397–8	157–8	55	78–9	426–7	197–8	101
9–10	398	158–9	56	79–81	426–7	198–9	102
10–12	398–9	159–60	57	81–2	427–8	199–200	103
12–14	399–400	160–1	58	82–4	428–9	200–1	104
14–15	400	161–2	59	84–5	429	201–2	105
15–17	400–1	162–3	60	85–7	429–30	202–3	106
17–18	401–2	163–4	61	87–8	430	203–4	107
18–20	402	164–5	62	88–90	431	204–5	108
20–1	402–3	165–6	63	90–1	431–2	205	109
21–3	403–4	166–7	64	91–3	432	205–6	110
23–5	404	167	65	93–4	432–3	206–7	111
25–7	404–5	167–8	66	94–6	433–4	207–8	112
27–8	405–6	168–9	67	96–7	434	208–9	113
28–9	406	169–70	68	97–9	434–5	209–10	114
29–31	406–7	170–1	69	101	437	211	115
31–2	407–8	171–2	70	102	437–8	212	116
32–4	408	172–3	71	103	438	212–13	117
34–5	408–9	173–4	72	104	439	213	118
35–7	409	174	73	105	439–40	214	119
37–9	410	175	74	106	440–1	—	120
39–40	410–11	175–6	75	107	441	—	121
40–2	411–12	176–7	76	108	442	—	122
42–4	412	177–8	77	109	442–3	—	123
44–5	412–13	178–9	78	110	443–4	—	124
45–7	413	179–80	79	111	444	—	125
47–8	413–14	180–1	80	112	445	—	126
48–9	414	181	81	113	445–6	—	127
50–1	414–15	181–2	82	114	446	—	128
51–2	415–16	182–3	83	115	447	—	129
53–4	416	183–4	84	116	447–8	—	130
54–5	416–17	184–5	85	117	448	—	131
55–7	417	185	86	118	448–9	—	132
57–9	417–18	185–6	87	119	449–50	—	133
60	419	187	88	120	450	—	134
60–2	419–20	187–8	89	121	450–1	—	135
62–4	420	188–9	90	122–3	451	214–15	136
64–5	420–1	189–90	91	123	451–2	215	137
65–6	421	190–1	92	124–5	452	215–16	138
66–8	421–2	191–2	93	125–6	452–3	216–17	139
68–9	422	192	94	126–7	453	217–18	140
69–71	422–3	193	95	127–8	453–4	218–19	141
71–2	423–4	193–4	96				

FUNDING SYSTEM

Supplement to Enc. Brit. (1820)	McCulloch's edition	Present edition	*Supplement to Enc. Brit.* (1820)	McCulloch's edition	Present edition
410	515	149	418	531–2	175
410	515–16	150	418	532–3	176
410	516–17	151	418–19	533	177
410–11	517	152	419	533–4	178
411	517–18	153	419	534–5	179
411	518–19	154	419–20	535	180
411–12	519	155	420	535–6	181
412	519–20	156	420	536–7	182
412	520	157	420–1	537	183
412–13	520–21	158	421	537–8	184
413	521–2	159	421	538	185
413	522	160	421	538–9	186
413	522–3	161	421–2	539–40	187
413–14	523–4	162	422	540	188
414	524	163	422	540–1	189
414–15	524–5	164	422–3	541–2	190
415	525–6	165	423	542	191
415	526	166	423	542–3	192
415	526–7	167	423–4	543–4	193
415–16	527	168	424	544	194
416	527–8	169	424	544–5	195
416–17	528–9	170	424	545	196
417	529–30	171	424–5	545–6	197
417	530	172	425	546–7	198
417–18	530–1	173	425	547	199
418	531	174	425–6	547–8	200

ON PROTECTION TO AGRICULTURE

Editions 1–4 1822	McCulloch's edition	Gonner's edition	Present edition	Editions 1–4 1822	McCulloch's edition	Gonner's edition	Present edition
1–2	457	257	209	13–15	463–4	265–6	217
3–4	459	259–60	210	15–16	464	266–7	218
4–6	459–60	260	211	16–18	464–5	267–8	219
6–7	460–1	260–1	212	18–19	465–6	268–9	220
7–9	461	261–2	213	19–21	466	269–70	221
9–10	461–2	262–3	214	21–2	466–7	270	222
10–12	462–3	263–4	215	22–4	467–8	270–1	223
12–13	463	264–5	216	24–5	468	271–2	224

ON PROTECTION TO AGRICULTURE (*cont.*)

Editions 1–4 1822	McCulloch's edition	Gonner's edition	Present edition	Editions 1–4 1822	McCulloch's edition	Gonner's edition	Present edition
25–7	468–9	272–3	225	59–60	482–3	293–4	248
27–8	469–70	273–4	226	60–2	483–4	294	249
28–30	470	274–5	227	62–3	484	294–5	250
30–1	470–1	275–6	228	63–5	484–5	295–6	251
31–3	471	276–7	229	65–6	485–6	296–7	252
33–4	471–2	277–8	230	66–8	486	297–8	253
34–6	472–3	278	231	68–9	486–7	298–9	254
36–7	473	278–9	232	69–71	487–8	299–300	255
37–8	473–4	279–80	233	71–2	488	300–1	256
38–40	474	280–1	234	72–4	488–9	301	257
40–1	474–5	281–2	235	74–5	489	301–2	258
41–3	475–6	282–3	236	75–6	489–90	302–3	259
43–4	476	283–4	237	76–8	490	303–4	260
44–6	476–7	284–5	238	78–9	490–1	304–5	261
46–7	477–8	285–6	239	79–81	491–2	305–6	262
47–9	478	286–7	240	81–2	492	306	263
49–50	478–9	287	241	82–4	492–3	306–7	264
50–1	479	287–8	242	84–5	493–4	307–8	265
51–3	479–80	288–9	243	85–7	494	308–9	266
53–4	480–1	289–90	244	89–90	495	311–12	267
54–6	481	290–1	245	90–2	495–6	312–13	268
56–7	481–2	291–2	246	92–3	496	313	269
57–9	482	292–3	247	93–4	497	313–14	270

PLAN FOR THE ESTABLISHMENT OF A NATIONAL BANK

Edition 1824	McCulloch's edition	Present edition	Edition 1824	McCulloch's edition	Present edition
v–vi	501	275	16–17	508	287
1–2	503	276	17–19	508	288
2–4	503–4	277	19–20	508–9	289
4–6	504	278	20–1	509	290
6–7	504–5	279	21–2	509–10	291
7–8	505	280	23–4	510	292
9–10	505–6	281	24–6	510–11	293
10–12	506	282	26–7	511	294
12–13	506–7	283	27–9	511–12	295
13–14	507	284	29–31	512	296
14–15	507	285	31–2	512	297
15–16	507–8	286			